A Village Goes to

To Dawn
Best Wishes
David Tattersfield

A Village Goes to War

A History of the men of Ravensthorpe
who fell in the Great War

By David Tattersfield

First published in 2000

Produced by Barkers Trident Communications,3 Marsden Park,
Clifton Business Estate, York YO30 4WX.
Tel: 01904 690882
Fax: 01904 690875
email: info@barkers.co.uk
Net address: http://www.barkers.co.uk

Printed by Maxiprint, Kettlestring Lane,
Clifton Business Estate,
York, YO30 4WX

ISBN 0 9534689 3 3

Set in Century Schoolbook

Their bodies are buried in peace; but their name liveth for evermore

Ecclesiasticus 44.14

This book is dedicated to the men named on the Ravensthorpe War Memorial.

May their names live for evermore.

Contents

Acknowledgements

This book could simply not have been written without the assistance of numerous people and organisations. In mentioning the following people, I hope I have included everyone who has contributed to producing this work; if anyone has been omitted, I sincerely apologise.

First of all I must mention the patience of my parents Roy and Ann Tattersfield, and my wife, Dawn, who have, at differing times allowed me to hide myself away for hours on end, seemingly only appearing at meal times; they have also accompanied me on numerous trips to France and Belgium, as did my brother, Stuart on the very first trip to the battlefields and on a memorable trip to Gallipoli.

The late Maurice Tattersfield provided useful gems of information about his uncle, Second Lieutenant Neville Tattersfield, I am only sorry Maurice did not live to see the book completed. I am also greatly in the debt of Lynne Duxbury who provided information about Alfred and John Duxbury, and Michael Hickling who filled in gaps in the story of Vivian and provided copies of his great-uncle's letters and paintings.

On my frequent trips to France I invariably stayed with Julie and Michael Renshaw of Auchonvillers, their hospitality and encouragement is much appreciated. Whilst there I was lucky enough to meet (and talk 'shop') with numerous fellow guests, all of whom showed interest in my work, but none more so than Derek and Jenny Clayton. Derek is himself writing a book on the 9th K.O.Y.L.I., and I have picked his brains mercilessly over several years.

As indicated elsewhere, other trips have been conducted under the auspices of Martin Middlebrook's battlefield tours; I am grateful to Martin for not only igniting my interest in this subject, but also for keeping it burning through his memorable tours. My thanks are also due to him for agreeing to write the foreword of the book.

One of the most single good strokes of fortune, however, was my making contact with Margaret Watson of the Dewsbury Reporter. Not only has she co-written the foreword and supplied numerous photographs of the men in the book, but encouraged me to believe that the publication of the book could be achieved, and put me in touch with other parties, through whom I have been able to obtain funding towards the printing costs.

The book would probably not have been published in this format if it were not for the grant funding. My thanks here are to Dennis Chaffer of the Royal British Legion, Dewsbury Branch, the branch being my partners in publishing, they enabled me to obtain funding from the Dewsbury Partnership's Single Regeneration Budget.

During the research for the book which took place between 1993 and 1999, I contacted many organisations which never failed to be courteous and helpful. I must therefore thank the staff of the Public Record Office (for access to war diaries and trench maps) and for permission to reproduce the copies of the trench maps; the staff at Dewsbury Library (for access to and the loan of valuable reference works including the back copies of the Dewsbury Reporter and Dewsbury News); and to Brian Haigh and Susan Gillooley of the Kirklees Community History Service for permission to reproduce photographs from the Hartley-Singleton photographic archive (This archive of photographs taken by F. Hartley and H.

Singleton in the early years of the twentieth century are available through a user friendly touch screen computer located in Dewsbury Library.) My thanks are also due to The Commonwealth War Graves Commission (who provided lists of casualties long before the information was available via the internet), and to Mr C. Patrick who undertook much research on the C.W.G.C.'s internet site when this became available.

The Headmaster of Ravensthorpe Junior School also kindly allowed me access to details of records of the old St. Saviour's Boys' School, and a former headmaster of the school, Trevor Robshaw, wrote a useful article about the history of the school itself.

Other material came in from the National Archives of Canada and the Memorial University of Newfoundland. The West Yorkshire Archive Service proved a useful source for old copies of the church magazine, without which I would have been unable to piece together the story of the construction of the memorial within St. Saviour's Parish Church. The former vicar, the Reverend Ian Wildey and the P.C.C. also provided me with the necessary letters to commence my research.

One of my early points of contact was Ronald Clifton, the Information Officer of the Western Front Association. His clear and concise answers to my lengthy lists of technical questions have been of use to me throughout the course of my research. Similar help has come from other members of the Western Front Association who are too numerous to name individually, but I am grateful to them all. Other assistance has come my way from various Regimental Secretaries principally Major D.L.J. Harrap of the Duke of Wellington's Regiment and Colonel J.S. Cowley of the K.O.Y.L.I. My thanks are also due to the Royal Artillery Historical Trust and the Royal Engineers Library.

I am grateful to the Society of Authors who, as the Literary Representative of the Estate of Laurence Binyon, gave permission for the quotation of an extract of his poem 'For the Fallen'.

My final and most sincere thanks are due to Alan Bull who has helped me in going through the numerous volumes of 'Soldiers Died in the Great War' (before these were available on CD-Rom), provided snippets of information, and made many useful suggestions. Besides spending much time browsing the C.W.G.C.'s internet site, he has, with infinite patience, proof-read and corrected my often errant typing in numerous drafts of the book. If any errors have crept into the text at this late stage these are my fault for amending the text after Alan's vetting of it.

My thanks are due to all of the above people and organisations. Any mistakes, omissions, misinterpretations or misconceptions that appear within this book are my responsibility alone.

Glossary

Army Structure

B.E.F. - British Expeditionary Force - (the army in France and Flanders).
Usually commanded by a Field-Marshal
E.E.F. - Egyptian Expeditionary force - the army in Egypt and later Palestine
Army - Written as, for example 'First Army' 'Second Army' etc. - Commanded by a General
Corps - Indicated by Roman numerals eg. I Corps, II Corps etc.
- Commanded by a Lieutenant-General
Division - Commanded by a Major-General
Brigade - (Infantry) Commanded by a Brigadier-General (see also below under Author's Explanation for details of Artillery Brigades)
Battalion - Commanded by a Lieutenant-Colonel
Company - Commanded by a Major or Captain
Platoon - Commanded by a Lieutenant or a Second Lieutenant, or even an N.C.O.

The term 'British army' has been used quite loosely to cover not only soldiers from the United Kingdom, but also those from the colonies and dominions, including Canada, Newfoundland (which at the time of the First World War was a colony and not part of Canada), Australia, South Africa and even a contingent from Bermuda. The term excludes India, which had an army structure of its own, units of which served on the Western Front in 1914 and 1915.

* * *

Regiments / Corps

K.O.Y.L.I. - King's Own Yorkshire Light Infantry
R.M.F. - Royal Munster Fusiliers
Duke's - Duke of Wellington's (West Riding Regiment) - shortened to 'Duke of Wellington's Regiment' (or occasionally Duke's)
D.L.I. - Durham Light Infantry
K.O.S.B. - King's Own Scottish Borderers

R.F.C. - Royal Flying Corps
R.A.M.C. - Royal Army Medical Corps
M.G.C. - Machine Gun Corps
M.M.G.S. - Motor Machine Gun Service (fore runner of the Tank Corps)
Anzac - Australian and New Zealand Army Corps.

Medals

V.C. - Victoria Cross. The highest award for gallantry in British & Empire armed services.
D.S.O. - Distinguished Service Order
D.S.C. - Distinguished Service Cross
M.C. - Military Cross
D.C.M. - Distinguished Conduct Medal
D.F.C. - Distinguished Flying Cross
M.M. - Military Medal

Other

C.I.G.S. - Chief of the Imperial General Staff
G.O.C. - General Officer Commanding (a division)
N.C.O. - Non Commissioned Officer (eg Sergeant, Corporal)
Bosche - German
A.I.F. - Australian Imperial Forces (the Australian Army operating within the B.E.F. and E.E.F.)
A.E.F. - American Expeditionary Force

Author's explanations

When I refer to casualties, this information will usually have come from a battalion's War Diary, in which case it will normally include those killed, wounded and captured. Alternatively the information may have been extracted from Soldiers Died in the Great War ('S.D.G.W.') which will break the figure down into those killed plus those who died of wounds on that day. S.D.G.W. is a series of binders originally published by H.M.S.O. listing by Regiment and Battalion all soldiers killed in the Great War. A separate binder (Officers Died in the Great War) was produced listing the officers who lost their lives. Rather than repeatedly differentiating between S.D.G.W. and O.D.G.W., I have used the term 'S.D.G.W.' to cover both works. The figures I have used for officer casualties may be somewhat inaccurate due to the men listed in this publication frequently being attached to other battalions or regiments. Towards the end of my research, the binders were reproduced in digital format (see Bibliography).

* * *

Each unit was obliged to keep a War Diary. These hardly ever mentioned individual soldiers or junior officers by name, nevertheless they are an invaluable record of the day to day activities of units of the British army. They were consulted extensively during the preparation of this book and are available for inspection at the Public Record Office in Kew, London. Quotations from War Diaries are too numerous to give each a specific source (each War Diary has, in the Public Record Office, a unique reference number); however all quotations that are from the War Diaries that can be found in the 'WO 95' series at the Public Record Office.

* * *

The army inevitably kept files on all its personnel, unfortunately, in 1941, the warehouse in which these files were being stored was bombed by the Luftwaffe. It seems that approximately 20% of the files survived the bombing and subsequent fire, although many of these were badly damaged. These documents relating to each soldier's service are now held on microfilm at the Public Record Office in Kew. Twelve of these service records had been located up to the time of publication (not all files were available, due to their being released in batches as soon as they have been copied).

* * *

Reference is often made to 'Kitchener's New Armies'. These were numbered in sequence (often designated by a 'K' number, so that the first New Army was K1). These were totally different from the Armies (First to Fifth) that operated in France. Kitchener's Armies were simply blocks of volunteers who came forward and were trained in the UK. Formed into battalions and divisions they were sent to France where they fought, depending on the sector in different Corps. Each Army (in France) had a number of Corps under it. These Corps were occasionally switched between the armies, and divisions often moved to different Corps, however divisions seldom had their battalions and brigades changed.

The division was the largest permanent force in the B.E.F., it contained three infantry brigades, each brigade containing (until 1918) four battalions. At full strength a battalion would contain about 1,000 officers and men. (In the reorganisation described more fully in Chapter 18, the number of battalions in a brigade was reduced to three, therefore reducing each division to nine infantry battalions.) The division was made up of about 20,000 men, just over half of whom would be infantry; each division also had numerous other units attached, including a pioneer battalion, medical units, field companies of Royal Engineers and brigades of artillery.

In addition to infantry divisions which the above relates to, there were also a number of Cavalry Divisions within the B.E.F. The Cavalry Divisions hardly feature in this book, and a description of these would not be necessary. There is occasional reference to Yeomanry Divisions, these were divisions comprising of territorial soldiers who performed the cavalry function within the Territorial Force.

As briefly mentioned above, most divisions had a Pioneer Battalion attached. Although still infantrymen, their primary role was digging, carrying and other physical tasks.

The artillery was made up of the Royal Field Artillery (R.F.A.) the Royal Horse Artillery (R.H.A.) and the Royal Garrison Artillery (R.G.A.). The first two (but particularly the R.F.A.) were constituent parts of an infantry division.

The guns were organised into artillery brigades, these were entirely different organisations than infantry brigades. An artillery brigade (which contained between 600 and 800 men) was the equivalent of an infantry battalion. Artillery within the B.E.F. was constantly being reorganised during the course of the war. Until the end of 1916 there had usually been four artillery brigades in a division, however at the beginning of 1917, this was reduced to two brigades; the 'surplus' brigades being removed from the control of divisions and placed under the command of the various armies. This change was made to ensure a reserve of artillery was created with which divisions who were in action could be reinforced. The artillery in each division was under the control of a Brigadier-General, who like the Brigadier-Generals in charge of infantry brigades, reported to the divisional commander.

The artillery brigade contained a number of batteries, each battery being made up of between four and six guns.

* * *

The Imperial War Graves Commission became The Commonwealth War Graves Commission ("C.W.G.C.") in 1960.

List of Illustrations

List of Maps

Foreword

I have made a rule - not to write introductions to other peoples books. It is, however, a rule I must sometimes break in exceptional circumstances. This work of my friend, David Tattersfield, is such a case.

No community, and very few families, escaped the ravages of that terrible First World War. Its effects have been described in a mass of literature. Some weighty tomes deal with the war in its entirety, usually viewing from the top, from the viewpoint of generalship, downwards. Some books deal with individual battles and find some space to describe the experiences of the ordinary soldiers who took part.

The most meritorious books, though, are probably those which view the war entirely from the bottom upwards, and it is such a book that David has laboured over these years to produce.

No one mattered more in the First World War than the ordinary soldiers who died and their families who were so cruelly bereaved.

In this book David has metaphorically put flesh on the bare bones of the names on the Ravensthorpe War Memorial.

I am delighted to break my rule and recommend this work to readers. I am grateful to him for thinking that I am worthy to do so.

Martin Middlebrook

* * *

Most stories about the First World War are written on such a massive scale that few ordinary people can identify with them, but this cannot be said about David Tattersfield's book which shows the horrors of war on a scale that we can all relate to.

In 'A Village Goes to War' we follow in the footsteps of 114 men from Ravensthorpe, most from working-class backgrounds who went to war and never returned. They were just a handful of fighting men amongst millions, but in this book they are plucked from obscurity and introduced to us one by one.

They are no longer anonymous, but flesh and blood men. We know their names, the streets where they lived, the schools they attended, the factories where they worked and the churches where they worshipped.

This remarkable book may draw a small picture of a big war but it is still a masterpiece of detail - a microcosm of the Great War and the devastating affect it had on the lives of ordinary people.

We owe David a debt of gratitude for providing us with a unique historical document which reminds us that world wars may be fought in foreign fields but they kill people who live down our street.

Margaret Watson

Preface

In 1990 I was persuaded to read a book entitled 'The First Day on the Somme' written by Martin Middlebrook. I had no idea that the personal repercussions of this would be so great.

Immediately after reading the book I had two requirements - to read more about the Great War and to visit the battlefields.

The following year, my brother and I spent two weeks in France. We visited the Normandy landing beaches, then moved on to the town of Albert, in the heart of the Somme Battlefield. Despite knowing little of the area (and having only a little knowledge of the French language) we were able to find our way around, and visit many of the sites mentioned in Mr Middlebrook's book. The friendliness of our welcome by the locals, other English visitors and by the caretaker of a memorial called the Ulster Tower, was extraordinary. However it was probably the countless Commonwealth War Graves Commission Cemeteries that made me determined to discover more about the events of 1914-1918.

Upon my return home I decided to inspect the War Memorial inside my local Parish Church at Ravensthorpe. As a child I had been a regular attender at the church and as the youngest choirboy had laid the wreath at the foot of the memorial on more than one Remembrance Sunday.

The inspection proved interesting, as towards the end of the list of names I discovered someone with my own surname, Second Lieutenant Neville Tattersfield of the Tank Corps. This was a surprising development. When I asked my father about this, he was unaware that there was anyone with our name on the memoral. This confirmed to me something that I had suspected; like everyone else, I took the War Memorial for granted. It was in the corner of the church, everyone could see it, but nobody looked at it.

I remembered that there used to be photographs of the men hung in three large frames near the memorial, these had been taken down some time ago. I soon discovered them on top of a cupboard. Unfortunately, there was no photograph of Neville Tattersfield.

Without knowing where such an act would lead, I copied the list of names from the memorial, and then compared this list with the photographs. There were 81 photographs, but the memorial contained 114 names.

I only then realised the significance of these photographs. The list of names immediately became a roll of men from Ravensthorpe who had lived, served and ultimately died in a conflict that had occurred 80 years previously. Without the photographs, the names were just a list, but now we could actually see what the majority of the men looked like.

Where were these men buried, what were their stories? I had to find out.

This started a quest for information that has led me back to the battlefields at least once per year in the years since my first visit. Many of these visits were on tours organised by Martin Middlebrook, whose grasp of the battlefields is second to none, and the friendships made on these tours is a lasting reminder of how other friends and comrades travelled these self same roads over 80 years ago, facing and often meeting death. Their legacy is the subject of this book. I hope that they would approve of this attempt at perpetuating their memories.

David Tattersfield

◂ 3. Ravensthorpe Parish War Memorial

▾ 4. The Cloth Hall, Ypres, 1919. Note the side of the bus advertising excursions to the battlefields. Pilgrimages to the Western Front started very soon after the end of the war.

Prologue

The Industrial Revolution of the late 18th Century came to the West Riding of Yorkshire largely as a result of the abundant supply of water that was, and still is available. The water drove the steam engines, washed and dyed the wool and provided the means for transport prior to the railways. West Riding mill owners felt that they needed to extend communication beyond Wakefield and this brought about the decision to build a canal into the Calder Valley. The canal (The Calder and Hebble Navigation) was started in 1767 by the Upper Calder Navigation Company. Although the River Calder was used for much of its route, there were numerous stretches of the river which were unusable to barges. Such stretches required the building of 'cuts'. One of these cuts was required to bypass the unnavigable loop of the River Calder on which the town of Dewsbury stands. This canal (the 'Long Cut') and further cuts of canal linked Dewsbury westwards to Mirfield and ultimately to Huddersfield.

The canal systems between Huddersfield and Lancashire which led to Manchester and the Mersey were therefore linked with the port of Hull and the North Sea.

Once the Long Cut was completed in 1824, the Upper Calder Navigation Company built a wharf and warehouse where the Long Cut joined the River Calder. This was in the belief that industrial activity may start here. With the discovery of coal, this speculation proved to be correct and in the 1850's textile mills were built. With industry came a new name for the area. Originally known as 'Little Mirfield' to the west, and to the east (where the first houses were built) as 'Newtown', the village of Ravensthorpe was created.

With the mills came houses; a council ('Local Board') was elected in 1864. The Parish of Ravensthorpe was created by separating it from the adjoining Parish of Mirfield in 1870.

▲ 5. A barge at the junction of the River Calder and the Shepley Bridge Cut. This cut is a stretch of the Calder and Hebble Navigation taking the canal from the western of Ravensthorpe into Mirfield. *Photograph courtesy of Kirklees Community History Service*

▲ 6. Drawing of St. Saviour's School in Church Street, by Ernlie Wrigglesworth

The education act of 1870 gave individuals and groups a period of two years in which voluntary schools could be built in order to make up the shortfall in school accommodation that then existed. Although there was a small private school in Ravensthorpe (in John Street), it was decided to build a Church School in the village. Land in Church Street, adjoining the church was purchased and the foundation stone laid in February 1871; the school was officially opened on 11th November that year. Further expansion of the school took place over the following years, and in 1890 a new school for 300 boys was opened in John Street.

A product of the Industrial Revolution, Ravensthorpe thrived over the next few decades, becoming part of the Municipal Borough of Dewsbury in 1909 (this became a County Borough in 1913). Its population grew steadily, the census of 1901 showed 5,609 living in the village, by 1911 this had grown to 6,376*.

The area was well served with railways. The Lancashire and Yorkshire Railway built the first station at the bottom of Scout Hill on the line from Bradford to Wakefield. The London and North Western Railway had a station (Ravensthorpe and Thornhill) south of the River Calder (this is the only surviving railway station) standing on the Leeds to Huddersfield line. Two other stations in Northorpe (technically Northorpe is part of neighbouring Mirfield) served Ravensthorpe. One was on another L&NW line which ran from Huddersfield to Leeds; the other, a L&Y station, was on the Huddersfield to Bradford line.

In order to serve the commuters of this period, a tramway was built at the turn of the century. Although only a single track (but with loops to enable the trams to pass), it ran from Dewsbury to the western end of Ravensthorpe. Due to low bridges, the trams themselves were single deckers and were powered by overhead electric lines; they had a maximum speed imposed of just 16 mph which was cut to 8 mph on the steep Scout Hill.

In 1991, the population of Ravensthorpe was 4,818.

The industry which made Ravensthorpe boom was dominated by the wool trade. Some of the firms who were present in Ravensthorpe in the early years of the twentieth century were:-

Henry Hamer & Sons - Made many varieties of cloth.
F. Doble & Sons - Manufactured eiderdowns.
Pickering & Greaves - Produced worsteds.
Rawdon, Briggs & Co. - Manufactured cloth for uniforms for the police and army officers.
Marshall, Kaye & Marshall - A firm of woollen manufacturers with two mills and 270 looms.
Jas Smith & Sons - Dyers and dry cleaners.
Smithson & Gledhill - Dyers and finishers.
J.H. Walker - Made bearskin and sealskin rugs.
Walker Brothers - Another branch of the Walker family, having a silk mill.
Armitage & Rhodes - Manufactured shawls. They arrived in Ravensthorpe in 1909 after their factory in the village of Delph burned down.

Dewsbury, two miles to the east of Ravensthorpe had become the centre of the Heavy Woollen area due largely to the Shoddy industry. (Shoddy is the process whereby wool fibre is reclaimed by carbonising old rags, it was invented in Batley in 1813.) This was to become an important industry in the near future*, and several firms in Ravensthorpe were involved in the process, these included: A. Grace & Co. and Lee, Nephew & Co. Other firms, such as Hirst and Gill were involved in the Mungo industry (this is the name of cloth made from second hand material. It is of slightly better quality than shoddy.)

Many other businesses were required to keep the mills operating, such as engineers (Bell Brothers; Morton, Son & Co.; and Edward Richardson & Co.); dyers (Yorkshire Chemical Dyework Co.); joiners (Preston & Burnett). Other associated industries included two coal mines (both owned by the same person), a gas works and a power station. There was even a piano manufacturer (Newsome Brothers).

At this time there were up to 90 local shops trading (although supermarkets had yet to arrive, the Co-operative movement - which could be said to be a forerunner of these - had a presence).

Religion played a much larger part in many people's lives than is now the case; the first churches were built in 1864, 1868 and 1875. Many of the community's social activities centred around the Parish Church (St. Saviour's); there were church outings, bible classes, the Church Institute, and many concerts. It was not just the parish church that was popular, the nonconformist churches had a strong representation in the area. Besides the Wesleyan Methodist Church in North Road, there was a Primitive Methodist Church on Huddersfield Road (the 'West

During the war it was an important method of keeping the army supplied with uniforms, old khaki being recycled into new jackets and trousers. One of the local newspapers, The Dewsbury Reporter, described how in 1917 at the height of the war one hundred truckloads of khaki was being received into Dewsbury's mills on a daily basis to be recycled. The process is now redundant due to the fact that man-made fibres are usually added to cloth making the process impossible.

▲ 7. A tram, making way for a procession on Webster Hill, Dewsbury. It is possible the procession may have been making its way to Crow Nest Park for the unveiling of the War Memorial there in 1924. *Photograph courtesy of Kirklees Community History Service*

▼ 8. The Co-operative building in Ravensthorpe at the junction of North Road and Huddersfield Road; opposite these shops is St. Saviour's Parish Church. *Photograph courtesy of Kirklees Community History Service*

▲ 9. North Road, Ravensthorpe. The Wesleyan Methodist Church is on the left. In the background can be faintly seen the outline of the Congregational Church. *Photograph courtesy of Kirklees Community History Service*

▼ 10. The Primitive Methodist Church, Huddersfield Road, Ravensthorpe. *Photograph courtesy of Kirklees Community History Service*

▲ 11. St. Saviour's Parish Church Ravensthorpe. *Photograph courtesy of Kirklees Community History Service*

End Methodist Church'). The United Methodist Church (also known as the 'New Connection Methodist Church') was also situated on Huddersfield Road, at the eastern (Dewsbury) end of the village. Finally, there was a Congregational Church at the northern (Northorpe) end of North Road. Other recreational activities outside the church were provided by the Conservative, Liberal and Working Men's Clubs. There were football, cricket and cycling clubs. Rugby League was played professionally at Dewsbury's Crown Flat ground. The club won the Rugby League Northern Union Cup (the forerunner of the Challenge Cup) in 1912.

Those interested in keeping fit and having a weekend away under canvas every year could join the Territorial Force; the Duke of Wellington's (West Riding Regiment) was a popular choice. This regiment had four territorial battalions, the 4th, 5th 6th and 7th. The 5th Battalion recruited one of its companies in Mirfield. This weekend soldiering was to seal the fate of many Ravensthorpe men in only a few years time.

Local political activity was dominated by the Liberal Party. The area's Member of Parliament was Walter Runciman who was elected in 1902 after losing his seat in Oldham to Winston Churchill. In 1914 Runciman served in the cabinet of Herbert Asquith's Government, holding the position of President of the Board of Trade*.

He was the last Dewsbury M.P. to serve on the Government's front benches until Ann Taylor became Leader of the House in 1997.

▲ 12. Walter Runciman, standing for election in 1908. *Photograph courtesy of Kirklees Community History Service*

The village of Ravensthorpe flourished. Although there was poverty (life was hard and wages were poor*) it was not suffered to the extent of that found in the big cities. The housing was high density, being largely of a 'back to back' nature, where (for example in Sackville Street) there were long rows of terraced houses. Each house not only had adjoining properties on either side, but also its back wall was the back wall of another house. This arrangement explains the reason for many addresses being, for example, 'Back Sackville Street'; access 'to the backs' being through passages at intervals along the terrace. There was some industrial pollution, but pleasant countryside was within strolling distance.

As the Victorian age gave way to the Edwardian era, there was no suggestion that just around the corner were momentous events that would change Britain, Europe and the world for ever.

* *The author's grandfather was one of ten children, the family lived in a two bedroomed house in Raven Street; the street, along with many others such as Sackville Street having been condemned some years ago and demolished.*

▲ 13. Huddesfield Road, Ravensthorpe looking west. To the right is Tanhouse Street. *Photograph courtesy of Kirklees Community History Service.*

▼ 14. Huddersfield Road, Ravensthorpe looking east. The large square property in the background is the Co-operative building

▲ 15. Clearly, despite the industries on its banks, rowing on the River Calder was an alternative recreational activity. *Photograph courtesy of Kirklees Community History Service.*

▸ Ordanance Survey Map of Ravensthorpe, 1907. *By courtesy of HMSO*

Introduction

Despite local prosperity, Britain's status in the world was under pressure; whilst school atlases were still showing the Red of the British Empire covering a large proportion of the Earth's surface, the expansion in trade of the mid-eighteenth century had slowed down. This was in direct contrast to the rapid expansion of Germany's economy which had started to grow after the unification of Germany under Count Otto von Bismarck and the defeat of France following the Franco-Prussian War of 1870-1871. In this war France lost two provinces (Alsace and Lorraine) which became part of the German Empire. This war upset the balance of power within Europe.

Germany, headed by Queen Victoria's grandson Kaiser Wilhelm, had colonial aspirations, not least in the Middle East. The building of the Berlin to Baghdad railway, through the Turkish capital of Constantinople, reinforced the idea within the British Government that Germany would want to have some influence in the oilfields.

The Kaiser had for many years been an annual guest of the Royal Family and had been envious of Britain's naval might. This, together with his military style upbringing, had strengthened his desire for Germany to become an industrial and world superpower by whatever means that may prove necessary.

Meanwhile, France was desperate to recover its lost provinces from Germany; this was to have a direct result on their military planning. The Austro-Hungarian Empire, headed by the elderly emperor Franz-Josef was in decline and faced problems from its subjects' nationalist aspirations, especially in the Balkans where Serbia (independent of the Austro-Hungarian Empire) was gaining in strength and unhappy over the Austro-Hungarian annexation of Bosnia and Herzegovina in 1908.

Russia under Tsar Nicholas II was allied to the Serbs, however the Russian Empire was crumbling, largely due to the Tsar's harsh regime and his inflexible attitude to even moderate political reform. He was an absolute monarch but, until 1917, retained a great deal of loyalty from his people. Like many of the European Royal families (including the Kaiser's) the Tsar was related to the British Royal family due to several of Queen Victoria's children marrying into the Royal Houses of Europe.

Britain had her Empire to look after, and in order to ensure the cost of this policing operation did not become excessive, the British Government entered into agreements with France and Russia (who were perceived as the major threats to the Empire). These agreements would avoid the requirement of maintaining large garrisons of troops throughout the Empire. It was because of this policy that the British Government entered into the 'Triple Entente' with Russia and France. Although Britain's obligations under this agreement did not extend to coming to the aid of the other parties if they were attacked, the result of the Entente was that Germany felt surrounded by potential enemies, with only the Austro-Hungarian Empire and possibly the Turkish (Ottoman) Empire as allies. The result of Germany's nervousness was the development of a plan, the underlying aim of which was to avoid, at all costs, a war with France and Russia simultaneously. This plan, the Schlieffen Plan, called for the rapid conquest of France, after which Russia could be defeated at leisure.

The overwhelming strength of the Royal Navy reinforced the British belief that the country's small, professional army (there was no National Service, unlike in France or Germany) would not need to become involved in any future European War.

Despite tensions, the first decade of the twentieth century passed peacefully, however disaster was to come from an unexpected direction.

*   *   *

In June 1914, the heir to the Austro-Hungarian throne, Archduke Franz Ferdinand and his wife paid a visit to the capital of the Empire's most southerly province, Sarajevo, in Bosnia.

Gavrilo Princip, a 19 year old Bosnian Serb was a member of 'Young Bosnia', a nationalist movement seeking to free Bosnia from Austro-Hungarian control and instead to be part of a union with Serbia. This group was supported by the Black Hand terrorist organisation (a Serbian secret society).

On the morning of Sunday, 28th June, a bomb was thrown by a member of the Black Hand organisation at the Duke's car as it travelled through Sarajevo. Whilst the explosion did not injure the Royal couple, the Archduke was most perturbed and changed the itinerary - this was to have fateful consequences. On the same afternoon other members of the gang were in the crowds watching the procession.

Gavrilo Princip could not believe his luck as the driver of the Royal car made a wrong turning and slowed down in order to stop and turn round. Seizing his chance, Princip stepped forward and shot the Archduke and his wife. Both died within minutes.

Although there was no proof that the Serbian Government was involved in the plot, Austria needed to be seen to be taking firm action against Serbia, and accused it of organising the assassination. In order to humiliate Serbia, Austria (after ensuring German support) presented a ten point ultimatum to Serbia on 23rd July, giving Serbia forty eight hours in which to reply. Although agreeing to most of their demands, Serbia refused to allow Austrian officials to enter Serbia to investigate the assassination. Austria rejected Serbia's response and exactly a month after the assassination, on 28th July, war was declared by the Austro-Hungarian Empire on Serbia. Two days later Russia, who was closely allied to Serbia, started to mobilise her armies.

Germany, backing Austria's action and sensitive about Russian mobilisation, threatened to mobilise too. On 1st August, after Russia had ignored a German demand to cease mobilisation, Germany declared war on Russia. France, whose obligations included that of mutual defence with Russia, therefore mobilised her armies on the same day.

Early in the morning of Sunday 2nd August, Germany invaded Luxembourg (an important railway ran through the Principality) and at 7pm that evening, gave a twelve hour ultimatum to Belgium, demanding free passage through that country. On this day, German patrols crossed into France, and Britain started the mobilisation of her army and navy. Germany declared war on France the following day, 3rd August.

Until this point, Britain had been hoping to keep out of any conflict, however due to numerous countries having guaranteed Belgian sovereignty, the Government felt obliged to go to Belgium's aid. Whilst Britain could have stayed neutral, there was a dilemma in so doing. If France and Russia were to lose to Germany, Britain would be isolated with no allies on the continent; however if Germany was defeated, France and Russia would not look favourably on Britain not having helped them, and could have repudiated the Triple Entente, therefore threatening the British Empire.

The British Government therefore felt obliged to stand beside France and Russia, and an ultimatum was given to Germany to pull her troops out of Belgium. Germany ignored Britain's ultimatum which expired on Tuesday 4th August 1914; at 11pm London time, Great Britain declared war on Germany.

Little more than five weeks after Archduke Franz Ferdinand was assassinated, much of Europe was in a state of war. The British Foreign Secretary, Sir Edward Grey commented *"The lamps are going out all over Europe, we shall not see them lit again in our lifetime"*.

Gavrilo Princip was thrown into jail, where he was to die of pneumonia four years later.

The car in which the Archduke and his wife were shot is now in a museum in Vienna. The registration number of the car is one of the strangest coincidences imaginable. It is A 11 11 18.

Chapter One

The Opening Engagements

Both Germany and France had prepared for a war against each other for many years. The dominating thought in French military planning had been the recovery of the two provinces of Alsace and Lorraine, which had been lost to the Germans in the Franco-Prussian War of 1870. The French plan (Plan XVII), called for a push into Germany along their common border in the east of France, so as to immediately regain this lost territory.

The Germans realised that the French alliance with Russia meant that in the event of a war with France, Germany would also have to fight the Russians. They also anticipated that French national pride demanded that the two provinces should be returned to France at all costs. It was therefore easy for the Germans to anticipate that the French would direct any attack straight into Germany in order to recover this territory.

With the knowledge that they would find it almost impossible to fight both Russia and France simultaneously, the Germans developed a plan which would allow any French attack to be absorbed, but at the same time aiming an overwhelming knock out blow at France. Whilst this was taking place the Russians whose army, it was known, would take several weeks to mobilise and become effective would be held off with a minimum of troops. Once France had been knocked out, the Germans could send all their armies to the east in order to deal with the Russians separately.

The plan was developed at the turn of the century by the then head of the German army, Alfred von Schlieffen. His plan, the Schlieffen Plan, called for a vast sweep of the bulk of the German armies through Belgium, thus outflanking the French armies. The advance would sweep round the west of Paris, and trap the French armies in the east of France where it was expected they would be. Unfortunately for Germany, the current head of the German army, General Helmuth von Moltke, tampered with details of the Schlieffen Plan; he decided to avoid violating Dutch territory and therefore chose not to pass the armies through the Maastricht appendix, a finger of Dutch land which reduced the length of the German/Belgian frontier significantly. This was to delay the German troops in their advance into Belgium. Von Moltke also reduced the strength of the right wing of the attack to ensure the predicted French advance into Alsace and Lorraine did not go too far. These alterations were to have disastrous consequences for the German army, and would result in them having to fight a war on two fronts - Britain and France on one front and the Russians on the other.

Upon the outbreak of war the French, in accordance with their Plan XVII, tried to advance into Germany, but were held at the frontier. The German army swept with overwhelming force into northern France via Belgium, although the tiny Belgian army managed to delay the German time-table by tenaciously holding out in their fortresses; these were eventually destroyed by massive German howitzers. In order to try and keep to the time-table and avoid having to

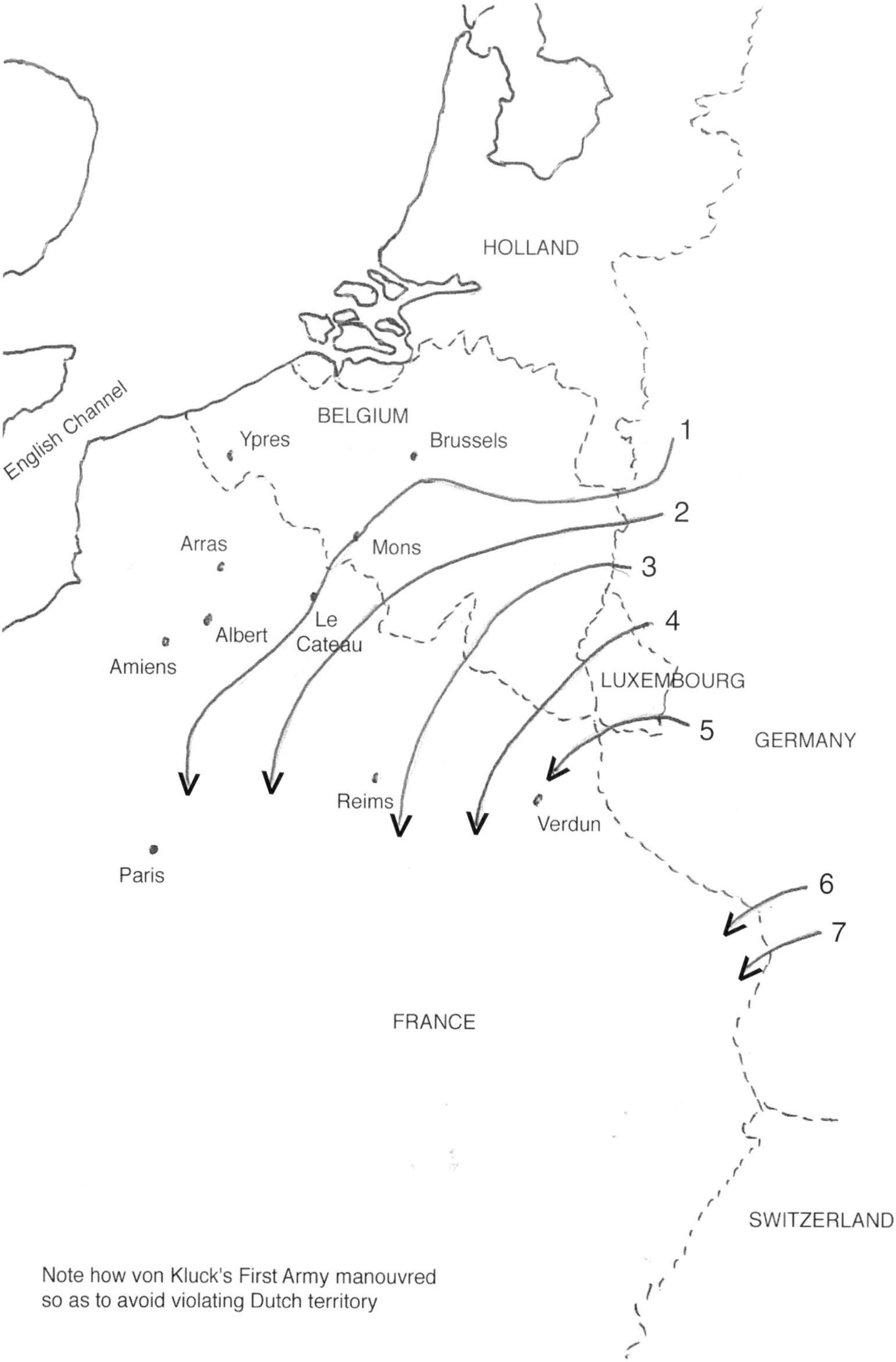

▲ Map 2. The Schlieffen Plan

leave large forces to look after the conquered territory, the Germans adopted harsh measures on the Belgian civilian population; this led to widespread stories of German 'frightfulness' in British newspapers which created an even stronger upsurge in anti-German feeling. One example of this German tactic was the destruction of the town of Louvain, with its famous medieval library. Other examples, possibly true, were graphic accounts of the execution of civilians.

Another mistake was now made by von Moltke; the original plan was for a retreat into Alsace and Lorraine, thus drawing the French armies into a trap. However he instead allowed his local commanders to inflict a heavy defeat on the French which stopped their advance in its tracks. This was to have the result in the forthcoming weeks of allowing the French to draw troops away from this area to reinforce the regions where the real German thrust was being made.

Meanwhile, the British Government under the Liberal Prime Minister Herbert Asquith had despatched a large proportion of the army under Field-Marshal Sir John French. The British Expeditionary Force, or B.E.F., was positioned on the extreme left of the French armies, therefore not being far from its ports of entry (Calais and Boulogne), and having fairly short lines of supply.

The B.E.F. comprised initially of four infantry divisions numbered 1,2,3 and 5 (the 4th and 6th Divisions were initially kept back at home) and a Cavalry Division. The arrival of the B.E.F. was carried out swiftly and secretly, the Germans were unaware of its arrival. As planned, the B.E.F. concentrated between the French towns of Maubeuge and Le Cateau. The only setback was the death, as a result of a heart attack, of the commander of the British II Corps, Lieutenant-General Sir James Grierson. His counterpart, and commander of I Corps was Lieutenant-General Sir Douglas Haig*. Unfortunately the site chosen as the concentration area was directly in the path of the advancing German armies. The first contact between British and German troops came at dawn on 22nd August when there were skirmishes between cavalry patrols.

The British divisions were pushed forward into Belgium along with the most northerly French armies. French military intelligence grossly underestimated the size of the German forces facing them; von Kluck's First Army numbered 320,000, on his left was von Bulow's Second Army which had 260,000 men. The British found themselves at the Belgian town of Mons on the afternoon of the 22nd August and formed a defensive position alongside the canal not knowing the French on their right were about to go into full retreat. The following day, 23rd August, the advance guard of the German First Army attacked the British. Due to the massed formations of the German troops and the highly trained musketry skills of the British, the Germans fell in their hundreds. However, the pressure from the Germans was relentless. It is likely that there was one soldier from Ravensthorpe, William Henry Kay, involved in this opening battle.

William Kay was born in Leeds in about 1884. He had been a regular soldier in the British army at the turn of the century serving in the Boer War in South Africa, which was the last of the small colonial conflicts of the 19th Century and had ended in 1902. Since then, William's period of service had ended and just prior to the Great War he had been working as a shunter on the Lancashire and Yorkshire Railway at Mirfield.

I Corps was made up of the 1st and 2nd Divisions; II Corps comprised the 3rd and 5th Divisions.

Although his period of service was over, discharged soldiers could, for a number of years after their service had ended, be called up again in the case of a national emergency. This is exactly what occurred on the outbreak of the war: in order to bring units up to their correct strength, many of these reservists were drafted straight into battalions and sent to France. Whilst these reservists, like William Kay, were trained soldiers, in the period since they had left the army, many would have lost some of their physical fitness - this was to have a serious effect over the following weeks.

Upon his call up William was drafted into the 1st Battalion of the Northumberland Fusiliers. The battalion was in 9 Brigade of the 3rd Division and had arrived in France on 13th August. William landed shortly after the majority of the battalion on the 15th August.

The 1st Northumberland Fusiliers were to the west of Mons, at the village of Mariette. Their task was to defend the canal and to hold a bridge over the canal. During the course of the day seven men of the battalion were killed, most of the casualties being incurred when a German field gun was used to try and force a party of the battalion away from the northern end of the bridge. German accounts of the battle talk of the British using many machine guns. This was not the case, the massive German casualties were caused by extremely rapid and accurate rifle fire.

The British army, although small by continental standards was manned by volunteers. The German and French, by comparison had a system of compulsory national service. Whilst the British army could not therefore match the strength of these other armies in numbers, it made up for this in morale, discipline and training. The Kaiser's remark of the B.E.F. being a *"Contemptible Little Army"* rebounded on him.

Despite the heroism of the British regulars, the sheer weight of numbers could not be held off and the right flank of the British line was forced back. A general withdrawal all along the line was ordered, which was carried out on the night of 23rd/24th August. The Germans pressed closely against 9 Brigade, and the 1st Northumberland Fusiliers lost, during the course of the 24th, a further twelve men killed.

Sir John discovered that the French, to his right, had suffered badly and had fallen back, but without consulting him. Unless he ordered his troops to conform with the French retirement, it was likely that the B.E.F. would be surrounded.

The retreat from Mons started.

At this time, von Moltke made a further mistake, again diluting the Schlieffen Plan by withdrawing troops from the right wing to send to the east as the Russians had mobilised more quickly than had been anticipated. Over the next couple of days the B.E.F., closely pursued by the advancing Germans, retreated southwards. On 26th August the commander of II Corps, Sir Horace Smith-Dorrien, who had been appointed by Lord Kitchener* to replace Grierson, and whom Sir John French disliked, decided that he must try to stop the Germans pursuing quite as closely as they were. He also believed that unless his men were rested, they would be unable to continue with the retreat. Smith-Dorrien, against Sir John's wishes, chose to

**** Field-Marshal Earl Kitchener of Khartoum was a hero in the eyes of the British public; he had fought several successful campaigns at the end of the nineteenth century, and on the outbreak of war was called back from going to Egypt and appointed Secretary of State for War.***

stand and fight at Le Cateau. Despite overwhelming odds, the weary British infantry held off the equally weary German troops for several hours.

Eventually the order to disengage was given, and the vast majority of the British infantry and artillery was able to withdraw, although the orders failed to reach some units which became surrounded and the men were killed or captured. Despite the German advance being halted, British losses were heavy; about 7,800 men became casualties, although this figure includes 2,600 men taken prisoner by the Germans.

The 1st Northumberland Fusiliers were not heavily involved at Le Cateau, losing six men killed.

Because of the unexpected defence put up by Smith-Dorrien's II Corps at Le Cateau, it took the Germans about twelve hours to get themselves sufficiently organised to continue their advance; although a breathing space had been gained, the retreat continued. The men had very little sleep and their feet were sore (this was even worse for the reservists whose new boots and soft feet would have taken more punishment than the regular soldiers' older boots and toughened feet). The constant threat of attack by German cavalry and the scorching summer sun took its toll. There were just two consolations, the Germans were suffering just as much and the supplies, organised by the Quartermaster General, Major-General Sir William Robertson* rarely failed to reach the troops.

The action at Le Cateau had confused the Germans into believing the B.E.F. was retreating in a south-westerly direction rather than due south, and the pressure on the British eased for a few days. Despite this, Sir John was in a state of depression and contemplated pulling the B.E.F. out of the line of the German advance and back to the Channel Ports. This was prevented by the intervention of Lord Kitchener. The retreat continued, much bravery and endurance was shown by the British troops, exemplified by an action at the village of Nery when three Victoria Crosses were won on one morning by men from 'L' Battery R.H.A.

On 3rd September, the B.E.F. crossed the River Marne; although the men did not know it, the end of the retreat was now in sight.

* * *

The intention of the original Schlieffen Plan was for the German armies to sweep to the west of Paris, but von Moltke made the last of his alterations to the plan and decided instead to turn the extreme right-hand edge of his advance south-east, thus turning away from Paris. This manoeuvre was spotted by the frail aeroplanes of the British and French air forces and the French Commander-in-Chief, Joseph Joffre (known affectionately as 'Papa' Joffre to the French troops), realising that this manoeuvre exposed the flank of the German armies to counter-attack, decided to halt the retreat.

**** Sir William Robertson - later Field-Marshal. He was the first man enlisting as a private soldier to become a Field-Marshal. Disliked by politicians (Lloyd George dismissed him in 1917) and liable to drop his H's he was obviously a very able man to have risen from private to the very top of the British army. He was promoted to be Sir John French's Chief of Staff in January 1915, replacing Lieutenant-General Sir Archibald Murray (see Chapter 17). Robertson later became Chief of the Imperial General Staff in London in December 1915.***

On the 5th September, Joffre asked Sir John French to order the B.E.F., in conjunction with the French Fifth and Sixth Armies, to turn around and counter-attack. Morale in the B.E.F. immediately soared. Since Mons, they had retreated 200 miles in nearly two weeks and had lost in the region of 15,000 men killed, wounded, and missing but now it was the German's turn to retreat.

The B.E.F. recrossed the River Marne on 9th September, and advanced slowly towards the Germans. The Battle of the Marne was really a series of engagements between the retreating German armies and the advancing French armies; the B.E.F. was not heavily involved. The Germans were pursued across several rivers, after about 60 miles they crossed the River Aisne. The advancing British approached the River Aisne on the 12th September. Aerial reconnaissance was made difficult due to the heavy rain which also turned the roads to mud. The German troops were exhausted and in urgent need of reinforcement. At the last moment, soldiers from the German VII Reserve Corps arrived to help their comrades.

At 11pm on 12th September the 4th Division, which had joined the B.E.F. on 25th August, started crossing, in single file, a damaged bridge across the Aisne; unfortunately, the advance was not supported by other British divisions due to the Germans having destroyed nearly all the bridges in their retreat. This was the first unit of the B.E.F. to start crossing the river.

The 3rd Division, containing William Kay's battalion, came up to the village of Vailly. Upon approaching the road bridge over the River Aisne in Vailly on 13th September, 9 Brigade (3rd Division) found the central span of the bridge destroyed, although a footbridge lay across it. The rail bridge was also destroyed and, according to a Royal Engineers officer, it could not be repaired until darkness had fallen.

A five hour delay therefore ensued as 9 Brigade had to wait for 8 Brigade to cross the road bridge. Two battalions of 9 Brigade (the 4th Royal Fusiliers and the 1st Lincolnshire Regiment) were sent forward as soon as they had crossed to occupy the high ground north of the bridge, on either side of a farm called La Maison Rouge. The countryside was steep, heavily wooded, covered in a damp mist and slippery underfoot.

At 4.30am on 14th September the remaining two battalions of 9 Brigade were 'Stood To'* in Vailly in case of a German attack; this passed off without incident. As they were cooking breakfast at 7.30am they heard the sound of heavy firing. The battalions, 1st Northumberland Fusiliers and 1st Royal Scots Fusiliers, were ordered to fall in and were led up the hill. The Northumberland Fusiliers were sent in support of the Royal Fusiliers on the left and, according to the Northumberland's War Diary *"succeeded in pushing forward well on the left through the woods"*. Due to heavy artillery, however, both these battalions had to be drawn back from their most advanced positions. To the right, the Lincolnshires and the Royal Scots Fusiliers both had to fall back as well. A total of 31 soldiers of the 1st Northumberland Fusiliers died on 14th September. The War Diary of 9 Brigade describes the losses for the day as *"Severe"*.

This was the end of the war of rapid movement. Up and down the line both sides, utterly exhausted, dug in and clung to their positions. Trench warfare had begun.

**** Throughout the war, one of the most likely times for the enemy to attack was at dawn; every morning at sunrise, therefore, the men were made ready to receive an attack. This was called being 'Stood To'.***

◂ 16. Vailly British Cemetery.

▾ 17. The modern bridge at Vailly.

It was on the 14th September, during the confused fighting around La Rouge Maison Farm that William Henry Kay was killed. Almost two years went by before the report of his death appeared in a local newspaper. On the 24th June 1916, the Dewsbury News stated that Mrs Gertrude Kay of 16 Aire Street Ravensthorpe had been informed that her husband was presumed to have been killed after being reported missing. The article describes how Mrs Kay had been trying, ever since her husband had been reported missing, to obtain news of him. She had even tried to obtain information through the King of Spain. The only news came via the Red Cross Society, and this seems to have come from one of his comrades who describes how he had last seen William lying on the ground, badly wounded by shrapnel, waiting for stretcher bearers to take him away. Presumably help never reached him in time and he died of his wounds.

When the Germans over-ran the advanced British positions on the 14th September, the least of their priorities would have been the identification of dead British soldiers. As a result William Kay, like 28 of the battalion's 31 casualties on 14th September has no known grave. He is named on the Memorial to the Missing at La Ferte sous Jouarre, where nearly 4,000 men are also commemorated. La Ferte sous Jouarre stands on the River Marne, where the German advance was halted. The Commonwealth War Graves Commission Cemetery at Vailly contains nearly 700 graves, including the three men of the 1st Northumberland Fusiliers who were killed on this day and who have known graves; it is possible that William is also buried here beneath one of the 'unknown' headstones which make up half of the graves in the cemetery.

*   *   *

On 14th September, General Erich von Falkenhayn took over from the discredited von Moltke. The Germans entrenched north of the River Aisne, on a ridge known as the Chemin des Dames*.

After the Battle of the Aisne, the lines stabilised and there followed a spell when the Germans and the Allies tried to outflank each other to the north. Once the English Channel was reached, this manoeuvring had to stop as there were no more flanks to turn. This period was called 'the Race to the Sea'.

In the meantime the expansion of the B.E.F. continued. The original strength of four infantry divisions (the 1st, 2nd, 3rd and 5th) plus a Cavalry Division were later joined by the 4th and 6th Divisions which formed III Corps under Lieutenant-General Pultney, being created on 30th August. The large Cavalry Division was split into two, and became the Cavalry Corps under Lieutenant-General Edmund Allenby. The 7th Division was formed in October and with the 3rd Cavalry Division became IV Corps. October also saw the introduction of the Indian Corps; the 8th Division arrived in November.

The army was also joined at around this time by a very unusual formation. After the call up of reservists on the outbreak of the war, the Royal Navy discovered it had more men available than ships in which they could serve, these surplus men were formed into battalions and trained as soldiers. The Royal Naval

Ladies Road which was built for the daughters of King Louis XV.

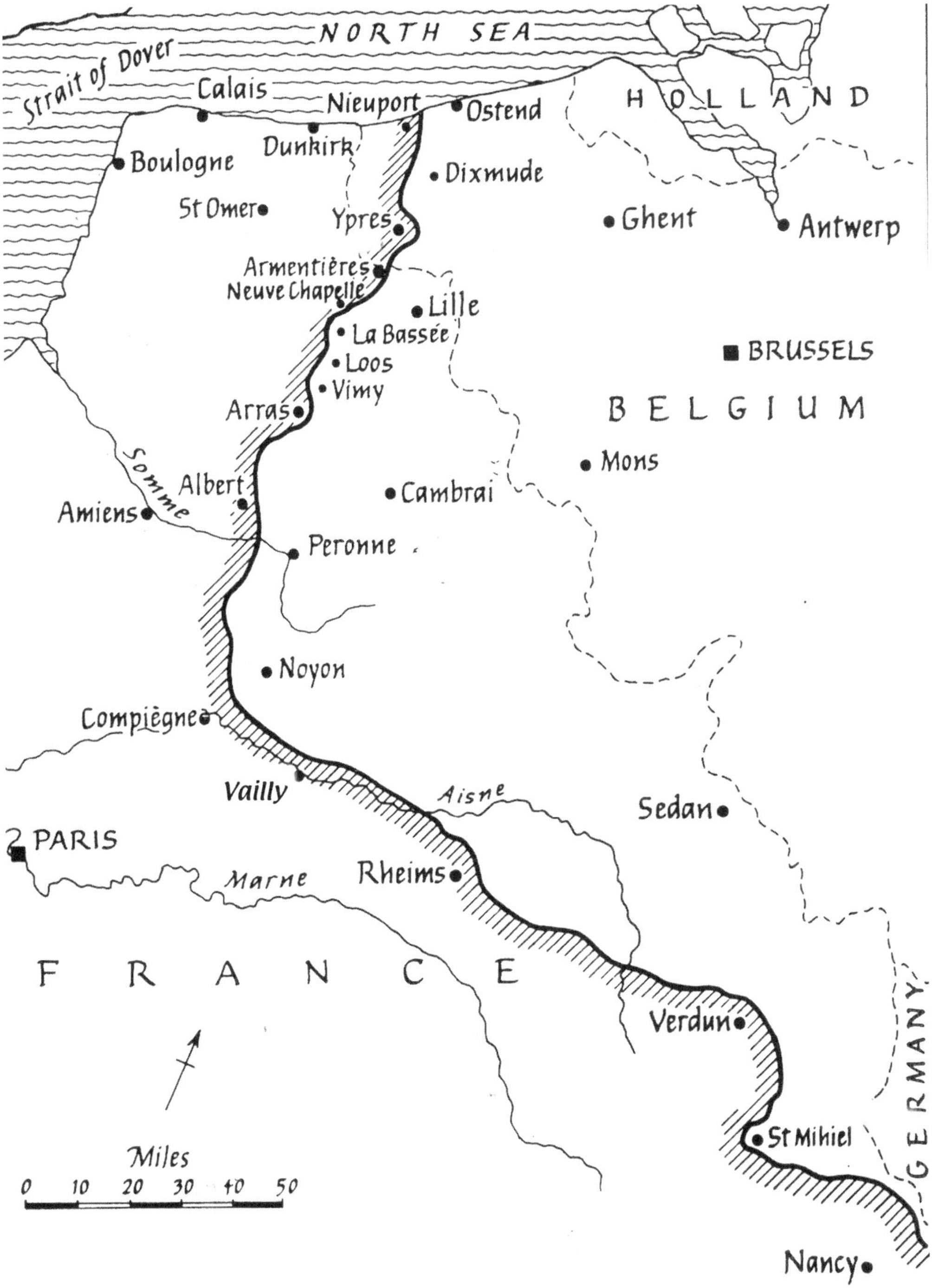

▲ Map 3. The Western Front

Division was therefore formed; although it was to come under army orders, and was organised on army lines it was nevertheless a creation of the Admiralty, in particular the First Lord of the Admiralty, Winston Churchill. Its members never forgot its origins and retained their naval ranks. The battalions of the division were named after famous sailors such as Drake and Nelson.

The Belgian army, having courageously held off the German invaders, fell back on the city of Antwerp. In an effort to save the city the British Government, after prompting by Winston Churchill, despatched the Royal Naval Division which arrived in the city on 4th October. It was soon realised that the situation was past saving and they were ordered to pull back. The first act of IV Corps, under Lieutenant-General Sir Henry Rawlinson, was to go to assist the Royal Naval Division and cover its withdrawal.

* * *

Sir John French realised that he should try and move the B.E.F. back to the north, near the coast where the lines of supply could be more easily maintained through the Channel Ports. Joffre agreed to this proposal and the transfer commenced on 1st October. By mid-October the British had moved from the Aisne and taken up position in northern France and the unoccupied corner of Belgium near the town of Ypres; this was most unfortunate for the British as the Germans were to launch their last attacks in this corner of Belgium, in a final attempt to win the war in 1914.

Following the fall of Antwerp, the Germans made an attack aimed at capturing the port of Calais; the Belgian army, assisted by the French, although resisting these attacks was forced to retreat. Realising that the Germans would be difficult to hold they decided to open the sluice gates at Nieuport, thus allowing sea water onto the low-lying area adjoining the coast. Although this action forced the Germans to fall back, they made another attack through Ypres. This was the start of the British association with this medieval Belgian market town, which had been for many years the centre of the Belgian cloth trade. In the centre of the town was the Gothic Cloth Hall and a magnificent cathedral.

The British were arriving at Ypres just as the Germans started to make their attack on 20th October. Although they had been ordered to advance, units found themselves being placed into the line in an haphazard fashion in an attempt at stemming the German attacks. As at Mons, the accurate rifle fire tore into the massed formations of the attacking German divisions as they made the first of their assaults north of Ypres near the village of Langemarck. By 24th October, the Germans had realised that this attack had failed.

A renewed attempt was made, starting on 29th October, to the south of the first attack; this reached crisis point on 31st October when seven fresh German divisions attacked the British 1st, 2nd and 7th Divisions at Gheluvelt. This village stood at a vital point, being on the road from Ypres to Menin; because it occupied the only (relatively) high ground, the Germans were desperate to take it because from this point the British were able to overlook their lines. Just before noon the

Germans captured Gheluvelt but once again, this time largely due to a counter-attack by the 2nd Worcesters which recaptured the village, the Germans were prevented from breaking through. The Germans did have some success, taking the Messines ridge south of Ypres, but further advances were prevented by the timely arrival of French reinforcements, and the front was stabilised.

It was on this day that the German artillery scored one of its most spectacular successes of the war. Hooge Chateau was the Headquarters of the 1st Division, and possibly noting a high level of activity, a German artillery gun opened fire on the Chateau on the afternoon of 31st October, killing seven staff officers, mortally wounding Lieutenant-General Samuel Lomax (G.O.C. 1st Division), and injuring several other officers including the G.O.C. of the 2nd Division.

A third and final attempt to break through was made on 11th November, this came close to success; had the Germans succeeded they would have been able to sweep into Calais, thus cutting off the B.E.F.'s escape route, as well as its lines of supply. Faced with mounting losses, the Germans were pushed back from Nonne Bosschen (Nun's Wood) by a force made up of little more than engineers, cooks and Headquarters clerks. This was the last line of defence, but it managed to hold off the German attack. There were further small scale actions over the next few days, but the First Battle of Ypres officially ended on 22nd November 1914.

The losses to the British army for the year of 1914 were enormous, but were tiny compared with what was to follow. The casualties of 1914 were however irreplaceable, being highly trained regulars. On the outbreak of war, the entire British army (excluding territorials) numbered just 235,000, with about half serving overseas in places such as India. The original B.E.F. that crossed into France in August 1914 was 84,000 strong, and whilst this number had been reinforced with the arrival of troops from all corners of the Empire, many of these reinforcements were needed just to keep the B.E.F. supplied with replacements for its ever-growing casualty list which, by the end of the year, amounted to 3,627 officers and 86,237 men (killed wounded or missing). It can be seen that a large proportion of the original pre-war army had been all but wiped out in five months.

It was with some relief that the first Christmas of the war was welcomed in the trenches on both sides, so much so that an unofficial truce occurred in some sectors, when men clambered out of their trenches and met in the middle of No Man's Land, exchanging cigarettes and tobacco, and playing a football match.

* * *

Back at home recruiting was being undertaken on an enormous scale. Lord Kitchener appealed for 100,000 men. Kitchener's face and pointing finger stating 'Your Country Needs You' appeared on recruiting posters up and down the country, this has become one of the most enduring images of the Twentieth Century. Although the initial target was met within a fortnight, these troops would take many months to be trained. In the meantime, territorial units were equipped and sent over to France as soon as possible. The first territorial troops to see a major action was the 14th Battalion, London Regiment (The London Scottish) who performed great heroics on the Messines Ridge during the First Battle of Ypres when they supported elements of the Cavalry Corps which was holding this sector*.

Fortunately for the Allies, the Germans, following their failure at Ypres, switched onto the defensive in France and Flanders, deciding to concentrate most of their resources in the east against Russia. This gave the British in particular time to reorganise over the winter.

Despite the early predictions that it would be 'All over by Christmas', it soon began to dawn on people that the war may last for a long time yet.

***** See Chapter 2 for a description of the expansion of the army, and the despatch of the territorial battalions. Earlier in September other battalions of the London Regiment had been sent to Malta to replace 'regular' battalions stationed there. Also, three divisions of territorials (the Home Counties Division and the 1st & 2nd Wessex Divisions) had gone to India to relieve the garrisons there. The arrival of these territorial units enabled the regular battalions to return home, these battalions were formed into the 7th and 8th Divisions.***

Chapter Two

1915: Early Battles

As has been described, the battles of 1914 had decimated the pre-war Regular Army. Whilst the 8th Division had been formed and despatched to the Western Front in November 1914, they were not the last soldiers of Britain's Regular Army. By the turn of the new year, the final battalions of regular troops had arrived from the far-flung outposts of the Empire and were formed into the last three regular divisions which were numbered 27, 28 and 29. The first two of these were sent to France in December 1914 and January 1915; the 29th Division was sent to the Dardanelles where it took part in the operation at Gallipoli (see Chapter 5).

The reason for these three divisions being numbered out of sequence was that Kitchener's appeal for 100,000 volunteers had been made immediately on the outbreak of the war. Whilst everyone else was expecting a short war, Kitchener was virtually alone in realising that this would not be the case. His appeal met with an overwhelming response, and within two weeks of it being made the first 100,000 men had enlisted. They were formed into the Kitchener's First New Army (abbreviated to 'K1') of six divisions, these became the 9th (Scottish), 10th (Irish), 11th (Northern), 12th (Eastern), 13th (Western) and 14th (Light) Divisions. It must be noted that the term 'New Army' is entirely different to the operational field armies fighting in France and Belgium. The New Armies were groups of six divisions created one after the other from the battalions formed from Kitchener's recruits.

These New Army divisions were loosely based on the administrative areas of the army; the Aldershot Command and London districts were ignored, and instead of the Southern Command having its own division, a 'Light' division was formed. This Light Division comprised of battalions from English light infantry regiments such as the Somerset Light Infantry, Oxfordshire & Buckinghamshire Light Infantry, Shropshire Light Infantry, Duke of Cornwall's Light Infantry, Durham Light Infantry and the Kings Own Yorkshire Light Infantry plus battalions from rifle regiments (The Kings Royal Rifle Corps and The Rifle Brigade).

A second appeal brought forward an equally quick response, and the Second New Army ('K2') with divisions from 15th to 20th was formed. Again the regional and 'Light' suffixes were used, although these were not used on the Third New Army, its divisions being numbered from 21 to 26. The Third New Army was raised soon after the Second during September 1914. By 15th September, half a million men had volunteered for the army.

In November the Fourth New Army was created, the K4 Divisions were numbered from 30 to 35 in the sequence after the 27th, 28th and 29th (regular) Divisions whose formation was mentioned above; however in order to create a pool of trained reinforcements for the eighteen divisions of the first three New Armies, the decision was taken in April 1915 to break up the six divisions of the Fourth New Army. (The resulting pool became the training reserve - see Chapter 13.)

Another result of this change was K5 (which came into being in December 1914) becoming a new K4, and its divisions' numbers being rearranged accordingly.

These new K4 divisions comprised of many battalions which had been formed by local councils and mayors, Members of Parliament, and other interested parties such as clubs and employers. By the end of 1914 there were 66 of these locally raised 'Pals' battalions; ultimately 148 battalions would be raised in this way, plus a further 68 reserve battalions, 84 artillery units and 48 engineer units. Examples of these battalions are numerous, but typically the 16th Battalion, K.R.R.C. was made up of past and present members of the Church Lads' Brigade and the 21st Battalion West Yorkshire Regiment was otherwise known as the Wool Textile Pioneers. The 15th, 16th and 18th Battalions of the West Yorkshire Regiment were the Leeds, 1st Bradford and 2nd Bradford Pals, and the 12th Battalion, K.O.Y.L.I. was formed by the West Riding Coal Owners' Association.

These locally raised battalions could not be taken over by the War Office until early in 1915 because the army's administration and training resources were under enormous strain due to the recruits already taken on in the first three New Armies.

The last of the New Army divisions were formed in August and September 1915 into a new K5. This Fifth New Army again consisted of six divisions, being numbered from 36 to 41; by this time the flow of recruits had slowed down, and alternative measures were being considered to ensure a continuing flow of men into the army (see Chapter 10).

Before Kitchener's New Armies could be trained, the commanders in France were desperate for their losses to be made up, and the soldiers of the Territorial Force were used to reinforce the surviving regulars in France and Flanders.

The Territorial Force had been formed in 1908 and its members were derided as 'weekend soldiers'. They had been created to guard Britain against invasion in the event of the Regular Army being called overseas. It was not long after the outbreak of war that the territorials were asked to waive their exemption from overseas duty; very few demurred. Prior to the outbreak of the war there were fourteen Territorial divisions, plus the same number of mounted brigades (the territorial equivalent of the cavalry, being Yeomanry).

Part of the original concept for the Territorial Force, as perceived when this organisation was formed, was that in the event of war, an unlimited expansion of the Territorials would take place; each battalion creating replicas of itself which, after training would be available for service. The battalions, after being despatched to the front, would leave behind a small cadre of men around whom a new battalion would form. The original battalion would become the first line battalion, the next the second line and so on.

As mentioned in the Prologue, the 5th Battalion Duke of Wellington's Regiment was Ravensthorpe's local territorial battalion, recruiting one of its companies in Mirfield. The 'original' 5th Battalion therefore became the 1/5th, and the new 'embryo' battalion was the 2/5th.

Kitchener did not rate the Territorials, and this resulted in him creating the New Armies previously mentioned, thus bypassing to a large extent the territorial organisation.

Despite the territorial organisation not being used to its full extent, many men volunteered for service in its battalions. There are a number of reasons for this, the one which may be the most relevant as far as Ravensthorpe is concerned was the fact that some areas of the country had strong local connections with the territorials. This, combined with the lack of any local 'Pals' type battalion meant that in many areas the territorial battalions filled up as quickly as their New Army equivalents.

As mentioned in Chapter 1, the first Territorials to see action were the London Scottish, a battalion of the London Regiment*; other Territorial units soon followed. The Territorial Force was based on regional lines; when mobilised and sent overseas these regional organisations were formed into divisions. The first complete territorial division to be sent abroad was the 42nd (East Lancashire) Division which went to Egypt, later taking part in the fighting at Gallipoli. It will be noted how this division was numbered after the last of the New Army divisions (the 41st).

Although the territorial divisions were numbered, they also retained their original local identity - thus there was the 46th (North Midland), 47th (2nd London)+, 48th (South Midland), 50th (Northumbrian), 51st (Highland) Divisions and many others; however it is the 49th (West Riding) Division that contained many of Ravensthorpe's Territorials. In May 1915 (when the first of Kitchener's New Army divisions arrived on the Western Front), these six territorial divisions were already in France and Belgium.

It has already been described how the B.E.F. had grown from its original two corps; in order to help the administration of the expanding B.E.F., an extra layer of command was created between Sir John French at General Headquarters ('G.H.Q.'), and corps level. This extra layer was the creation of two armies (later to be expanded to five). Sir Douglas Haig and Sir Horace Smith-Dorrien became commanders of the First and Second Armies respectively.

* * *

The first battle of 1915 was at Neuve Chapelle in March 1915. Sir John French hoped that he could pierce the German trench lines and advance towards the city of Lille. The attack was accompanied by a major artillery barrage, which, although puny compared to barrages later in the war, was impressive at the time; more shells being fired in the opening 35 minute barrage than in the whole of the Boer War.

The British and Indian troops attacked on 10th March, it was their first offensive of the war against German troops who were defending well entrenched positions. Rawlinson's IV Corps attacked on the left, with the Indian Corps on the right. The attack was quite successful as four lines of German trenches were captured as was the village of Neuve Chapelle. It is likely that more could have

**** This was one of the few all Territorial Regiments. Each battalion of the London Regiment had a subtitle depending on its location or its source of recruits. There were the Post Office Rifles, Civil Service Rifles as well as the Poplar and Stepney Rifles and the Blackheath Rifles.***

+ This, although the 2nd London Division, was the first from London to be formed into a division. The 1st London Division was the senior of London's two territorial divisions and comprised of units like the London Scottish which had been sent piecemeal to assist the regulars at the First Battle of Ypres. Because the units had been sent on an ad-hoc basis to the Western Front, it was not until later that the battalions were able to be withdrawn. The 1st London Division was sent to France in February 1916, being given the number 56.

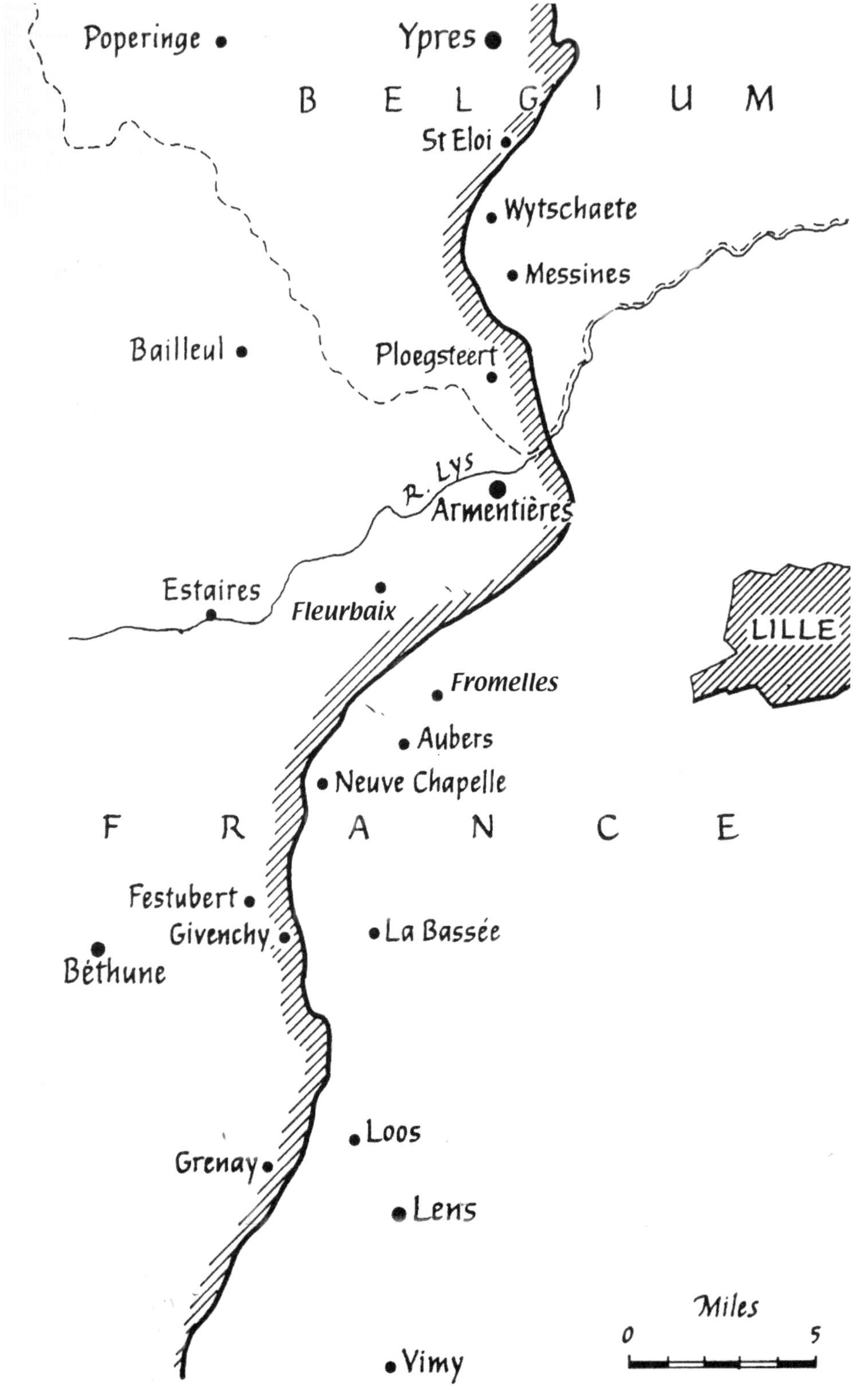

Map 4. The Front, northern France and southern Belgium

been achieved if communication between the attacking troops and the generals conducting the battle had been maintained. This problem was not to be fully overcome during the entire war. British and German casualties were approximately even - 12,000 each. Both sides claimed a victory, the British because of the ground that had been gained, whilst the Germans were pleased that, by rushing up reinforcements and counter-attacking, they had prevented a breakthrough. Although the battle lasted three days, all the ground gained had been taken in the first few hours of the attack. The Battle of Neuve Chapelle petered out; by 13th March a small salient had been created in the German lines.

Whilst the Battle of Neuve Chapelle will have meant little, if anything, to the people of Ravensthorpe, the departure of the 1/5th Battalion Duke of Wellington's Regiment, one of the battalions within the 49th (West Riding) Division, would have affected numerous families as many men from Ravensthorpe served in this battalion.

On 12th April, as part of the departure of the 49th Division, the 1/5th Battalion Duke of Wellington's Regiment sent its transport and machine gun section ahead of the main contingent. The battalion travelled in trains from Doncaster to Folkestone and on the evening of 14th April they crossed the English Channel on the steamer 'Victoria', arriving in Boulogne at 11.15pm.

A march up the hill out of town saw the battalion arrive at St. Martin's camp at 12.45am on the 15th. Despite the intense cold, only one blanket per man was issued. The War Diary describes how most of the men had given up any attempt at sleep by 3.30am.

After breakfast the battalion moved off at 10am, however their woes continued; the march was difficult, the day turned out to be hot, the roads were bad (the French variety of cobble stones - called Pave - made marching difficult) and the new boots the men had been issued with two days before departure had not been broken in. The War Diary complains bitterly: *"Many bad feet, before issue they were marching grandly. Everything left to the last moment - boots, harnesses, clothes, equipment, rifles, horses, carts, everything. Also issued with a range finder. Not one man in the battalion had ever seen a range finder before, a very difficult instrument to use...."*

The battalion's experiences upon arrival in France were probably similar to that of many other newly-arrived battalions, there was some confusion as inexperienced officers tried to organise the unit's movements. On 16th April the battalion was despatched by train to the town of Estaires. The War Diary reveals how two engines were required to pull the train, the men were in cattle trucks - 44 in each, whilst the officers did at least have carriages to travel in. After arriving in Estaires, billets were found to accommodate the men, these would have been farm out-buildings and barns and other properties abandoned by their former owners. On 19th April a total of 42 officers and senior N.C.O.s left for a short period of instruction in nearby trenches. The battalion went into the front line for the first time in May and took over a stretch of the trenches at Fleurbaix.

Whilst this introduction to the trenches was going on for the 1/5th Duke of Wellington's, a crisis was occurring to the north.

* * *

After the short battle of Neuve Chapelle in March, the next major event on the Western Front that concerned the British army was a renewed German attempt to break through to the Channel Ports. They had again selected Ypres as the battleground. On this occasion the Germans used a new weapon - gas. The attack had been delayed for several days whilst the Germans waited for a favourable wind to carry the chlorine gas in the direction of the Allied trenches; eventually an opportunity presented itself and the taps on the gas cylinders were opened at 5pm on 22nd April.

The soldiers lying in the path of the gas cloud were a division of French territorials and a division of French colonial (Algerian) troops. They can hardly be blamed for their reaction to the poisonous waves of greenish-yellow gas that engulfed them. Choking and drowning due to the liquid in their lungs, those that were able fled; the line collapsed and a gap of nearly five miles in the Allied front was created. Fortunately a German breakthrough was prevented partly due to their own timidity in advancing as they were surprised at the success of the gas, and the bravery of Canadian soldiers who took over the abandoned trenches. Crude gas masks were improvised by the Canadians - they were told to urinate on their socks and hold this against their faces. Within days the first purpose made, but basic, gas masks were made, being pads of gauze soaked in bicarbonate of soda.

Although the line was driven back, the Germans were held. Fighting during this Second Battle of Ypres continued for over a month until 25th May. Had the Germans managed to break the line here, it is likely that the Channel Ports would have been lost; with the line of retreat cut and resupply made difficult, defeat would have been a distinct possibility for the B.E.F. Although the line eventually stabilised, the position was difficult for defence and General Smith-Dorrien urged the Commander-in-Chief, Sir John French, to withdraw behind Ypres. Sir John had not trusted Smith-Dorrien ever since, against orders, he had fought the battle of Le Cateau. Because of his wish to give up ground, Smith-Dorrien was sacked* being replaced on 6th May by General Herbert Plumer who had until then been in command of V Corps. Plumer was to become one of the most respected British generals of the entire war.

Further gas attacks were made, but the element of surprise had been lost, and only a little ground was given up by the British. The Ypres salient was now formed and was to remain a very dangerous place for the British troops as it was overlooked on three sides by German positions.

* * *

Immediately after the Battle of Neuve Chapelle, Sir John French had held talks with General Joffre with a view to a joint offensive against the Germans; although

**** Smith-Dorrien received the news on the telephone from the C.I.G.S., Sir William Robertson with the words " 'Orace, you're for 'ome". In December 1915 he was appointed to command British forces in a campaign against the Germans in their East African colonies. He embarked for Cape Town on Christmas Eve 1915, on his first day at sea he caught a chill which developed into pneumonia. When his ship docked at Cape Town he was taken to hospital. Although on the road to recovery, he left hospital prematurely and recommenced work. He suffered a severe relapse and was forced to return to England.***

the preparations were interrupted by the German offensive at Ypres, once the first crisis was over, planning went on. It was hoped that the French would take the prominent feature of Vimy Ridge which commanded the landscape for miles around. The British would cooperate to the north towards a small rise in the ground at the village of Aubers; this was just behind the village of Neuve Chapelle which had been attacked a few weeks earlier.

As well as being flat, the area also had a very high water table, this meant that it was impossible to construct trenches; it was therefore necessary to build breastworks above the ground which offered much less protection than trenches.

The British attack on Aubers was to be a pincer movement, the northern assault being launched from the Fleurbaix area southwards towards Fromelles, and the southern attack from Neuve Chapelle. The attack which was to converge at Aubers was launched on 9th May. The Germans had learned the lesson of Neuve Chapelle and had strengthened their defences, siting concealed machine guns every few yards.

Because of the expenditure of ammunition at Neuve Chapelle, when 15% of the whole of the B.E.F.'s supply of artillery shells had been fired off, and the desperate fighting at Ypres, the bombardment could only last 40 minutes. Unfortunately the high explosive shells needed to destroy the German breastworks were in particularly short supply, the vast majority of the shells were shrapnel. Whilst these were deadly against troops in the open, the effect on troops in trenches or between breastworks was minimal; to make matters worse many of the shells were duds, this was due to the manufacturing process having been speeded up, unfortunately quality had declined as a result. The guns were also becoming worn, resulting in many shells being inaccurately aimed.

The German defences were only lightly damaged and were able to withstand the British assault which commenced at 5.30am. Machine guns mowed down hundreds of British and Indian troops as they advanced. Despite the failure of the first assault, Haig (in command of the First Army, under whose control the battle was fought) ordered another attack that afternoon. This attack also failed. Another assault ordered by Haig that night was cancelled after Haig's subordinate generals persuaded him that such an attack would be futile. The one day battle had cost 12,000 casualties without any gains to show for it.

To the south, in the French sector, gains had initially been made, but after desperate fighting for over a week, Vimy Ridge was still in German hands.

In order to support the French, a further attack was planned to take place at Festubert, just north of the La Bassee Canal. The assault, after a three-day bombardment was launched at 11.30pm on 15th May. This was the first night-time attack by the British. Again it was a two pronged assault. The southern attack was successful, but to the north (or left) the initial assault was repulsed. After much heavy fighting, the Germans withdrew their line slightly. The battle was brought to a close after ten days; it was the first time in the war that the Territorials were used in large numbers, with the 47th (2nd London) Division being involved in the closing stages.

The poor performance of the B.E.F. in these battles was blamed by Sir John French on a shortage of artillery shells; this information was reported in The Times (after Sir John had deliberately leaked the information) and brought about the collapse of Asquith's Liberal Government, this was replaced by a Coalition Government formed between the Liberals, Conservatives, and for the first time, the Labour Party. Sir John's actions in leaking information to the press were to rebound on him later - see Chapter 3.

Although the 49th (West Riding) Division had not been involved in any of these battles, they had been in reserve at both Aubers Ridge and Festubert, and would probably have been thrown in to the battle had either attack proved successful.

A total of four fatal casualties were incurred by the 1/5th Duke of Wellington's on 9th May, and a further seven on 15th May. Having been introduced to the trenches at Fleurbaix in May, and after a period in Brigade Reserve and then in Divisional Reserve, the battalion was back in the trenches in mid-June. It was during this second spell in the trenches that the next Ravensthorpe soldier to die in the war was killed.

William Astbury was born in January 1893, probably in Liverpool and educated at the Holy Trinity School, Grafton Street in Liverpool. William was orphaned, and having no relatives was adopted by Mr and Mrs Walton who lived in Norristhorpe, a small village near Heckmondwike. It is not known when or how this adoption came about - the distance between Liverpool and the West Riding of Yorkshire indicates there being some connection between Mr and Mrs Walton and that city.

Mr Walton was a miner working for the Mirfield Colliery Company. While the family lived at Norristhorpe, William attended the Congregational Sunday School in the village and gained a prize in 1913 for the best bowling average in the Sunday School cricket team. He started attending the Ravensthorpe Congregational Sunday School when the family moved to 4 Craven Street, Ravensthorpe, in 1914.

Before the war William was a territorial in the Duke of Wellington's Regiment. On 14th December 1914 he volunteered for overseas service and after being examined by a doctor who recorded his height (5' 5") and chest expansion (36"), passed him fit. Leaving his job (in the Dewsbury Reporter he was described as a 'labourer'), William was allowed four days leave at Easter and was then sent abroad with the 1/5th Battalion, arriving in France on the 14th April.

Besides letters from his family, William received a printed letter from the Yorkshire Congregational Union and another one from a governor of his old Liverpool school which informed him that 220 'old boys' of the school were at the front. He wrote home on 11th June when he reported that he was in good health, but looking forward to being relieved so as to get a decent night's rest. He also described how they had been in the trenches for the past six days, and *"...taking all things into consideration.....had had a lively time."* The weather was hot but cool at night, the countryside *"...that is what we see of it looks very well and it is a great shame and disgrace to civilisation that such a war goes on."* Clearly eager for news from home, he asked for a weekly newspaper to be sent.

His last letter home was written on 13th June 1915. Possibly having a premonition of his death, he tells in the letter how he had been reading from his pocket bible. His letter concluded with the quote: *"Be prepared for you neither know the hour nor the day when the Son of Man cometh."*

The next letter Mr and Mrs Walton received was from Lieutenant Sykes. He wrote that he was *"...sorry to inform them that Private Astbury died that morning - 16th June - having been shot in the head whilst on sentry duty. He was buried along with an officer by his comrades near the trenches."* The War Diary names William Astbury and Second Lieutenant Crowther as having been killed, with another private being seriously wounded.

William Astbury is buried in Rue David Cemetery, Fleurbaix, alongside Second Lieutenant Leslie T. Crowther, who was killed on the same day. The early casualties of the battalion are buried in this cemetery, these include the first soldier of the battalion to be killed, Thomas Sheard of Mirfield who died on 29th April. The Division's first casualties had been incurred a week earlier on 22nd April, when two men, one from the 1/4th Duke of Wellington's Regiment and one from the 1/4th York and Lancaster Regiment were killed (one of these soldiers is buried at Rue David Cemetery, the other at Sailly-sur-la-Lys Canadian Cemetery). Rue David Cemetery contains nearly 900 graves, including 17 from the 1/5th Battalion, Duke of Wellington's Regiment.

The next two men commemorated on the War Memorial did not die as a result of enemy action. John Henry Davill, like William Astbury was a territorial soldier; John however was in the Royal Garrison Artillery*; he was born in York in February 1893, the third of nine children of Harry and Mary Davill.

▲ 18. William Astbury

▲ 19. John Davill

** The artillery was split into three main components. The Royal Field Artillery (R.F.A.) served the infantry and the Royal Horse Artillery (R.H.A.) were primarily assigned to Cavalry Divisions. The Royal Garrison Artillery (R.G.A.) were however controlled from Army Headquarters rather than at divisional level. The R.G.A.'s enormous siege guns were capable of firing very heavy shells; the importance of their weapons was to grow as the German trenches became ever stronger during the course of the war. There was a fourth artillery component; the Honourable Artillery Company (the oldest regiment in the British Army) not only provided artillery but also supplied an infantry battalion.*

On 20th May 1912 John joined the territorial Royal Garrison Artillery. His medical records from his enlistment state he was 5' 6" tall with a 36" chest measurement. Many men joined the territorials in order to enjoy the annual manoeuvres which, for many of them, would have passed for holidays. John took part in three of these annual camps: for seven days in August 1912, with further fortnight long camps in June 1913 and June 1914.

By the time of the outbreak of war, the Davill family had moved to Ravensthorpe, living at 79 Sackville Street. John would have volunteered for overseas service, and was posted to France, arriving with his unit, the West Riding Heavy Battery, R.G.A. on the 17th April 1915. The battery was attached to the 49th (West Riding) Division between 13th May and 28th June - probably to assist the Division in the part it would have played in the Battle of Festubert. The War Diary of the battery surprisingly mentions John's name, recording on the 19th August *"Driver J.H. Davill died from pneumonia on 28th July. Buried at Merville."* Although the place of his burial was correct, John was admitted to the 82nd Field Ambulance on that day; he actually died on the 31st July and was buried the following day. John was aged 22 at the time of his death, and is buried at Merville Communal Cemetery. This tragedy did not prevent his younger brother, Henry (aged about 18) joining up within a year.

As has been mentioned earlier, the 2/5th Battalion, Duke of Wellington's Regiment was formed following the creation of the 1/5th Battalion; most of the original members of the 5th Battalion would have been posted to the 1/5th Battalion with more recent recruits going to the 2/5th Battalion. The training of the new 2/5th Battalion would have commenced immediately.

Hubert Oxley was one of the more recent recruits, joining up (and volunteering for overseas service) on 25th January 1915. Hubert's service record exists and we know that at the time of his enlistment he was 21 years and 10 months old, 5' 4½" tall, and had a 35" chest expansion. Initially part of the 5th battalion, he was posted to the 2/5th Duke of Wellington's when this unit was created, probably on 22nd February. Hubert was promoted to lance corporal on 3rd June 1915.

It was whilst undergoing his training in the U.K. that Hubert was taken ill. A medical report within his file indicates that he reported sick on the morning of 6th September; it goes on to describe how his condition deteriorated, and he was therefore taken to Sheffield General Hospital. His condition continued to worsen and on 12th September he was operated on, and his appendix was removed. It was too late; at 3pm that day, Hubert died.

Hubert's parents, John Henry and Adelaide Oxley of The Station Hotel 130 North Road, Ravensthorpe, chose to have their son buried in Edgerton Cemetery, Huddersfield.

* * *

The continued expansion of the British army* meant a further fifteen miles of the front line stretching south of Arras to the River Somme, could be taken over from

**** Between February and September 1915, besides the six territorial divisions previously mentioned, fifteen 'New Army' divisions arrived in France and Flanders. The 1st Canadian Division had the honour of being the first non-regular division to arrive in France on 15th February 1915; this division together with the 2nd Canadian Division formed the Canadian Corps.***

the French in August. This became the responsibility of the newly formed Third Army, under General Monro. (Monro had previously stepped into Haig's shoes as commander of I Corps when two armies were formed at the end of 1914.) The French continued to hold some of the line around Arras, this would not be taken over by the British until early in 1916

Meanwhile, the 49th Division had at the end of June moved northwards to the Ypres Salient. (Nervous of the Germans launching further gas-attacks, the division's War Diary records *"Sufficient anti-gas helmets for the whole of the division were received and distributed".*)

On 16th July the 49th Division lost its first commanding officer; Major-General T.S. Baldock was severely wounded in the head by a fragment of an artillery shell which was fired at his headquarters (Trois Tours near Brielen, north-west of Ypres) at 4.15pm. Although the injury was not fatal, he was unable to resume command and retired from the army the following year. His replacement as G.O.C. of the 49th Division was Major-General E.M. Perceval.

The good weather mentioned by William Astbury had by September changed to heavy rain. Water, two feet deep stood in trenches; in several places the parapets of the trenches were washed away and had to be rebuilt with sandbags. By the middle of September, the weather had improved slightly. The 1/5th Duke of Wellington's spent, according to the War Diary, *"...a quiet time on the canal bank"* between the 10th and 15th September (between the 25th August and 17th September, the battalion only suffered two fatal casualties). The canal in question, the Yser Canal, ran northwards out of the town of Ypres towards the coast. The War Diary continues *"Weather very fine, and it was possible for the men to indulge in swimming in the canal. The battalion provided working parties daily and nightly. Evenings very quiet and there were few casualties. Major Rendall, Adjutant, had to go to hospital on September 14th with a chill."*

What the War Diary fails to mention is that on the 14th, besides Major Rendall catching a chill, Ernest Beckett was killed. Ernest was born in May 1890, the son of William and Sarah Beckett who lived at 12 Calder Road, Ravensthorpe. Besides Ernest, Mr and Mrs Beckett had a further two sons and two daughters; Ernest was, however, the oldest of the Becketts' children.

Again, the service record exists; we know that Ernest, when he volunteered for overseas service on 14th December 1914 was 5' 4½" tall. (As William Astbury also agreed to serve overseas on this day, it seems likely the battalion volunteered en-masse on the same day.) Before the war he worked as a spinner for Armitage & Rhodes; like many other men on the memorial he had strong connections with the parish church, being a member of the Church Institute, and also in the choir. He went to France with the first draft of the battalion, arriving on 13th April. His last letter home was received on Thursday 16th September, two days after his death; part of the letter was reproduced in the Dewsbury News on 25th September and reads:- *"I am in the pink, we are having lovely weather just now. It is hot but the nights are getting longer now - but we must only expect that."*

Also on 25th September, the rival newspaper for the district, the Dewsbury Reporter published a letter from Stanley Gawthorpe, another Ravensthorpe soldier, to his parents describing how Stanley and his pals had *"received quite a shock by Ernest Beckett being killed whilst trying to get a mate away from the path of a shell."*

▲ 20. Hubert Oxley

▲ 21. Ernest Beckett

▼ 22. Calder Road, Ravensthorpe. Ernest Beckett's parents' house is one of those in the right foreground. *Photograph courtesy of Kirklees Community History Service*

Ernest's parents received at least three letters concerning their son's death, and all tell a similar story. Second Lieutenant Rippon, Ernest's platoon commander wrote on the 14th, the day of Ernest's death, telling how a shell landed only one yard from Ernest. He described Ernest as a thoroughly good soldier, and went on *"I have never heard your son making any complaints."* The following day, a letter was sent by Walter Garfitt, Albert Mason, Albert Jewsbury, Stanley Gawthorpe and Jack Crowther (three of these five were to be killed within a year) who reported that Ernest was killed instantaneously whilst on a working party. The last letter, however, may have come from the soldier whom Ernest had saved; Private T. Hardy wrote to Mr and Mrs Beckett:- *"I am sorry to tell you that your son Ernest was killed this afternoon. We were stood talking to one another, your son and I awaiting instructions from the corporal in charge of our party when we heard a shell coming over. We dropped together into the trench bottom, but the shell burst between us; Ernest was struck in the head and died in a few minutes. You must try to bear up in your great sorrow and know that he suffered no pain as he never recovered consciousness. We buried him in a quiet little cemetery behind the firing line and most of us in the same platoon attended the funeral to pay our best respects to a true soldier...."*

Private Ernest Beckett, aged 25 was killed in action on 14th September 1915 and is buried in Bard Cottage Cemetery, to the north of Ypres. The cemetery contains about 1,700 graves including ten men of the 1/5th Duke of Wellington's. One of these ten is Second Lieutenant Norris Rippon who was killed on 18th November 1915. The cemetery is just a few yards west of the canal where the battalion had been resting.

Chapter Three

The Battle of Loos

The Battle of Loos in September 1915 was the most important offensive battle fought by the British on the Western Front in that year; it was also the first time in France that Kitchener's New Armies had been ordered 'over the top'; however the most significant effect of the battle was that it precipitated a change in the leadership of the British army, thus affecting the way the army fought for the rest of the war.

Like the attacks earlier in the year, the battle was instigated in order to conform with the actions, or intended actions, of the French army who were to assault the high point of Vimy Ridge. Sir John French was far from happy about the proposal as the ground over which the British army was to attack was flat, full of small villages which had been fortified by the Germans, and dominated by the slag heaps from the coal mines in the area. From these slag heaps the Germans would be able to observe all movement, and fire upon the attacking troops. The British antipathy towards the plan was exacerbated by the continuing shortage of artillery and ammunition; nevertheless Sir John agreed to go along with the French plans. General Haig, commanding the First Army, was also against the plan but was forced to carry on despite his prediction that heavy losses would be incurred.

A total of six British divisions were to be used in the attack; on the southern end of the front was placed the 47th (2nd London) Division*, to the north, attacking Loos village itself was the 15th (Scottish) Division; further north still came the 1st, 7th, 9th (Scottish), and 2nd Divisions. Other divisions were held in reserve; their deployment was the most controversial aspect of the battle.

A total of 75,000 British troops were to be used against 10,000 Germans, however the Germans, anticipating an attack, had strengthened their trench lines using barbed wire and machine gun posts. Previously a single line of trenches, consisting of a main front line with communication trenches leading back to support and reserve lines had been thought to be sufficient for defence. The Germans, however, had been busy, building a second line of trenches, again with front, support, and reserve lines; during the next twelve months, a third line of trenches was started.

As the Germans had advanced far into France and Belgium, they had the luxury of being able to choose the best sites for the location of their defences; a small tactical withdrawal in order to take advantage of local conditions was therefore always possible to the Germans (thus enabling them to make their defensive positions even stronger), whereas to the British, but even more to the

From now on I will not be differentiating between Regular, Territorial and New Army Divisions. The type of division can easily be worked out. Regular Divisions were numbered 1 to 8 and 27,28 and 29. The New Army Divisions were 9 to 26 and 30 to 41. All the others were Territorial except the 63rd (Royal Naval) Division - see Chapter 1, and the 70th to 75th Divisions.

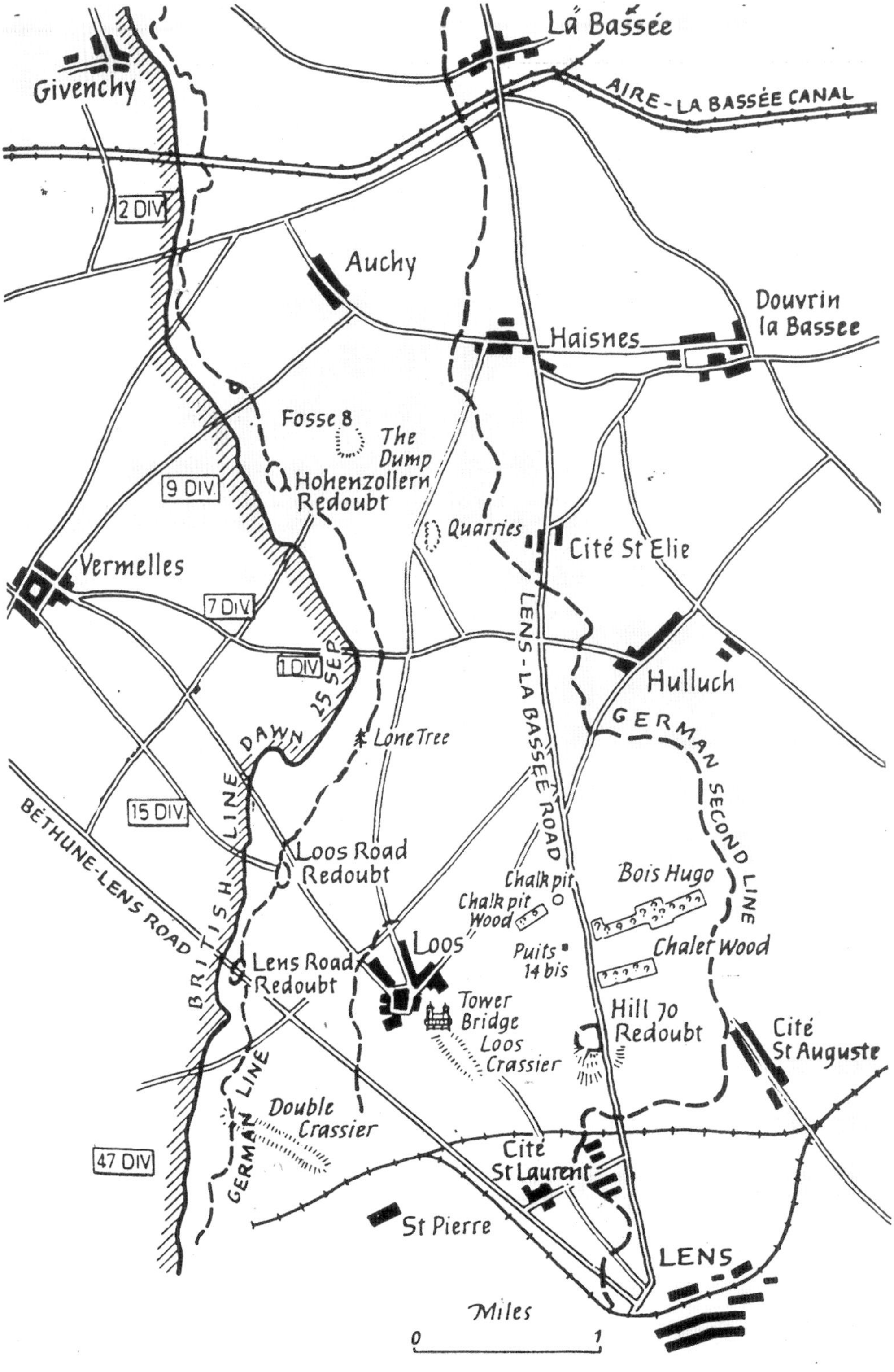

▲ Map 5. The Battle of Loos

French, every yard of ground held by the enemy had to be challenged for the sake of national pride.

The Battle of Loos was the first time the British were to use poisoned gas in the war, however, right until the last moment it was not certain, due to the direction of the wind, whether the gas would be discharged. At 5am on Saturday 25th September, General Haig, along with his staff, climbed a wooden observation tower that had been built, in order to make the final decision on the release of the gas. A cigarette was lit, the smoke drifted in a north-easterly direction, and the decision to release the gas was made.

The preliminary bombardment by the British artillery had lasted for four days, it was hoped that this, along with the gas would sufficiently subdue the German defenders. At 6.30am on 25th September, the six divisions attacked behind the somewhat fitful gas cloud; early morning drizzle had cleared, leaving a little ground mist. The gas had been discharged intermittently for forty minutes before the attack. When gas was not being discharged, smoke was deployed to confuse the enemy into believing the discharge of gas was continuous. (This was due to there being insufficient gas for the full forty minutes; it was however necessary for the discharge to be this long to ensure the Germans kept their gas masks on - it was known that the masks would only be effective for about half an hour, and any discharge for longer than this would ensure the wearer received a dose of gas poisoning.)

Unfortunately the plan did not work; in many places the wind was not strong enough to carry the gas towards the German lines, and it hung around near the British trenches, causing heavy casualties to the attacking troops.

Despite the problems with the gas, on the right, the 47th (2nd London) Division broke through the German front line. To their left, after much bitter fighting, the 15th (Scottish) Division took the village of Loos. The success of these two divisions was partly due to the fact that the gas travelled reasonably well in the wind at this end of the battlefield. Unfortunately, in the 15th (Scottish) Division, many officers had been killed; this probably explains how battalions of the division lost direction and many, who should have been attacking outside the village, ended up in Loos itself. It took some time for the now thoroughly intermingled battalions to leave Loos (where they were prising Germans out of the cellars) and set off in a south-easterly direction towards Hill 70, which was an important position commanding a large part of the battlefield, dominating the town of Lens as well as Loos village.

Hill 70 was only lightly defended and the Germans ran off at the approach of the British troops. Things however soon started to go wrong for the British. After taking Hill 70, the troops turned south towards Lens, this was a mistake and not in accordance with the plan. The Germans took advantage of this confusion, and from their positions in the second line, poured fire on the Scottish battalions who were therefore pinned down in front of the German second line positions. Later in the day, the Germans counter-attacked and retook Hill 70.

Further to the north, the attack had not been as successful. Although some troops from the 1st Division had also managed to break through the German front line and advance towards Hulloch, elsewhere on the Division's front, opposite the position known as the Lone Tree, the advance was stopped in its tracks. The commander of the 1st Division, rather than trying to push through the gap made near Hulloch, chose instead to reinforce the failed push at the Lone Tree. As a result, the success here was not exploited and the breach in the enemy lines was plugged by the Germans bringing up reinforcements. Had the two successful advances on either side of the Lone Tree at Loos and Hulloch been exploited, the Lone Tree position would probably have fallen anyway due to it being virtually surrounded.

Further north still, the 7th Division's attack on a position known as The Quarries was successful in its early stages, as was that of the 9th (Scottish) Division against the Hohenzollern Redoubt and Fosse 8 (a large slag heap). Unfortunately, initial gains here could not be held and German counter-attacks were successful.

The only troops in the area that had not been committed was a reserve of three divisions (formed into XI Corps). XI Corps contained, besides the 21st and 24th Divisions, the newly formed Guards Division. The Guards Division had been formed by removing battalions of Grenadier, Coldstream, Scots and Irish Guards from their original divisions. (The newly created Welsh Guards also contributed a battalion to this new division.)

The two New Army Divisions, the 21st and 24th, had only been in France for a fortnight, and had received very little training in England; they had few experienced officers and had only received their rifles two months previously. In the days and nights immediately preceding the battle, the reserve divisions were marched rapidly to the front.

Sir John French had decided against using these divisions in any frontal attack (they were to pursue the enemy once the front lines had been breached) and so kept them under his personal control at G.H.Q. As the battle was organised, once again, by Sir Douglas Haig's First Army, he tried to persuade Sir John to allow the reserves to be placed under his control, but Sir John refused. After the news of the successes near Loos on the morning of the 25th Sir John decided to release XI Corps to Haig in the hope that the fresh impetus would tip the balance in favour of the British. Unfortunately, it was not until 1.20pm on the 25th that XI Corps was released to Haig (which, according to Haig, was far too late).

It was decided that the 21st and 24th Divisions would be pushed up with the Guards Division in reserve; however the divisions were scattered throughout the countryside, up to sixteen miles behind the front, and it took a long time for them to be assembled.

That night (the 25th/26th September) the 21st and 24th Divisions were marched forward, through a countryside heavily congested with troops moving in both directions, ambulances and convoys of ammunition. There was much confusion as hasty orders for the divisions to move up were given by inexperienced officers, on routes that had not been reconnoitred, in the dark and in pouring rain. The crossing of derelict trenches on the way up to their jumping off positions was time consuming and tiring. The wet and exhausted troops, without any food (the mobile kitchens had to be left behind) were expected to take, in broad daylight, positions which more experienced troops had been unable to take despite the assistance of an artillery bombardment* and gas attack.

The artillery of the 21st and 24th Divisions became lost on the night of the 25th/26th. At daybreak they found they had advanced too far, and as a result were subjected to severe German artillery fire, and were effectively neutralised. When the infantry of the two divisions came to advance, they found they had inadequate artillery support.

Without being aware of the full situation, the British High Command believed that a push against the second line trenches would result in a clean break being made in the German line and enable exploitation of the countryside behind by the cavalry. Whilst the second line trenches were held in places by the British (this had been the case since early on the 25th) the Germans had, in the intervening twenty-four hours, rushed up reinforcements, and in many cases recaptured their second line positions. The plan was for the 21st and 24th Divisions, marching side by side, to attack the Germans between Hill 70 and Hulloch.

When, on the morning of the 26th, the first of the attacks by these troops went in, their massed formations were cut to pieces by German machine gun fire. They soon came up against the barbed wire entanglements, and found their route blocked; desperately they tried to force a passage through the four-foot high barrier, but to no avail. Thousands of troops were cut down during this initial advance; attacks were again made later in the day.

* * *

Four men from Ravensthorpe were killed whilst serving in units of the 21st and 24th Divisions. Philip Chapman was in the 9th Battalion, Norfolk Regiment (71 Brigade, 24th Division); Alfred Gardiner and Fred Smith were both in the 9th Battalion, King's Own Yorkshire Light Infantry (64 Brigade, 21st Division); John Pattinson was in the 10th K.O.Y.L.I. (also 64 Brigade, 21st Division).

The 24th Division attacked on the left of the 21st Division between Bois Hugo and Hulloch. The War Diary of 71 Brigade states that at 1am on the 26th the brigade was ordered to send one of its battalions to attack The Quarries in front of Hulloch. This is confirmed by the War Diary of the 9th Norfolks which indicates that they were ordered at 3.30am on the 26th to assist 20 Brigade (7th Division). It was never easy for troops to be taken out of their usual command structures and to be placed under the orders of a different formation; for this to happen on the eve of their first action and with very little notice was most unfortunate.

The 9th Norfolks arrived in what had been the German front line trench at 5.30am. According to the War Diary *"The attack was launched at 6.45am, but owing to the heavy fire.....no progress was possible, and so cover was taken once more in the trenches. Later the 2nd Worcesters* [5 Brigade, 2nd Division] *passed through the battalion to attack The Quarries."*

At about 7pm the battalion was forced to retire to some trenches further back when the Germans opened heavy fire on them. The battalion was relieved that night by troops from the Guards Division. In the confusion the War Diary originally indicated that the day's losses were 19 officers and men killed, 70 wounded and 335 missing; this was later amended to 39 killed, 130 wounded (8 of whom by gas - presumably British) and 34 missing. Although giving no indication of numbers wounded, 'Soldiers Died in the Great War' ('S.D.G.W.') lists 60 men from the Battalion killed on the 26th September. One of that number was Philip Benjamin Chapman.

Philip was born in Norwich to William and Amelia Chapman. His parents (who still lived at Middle Street in Norwich) had five sons; Philip who was aged 35 when killed was the second of the Chapmans' children. It seems that before the war he worked as a stoker at the Mirfield Gas Company in Ravensthorpe, and was a member of the Working Men's Club. He was probably a pre-war reservist and joined his regiment on 7th September 1914. Philip arrived in France on 30th August 1915, less than four weeks before his death. His last letter home stated that he had not come across his brothers Jim or Tom, who were also serving at that time in France; after asking for some 'fags', he concluded *"I shall see you before long."*

In early October, his parents received a letter from Lieutenant M.J. Spurrell who wrote as 'the only surviving officer in 'C' Company' to say Philip had died fighting bravely; while this may have been a comfort, it is unlikely that Lieutenant Spurrell really had any idea what had happened to Philip. Philip Chapman has no known grave and is therefore named on the panels of the Loos Memorial to the Missing, which stands on three sides of Dud Corner Cemetery, on the Lens - Bethune Road, less than a mile from Loos village. The Memorial commemorates about 21,000 men with no known grave, the majority of whom fell during the Battle of Loos.

Meanwhile the 21st Division was alongside and slightly to the south or right of the 24th Division. (The 21st Division had, like the 24th Division, been reduced to just two Brigades with 62 Brigade having been sent to support the 15th (Scottish) Division.) The night-time advance of the 21st Division was led by 63 Brigade with 64 Brigade to their rear. Immediately to their left should have been 72 Brigade of the 24th Division (unfortunately they failed to advance - this was to cause problems later on). It is with 64 Brigade that the three Ravensthorpe K.O.Y.L.I.s were serving; the brigade contained the 14th and 15th Battalions, Durham Light Infantry besides the 9th and 10th K.O.Y.L.I.

In the hours before dawn on the 26th, the 21st Division moved forward, but only with great difficulty owing to the confusion and congestion. By 3am, 64 Brigade found itself east of the original German front line trench system; it was only at daybreak that its exact position was established; 63 Brigade (with whom 64 Brigade had lost touch during the night) were found to be entrenched on the Lens to Hulloch road, just north of Bois Hugo, with 64 Brigade a little to their rear.

At 9am an attack on Hill 70 was launched by the 15th (Scottish) Division, along with 62 Brigade (it will be remembered that the Germans had retaken Hill 70 the previous day). The attacking troops managed to advance some way up the hill, but could not advance any further. Reinforcements were called for, so 64 Brigade sent up the 14th D.L.I. At this point, 63 Brigade retired, taking with them the 14th D.L.I.; a general retirement also took place from Hill 70, which was then shelled by the British artillery on the assumption that no British troops remained on the hill. (While attempting to stop this retirement, Brigadier-General Nickalls, the commander of 63 Brigade, was killed; he has no known grave and is commemorated on the Loos Memorial to the Missing.)

The retiring troops rallied behind 64 Brigade; another assault was then organised, this time with both the 14th and 15th D.L.I. taking part, they were to attack the Germans at Puits 14 Bis, west of the Lens-Hulloch road. Unfortunately the D.L.I. were drawn to the right and attacked in the direction of Hill 70, this caused many casualties to the attacking battalions. This second attack wavered and at about 12.30pm, there was another retirement. Once again the retiring troops were rallied, again behind the 64 Brigade's reserves (being the 9th and 10th K.O.Y.L.I.).

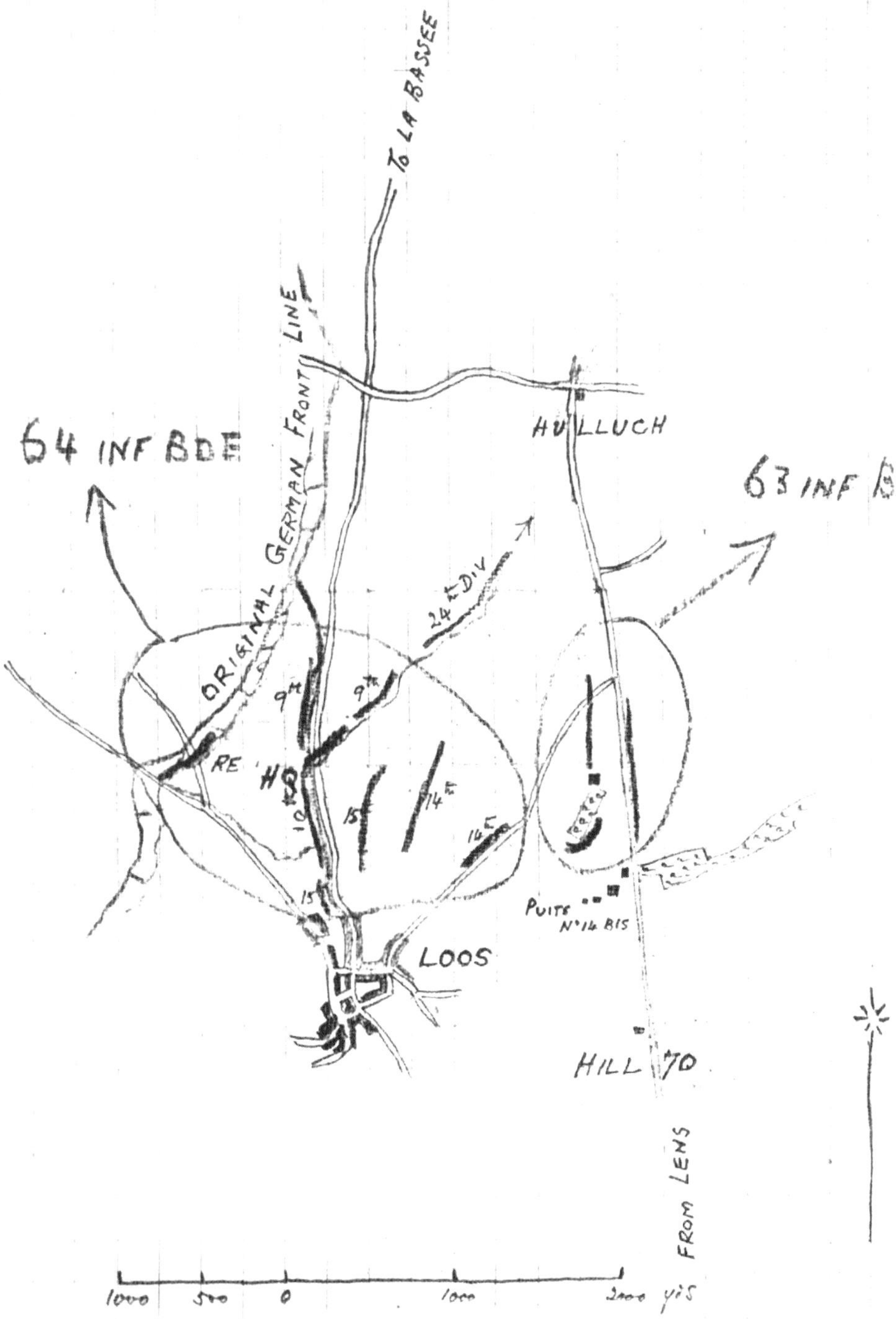

▲ Map 6. Trench Map of Loos. *Courtesy of the Public Record Office*. Reference WO 95/2159

A third attack was then organised; this was to be undertaken by the 9th and 10th K.O.Y.L.I. together with as many other troops as could be mustered together. Just as this attack was being organised at Brigade Headquarters, it was noticed that the 9th K.O.Y.L.I. was moving forward without any orders*. Their commanding officer dashed off to try and stop this unauthorised attack. The 10th K.O.Y.L.I. was ordered to follow. Mixed parties of men from the two D.L.I. battalions and units of 63 Brigade followed the two K.O.Y.L.I. battalions - some of these men were attacking for the third time that day. The attack pressed up the slopes of Hill 70, all the time under heavy machine gun and artillery fire. Once again the attack withered.

Incredibly, all the attacks had been made under the assumption that Hill 70 was entirely in the hands of the Germans; this was not the case. The first retirement from Hill 70 (by the 15th Division and 62 Brigade) had not been a total retirement, many troops had been left hanging onto trenches halfway up the hill all day, and had been bombarded by British artillery as well as German. The attacks had therefore been aimed at taking positions which were largely in British hands.

The Guards Division arrived that night to relieve the 21st Division whose casualties were about 4,000. An analysis of S.D.G.W. for the two K.O.Y.L.I. Battalions reveals that the 9th K.O.Y.L.I. suffered far more casualties (43 killed, plus three more who died of wounds in the following days) than did the 10th K.O.Y.L.I. (21 killed, plus two who later died of wounds).

As with Philip Chapman, what happened to Fred Smith, Alfred Gardiner and John Pattinson, the three Ravensthorpe K.O.Y.L.I.s, is not known in much detail.

John T. Pattinson+ who, it will be remembered, was in the 10th K.O.Y.L.I., was born in Liversedge; before the war he worked as a canal boatman. He enlisted in September 1914, leaving behind a wife and five children. It was not until September 1916, a year after his death, that his widow received, at their home at 18 Duke Street, Ravensthorpe a letter about John, confirming that "*...as no further information concerning him has been received, it has been presumed for official purposes that he died on or since that date* [ie 26th September 1915]." John was aged 38 when he died.

Born in Fleetwood, Lancashire, before the war Fred Smith worked in the pressing department of Marshall, Kaye and Marshall's Mill; he attended St. Saviour's Church and was a member of Ravensthorpe United football team. He lived with his parents at 21 Hebble Street, Ravensthorpe. Fred's parents were initially told that their son may have been injured; a letter was published in the Dewsbury Reporter on 2nd October 1915, the writer, a soldier from Mirfield, said that Fred had been shot in the leg, but he believed that he had been 'picked up by ambulance men'.

Three weeks later, a further article appeared reporting that Fred's parents had received a letter from a stretcher bearer who had written to say that he had found the body of their son on the battlefield at Loos - the identification being made from documents found in his pockets. The article went on to say that despite this (and the fact that his parents had received a returned letter marked 'location unknown'), his mother clung to the belief that Fred had not been killed; two weeks

---

***** *The Official History lays the blame for this with a Staff Officer who urged the attack to take place.***

+ The War Memorial misspells his name as 'Pattison'.

AN EXTRAORDINARY CASE.

NO NEWS FOR A YEAR.

RAVENSTHORPE SOLDIER KILLED.

Over a year ago news was received by his relatives that Pte. J. T. Pattinson, of the K.O.Y.L.I., No. 18, Duke Street, Ravensthorpe, was missing, and up to September 25th of this year no further news had been received, when on that date an an official intimation came to hand which stated that "as no further information concerning him has been received, it has been presumed for official purposes that he died on or since that date." With the letter a copy of the King and Queen's sympathy was enclosed. Pte. Pattinson was 38 years of age, and leaves a widow and five children to mourn his loss. He enlisted in September, 1914, and went to France twelve months later. He had only been at the Front a fortnight when he was reported missing. In civilian life he was a canal boatman.

Pte. J. T. Pattinson, K.O.Y.L.I., Ravensthorpe (killed).

▲ 23. John Pattinson

▲ 24. Fred Smith

later Fred was officially reported 'wounded and missing'. In early December, Fred's parents received a letter from the War Office stating that their son, who was aged 25, had been killed.

The notification from the War Office was duly reported in the Dewsbury News on 11th December, together with a letter from a Lance Corporal Crossley who wrote from hospital "*...he* [Fred] *was wounded on the 26th September just before I got hit. After I got wounded I started to crawl to a place of safety, and as I was crawling along Fred called for me to give him a helping hand, also to dress his wound which was a gunshot wound in the left thigh. I was so badly wounded that when I got to Fred I was so weak that I rolled onto my back, and I was helpless for a few minutes, but I could see that your dear son needed attention more than I did so I pulled myself together and dressed his wound which, although not a big one, had caused the loss of a lot of blood. My only regret is that I could not get him away with me. I was hit in the left thigh, both hips and both buttocks....*"

Also in the 9th K.O.Y.L.I. with Fred was Alfred Gardiner. Alfred was just 21 when he died. He had four brothers who also served in the war. His parents, who lived at 9 Armitage Street Ravensthorpe, received a letter from him on 27th September saying he was 'quite well'. It was not until late November that they received notification that Alfred had been killed on the 27th September*. Although

**** This is incorrect. Both Fred Smith's and Alfred Gardiner's parents were told that their sons had died on 27th September. 'Soldiers Died in the Great War' quotes this date for virtually all the battalion's casualties. The C.W.G.C. and the Medal Rolls at the Public Record Office also state the 27th September; however the battalion saw no action on this date (they were relieved at 3am on the 27th). The correct date was, of course, the 26th September which was the worst day of the war for Ravensthorpe (equalled only by 3rd May 1917).***

◂ 25. Alfred Gardiner wearing a uniform which seems to be too small. The bugle is misleading. It was not unusual for photographers to give their subjects superfluous pieces of equipment so as to make the photographs more interesting.

▾ 26. The Loos Memorial to the Missing, which surrounds Dud Corner Cemetery. *Photograph courtesy of Mrs D. Tattersfield*

attending Ravensthorpe Primitive Methodist Church, Alfred was apprenticed to Bagley's Glass Works in Knottingley (the town where he was born), which is some 20 miles from Ravensthorpe. Tragedy struck Alfred's parents again, just over 12 months later when another son, Ernest (aged 14) was drowned in the canal.

Like Philip Chapman, all three K.O.Y.L.I.s have no known grave and are commemorated on the Loos Memorial to the Missing.

The next Ravensthorpe casualty was a brother of Philip Chapman; it has not been possible to establish when Jim Chapman was injured, it may have been on 26th September, but it is equally possible he was wounded some time after this date.

Aged 33 in 1915, Jim had three older brothers (Philip, Tom and William) and one younger brother (Albert, aged 18). Of the five brothers, only Albert and William survived the war. (It has been a little difficult to unravel the family connection here as Jim's Christian names were James Albert; unfortunately the military authorities reversed his names and recorded him as Albert James, which initially caused me to confuse him with the youngest brother!)

Before the war, Jim worked at the Yorkshire Electric power station at Thornhill, and was a member of Ravensthorpe Working Men's Club. He joined the Royal Field Artillery at the outbreak of the war (he was a pre-war Royal Garrison Artillery territorial), and arrived in France on 18 March 1915.

Serving in the 21st Trench Mortar Battery, R.F.A., and attached to III Corps which held the northern end of the First Army's frontage, it can be assumed he took part in one of the three subsidiary attacks that were effectively diversionary attacks for the Battle of Loos.

III Corps' subsidiary action was carried out by the 8th Division at Bois-Grenier north of the main attack front at Loos. It is possible that his battery, which was armed with four 1.5 inch mortars assisted the 2nd Rifle Brigade, part of 8th Division, in beating off German counter-attacks. The result of this attack was the capture of the German front line trench for eleven hours, and the taking of over 120 prisoners. It cost the 8th Division, however, more than 1,300 casualties.

As mentioned earlier, it is by no means certain that he was wounded in this attack, his injuries may have been incurred some time after this action. The wound he received in his arm was probably not life threatening, and after spending some time at one of the large base hospitals on the French coast, it was decided to send him home either for further treatment or to complete his recovery.

Jim was put on board the hospital ship 'Anglia'* which set sail from Boulogne at 11am on Wednesday, 17th November. Upon approaching Folkestone the Anglia hit a mine which had been laid by a German submarine. The shock of the explosion broke the wireless set, so no S.O.S. signal was able to be sent, and the engine room had to be abandoned. Lifeboats were launched from the Anglia (one of which sank due to being overloaded), and the destroyer H.M.S. Ure came alongside and took many people off, a task which was made more difficult due to the Anglia circling helplessly as its engines were still running. Another ship - a steam collier called 'Lusitania' - came up to help with the rescue; just as the first men were boarding from the lifeboats, this ship also hit a mine.

Anglia belonged to the London and North West Railway Company and had been requisitioned and converted into a hospital ship. On 1st November it had brought King George V back to England after he had been injured following a fall from a horse whilst inspecting troops.

The death toll of approximately 150 (including a number of female nurses) would have been less had it been possible to stop the Anglia's engines. Many of the wounded on the ship were stretcher cases on their way to 'Blighty' and would have had no chance of escape when the ship started to go down. It is not known if Jim Chapman was one of these stretcher cases, but he was one of those who lost their lives.

Jim's body was never recovered, and his name is therefore recorded on the Hollybrook Memorial in Southampton. The memorial records the names of 1,868 sailors, soldiers, marines and airmen who were lost in home waters and who have no grave but the sea.

* * *

After the Battle of Loos had ended, serious doubts were raised over the suitability of Sir John French as Commander-in-Chief of the British armies on the Western Front. Prone to swings of mood from undue optimism to serious depression, he had made a number of questionable decisions including the sacking of General Smith-Dorrien (see Chapter 2). It was however his refusal - until it was too late - to release the reserve divisions under his control to Sir Douglas Haig that caused the most concern. The final straw for Haig was when The Times reported details of the battle and criticised Haig's handling of it. Much of the information that The Times used was inaccurate and had come straight from Sir John who was trying to cover up his own mis-management. Haig wrote to Sir John asking for the inaccuracies to be corrected. Although Sir John refused, there was by now a growing feeling within the Cabinet that Sir John had to be replaced (they had not forgotten his leaking information about the shell shortages earlier in the year); he was eventually removed from his command in December 1915. It was not surprising when Sir Douglas Haig was appointed as his successor as Commander-in-Chief of the B.E.F. in France and Flanders.

Haig's replacement as Commander of the First Army was General Sir Charles Monro (who was currently in charge of the Third Army) but before he was able to take up this appointment Monro was sent, in October 1915, to Gallipoli - see Chapter 5. (Upon his return from Gallipoli, Monro took command of the First Army, but did not stay long in this post as in August 1916 he was sent to be Commander-in-Chief in India.)

Chapter Four

Holding the Line at Ypres Winter 1915/1916

Although the 49th (West Riding) Division did not take part in the Battle of Loos, they did, as the year of 1915 drew to a close, continue to hold a sector of the front line on the canal bank north of Ypres. Whilst there were no major battles, the daily wastage of casualties continued.

Since mid-September when Ernest Beckett had been killed, the weather had deteriorated and life in the trenches had become unpleasant for the men from Ravensthorpe in the 1/5th Battalion, Duke of Wellington's Regiment. Even periods of so-called rest in the rear involved much fetching and carrying for the troops holding the front line trenches; nevertheless, the men did have time to write home, as evidenced in letters printed in the Ravensthorpe Parish Church Magazine in September 1915. The sentiments in the magazine seem to have been an attempt to embarrass those men still at home who had not joined up. The letters, from Walter Garfitt, William Harrison, Albert Jewsbury, Albert Mason, Stanley Gawthorpe and Lawrence Morton, describe the conditions: *"We have had a lot of rain recently and the trenches are in an awful mess."* But later: *"We are now billeted in some old barns that have in turn been occupied by all the armies in the world, each having left its own peculiar souvenir to tell the tale. The billets are about eight miles from the firing line, and we can hear the guns when there is a bombardment on."*

After a heavy bombardment on 1st October, when four fatal casualties were incurred, the 1/5th Duke of Wellington's was relieved by the 1/5th K.O.Y.L.I. the following day. Inspections by Brigadier-General Brereton (officer commanding 147 Brigade) and Major-General E.M. Perceval (the Divisional Commander) took place on the 11th and 12th October - this, no doubt, involved much polishing up and other such 'bull' - much to the troops disgust!

The battalion was not to stay in reserve long as on 14th October they relieved the 1/8th West Yorkshire Regiment, probably in the support trenches on the canal bank.

The 1/5th Duke of Wellington's War Diary for the 17th to 20th October simply says *"On canal bank. Numerous working parties; considerable activities of enemy."* Another brief rest occurred on the 21st October when the battalion was relieved and marched back to Elverdinghe Chateau, arriving at 9pm. Any thoughts of a longer period at rest were rudely shattered when, on the following day, the battalion was marched *"....in platoons at five minute intervals"* a distance of about three miles to the front line trenches; these trenches were numbered F31 to F35.

Although the War Diary describes the 23rd and 24th October as being quiet days (a visit by ammunition workers from Glasgow is recorded), two fatal casualties were incurred on Saturday 23rd October. One of these was Albert Jewsbury.

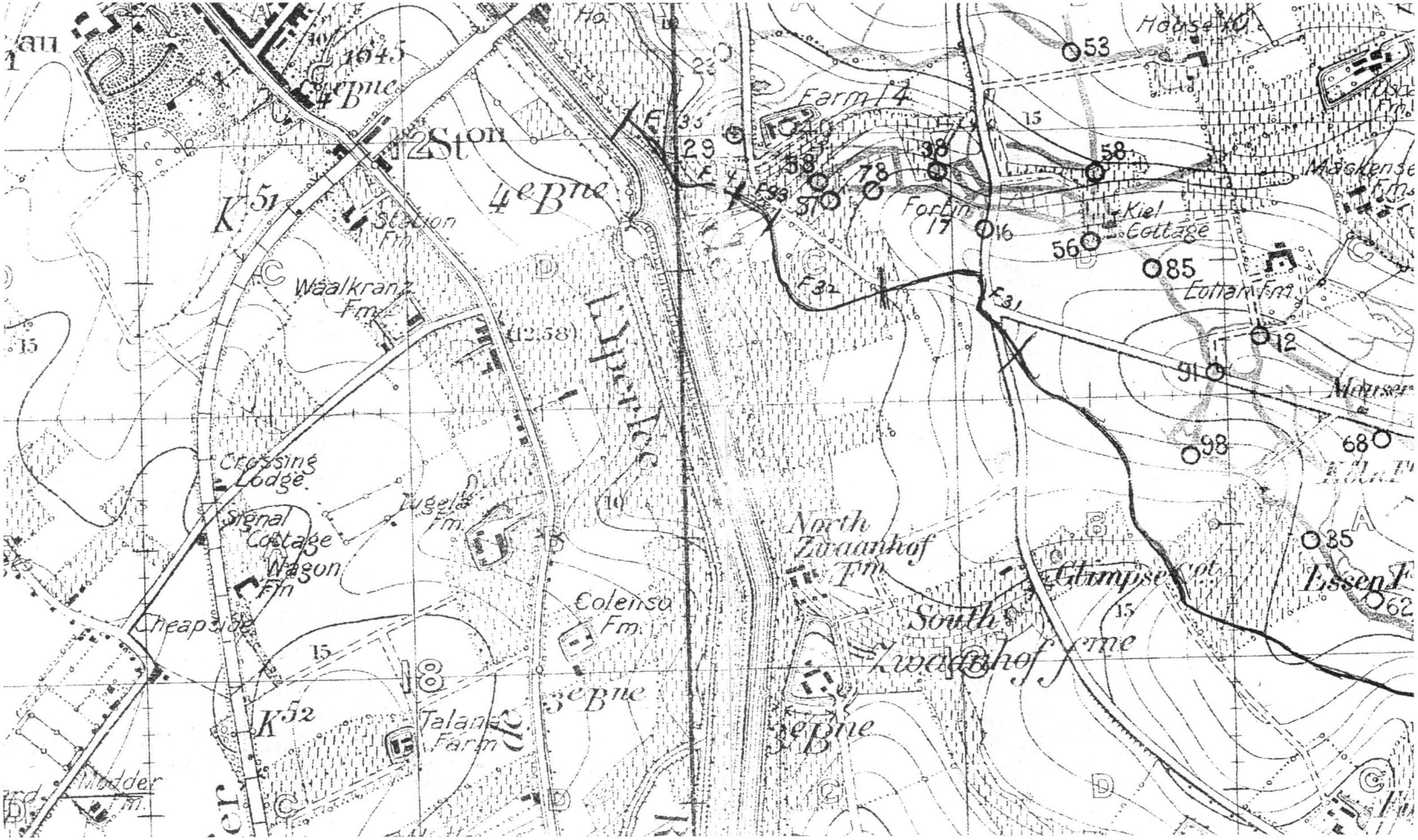

▲ Map 7. Trench Map of Ypres. *Courtesy of the Public Record Office.* Reference WO 95/2800

Albert, aged just 19, was born in Swinton, Lancashire, moving to Ravensthorpe in about 1912. He lived with his mother and stepfather, Mr and Mrs Holloman, at 30 Broomer Street Ravensthorpe. Albert worked with his stepfather as 'an electric cable jointer' for the Yorkshire Electric Power Company. He was closely associated with the Parish Church, being a member of the Bible Class, Church Institute, and St. Saviour's Young Men's Club.

Frederick and Edith Holloman received news of their son's death the following Tuesday (26th October); the letters from his Company Commander, Major Gilbert Norton, and another from his two friends, Albert Mason and Stanley Gawthorpe both confirm the circumstances of his death. The letters explain how Albert was shot at 8.30am *"...through the head by a sniper's bullet while in the open behind the trenches."* He died instantly. On the same day as Albert's parents received the news of their son's death, another of Ravensthorpe's soldiers was killed by a sniper.

George Arthur Hammond, like Albert Jewsbury had arrived with the first draft of the battalion and was in 'A' Company. Over the previous few days the battalion had endured poor conditions in the trenches, which the War Diary described as *"filthy"* owing to the heavy rain; it had also turned very cold.

Major Norton had the unenviable task of writing to George's parents who received the news at their home at 1 Garden Street, Ravensthorpe on Friday 29th October. Major Norton again describes the incident as one where no pain was suffered *"George died almost immediately, and never regained consciousness, as he was shot through the head."* The news was broken in the local newspapers the following day (30th October); the obituaries describe George as being *"....well known in footballing circles"* and go on *"...A remarkably well developed youth, deceased measured 41 inches round the chest when he went to the recruiting*

▲ 27. Albert Jewsbury

▲ 28. George Hammond

sergeant. Before the war, Hammond was employed by his uncle, Mr A. Algate, tailor, Ravensthorpe."

George (who attended the Ravensthorpe United Methodist Church) had written home on Saturday 23rd, the same day as Albert Jewsbury was killed: *"We Ravensthorpe boys are getting a good share of it now as we have lost two. One is Jewsbury and the other is Smith*...he was hit in the head and died a few minutes after. We are having it a little bit cold, but we can stand cold better than the shells. My mate is S. Gawthorpe of Ravensthorpe. He is only a new chap in the trenches +. We have only four days to do in the trenches, and then we go back into the woods for three days on reserve, about six miles back..."* It was on the last of these four days that George was shot.

George Hammond was buried alongside Albert Jewsbury at Talana Farm Cemetery. Although their graves were placed in different plots when the cemetery was tidied up after the war, Albert and George still lay next to each other just as they were buried in October 1915. They are the only men on the Ravensthorpe War Memorial who are known to lay side by side in a Commonwealth War Graves Commission Cemetery.

As George Hammond had predicted in his letter, front line duties for the month ended with the battalion being relieved on Tuesday 26th October by the 1/7th Battalion, Duke of Wellington's Regiment.

The first week in November found the battalion in Brigade reserve in the 'Farms Sector'; it seems that the numerous farms in the area (such as Modder, Saragossa, Pelissier, Malakoff and Hull's Farms) contained extensive dugouts which, compared to the front line trenches, must have been reasonably comfortable. These farms were all west of Talana Farm Cemetery and Bard Cottage Cemetery.

On the 7th November the battalion again took over the front line trenches between F31 and F35, all four companies being in the front line. 'A' Company took over the extremely crooked F31 sector on the right of the battalion's front. On this first day back in the trenches the battalion suffered two men killed, one of whom was a Ravensthorpe soldier.

William Ewart Popplewell was born in Mirfield in about 1896 to Edwin and Louisa Popplewell of Primrose, Mirfield. Ewart, as he was known, lived most of his life in Mirfield, but the family moved to 73 Garden Street, Ravensthorpe, probably in 1914. A regular attender at Mirfield Parish Church, he worked in the shoddy industry for Fred Ellis Ltd in Dewsbury. After arriving in France with the same draft as Stanley Gawthorpe on 29th June 1915, Ewart's last letter to his parents, saying he was *"in the pink"* was received a fortnight before his death. The Dewsbury News of 13th November carried an article which reproduced a letter of condolence from Lieutenant Sharp, which said that Ewart had been killed *"....whilst carrying rations. He died almost immediately and suffered no pain."* The letter continued *"Although your son has not been out here long, he has become very popular in the platoon on account of his cheery disposition and his readiness to help any of his pals at any time. Personally, I feel that I have lost one of the best men in my platoon. The only consolation I can offer you in your terrible sorrow is that your son died fighting for his King and Country and surely his life could not be given for a better cause."*

**** Private Douglas Smith - not named on the Ravensthorpe War Memorial; buried at Talana Farm Cemetery.***

+ Stanley Gawthorpe had arrived with a draft of reinforcements at the end of June.

▲ 29. Huddersfield Road, Ravensthorpe. Garden Street, where George Hammond and Ewart Popplewell both lived is on the right. *Photograph courtesy of Kirklees Community History Service*

A further letter from Lance Corporal Smith describes how Ewart was killed at about 11.30pm "*.....we had nearly reached the firing line when the machine guns were turned on us. We all dropped down and on rising again we found Ewart had been hit by a bullet and killed instantaneously.....*"

Along with Albert Jewsbury and George Hammond, Ewart is buried at Talana Farm Cemetery, this cemetery contains over 500 graves, including 17 from the 1/5th Battalion, Duke of Wellington's Regiment. Besides being commemorated on the Ravensthorpe Parish War Memorial, due to his strong ties with Mirfield, Ewart's name is also listed on the Mirfield Parish Memorial.

Exactly a month was to pass before the next injury was incurred by a Ravensthorpe soldier. Private William Beckett, although not a brother of Ernest Beckett (see Chapter 2), was probably related to him (there is certainly a resemblance in their photographs). The confusion is compounded by the fact that the two Becketts had parents with similar names: Ernest's parents were William and Sarah who, as previously mentioned, lived at 12 Calder Road; William's parents were Walter and Sarah Ann of 450 Huddersfield Road.

Unlike Albert Jewsbury, Ernest Beckett and George Hammond who had arrived with the battalion in April 1915 (and Ewart Popplewell and Stanley Gawthorpe who both disembarked on 29th June), Willie Beckett was a much later arrival. He set foot on French soil for the first time on 19th August, probably as part of a draft of 41 reinforcements which the War Diary of the 2/5th Battalion, Duke of Wellington's Regiment indicates were despatched on 14th August.

It was some months later, on 7th December that he was injured whilst on sentry duty. The 1/5th Duke of Wellington's had again moved up from the 'Farms' Sector to man the front line trenches on the 5th December (it seems that this time

▲ 30. Ewart Popplewell

▲ 31. Willie Beckett; although the photograph indicates he was 25 years old, the C.W.G.C. state he was 24 when killed.

only F34 and F35 were occupied by the battalion). On the night of 7th December patrols were sent out to investigate the strength of the German defences. The War Diary states *"They found the German wire fairly good,"* and went on to report that *"a German searchlight position was located apparently mounted on a motor car opposite the village of Boesinghe on a road running parallel with the canal."*

Although there is no mention of casualties, Willie Beckett may well have been acting as a lookout in the trenches, awaiting the return of the patrols when he was shot.

On the day he was injured, Willie wrote his last letter home (he had just received a parcel from St. Saviour's Boys' School); his letter included the following passage: *"It would be grand if I could get home for Christmas. We have a right to do, but never mind, keep smiling. The war will finish some time. It is grand when I get a parcel in the trenches."* Unfortunately Willie did not get home that Christmas.

The first his family knew about Willie's injury was when a telegram was received by his mother, Sarah Ann Beckett at their home at 450 Huddersfield Road, Ravensthorpe on Tuesday 14th December, which stated that Willie was dangerously ill with a gunshot wound in the head. After being shot on Tuesday 7th December, Willie was transferred to a hospital at Wimereux (just north of

Boulogne) on Sunday the 12th; Sister M. Philips wrote on this day to Willie's parents, describing his condition as *"very serious"*. She wrote again the following day: *"I am very sorry to say that your son is worse. He has had several fits and it has been found necessary to operate on his head. There was no improvement."*

Despite all the efforts of the doctors and staff at the Number 14 General Hospital, Sister Philips was forced to write again on Friday 17th December to say - *"I am very sorry indeed to have to tell you that your son died today at 1.10pm. He was quite unconscious and I don't think he suffered any pain...."*

The Commonwealth War Graves Commission Cemetery at Wimereux is quite unusual - due to the soft nature of the soil, the headstones are laid flat. Besides containing the grave of Willie Beckett, the cemetery also contains the grave of Lieutenant-Colonel John McCrae, a Canadian doctor. During the war McCrae wrote 'In Flanders Fields', one of the most famous poems to come out of the First World War; it was written in 1915 whilst he was stationed at Essex Farm Dressing Station on the canal bank outside Ypres. The poem was to inspire the idea to make the poppy the emblem of remembrance after the war.

Essex Farm is now the site of a Commonwealth War Graves Commission Cemetery. It is only two miles south of the sector where Willie Beckett and the rest of the 1/5th Duke of Wellington's were stationed in the autumn of 1915. Adjacent to the cemetery, and overlooking the canal is a memorial to the 49th (West Riding) Division.

The next Ravensthorpe casualty, whilst also in the 49th Division, was not a member of the 1/5th Battalion, Duke of Wellington's Regiment.

* * *

The King's Own Yorkshire Light Infantry had strong ties with the West Riding of Yorkshire; it had two territorial battalions, the 4th based in the Wakefield/Dewsbury area and the 5th which recruited in the Pontefract/Castleford/Doncaster area.

Although more Ravensthorpe soldiers served in the 1/5th (and 2/5th) Battalions of the Duke of Wellington's than in any other battalion (nineteen men on the War Memorial served in these two battalions - twelve being killed whilst serving in the 1/5th), more men served in the various battalions of the K.O.Y.L.I. Regiment than in the Duke of Wellington's Regiment*. A total of seven men served in either the 1/4th or 2/4th K.O.Y.L.I., and a further three served in the 1/5th or 2/5th K.O.Y.L.I., although this ignores men who may have passed through these battalions and died whilst serving in another regiment.

James Midgley Goodfellow was born in Chapeltown, Leeds to William and Annie Goodfellow in about 1888. Jim was employed as a stacker by Hirst & Gill, mungo manufacturers of Calder Wharf Mills, Ravensthorpe; he was married and lived with his wife Eveline in Bridge Street, Ravensthorpe. As a boy he went to Westtown Church School, but rather than going to church in Ravensthorpe,

**** At the time of their deaths, 25 men on the Memorial were serving in the K.O.Y.L.I. (This includes Matthews but ignores Duxbury - see Appendices 1 and 2.) The Memorial lists 22 men from the Duke of Wellington's Regiment.***

attended Thornhill Lees Wesleyan Chapel. A pre-war territorial, he arrived in France on 13th April 1915 with the 1/4th K.O.Y.L.I.

The 1/4th K.O.Y.L.I. was in 148 Brigade as opposed to the 1/5th Duke of Wellington's 147 Brigade, but as part of the 49th (West Riding) Division their story is very similar to that of the Duke's. In mid-December 1915 the 1/4th K.O.Y.L.I. was on the canal bank, north of Ypres. The battalion's War Diary for the 19th December gives an excellent description of events:

"4.50am: A hissing noise like a fast running motor car was heard in the German lines. Very shortly after the presence of cylinder gas, said to be Fossgene [Phosgene] *was detected in the air. Warning was given* [to put on anti-gas helmets] *and rapid fire opened on the enemy's parapet with rifles and machine guns. 'S.O.S. Gas' was sent to the artillery* who immediately opened fire. No infantry attack was made* [by the Germans] *but later a German patrol numbering about ten was seen advancing towards our trenches. Rifle fire was opened on them and they dispersed, only one man being seen to regain the German trenches...."*

The battalion was relieved that night. The War Diary records one officer and 23 other ranks died of gas poisoning, plus six other ranks killed in action. S.D.G.W. records 17 men killed in action plus one died of wounds for 19th December. On the subsequent three days a further 14 men died of their wounds.

The Dewsbury News made an attempt on 1st January 1916 to stem what may have been a rising tide of panic in the Dewsbury area:- *"Whilst the list of casualties to the local territorials as a result of a German gas attack on December 19th is serious, we are asked to deny a rumour that many men are dead."* Unfortunately one of the victims was Jim Goodfellow. Jim's wife received letters of condolence from the battalion's commanding officer, Lieutenant-Colonel Haslegrave, and also from Mrs Haslegrave. A boyhood pal wrote to Jim's mother at 23 Scout Hill, Dewsbury to express his sympathies, as did another comrade, Arthur Purden who was also injured in the gas attack.

James Goodfellow is buried at Bard Cottage Cemetery, nearby is the grave of Ernest Beckett.

Private Arthur Gill of the 1st Battalion, West Yorkshire Regiment sustained fatal injuries on the same day as Jim Goodfellow was killed. Born in Cleckheaton in 1895, before the war Arthur was employed by Rawdon, Briggs & Co. He joined up in Leeds on 22 February 1915 and after a period of training at York and Whitley Bay, was posted overseas, arriving in France on 20th July 1915.

The 1st Battalion, West Yorkshire Regiment was part of the 6th Division and in December 1915 was on the canal bank to the south (right) of the 49th Division. The division was 'stood to' during the gas attack on the 19th but was not as seriously affected as the units to the north. During that evening the Germans heavily shelled the 6th Division, and 'D' Company of the 1st West Yorkshires had two of its dugouts destroyed, causing eighteen casualties. It is likely that Arthur Gill was one of these casualties.

Sister M. Wharton of the 17th Casualty Clearing Station - which was located at Remi Sidings, Lijssenthoek - wrote on the 20th December to Arthur's mother, Cecilia, at 33 Low Mills, Ravensthorpe: *"I very much regret having to send you very bad news of your son who was admitted last evening suffering from internal injuries caused by the falling in of a dug out. His condition is most critical. You may*

**** Flares of different colours were used to communicate with the artillery.***

▲ 32. James Goodfellow

▲ 33. Arthur Gill actually died on 21st December not 11th December as stated on the photograph

rest assured everything will be done that can be done for him. He sends his love and best Christmas wishes."

Sister Wharton wrote again the next day to say that Arthur had died that morning (the 21st) at 11am.

Arthur Gill is buried at the large but rarely visited Lijssenthoek Military Cemetery.

The last Ravensthorpe casualty of 1915 was Herbert Greenwood. Born in August 1896 and educated at Warwick Road School, Batley Carr, he was a regular attender at the United Methodist Church and before the war was employed as an under-tuner at Henry Hamer and Sons.

Like so many others he was a pre-war territorial, although he only joined the 5th Duke of Wellington's in June 1914. After volunteering for overseas service he arrived in France on 13th April 1915, being promoted to lance corporal some time later.

Writing home just after the gas attack, he describes the British artillery retaliation *"We are going into the trenches again tonight. I dare say you'll have seen the papers about the gas attack. Well our lads were in it. You talk about knocking up: I can tell you our gunners caught the Germans on the hop and flattened their trenches on a front of about 18 or 20 miles, so they got a good return for their gas."*

The War Diary describes how the battalion relieved the 1/6th Duke of Wellington's on Tuesday 21st December, the relief being completed by 9pm. During the relief one man was killed. The following day was 'generally quiet', but that night (Wednesday 22nd / Thursday 23rd December) the War Diary reports how a German machine gun *".....known as Mad Alec* [was] *rather active during the night, with plenty of rifle fire."* One of the two men killed that night was Herbert Greenwood.

It was Christmas Eve when Captain Wheatley wrote to Herbert's parents, William and Elizabeth Greenwood of 113 Sackville Street. He informed them (inaccurately) that Herbert was killed on the afternoon of Thursday 23rd December. However Corporal Clarkson of 'D' Company, who also came from Ravensthorpe, also writing on Christmas Eve was more accurate:- *"It is with deepest regret that I write to tell you that Bert got killed on Wednesday night, about 11pm. He was hit on the head with a bullet and died instantaneously, suffering no pain. I had only just left him when some men brought a fresh supply of bombs, and as he was in charge of the bombers he had to attend to them. He had put the boxes of bombs in the dug out and must have stood up unconsciously with his head too high above the firing parapet.......We carried him out of the trench and buried him beside some of his fallen comrades."*

Herbert Richardson Greenwood was aged just 19 when he was killed; he is buried at Talana Farm Cemetery.

*　　*　　*

▲ 34.Herbert Greenwood

▲ 35.Talana Farm Cemetery.

The new year started quietly for the men from Ravensthorpe, no fatal casualties were incurred in January, the first death of 1916 was that of Horace Wright Davies Oldroyd. Born in October 1897, after the death of his mother Horace, together with his two sisters, went to live with his grandmother at 49 Garden Terrace, Ravensthorpe. Before the war he was employed by Marshall, Kaye and Marshall as a cloth finisher; he was also a member of St. Saviour's Men's Bible Class.

On 23rd August 1915, aged 17, he enlisted (under age) into the 7th Battalion, Yorkshire Regiment. The battalion was part of 50 Brigade, 17th (Northern) Division which had been sent overseas in July 1915. Horace, however, was a later reinforcement, only arriving with his unit in January 1916, joining 'C' Company.

In early February, the division arrived in the Ypres salient, and was sent to the south-west of the town, the 7th Yorkshires taking over some billets in the Dickebusch area. On 7th February, the battalion's War Diary reported things 'very quiet'. On Monday, 14th February the battalion prepared to take over the front line from the 12th Battalion, Manchester Regiment (52 Brigade, 17th Division).

Whist the battalion was making these preparations and the leading company was setting out to make the relief, shells began to fall injuring, according to the battalion's War Diary, two officers. The battalion moved up in anticipation of making the relief, but at the last moment the move was halted. The Germans had made an attack on a position known as 'The Bluff'* and captured about 600 yards of trenches. The battalion's bombers and machine gunners were already in the trenches. Two companies ('A' and 'D') were ordered to support another battalion (10th Lancashire Fusiliers), whilst the rest of the battalion were detailed to carry bombs to the front line troops.

Although casualties in the 7th Yorkshires were not particularly heavy, Horace Oldroyd was one of the five fatalities incurred by the battalion on that day.

Horace had been writing regularly to his grandmother, and she became concerned when she did not hear from him after his last letter, which was written at the end of January. On Tuesday, 1st March, she received notification that Horace had been killed in action.

Horace Oldroyd is one of the four men, out of the five to be killed, who have no known graves, and is therefore commemorated on the Menin Gate Memorial to the Missing in Ypres.

**** This was a narrow ridge on the north bank of the Ypres-Comines Canal, about a mile east of St. Eloi. (See Map19 on page 208.)***

◂ 36. Horace Oldroyd

▾ 37. The Menin Gate Memorial to the Missing, Ypres, in the 1920's or 1930's.

Chapter Five

Gallipoli. A short cut to victory?

The year of 1915 had finished in a frustrating manner for the Allies on the Western Front, but in another theatre of the war, the year had started out with the possibility of great success. The one great strategic concept, that was the only realistic alternative to what was to become the war of attrition on the Western Front was conceived, executed and ultimately squandered during 1915 in the Eastern Mediterranean.

On 4th August 1914, the day war broke out, but before the expiry of the ultimatum that Britain had given to Germany, the Royal Navy's Mediterranean Fleet sighted and shadowed the German battlecruiser the *Goeben* and her escort, the *Breslau*. That night, however, under the cover of darkness, the German ships managed to slip away and escaped into the Black Sea through the narrow waterway known as the Dardanelles; they docked in Constantinople where they were given a warm welcome.

Constantinople was the capital of Turkey whose vast Ottoman Empire spread throughout the Near and Middle East, including Palestine and Mesopotamia (now Israel and Iraq). Britain had traditionally enjoyed good relations with Turkey, but in the years prior to 1914 Germany had been courting Turkey, hoping to secure her as an ally. Part of this alliance between Germany and Turkey involved German generals being sent to overhaul the Turkish Army.

Before the war Turkey had placed an order for two battleships with Armstrong's Shipyard on the Tyne. The money had been raised by public subscription within Turkey - there was much patriotic feeling in favour of the purchase as this would do a lot to raise the standing of Turkey generally, and the Turkish Navy in particular.

When war was declared with Germany, the British Government requisitioned all warships currently under construction, so they could be taken onto the strength of the Royal Navy. Public opinion in Turkey was outraged, and to make matters worse, Germany, realising that their two ships were effectively out of the war (being bottled up in the Black Sea) pulled a public relations masterstroke and made a gift of the *Goeben* and *Breslau* to Turkey in order to replace the two requisitioned ships.

This diplomatic coup by Germany put Turkey very much in Germany's camp. When, at the end of October 1914, the two ships (still crewed by German sailors) went off to bombard Russia's Black Sea ports, Russia, closely followed by Britain and France, declared war on Turkey.

Winston Churchill who was, as First Lord of the Admiralty, the political head of the Royal Navy ordered the Mediterranean Fleet to bombard the Turkish forts on the Gallipoli peninsular at the entrance to the Dardanelles. This action was, in hindsight, a serious mistake as it alerted the Turks as to Britain's future intentions, and made them realise how vulnerable these forts were.

Churchill's plan for the Dardanelles was probably the only chance of cutting short the war with Germany, although it depended on many factors and has been argued about ever since; his thought process was as follows:-

Russia's land borders with the west were now inaccessible to trade due to the war with Germany, Austria and Turkey, and the only way of supplying Russia was therefore by sea. The sea route to the north was long and, particularly in winter, very arduous. A much easier route would be through the Mediterranean and into the Black Sea. To secure this route the Dardanelles would have to be kept open, which meant that Turkey would have to be removed from the war. Turkey's Government was weak, and if the Royal Navy arrived off Constantinople and made a brief bombardment, panic would ensue and the Government would collapse. The Turkish empire would then be divided between Britain and France. With Turkey out of the war, the southern European states would fall into the British and French alliance and threaten Germany and Austria.

Surrounded on three sides (Britain and France in the West, Russia in the East, and Italy Rumania, Serbia etc. in the south) Germany and Austria would see the futility of their position and seek peace terms.

Churchill put forward a plan which involved, quite simply, a force of Royal Navy battleships sailing up the Dardanelles, arriving off Constantinople and shelling warehouses on the waterfront. In the early weeks of 1915 there was much debate in the British Cabinet about Churchill's plan. The army was demanding that all available troops should be sent to France, so the Royal Navy would have to execute the plan on their own; however Kitchener eventually decided, on 16th February, to make some troops available, and the 29th Division (made up of the last of the pre-war Regulars) was allocated. Immediately protests broke out from the Western Front generals and the decision was reversed; it was decided that the Australian and New Zealand Divisions (later known as Anzacs) who were training in Egypt would be sent instead. The ships that were to have transported the 29th Division were dispersed.

On 19th February the forts were again bombarded and landings were briefly made by sailors and marines from the warships. These landings were virtually unopposed, but the Turks did not ignore what was obviously being planned, they rushed up troops and took steps to strengthen fortifications, but most crucially they laid mines in the waters of the Narrows of the Dardanelles.

In early March fishing trawlers crewed by civilians were used by the British to try to clear these mines; the trawlers were bombarded by the Turkish batteries on shore and were forced to retire. At the same time General Sir William Birdwood, who commanded the Anzacs, reported that in his opinion the Royal Navy could not force the Dardanelles on their own, and that the army would be required to assist. On 10th March the decision was made to definitely send the 29th Division together with the Anzacs, the Royal Naval Division and a French Division; this meant that the army's contribution would be around 70,000 men. Delays ensued as ships had to be re-found to transport the 29th Division.

This decision was made because the Royal Navy claimed they could not clear the mines until the shore batteries on the peninsular were stopped from firing at the minesweepers. The mines had to be cleared to enable the battleships to pass through the Narrows without sustaining crippling losses. The reluctance on the part of the navy to risk the loss of a few elderly battleships (the Mediterranean Fleet had been given older ships - the newer battleships had been retained in the Grand Fleet to protect home waters) was to be shown in the following months to be a mistake when thousands of casualties were incurred in trying to take the peninsular. The minefields did not prove to be large and could possibly have been forced with a firm push by the Royal Navy. Many of the battleships that were being so carefully protected had been destined for the scrapyard before war broke out. The expendability of these ships had not been driven home to Vice-Admiral Sir Sackville Carden, the commander of the Mediterranean Fleet, who feared a reprimand or worse in the event of him losing battleships.

This was the start of much delay, hesitation and timidity which was to plague the whole of the campaign. When Carden's health broke down he was replaced by his deputy, Vice-Admiral Sir John de Roebuck, but there was still no change in the Royal Navy's policy of waiting for the army. Sir Ian Hamilton arrived in the Eastern Mediterranean in mid-March; he had been appointed by Lord Kitchener to take command of the army (designated the Mediterranean Expeditionary Force) in the forthcoming operation.

Hamilton arrived in time to hear of de Roebuck's last attempt to force the Dardanelles without the army's assistance. On 18th March a renewed bombardment had taken place of the Turkish forts and once the fire from the Turkish batteries was subdued, the minesweepers were ordered forward. Suddenly three battleships (two British and one French) hit mines and were badly damaged. The fleet was ordered to retire but during this manoeuvre a fourth battleship hit a mine. The Turks could not believe their luck, they were on the point of defeat and had virtually no ammunition left when the British withdrew.

It was now up to the army to take the peninsular, Hamilton therefore started making his plans. One of his first discoveries was that the ships sent with the army's supplies had been packed in such a disorderly fashion that they needed to be totally unloaded and repacked; this could only be done at Egypt. Further delays therefore ensued. All the time the Turks were strengthening their defences. Hamilton, meanwhile, had other problems; not only had he no accurate maps of the Gallipoli peninsular, he also had no information about the supply of fresh water that he expected to find when ashore.

There were islands nearby which were to be used as bases for re-supply, administration and for medical units. These islands, however, were not suitable for these roles. Due to there being no docks (although a deep harbour was available at Mudros) it was difficult to load and unload the transport ships; the tranquillity was to prevent the staff from appreciating the difficulties of life for the soldiers on the peninsular; and the medical facilities were too small to cope with the thousands of casualties that were to be incurred.

Hamilton was advantaged by having the 29th Division available, they were known to be of high quality and could be relied upon. The Anzacs were an unknown quantity, they had already, during their training period in Egypt, acquired a reputation for insubordination, but they were to prove themselves in battle. The Royal Naval Division were regarded as a questionable asset. Made up of Royal Naval Reservists called up on the outbreak of war, they had found themselves confined to land as the navy did not have enough ships for them. Despite their high average age, they acquitted themselves well during the following months.

It was not until 24th April that Hamilton felt able to launch his assault*. With French troops alongside, landings were made along the tip of the Gallipoli peninsular by the 29th Division. These landings at Cape Helles were accompanied by landings further up the coast by Australian troops. At Helles some landings were virtually unopposed, whilst others met with fierce opposition. Unfortunately rather than reinforcing the successful beach landings, Major-General Hunter-Weston (G.O.C. 29th Division) became transfixed by the failed landings. Eventually the Turkish defences were overrun, but not before Turkish reinforcements had arrived and pushed the previously successful (but un-supported) British troops back into the sea. Like the naval operations before, the Helles landings were a case of missed opportunities.

The Australian troops meanwhile had been landed in the wrong place. Rather than being faced with fairly gentle hills, they had been put ashore at the foot of a steep cliff where, not surprisingly, the Turks had not expected landings to be made. The Australians charged ashore and started climbing the cliffs. The momentum of their assault carried them inland; amid the gullies, sheer cliffs and valleys, their advance inevitably petered out as the troops lost touch with one another. Control from higher command was impossible and the nature of the terrain prevented meaningful communication; however the Australians with their independent spirit used their initiative. Against stiffening opposition, they dug in and managed somehow to hold a thin strip of high ground, the crest of which, if lost, would mean the immediate destruction of the entire force at the beachhead. This beachhead was to become known as Anzac Cove.

The advantage of surprise in both the Anzac and Helles sectors was lost and the fighting degenerated into the familiar one seen on the Western Front - that of trench warfare. The difference here was that there were also the enemies of thirst, heat and disease to contend with.

At Helles, on three successive days, three frontal assaults were made in broad daylight towards the village of Krithia, and the vital hill known as Achi Baba. Losses were massive and there was virtually no gain in ground. Realising that a fresh attempt had to be made, Hamilton asked for reinforcements; these were reluctantly sent by Lord Kitchener.

Hamilton planned to outflank the Turks by breaking out at Anzac, this was to be carried out along with a simultaneous landing at Suvla Bay. This new attack would cut the peninsular in half, trapping the Turkish army (most of which was now concentrated on the peninsular) and thus enabling the Narrows to be swept without any interference.

It is the landing at Suvla that claimed the life of the only Ravensthorpe soldier to die in the Gallipoli campaign.

* * *

The landings were made just after the Germans had launched their gas attack at Ypres. (The Second Battle of Ypres commenced on 22nd April.)

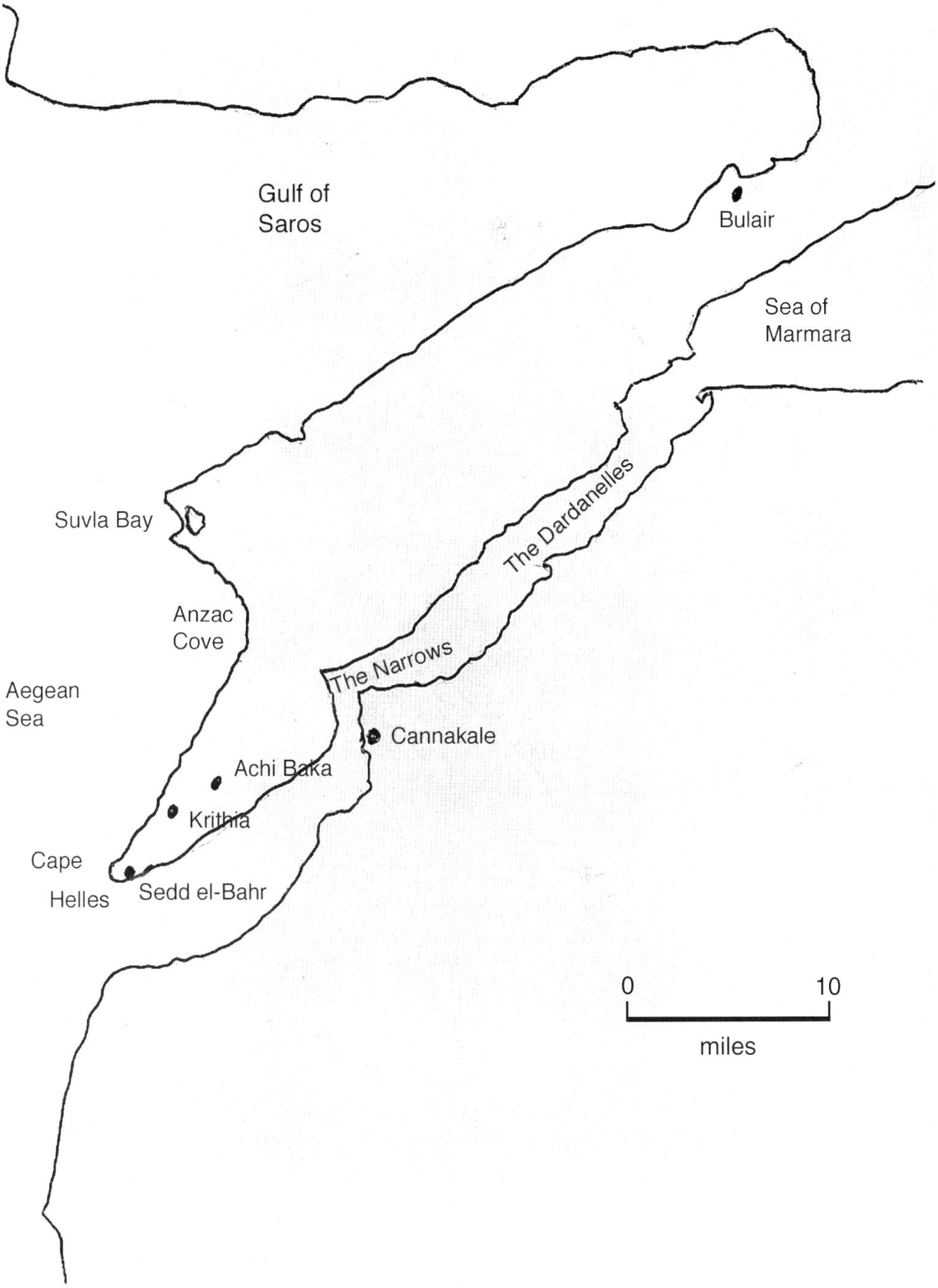

▲ Map 8. Gallipoli

Henry Ellis was born in Dewsbury in about 1892. He attended St. Saviour's Boys' School* but very little else is known of him. His widowed mother seems to have remarried, whilst Henry married and lived with his wife and child at 71 Albion Street, Ravensthorpe.

Recruiting across the British Isles was very brisk in the early weeks of the war. Enthusiasm and the rate of volunteering first saw signs of waning in Ireland and as a result some half-full Irish battalions had to be topped up with English drafts. The 7th Battalion, Royal Munster Fusiliers was such a battalion, much of its strength coming from soldiers who had originally joined the K.O.Y.L.I. or the York and Lancaster Regiment. Although there is no direct evidence, it is likely that Henry initially joined the K.O.Y.L.I., and was one of the drafts sent to reinforce the 7th Royal Munster Fusiliers.

The 7th R.M.F. formed part of the 10th (Irish) Division. This division, together with the 11th (Northern) and the 13th (Western) Divisions made up IX Corps. This was the reinforcement chosen to be sent to Hamilton. The command of IX Corps was given to Lieutenant-General Sir Frederick Stopford, an infirm, retired soldier who was an expert in ceremonial.

In great secrecy the renewed offensive was planned. The main thrust of this attack was to be the responsibility of New Zealand troops who were to break out of the gullies and ravines (which the Turks believed to be unclimbable) in the area between Anzac and Suvla. The Suvla landings were, nevertheless, a fundamental part of Hamilton's plan to overwhelm the Turkish defenders by simultaneous assaults all along the front line. The attack across the flat Suvla plain was entrusted to the 10th+ and 11th Divisions.

Before any of these new troops stepped ashore, the first of many mistakes had already been made. The decision to appoint someone as unsuitable as Stopford to command IX Corps was probably the most fundamental mistake of all. Because the 10th (Irish) Division was commanded by a Lieutenant-General (Sir Bryan Mahon) rather than a Major-General, it was felt that his corps commander could not be junior to him; there were only two possible candidates, and Stopford was chosen ahead of Lieutenant-General Ewart.

Another serious mistake was down to the secrecy that Hamilton had insisted upon. As the details of the new landings were known only to a few men, no one was in a position to prevent the inoculation of the troops against cholera just before they were ordered to embark for the landings. Although such inoculations were necessary, the side effect was that the men were extremely groggy for some time afterwards; this was to seriously affect their fighting ability.

Despite these and other problems, there should not have been much difficulty in achieving a good landing and then advancing inland to take the heights of Tekke Tepe, the large hill dominating the Suvla plain, control of which would mean control of the central part of the peninsular.

In the issue of the Dewsbury Reporter published on 2nd January 1915, a list was published totalling 103 former pupils who were, at that time, serving in the army or navy. Obviously more former pupils served later in the war, but of these 103 listed, 15 are named on the Parish War Memorial.

+ The 10th Division arrived on the island of Lemnos on 19th July. The 7th Royal Munster Fusiliers were quickly reduced from 1,000 strong to just 700 due to disease.

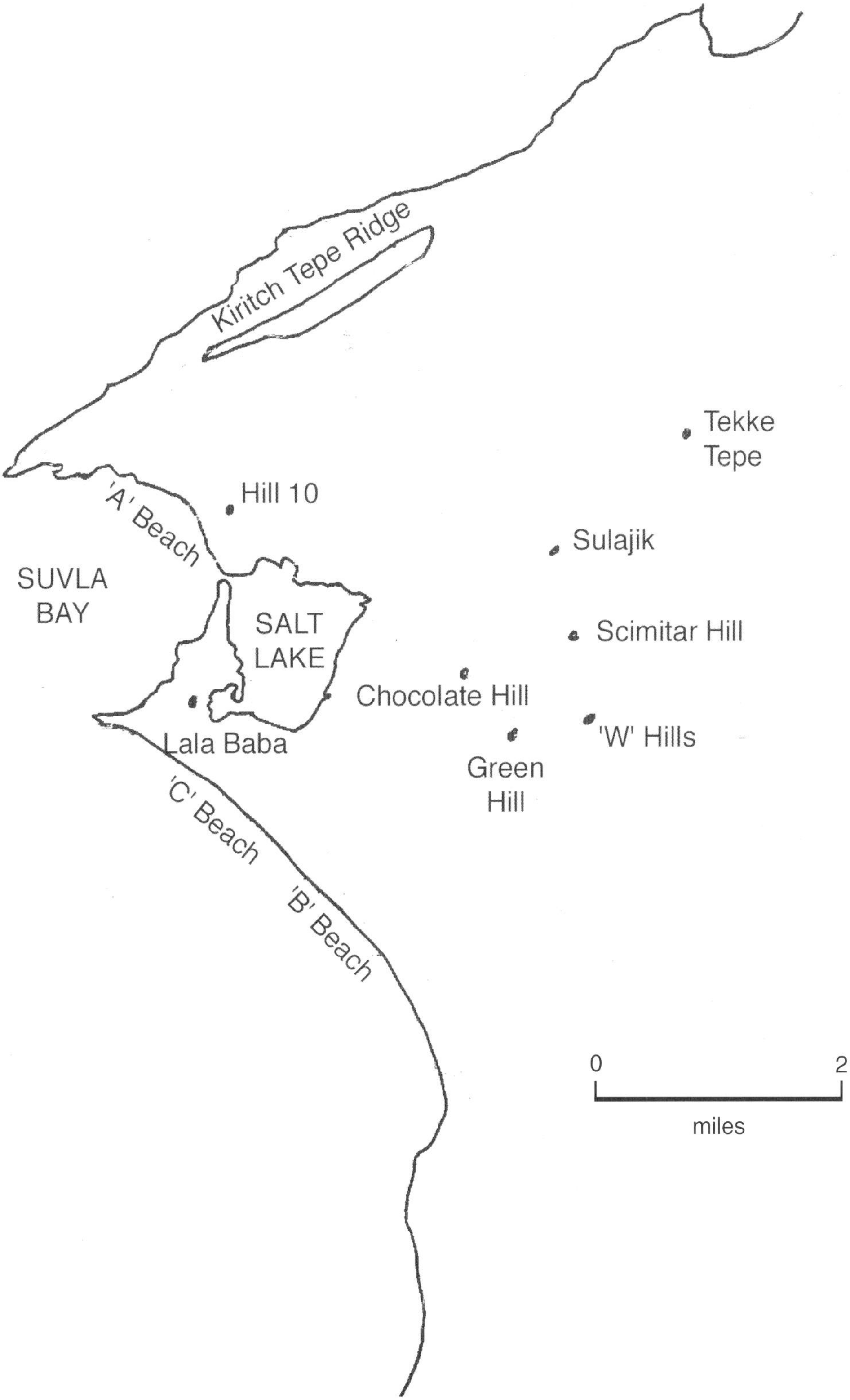

▲ Map 9. Suvla Bay

The Turks were not expecting a landing and had stationed only 1,500 men in the area. Reserves were more than thirty miles and many hours march away. Surprise was to be total.

Regrettably, the landings started to go wrong immediately they were underway. The first troops, from the 11th Division landed at midnight on 6th/7th August. Although meeting little opposition, because of the lack of preparation (due to the secrecy) and - in many cases - being put ashore in totally the wrong place, there was much confusion and the command structure broke down. No one was able to get a grip on the situation in order to sort matters out.

The few Turks in the vicinity caused many casualties through their sniping (made somewhat easier by the order issued for all the troops in the 11th Division to wear white armlets as a means of identification). Eventually a small mound (Hill 10) was taken. The commander of 34 Brigade, Brigadier-General Sitwell decided to entrench and hold the ground gained. This was not an appropriate course of action; despite the confusion and lack of coordination, the Turks were in no position to attack such an overwhelming force (less than 1,500 Turks opposed 20,000 British).

Into this confusion was landed, at dawn on the 7th August, the majority of the 10th (Irish) Division, once again in the wrong place. Nearly all the troops had now been landed on top of each other, to the south of the dry Salt Lake. The plan had been for the 10th Division under Lieutenant-General Mahon to land to the north of the Salt Lake and then advance north-eastwards and take the Kiritch Tepe Ridge. This action would secure the northern flank of the landing (a similar move south-eastwards by units of the 11th Division would secure the heights known as Chocolate Hill and Green Hill).

Because the majority of his division had been landed in the wrong place, Mahon had only three battalions of his division available to him instead of the twelve infantry battalions he would normally have. One of these battalions was the 7th R.M.F., containing Henry Ellis who found himself crawling along the Kiritch Tepe Ridge along with the rest of his battalion.

Sir Bryan Mahon, whilst a competent general, had a fiery temper. Matters had gone from bad to worse for Sir Bryan. First of all he was displeased at only having a division to command (however as he had raised and trained the division himself, it was not inappropriate for him to be its commander); when his division embarked for the attack, he found himself stranded without transport on one of the island bases. Eventually catching up with his division, he discovered that he only had three battalions at his disposal, the 6th and 7th R.M.F. plus the divisional pioneer battalion, the 5th Royal Irish Regiment.

Undaunted, he ordered the two Royal Munster Fusiliers battalions to advance up the rocky Kiritch Tepe Ridge, keeping the pioneer battalion in reserve. The 6th and 7th R.M.F. joined up with the 11th Manchesters (11th Division troops who had been landed in the wrong place and had advanced independently onto the ridge). The ridge itself was rocky; erosion had caused razor-like ridges and steep gullies to riddle the area. There was little topsoil, but sharp shrubs still managed to grow in profusion. It was almost impossible to maintain a steady direction. It was, however, ideal ground for snipers.

Although the two Irish battalions and the Manchesters managed to climb to the top of the ridge and started to advance along it, they were without support and virtually without water (they only had the water in the bottles they carried). There were simply insufficient troops to flush out the 700 or so Turks who were on the ridge. Despite all the adversities they had done as well as could be expected under the circumstances.

The War Diary of the 7th Royal Munster Fusiliers describes the day's events in further detail. After landing at 2pm on 7th August without incurring any casualties, the battalion advanced on the eastern (inland) side of the ridge. During the advance a number of dead of the Manchester Regiment were observed. This, together with the long range sniping would have unnerved the men who had not been under fire before. After 1½ miles (through country which the War Diary describes with a degree of understatement as being 'very broken up') the 6th R.M.F. were held up and unable to advance. The 7th Battalion therefore *"Got into position on a small hillock and ridge, closing from the south side of a valley running along the foot of the Kiritch Tepe Ridge on its east side. 'A' Company were ordered to endeavour to turn the Turks who were occupying ground at the north-east end of the valley and from there checking the advance of the 6th R.M.F."* Unfortunately no advance was possible due to the fire from a small, well-concealed Turkish trench. Many casualties were suffered here. The battalion therefore entrenched on high ground, blocking the south end of the valley. The War Diary puts the casualties for the day at eleven killed, 60 wounded and five missing.

The following day, 8th August, the battalion were sniped at all day and suffered two casualties, both wounded*. The 6th R.M.F. advanced about 800 yards and captured the western tip of the highest ridge in the area. This was named 'Jephson's Post' after the second-in-command of the 6th R.M.F. who led this attack+. This was the only advance on the Kiritch Tepe Ridge during the entire second day of the landings, there was similar inactivity all day in the rest of the Suvla area.

The Turkish reserves, meanwhile, were being marched at a furious pace from the north. Victory for the British was still possible but precious time was being lost.

Mahon's command had, by now, been reinforced. The three battalions of the 10th Division plus the 11th Manchesters had been joined by the 5th Royal Inniskilling Fusiliers who had also been landed in the wrong place. Mahon now had five battalions under his control: the 6th and 7th R.M.F. (30 Brigade, 10th Division), the 5th Royal Inniskilling Fusiliers (31 Brigade, 10th Division), the 5th Royal Irish Regiment (10th Division Pioneers), and the 11th Manchesters (34 Brigade, 11th Division). Although still well short of his full complement of troops, Mahon was ordered into action on Monday 9th August; this was to be a continuation of the advance along the ridge.

Although this advance was not the main axis of the British attack at Suvla (this and a similar one to the south were flanking moves for the main thrust through the centre against the Tekke Tepe Ridge), unbeknown to the British, the main Turkish ammunition dump for the whole of the peninsular was positioned just beyond the ridge. If this was to be captured or destroyed the Turks could yet be defeated.

Despite being scheduled to commence its attack at dawn, it was not until 8am that the 7th R.M.F. received its orders. These orders were issued and eventually at 9.30am the battalion advanced. Even despite this delay, the mens' water bottles,

**** S.D.G.W. indicates the casualties for the 7th R.M.F. on the two days as being - 7th August: 5 killed; 8th August: 4 killed.***

+ Major John Jephson was injured on 15th August and died of his wounds on 29th August. He is buried at East Mudros Cemetery on the island of Lemnos.

which had been sent to the beach for refilling, had not been returned. In the 100°F. heat of midsummer this lack of water was a serious omission.

The War Diary notes that the battalion was forced to alter direction due to the advance of the 5th Dorsets across their front (the 5th Dorsets were 11th Division troops who were attacking a position known as Kidney Hill, to the east of the ridge). Because of this and the broken up ground, communication between the battalion's companies was lost. Meanwhile on the top and the western (seaward) side of the ridge the 6th R.M.F. were advancing, but became held up at Jephson's Post. Although the position was taken, they were unable to advance any further.

The War Diary of the 7th R.M.F. describes how, *"At about 13.30 a message was received from G.O.C.* [Mahon] *urging the advance. Owing to the lack of cohesion* [within] *the battalion and with other units* [presumably the 6th R.M.F.] *and the general ignorance of the situation, of the enemy, and what was required, this was impossible to carry out......At about 15.30 the order to retire was given."* Unfortunately this order did not reach 'C' Company who clung onto their positions.

The 7th R.M.F.'s War Diary reported casualties for the 9th as being 34 officers and men killed, 83 wounded and 10 missing. (S.D.G.W. indicates 24 men killed and died of wounds that day.) Evacuation of casualties was made even more difficult due to the Turks firing not only at the stretcher bearers, but at those men who were lying wounded.

Although Henry Ellis may have been injured on this day, it is possible that he survived this battle unscathed.

The attempt at capturing the Tekke Tepe Ridge failed and the Turkish reinforcements arrived. The campaign once again degenerated into one of attrition. Hamilton, bitterly disappointed and blaming, with some cause, Stopford for the failure of the Suvla landing took steps to have him removed. It was at this moment that Stopford, quite out of character, ordered, on 15th August, the launching of a renewed offensive, the main thrust of which was along the Kiritch Tepe Ridge where he believed, incorrectly, that the Turks had not been reinforced. The attack was made by the 10th Division which had been reinforced by the troops who had earlier been landed in the wrong place. The 6th and 7th R.M.F. were on the left of the attack between the crest of the ridge and the water's edge. Only slow progress was initially made, but a charge by the 6th R.M.F. at 4.30pm enabled the 7th Battalion to advance *"without opposition through very dense scrub and over very steep gullies."* Although progress had been made, the attack ground to a halt; no further advance was possible. On the other side of the ridge the attack had failed. (The attack caused great concern to the Turks as they had no reserves and the British were getting closer to their ammunition dump.) The failure of the right side of the attack plus the Turkish resistance on the ridge were important factors, but crucially at this point, Stopford was sacked. His replacement, Major-General Sir Beauvoir de Lisle, was junior to and disliked by Mahon, who promptly resigned. In the middle of the battle, there was suddenly no one in command.

The following day (Monday 16th August) the 7th R.M.F. were subjected to prolonged shelling, and were forced to abandon much of their gains. They retired to behind Jephson's Post. The War Diary gives casualties as - 15th August: 13 killed, 45 wounded, 7 missing; 16th August: 19 killed, 63 wounded, 12 missing*.

**** S.D.G.W.: 15th August - 23 killed; 16th August - 23 killed plus 1 died of wounds.***

◂ 38. The Helles Memorial to the Missing, Gallipoli. *Photograph courtesy of the Commonwealth War Graves Commission.*

▾ 39. Suvla Bay.

We will never know what happened to Henry Ellis. It was reported that he died of wounds on 17th August. These may have been sustained at any time subsequent to the landing, but are perhaps most likely to have been incurred on the 15th or 16th August. Henry was buried at sea from a hospital ship. Having no known grave but the sea, he is one of the 20,000 men commemorated on the Helles Memorial to the Missing.

* * *

For various reasons, this renewed offensive failed. Hamilton asked for some more reinforcements but these were refused as the Western Front needed every available soldier.

The Gallipoli campaign was abandoned. When asked how many casualties would be incurred if the peninsular was to be evacuated, Hamilton reacted badly, estimating enormous casualties, and was therefore removed from command in October, being replaced by General Sir Charles Monro.

Over the winter, the Allied troops were evacuated in two stages with virtually no casualties in what was, ironically, the best planned and executed operation of the campaign. If previous efforts had been carried out only half as successfully, the Gallipoli campaign may have succeeded, and the one great strategic alternative to the Western Front may have turned the war decisively in the Allies' favour in 1915. This was not to be; instead the country's efforts were concentrated in France and Belgium where the war was to carry on its bloody course for the next three years. One final casualty of the Gallipoli campaign was Winston Churchill; he was removed from high office and went to France where he took over command of a battalion of Royal Scots Fusiliers.

Chapter Six

The War at Sea

Britain's sense of world superiority had, in the last years of the reign of Queen Victoria, been largely expressed by the might of the Royal Navy. It protected the empire, was the principal means of defending Britain's shores, kept the shipping lanes free from the threat of interference, and was openly envied by the Kaiser. Upon coming to power in 1888, the Kaiser immediately set about building a fleet to challenge the Royal Navy. This obviously did not go unnoticed by the British and was a contributory factor in the tensions that were to build up in Europe over the following years.

The Royal Navy's power, and its perceived ability to defeat the navy of any other nation, meant that immediately upon the outbreak of the war, the Government was in a strategic dilemma over its role. The fear was that if the German fleet in the North Sea (the High Seas Fleet) came into contact with the British Grand Fleet (the Royal Navy's principal battle fleet) and defeated it, the Germans would have control of the world's seas and thus enforce a blockade that could knock Britain out of the war. As Winston Churchill put it, Admiral Sir John Jellicoe (the commander of the Grand Fleet) was the one man who *"could have lost the war in an afternoon"*. This overriding concern was to ensure that Jellicoe, with the Government's approval, maintained a 'safety first' policy. Jellicoe's policy was criticised after the war as not being sufficiently offensive towards the German Navy*.

The British Grand Fleet was at an immediate advantage upon the outbreak of war; for a number of months, a test mobilisation had been planned for July 1914. When the Balkan Crisis erupted, rather than dispersing the fleet at the end of the exercises, it was held in readiness and was therefore fully equipped and ready for action when war broke out.

Despite this level of readiness, because of the safety first policy, Jellicoe did not sail into the North Sea and offer battle to the High Seas Fleet. Meanwhile the Germans decided that under the circumstances, their fleet should remain in harbour. The Kaiser, despite his attempts to build a fleet to rival Britain's, was acutely aware that this ambition had not been fulfilled. His navy was inferior in numbers to the Royal Navy, but it was modern and well trained; whilst it was intact it was a great threat to the Royal Navy. The Kaiser therefore made sure that there was no chance of his precious fleet being destroyed, and kept it ready for use until the time came when the Royal Navy's superiority had been eroded through

**** Jellicoe had succeeded his superior as commander of the Grand Fleet immediately on the outbreak of the war, as the outgoing commander (Callaghan) was considered too old for the task. It is ironic that the Commander-in-Chief of the B.E.F. (Haig) was to be criticised for being too ambitious in his plans and wasteful of his mens' lives, whilst the opposite criticism was levelled at Jellicoe. As Jellicoe fully explained his policy to the Government via the Admiralty, the Government, by not disagreeing with the policy, was ultimately responsible for it.***

the German's use of mines* and submarines and there was therefore a more likely chance of the German Navy inflicting a crushing defeat on the Royal Navy.

This German strategy was evidenced as early as 5th August 1914 when the British light cruiser, H.M.S. Amphion was sunk in the Thames after hitting German mines. Three more cruisers were sunk on 22nd September off the Dutch coast by torpedoes from a German submarine, with a loss of 1,600 lives. The German naval presence in the Mediterranean meanwhile has been described in the preceding chapter.

The First Sea Lord (who was the military head of the Royal Navy) was Lord Fisher. He had a volatile temper and his relationship with the political head of the Navy, Winston Churchill (the First Lord of the Admiralty) was uneasy. There was to be, in May 1915, a dramatic outcome to the relationship between these two powerful men.

* * *

As the immediate threat to both countries' fleets had been eliminated by similar defensive strategies, it was the protection of Britain's trade routes that became a top priority for the Admiralty. In 1914, 64% of the country's food supplies came from overseas. There were early worries about losses of merchant shipping to the German Navy as eight German cruisers were patrolling the oceans; steps were therefore taken to stop them using ports on German owned islands for refuelling purposes.

Five of these cruisers were under the command of Admiral Count von Spee, operating from China. One of his cruisers, the *Emden*, was detached from von Spee's squadron and went to the Indian Ocean where it operated for some time in the Bay of Bengal. Whilst in this area it captured thirteen merchant ships and bombarded oil tanks at the port of Madras. The *Emden* moved south and captured three more vessels including a vital collier, whose cargo she desperately needed. A further run south of one thousand miles brought the *Emden* to a remote British island called Diego Garcia, where on 4th October 1914 the ship was resupplied by the islanders, unaware that a war had broken out.

Subsequently, a further seven merchantmen were captured by the *Emden*; in addition, whilst coming up to the harbour at Penang (Malaysia), a Russian cruiser and a French destroyer were sunk. However on 9th November, whilst approaching Cocos Island (500 miles south-west of Java) with the intention of destroying an important British wireless station on the island, the *Emden* was spotted and the wireless operator managed to send a signal reporting the her position. An Australian cruiser, (the Sydney) was despatched from a convoy it was escorting nearby and sank the *Emden*.

The *Emden* was the most successful of the German commerce raiders. The other cruisers in von Spee's squadron the *Scharnhorst*, *Gneisenau*, and *Nurnberg* raided

**** Possibly the most significant loss by use of mine in terms of the ship itself rather than those on board occurred on 27th October 1914 when the brand new battleship H.M.S. Audacious hit a mine off the Northern Irish coast.***

islands in the western Pacific until they moved to the western coast of South America where they were joined by the *Dresden* and *Leipzig*. Admiral Craddock was ordered to intercept von Spee and collected a squadron of ships at the Falkland Islands. From there he rounded Cape Horn into the Pacific. The two fleets met on 1st November 1914; Craddock was hampered by being without the slow but heavily armed battleship H.M.S. Canopus. In the ensuing battle (The Battle of Coronel) the British lost H.M.S. Good Hope and H.M.S. Monmouth; only H.M.S. Glasgow escaped.

After this heavy defeat Lord Fisher and Winston Churchill, at the Admiralty in London, made arrangements that when von Spee was next encountered, he would be met with a superior force. The Germans rounded Cape Horn into the Atlantic and approached the Falkland Islands with the intention of attacking this important British base unaware that Admiral Sturdee was lying in wait with a larger force (Invincible, Inflexible, Carnarvon, Cornwall, Kent, and Bristol together with the Glasgow which had escaped from the Battle of Coronel). On 8th December in calm seas and good visibility Sturdee chased von Spee's ships down. Although it took a little while to sink the German ships due to faulty armour piercing shells, in the ensuing battle, The Battle of the Falkland Islands, only the *Dresden* escaped destruction.

Of the other German cruisers, the *Konigsberg* was blockaded in a river delta in East Africa and the *Karlsruhe* was accidentally blown up in the West Indies. Together these eight German Cruisers sank 50 British merchant ships, but by December 1914, seven of these cruisers had been destroyed; the eighth, the *Dresden* was sunk by the Royal Navy in March 1915.

* * *

With the early destruction of these German commerce raiders, there started an aspect of the War at Sea that was to last for the entire period of the conflict, and which was to have enormous consequences. Britain and Germany both knew that an effective blockade would reduce the ability of the opponent to wage war. Although Germany was not wholly reliant on sea-borne imports (many goods came through neutral Holland), there was still a large dependency upon goods from overseas. Whilst coal and iron ore could be transported across the Baltic Sea with no chance of the Royal Navy being able to stop this, goods coming to Germany from America and elsewhere were a different matter. The Royal Navy cordoned off the English Channel very easily and was able to patrol the North Sea between the Shetland Islands and Norway - this was 190 miles wide - and stop and search neutral shipping. If Germany was suspected as the ultimate destination of the goods, the ship was prevented from completing its journey.

The German blockade of Britain was different, and relied upon submarines to succeed. The destruction of the commerce raiders had made the Kaiser realise that the only way of starving Britain out of the war would be through submarine warfare. Such a strategy meant that neutral shipping was just as likely to be sunk as was Allied shipping, although it must be said that German submarine captains in the early part of the war rarely attacked merchant ships without warning.

One submarine attack that was made without warning however was made in May 1915; the British liner the Lusitania, homeward bound from New York, and sailing close to the southern Irish coastline was sunk by torpedoes fired from a German submarine. Of the 1,198 victims, 128 were American citizens. This act very nearly brought the U.S.A. into the war, but President Wilson (who was keen to keep his country out of the conflict) was able to avoid this by obtaining a promise from Germany not to sink any more liners without warning.

The Germans claimed the Lusitania was carrying ammunition, this was denied by the British, but the fact that the liner blew up so readily after the torpedo strike ensured controversy has surrounded the event ever since.

The wreck of the Lusitania was surveyed in the 1990's by Dr Robert Ballard (the ocean explorer who discovered the wreck of the Titanic) and his conclusion that the vessel probably blew up due to the highly explosive coal dust that was in the ship's bunkers has gone some way to solving the puzzle. The sinking of the Lusitania was a serious error by the Germans, but their hope in attacking ships like this was to sink a troopship, the first of which to be sunk was on 13th August 1915 when the Royal Edward was sent to the bottom of the Aegean Sea off Crete, with over 800 men being drowned.

The sinking of troopships was not always the outcome of a German submarine's attack. The loss of the hospital ship 'Anglia' mentioned in Chapter 3 is one of a number of examples of hospital ships being sunk. Perhaps the most famous hospital ship to be sunk was the Britannic, a sister ship of the Titanic.

The Britannic was launched in February 1914, nearly two years after the Titanic hit an iceberg in the north Atlantic. Lessons were learned from the loss of the Titanic, and the Britannic was a much safer design than her sister. The ships requisitioned (mainly from the Union Castle Line) for hospital ship duties were found not to be large enough, and so larger ships were pressed into service, including the brand new Britannic, which had not even carried a fare-paying passenger.

The Britannic successfully made five trips to the Mediterranean, each time carrying back home up to 3,000 wounded soldiers. On 21st November 1916, on her sixth outbound voyage and only a few hours away from Mudros for where she was heading, she was passing close to the island of Kea, north of Crete when she struck a mine and sank in less than an hour. Thankfully the loss of life was minimal due to there being no casualties on board at the time. (S.D.G.W. indicates one officer and eight men all from the Royal Army Medical Corps were lost, in addition there was a small loss of life amongst the ship's crew.)

* * *

Back in the North Sea, the German High Seas Fleet, although largely bottled up did, at the end of 1914, make quick raids on the British coast; the first of these was on 3rd November and was made on Yarmouth; the second raid is more well known. On 16th December 1914, German warships bombarded Whitby, Scarborough and Hartlepool, killing many civilians in the process, and managed to evade the British ships that were sent out to intercept them. These British ships (commanded by Rear-Admiral David Beatty) were believed to be an overwhelming force for the task, however it was not realised that the Germans had sent out their entire High Seas Fleet. Had the fleets met, it is likely that the superior German force would have destroyed the British squadron, thus in one stroke wiping out the numerical superiority in capital ships that the British enjoyed.

Besides the laying of a minefield off Scarborough, which was to prove to be a hazard to British shipping for weeks to come, the casualties of the raid amounted to 500 (mainly civilians) including over 100 killed. Some of the casualties were not civilians, six men of the 18th Battalion, Durham Light Infantry (part of 31st Division) were killed. These men, who were manning the defences at Hartlepool had the dubious distinction of being the first of Kitchener's volunteers to be killed by enemy action, being eight months earlier than the men from the 11th (Northern) Division who were to be killed at Gallipoli at midnight on 6th/7th August 1915 (see Chapter 5).

It is possible that the German habit of laying mines in the North Sea may have led to the death of Willie Mellor from Ravensthorpe. Willie was born in Ravensthorpe in 1875, and had presumably settled in Hull, where he lived, at 6 Glasgow Street, with his wife. In July 1915, Willie signed up with the Great Northern Company, who were owners and operators of fishing boats, as First Engineer on the company's steam trawler, the 'Earl'. The 'Earl' was seventeen years old, having been built at Govan on the Clyde in 1898. The boat was 104 feet long, with a displacement of 168½ tons. Powered by coal, its engines generated 40 horse power.

After completing the first trip, lasting less than two weeks, Willie signed on again for another ten trips, the first of these, later in July 1915, being under a new skipper, W.D. Coates. Although the skipper and the 'second hand' earned a proportion of the catch, Willie, as First Engineer was the highest salaried individual on board, earning the very respectable sum of 47 shillings, 6d per week.

40. Willie Mellor

In early January 1915, the Earl commenced its last journey. As in previous fishing expeditions, it carried a total of nine crew, including the skipper's son, also called W.D. Coates.

Nothing is known of the fate of fishing vessel H436 'Earl'. The ship is simply recorded as 'missing'. The crew of nine, including Willie Mellor are recorded as having been 'presumed drowned' on 21st January 1915. Willie Mellor is the only civilian named on Ravensthorpe's War Memorial.

The names of Willie Mellor and the rest of the crew of the 'Earl' are recorded on the Tower Hill Memorial in London. The Memorial commemorates 12,649 men of the Merchant Navy and Fishing Fleets who died in the First World War and who have no known graves.

The next raid by the Germans was on 28th January 1915. It was their intention to sink fishing boats operating in the area of the North Sea known as the Dogger Bank. The Admiralty had decoded the German signals and sent two forces to intercept the Germans. The force led by Rear-Admiral Beatty made contact with the Germans and a running battle ensued as the Germans headed for the safety of their coast. Although one German ship was sunk, due to poor signalling by the British ships, the others managed to escape.

There was no further action in the North Sea in 1915.

* * *

As has already been described, the relationship between Lord Fisher and Winston Churchill was uneasy; following disagreements about the conduct of the Gallipoli campaign, Lord Fisher resigned as First Sea Lord in May 1915. This, together with the shortage of shells - the so called 'shell scandal', briefly mentioned in Chapter 2 caused Asquith's Liberal Government to collapse and a Coalition Government (but with Asquith still as Prime Minister) took over. Churchill was forced out of his job as First Lord of the Admiralty during this political shake up (being replaced by Arthur Balfour, a former Prime Minister), although he continued to hold office within the Government, as Chancellor of the Duchy of Lancaster, until being removed at the end of the year as a direct result of the Dardanelles disaster.

The year ended with the British blockade of Germany continuing with the English Channel cordoned off and virtually all shipping in the North Sea being intercepted (a total of 3,098 ships were intercepted and searched in the North Sea by the Royal Navy in 1915; only 19 slipping past the patrols).

German submarines were operating off the Gallipoli coast, several old battleships were sunk and the fleet was forced to retire to the safety of Mudros harbour; this significantly reduced the morale of the troops fighting on the peninsular.

* * *

In 1916, following the appointment of Admiral Rheinhard Scheer as the commander of the High Seas Fleet, there was a change in policy by the Germans.

With their submarines lying in wait outside naval bases such as Rosyth, Scheer hoped that by interfering with merchant shipping off the Norwegian coast, the Grand Fleet would be tempted into action. On 31st May the British Grand Fleet (now with 24 battleships) and the German High Seas Fleet met in the one major sea battle of the war - The Battle of Jutland.

Once again it was Rear Admiral Beatty's ships which played an important part in the battle. One of the ships in Beatty's squadron sighted smoke on the horizon and believing it to be from a German ship, vessels were despatched to investigate. The smoke turned out to be from a Danish merchant ship; however the Germans had also sighted the smoke and sent ships of their own to investigate. It was therefore only by chance that the two forces came into contact.

Beatty's stronger flotilla chased the Germans who despite being weaker, shot more accurately than the British*. Two British ships were sunk in this exchange - the Queen Mary and the Indefatigable - but the pursuit continued until the British sighted the entire German High Seas Fleet sailing towards them. The roles were suddenly reversed, and Beatty's squadron was chased northwards. Little did the Germans realise that Jellicoe, with the rest of the Grand Fleet was sailing to Beatty's aid following Beatty sending news by wireless.

Upon sighting the Germans, Jellicoe deployed the Grand Fleet in such a way as to "Cross the German 'T' "- that is to enable the British ships to fire broadside against the Germans who were deployed in column and who could not therefore fire anything other than their forward facing armament. The German ships' formation also meant that the fire of the ships at the rear of the column would be restricted by the ships in front. From the British perspective, this was the ideal tactic to be accomplished.

In fading light the German ships managed to disengage from the battle, all the time inflicting heavy damage on the British ships. By some fluke, shortly after this the Germans again stumbled into the British fleet, but before they suffered too much damage, they again disengaged and disappeared into the gathering gloom.

Despite Admiral Jellicoe managing to manoeuvre the Grand Fleet into favourable positions, poor gunnery and unreliable shells, together with the strong armour of the German battleships meant the German losses were much fewer than British losses. However, the High Seas Fleet was forced to escape back to port, leaving the British in command of the North Sea again; the Germans realised that although they had sunk more ships+ they had little hope of winning a major fleet action. Although they could claim a tactical victory, with their withdrawal back to harbour, the Germans had suffered a strategic defeat.

The High Seas Fleet remained in harbour for much of the rest of the war. The Germans turned once again to their submarines in a renewed attempt to starve Britain out of the war.

There was one further development immediately after the Battle of Jutland that had major implications for the way the war was run. Lord Kitchener, whose power and influence although declining, was still a significant figure in Government circles. It was decided that he ought to go to Russia in order to bolster their war

**** The superior German shells and range finding equipment were telling factors.***

+ British losses - 3 battlecruisers, 3 cruisers, 8 destroyers (115,000 tons of shipping) and nearly 7,000 men

German losses - 1 (old) battleship, 1 battlecruiser, 4 cruisers, 5 destroyers (61,000 tons) and just over 3,000 men.

effort; he set sail to Russia the week after Jutland, on board H.M.S. Hampshire. Shortly after setting sail the ship hit a German mine off the west coast of Orkney. Kitchener was drowned along with all but twelve of the crew.

* * *

George Hoggarth was the next Ravensthorpe casualty to be incurred at sea. He was born on 10th July 1896 in Barrow and at the time of his death was a crew member on board the destroyer H.M.S. Mounsey. The ship (a Yarrow 'M' Class vessel) was constructed between September 1914 and November 1915; it had a top speed of 35 to 36 knots and a crew of 79*.

George had volunteered for navy service and enlisted in August 1915 at Huddersfield whilst working for the Mirfield Colliery Company; previously he had been employed in the shipyard at Barrow - which probably explains his decision to join the navy.

◂ 41. George Hoggarth

* *The ship was sold in 1921 and broken up, ironically enough, in Germany.*

Although he came through the battle of Jutland unscathed, it was during routine operations that George was drowned. On Sunday 8th October 1916, H.M.S. Mounsey left the Naval base at Scapa, in the Orkneys, for a routine exercise. The following day, in conjunction with H.M.S. Erin, the Mounsey (according to the ship's log) carried out exercises, commencing at 2pm. The log records that at 5.30pm a man was reported overboard on the port (left) side; this was George Hoggarth. The ship was stopped and the lifeboat launched. A search was carried out at slow speed for the next forty minutes but to no avail. No trace could be found of George. At 6.10pm the ship rejoined the flotilla and returned to Scapa the next day, 10th October.

The Dewsbury Reporter published an article two weeks later, reproducing a long letter to George's mother at 24 Bell Street, Ravensthorpe, from Lieutenant Frank Butt of H.M.S. Mounsey. He described how George was *"...walking on the upper deck, just before dark* [with a] *heavy sea running. He had got about halfway along the ship when we took a sea forward which washed along the deck and knocked him off his feet. He was seen to go over the side. The ship was turned quickly and the lifeboat got ready for launching and everything possible was done to find him. He was never seen again after he was washed overboard. He had sea boots and oilskins on at the time which would have made it impossible for him to keep himself afloat at all."* Lieutenant Butt goes on to say how, despite the state of the sea, there were more than enough men who immediately volunteered to crew the lifeboat in an attempt to find him.

He finishes *"I understand that your son was in the habit of sending you part of his pay, so I am enclosing a note from myself which I hope you will accept in the spirit in which it is offered."*

George Hoggarth, who was 20 years old, has no known grave and is commemorated on the Plymouth Naval Memorial. The memorial is one of three built to commemorate the men of the Royal Navy who died at sea and who thus have no known grave. These memorials, at Chatham, Portsmouth and Plymouth, were located at each of the navy's manning ports. The Plymouth Memorial lists the names of 7,256 men of the Royal Navy who have no known grave but the sea.

* * *

In November 1916, Jellicoe became First Sea Lord and the flamboyant Rear Admiral Beatty was promoted to take command of the Grand Fleet.

The following month, Asquith was replaced as the Prime Minister by David Lloyd George, and as part of his shake up of the Coalition Government he appointed the leader of the Ulster Unionists, Sir Edward Carson, as First Lord of the Admiralty, despite his knowing little of naval matters.

It was also in December 1916 that the Germans put forward peace proposals; these were rebuffed by the Allies and this, together with the previously described failure to defeat the Royal Navy at Jutland, made the Germans turn once again to submarine warfare. On 1st February 1917 they declared that any ship approaching the British Isles was liable to be attacked. The following month five American ships were sunk by German submarines. This, together with the discovery of a German attempt to persuade Mexico to agitate on the U.S.A.'s southern border, resulted in America declaring war on Germany in April 1917.

Although the U.S.A.'s entry into the war on the Allied side, and the opening of the Battle of Arras (see Chapter 12) were the most significant events of the month, it was also in April 1917 that an action took place in the English Channel off the coast of Dover. It had been recognised from the outset of the war that the Straits of Dover were a highly sensitive area; in this passage of water sailed the numerous ships which transported not only men but the supplies needed to keep the B.E.F. fighting. Occasional German raids on shipping in this area were invariably successful, but they never succeeded in penetrating the cordon maintained by the ships of the Dover Patrol, which guarded the troopships. These raids were somewhat of a nuisance, and were often against easy targets such as trawlers. It was such a raid on the night of 20th/21st April 1917 that was intercepted by two Royal Navy destroyers, the Broke and Swift. Twelve German destroyers had set out from the German occupied port of Zeebrugge on the Belgian coast with the intention of attacking British trawlers. They were intercepted and attacked by the British ships which managed to beat off the attack, sinking or damaging three of the German destroyers. As a result of this action, there were no further raids by the Germans until 1918.

* * *

This successful operation in the English Channel did not however disguise the crisis that was being caused by the continued losses of merchant ships. These losses, together with fewer neutral ships daring to run the gauntlet of the submarine menace meant that the vital imports needed to sustain Britain were falling. The British were also failing to keep up with the Germans in the manufacturing race; the building of merchant shipping in Britain was diminishing, whilst the Germans were building more submarines of better design: in 1917 there were about five times more German submarines available than the mere 24 that there had been in 1915.

The Royal Navy's answer to the submarine threat was the development of Q-ships. These ships were merchant vessels, but armed with concealed guns and torpedoes. They took advantage of the German submarine commanders' usual tactics of surfacing near lone merchant ships in order to sink them by either landing a party from the submarine in order to scuttle the vessel, or sinking them via gunfire, both of which ensured their supply of torpedoes was maintained.

The Q-ships sank eleven submarines between July 1915 and the autumn of 1917 when they were finally withdrawn.

The declaration of 1st February 1917 that unrestricted submarine warfare would commence, and the resulting losses of shipping, very nearly knocked Britain out of the war. In April it was said that there was just six weeks supply of corn left in the country, the answer was the convoy system; the Royal Navy objected to this as each convoy would be reduced to the speed of the slowest ship, and they said they would be unable to provide the required number of escorts*.

**** The dwindling supply of food and the desperation of Jellicoe to destroy the submarine bases were contributory factors in the way Haig decided to prosecute the campaign in Flanders in 1917. Haig was told (inaccurately) that most of the submarines were operating from the Belgian ports that were in German hands (see Chapter 13).***

Despite these objections, Lloyd George, prompted by Sir Maurice Hankey, the highly regarded secretary to the Cabinet, forced the Royal Navy in May 1917 to adopt the convoy system. Although losses continued, they were at a gradually reducing rate. With America's entry into the war, more warships became available for escort duty and American shipyards began to turn out vast quantities of new merchant ships to replace lost ones.

Sir Eric Geddes replaced Sir Edward Carson as First Lord of the Admiralty in July 1917 (as a result of his predecessor's reluctance to introduce the convoy system). Geddes was far more effective than Carson had been, but he disagreed with, and subsequently dismissed Jellicoe as First Sea Lord in December 1917 and replaced him with Vice-Admiral Sir Rosslyn Wemyss.

* * *

One of the most daring naval actions of the entire war took place on 23rd April 1918, nearly a year to the day after the action involving the Broke and Swift. Vice-Admiral Roger Keyes had taken over command of the Dover Patrol and planned a raid on the ports of Zeebrugge and Ostend, which were used as bases for German submarines. Both of these ports were connected by a canal network to the inland port of Bruges, where more German destroyers and submarines were located.

The plan was for three old cruisers, filled with concrete, to be sunk in the narrow part of the canal entrance in Zeebrugge, and for a further two to be sunk at Ostend. The Zeebrugge raid was partially successful, two of the ships being sunk, but they failed to totally block the canal. The Ostend raid failed. Around 75 ships took part in the raid, together with about 200 Royal Marines who were to be landed from a further obsolete cruiser, H.M.S. Vindictive in a diversionary attack against the Zeebrugge mole. A total of eight V.C.s were awarded, but losses were heavy, with nearly 200 British dead and a large number of others wounded.

Despite the failure of the raid, the German submarine menace was being slowly overcome; increasing numbers of German submarines were sunk and from May 1918 onwards, more merchant ships were turned out from British and American shipyards on a monthly basis than were destroyed by German submarines. The menace of starvation was averted and although rationing had to be introduced, by the end of the war it was the German civilian population that was on the verge of starvation and not Britain's.

The blockade of Germany by the Royal Navy helped to bring about civilian discontent within the country, and so no doubt speeded up the collapse of the German will to fight on in 1918. However as will be seen, it was the defeat of Germany's army that brought about the Armistice. Had the Royal Navy brought about a crushing defeat on the German Navy, it is doubtful if the war would have been shortened by much; however, had the Battle of Jutland or any other major sea battle been lost, the war could easily have been won by Germany as Britain would surely have been starved into submission.

Chapter Seven

The Somme (1) - July and August

Following the dismissal of Sir John French as Commander-in-Chief and Sir Douglas Haig's appointment on 19th December 1915 as his successor, Haig's first task was to attend the second of two conferences at the French town of Chantilly on 29th December (the first one having been held on 6th December).

At this conference, much against Haig's wishes, it was decided that a combined thrust by the French and British armies would be made against the Germans at the point where the French and British armies met. This point was between the town of Albert and the River Somme in the Picardy region of northern France. Albert was to become the symbol of the forthcoming battle for many British soldiers; passing through the town on the way to the front line trenches the British troops invariably passed below a statue of Mary and the infant Jesus. This statue had hung in a precarious horizontal position from the tower of the town's Basilica ever since being hit by German artillery fire earlier in the war.

Haig's opposition to this plan was largely due to the fact that a push here, even if successful, would have no strategic value. There were no important cities, railway junctions or even railway lines behind the German front line. Although forced to comply with the French wishes (his instructions from the British Government were vague but made it clear he would have to conform to the French in terms of strategy) he instructed Sir Herbert Plumer (commanding the Second Army) to make preparations for an offensive in the Ypres sector which was Haig's preferred battleground.

The French plan for the offensive on the Somme involved their armies making the largest contribution (although the New Armies of Kitchener's volunteers were arriving in force, the B.E.F. was still the junior partner in the coalition); the French were to launch nearly forty divisions on the opening day. With the British in support, together with attacks on other fronts it was hoped that German resistance would begin to crumble.

Before the Allied plans were far advanced, the Germans launched a surprise blow against the French at the town of Verdun. During 1915 the Germans had stood on the defensive in the west, concentrating instead on the Russians in the east. The attack at Verdun, which commenced in February 1916, took the initiative away from the Allies. It was designed by the Germans to decimate the French armies. They guessed, correctly, that the French would be unwilling to surrender the town at any price - it had stood as a symbol during the Franco-Prussian War; it was the German intention to 'bleed the French white' by destroying their troops through the use of massed artillery. The German tactics worked and French reserves were drawn into the battle in vast numbers; the French managed, despite enormous German pressure, to hold off the attacks. Despite the original concept of using artillery to destroy the French, the Germans became sucked into the battle in increasing numbers, and both sides started to lose troops at an enormous rate.

The French, because of their commitment at Verdun, could not fulfil their intended role alongside the British on the Somme; their participation had to be scaled down and the British involvement was therefore increased. The main burden of the offensive now fell on Haig, but despite this, matters were too far advanced for a switch to Haig's favoured battleground in Flanders. With continuing attacks on their defences at Verdun, the French appealed in ever increasing desperation for the Somme attack to be launched so as to take the pressure off their troops at Verdun.

In order to assist the French, during March Haig agreed to relieve the French Tenth Army in front of Arras, this resulted in an uninterrupted British front line stretching from Belgium down to the Somme. Haig did not, however, consider he would have Kitchener's New Armies sufficiently trained until late summer, but in view of the French plight he brought the attack forward to late June.

The B.E.F. had by now expanded to 58 Divisions including battalions from Australia, New Zealand, Canada, South Africa and India. These were organised into armies under Monro, Plumer, Allenby and Rawlinson. Rawlinson's Fourth Army (which came into being on 1st March 1916) was joined in May 1916 by a brand new 'Reserve' Army under Lieutenant-General Hubert Gough; this Reserve Army was to be used to exploit the breach that it was hoped would be created in the German lines.

Although Haig was in overall command of the British Armies in France, the detailed planning of the attack was left to General Sir Henry Rawlinson who believed that the troops he had been allocated were insufficiently trained and could not be relied upon to undertake complicated manoeuvres. This, together with his confidence in the artillery, led him to evolve a simple plan. The artillery would pound the German lines until their trenches were destroyed, the infantry would then advance slowly in straight lines and occupy the destroyed trenches. The exercise would be repeated as often as necessary, against successive lines of German trenches.

Unfortunately, there were fundamental flaws in Rawlinson's plan. The Germans, realising an attack was imminent had strengthened their trenches and built very deep dugouts in which the troops garrisoning the trenches could shelter, the strength of these defences was underestimated by the British. There were also serious inadequacies in the artillery fire plan; although the barrage was heavier than any previous one, there was a lack of the guns of the largest calibres. The medium sized guns were incapable of destroying the deep dugouts, and the sheer quantity of shells they fired would not alter that fact.

Not only was the artillery responsible for destroying the trenches and dugouts, they also had to destroy the barbed wire entanglements that were stretched in depth in front of the German trenches. The art of destroying these entanglements was complicated; because of worn out (therefore inaccurate) guns, unreliable ammunition and undertrained gunners, the barbed wire was, despite all the artillery's efforts, not cut in enough places to allow the majority of the troops to pass through.

The final problem which occurred was the time of day chosen to launch the attack. The usual time for such offensives to be launched was at dawn. The French had decided that artillery observation would be made easier if the attack was made at a later hour, in broad daylight. A time of 7.30am was therefore decided upon. Although it is undeniable that artillery observation would be made significantly easier at this time, the benefit gained by this later hour of attack was incapable of being taken advantage of, due to the inflexibility of the artillery fire plan. The artillery was ordered to change its objectives at pre-determined times, the infantry simply following the shellfire from one objective to the next. These 'lifts' were to be made regardless of whether the infantry had kept up. It was assumed (because of the weight of the shellfire) that the infantry would not have a problem in keeping up.

It was not possible for anyone at a low level of command to alter the artillery lifts to bring the guns back to fire at any part of the German defences that was causing a hold up. Such decisions were only able to be made high up the chain of command, and would thus be delayed; for these reasons, therefore, the benefit of the improved visibility was wasted. The Germans were advantaged by this decision over the time of the attack; their machine guns were brought up out of the undamaged dugouts and would have excellent observation of the slowly advancing British troops.

Although an over-simplification, the attack could be described as a race between the British (coming across No Man's Land) and the Germans (clambering out of their dugouts). Whoever arrived at the top of the German trenches first would win. It was a race into which Rawlinson did not enter his troops.

The British soldiers were hampered not only by orders to walk slowly in rigid lines against the 'destroyed' German defences, but also by the misguided logic that formed Rawlinson's plan. As the German defences were going to be destroyed, and the attacking troops would simply have to occupy them, they may as well take over with them the equipment needed to repair the trenches, and make them defensible against German counter-attacks. The attackers were therefore weighed down with heavy loads which made a race to the German parapet (even if allowed within their orders) almost impossible to win.

The Battle of the Somme was launched using the Citizen Army raised by the late Lord Kitchener containing the most patriotic of Britain's male population. Casualties were enormous. On the first day there were 60,000 killed missing or wounded; of these 20,000 were dead. These first day casualties were more than the British army suffered during the Crimean, Boer and Korean Wars combined. The majority of the casualties were incurred in the first hour when along most of the 18 mile long British front there was a near total failure to breach the German trenches.

Success was gained on the right flank where the British attacked alongside the French. The success could be put down in part to the French heavy artillery (which was not in such short supply as British heavy artillery) firing across the boundary of the two armies' attacks, thereby helping to destroy many of the German dugouts.

The only other notable success was on the front of the 36th (Ulster) Division where the troops attacked, against Rawlinson's orders, at a rapid charge; the Germans were overwhelmed but due to their success being unsupported on either flank, the Ulster Division's gains could not be held.

There were a number of Ravensthorpe men involved in this opening day's attack. Two were killed, and four wounded, however there was another casualty that was incurred before the attack even commenced.

*   *   *

John Thomas Walker originally enlisted in the King's Royal Rifle Corps; this regiment was extremely proud of its history and was probably second only to the Guards Regiments in terms of status. However, after the photograph was taken, Jack (as he seems to have been known) was transferred to the Royal Engineers, where he became a member of the 'Special Brigade'. This unusual title was given to the arm of the Royal Engineers that was responsible for discharging poisoned gas towards the Germans by means of the 'Gas Cloud'.

This type of attack was made by having the gas discharged from cylinders situated in the front line trenches; it was obviously important that the wind was blowing in the correct direction to ensure the cloud, upon it being discharged from the cylinders, did not linger and instead travelled across No Man's Land towards the German trenches. (The other method of using poisoned gas was via shells which were fired by the artillery. These, on exploding, discharged the gas directly at the point of impact.)

The Special Brigade, Royal Engineers, was split into four battalions, Jack being in the Fourth.

◂ 42. Jack Walker in his K.R.R.C. uniform

In the days leading up to the battle, the 4th Battalion, Special Brigade, R.E. was operating in the area of VI Corps, and had responsibility for the part of the front line held by the 14th, 55th, and 37th Divisions; this was to the north of a diversionary attack at Gommecourt, which itself was to the north of the main front to be attacked on the opening day of the Battle of the Somme. Although these divisions were not directly involved in the Battle of the Somme there was a requirement to keep the Germans guessing as to where exactly the attack would be delivered (although the massive artillery bombardment would have left the defenders in little doubt that they would soon be under attack), and so many methods were used to try to make the Germans believe an attack was imminent elsewhere.

On 27th June the order was given that gas should be released as soon as a favourable opportunity presented itself, and during that afternoon gas was released on the fronts of the 14th and 37th Divisions. The wind continued to be favourable the next day (28th) and the discharge of gas would probably therefore have continued.

Due to the large area covered by the 4th Battalion of the Special Brigade (the other three battalions had similar lengths of line), there is no detail in the battalion's War Diary of any incidents during these days. There is, however, a brief summary of casualties; this reports that on the 27th the battalion suffered five killed (including died of wounds) and 24 wounded. The following day there were nine deaths plus 44 wounded and 11 missing*. The majority of these fatalities were as a direct result of gas poisoning (it is likely leakages and sudden shifts in wind would have caused these casualties). Jack Walker was one of the eight who died of wounds on 28th June. He is buried at Avesnes-le-Comte Communal Cemetery Extension.

There is very little detail in either of the local newspapers about Jack. Born in Dewsbury in about 1897 to Ephraim and Rachel Walker, it seems that after the death of his parents he and his sister were adopted by their aunt, Mrs Leak of 53 Sackville Street, Ravensthorpe. His sister went into domestic service while Jack went to work as a platform porter at Thornhill's Lancashire & Yorkshire Railway station until about December 1915 when he enlisted in the K.R.R.C.

*   *   *

As previously mentioned, the Battle of the Somme commenced on Saturday 1st July; in the minutes before the attack was launched, the bombardment redoubled its ferocity as trench mortar batteries joined in. At 7.28am a series of mines were exploded beneath German strong points, although the one at Beaumont-Hamel was detonated a few minutes earlier at 7.20am. The largest of these mines, the Lochnagar Mine, was at the village of La Boiselle which was just to the south of the road leading from Albert to Bapaume. This road was vital as it was to be the axis of the main advance by the British.

**** S.D.G.W. states on the 27th - 3 killed in action plus 1 died of wounds; 28th - 3 k.i.a. plus 8 d.o.w.; 29th - 2 k.i.a. plus 2 d.o.w.***

▲ Map 10. The Somme

The British troops were full of confidence, there seemed to be no way that anything could survive the bombardment. At 7.30am precisely the bombardment fell silent as the gunners paused whilst the aim of their weapons was lifted to the next line of German trenches. In the momentary silence, larks could be plainly heard singing in the cloudless skies above the battlefield. Officers' whistles signalled the men to clamber out of the trenches, and all along the front the men formed neatly into lines as ordered and stepped forward.

Just south of the village of La Boiselle and only a few hundred yards from the Lochnagar Mine was the 21st Division. Since its baptism of fire at the Battle of Loos ten months previously, it had been made back up to full strength; 64 Brigade still contained the 9th and 10th K.O.Y.L.I. and the 15th D.L.I., however the 14th D.L.I. had been exchanged for a regular battalion from the 6th Division, the 1st Battalion, East Yorkshire Regiment. This was part of a deliberate policy of strengthening Kitchener's Divisions with regular troops.

For the purpose of the opening assault, the 21st Division had two brigades in the assault (63 and 64 - with 62 Brigade being in support); the division had also been strengthened by the loan of 50 Brigade (from the 17th Division). It is, however, the attack of 64 Brigade that directly concerned Ravensthorpe. The first wave of 64 Brigade's attack was made up of the 9th and 10th K.O.Y.L.I.; in support were the 15th D.L.I. and 1st East Yorks.

In order to reduce the width of No Man's Land to a minimum, a Russian sap was dug* the roof of which was blown in prior to the attack, this reduced the width of No Man's Land at this point to 180 yards. At 7.25am parties from the two K.O.Y.L.I. battalions crawled out from the Russian sap and laid out in front of the British trenches waiting for the barrage to lift. Unfortunately, in spite of the barrage the Germans (warned by look-outs manning their trenches) brought up machine guns from the dugouts in response to this activity and fired on the K.O.Y.L.I.s.

Despite these casualties, the variation to General Rawlinson's plan worked and the leading troops were quickly able to overwhelm the German front line trenches at this point. Although losses were heavy the leading waves pressed on and supported by troops from other battalions the objective of the sunken road leading north out of the village of Fricourt was taken. The troops had became seriously mixed and the Brigade Commander, Brigadier-General Headlam was forced to come forward at 8.20am to ascertain the exact situation; after a while he had to return to his headquarters to report to his divisional commander, leaving Lieutenant-Colonel Fitzgerald (the commanding officer of the 15th D.L.I.) in charge of the now totally intermingled troops.

The situation was far from good; on the 21st Division's left, the 34th Division (whose front straddled the Albert-Bapaume Road) had failed to break through, therefore the 21st Division's left flank was, in the jargon of the army 'in the air', this meant that their advance was not supported and it was in danger of being attacked from the direction of the 34th Division's failed assault. Although the 9th and 10th K.O.Y.L.I. had reached the sunken road, the ultimate divisional objective was beyond this, being Crucifix Trench; some troops had managed to take this

A tunnel dug out from the British trenches into No Man's Land, the roof of which, when destroyed, would transform the tunnel into a rudimentary trench leading into No Man's Land.

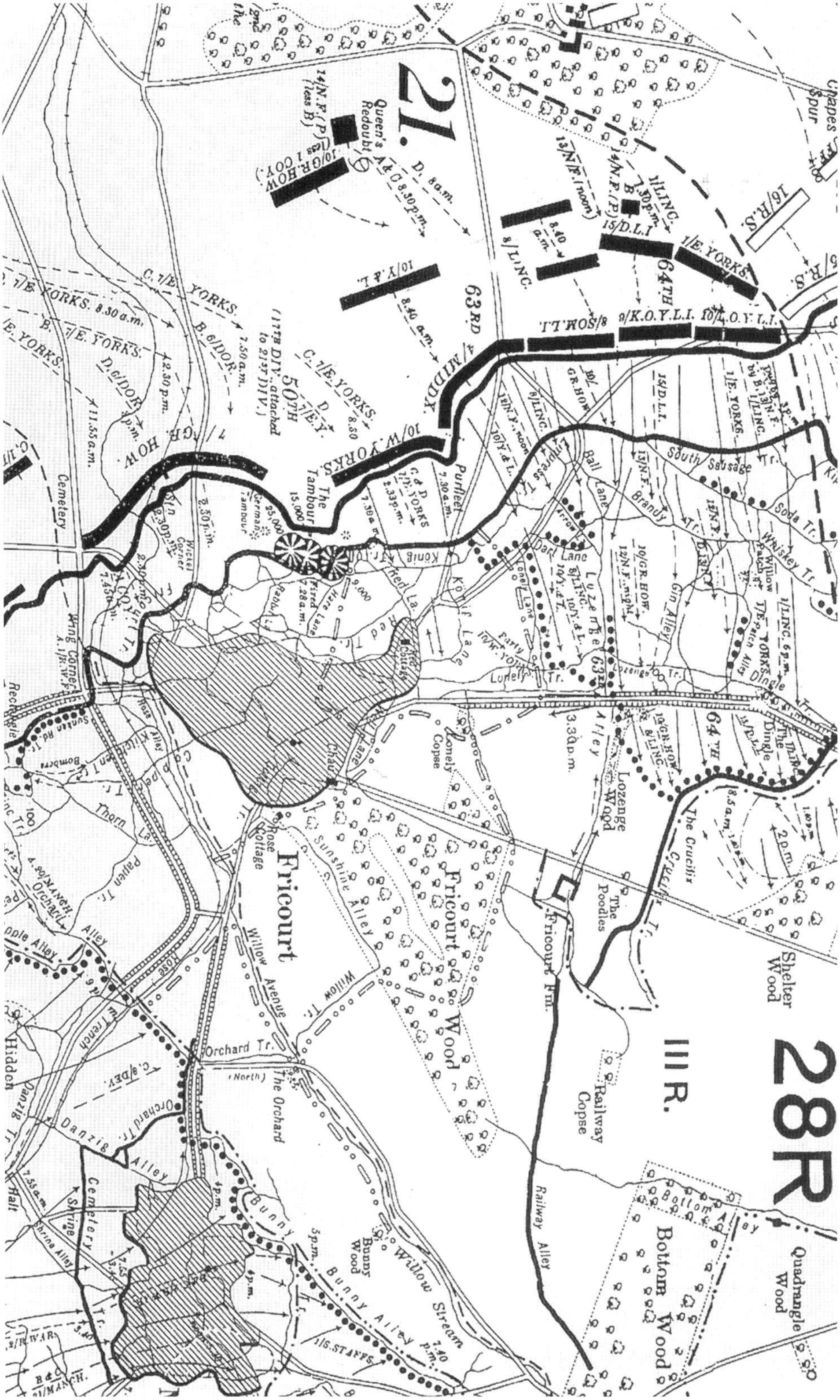

Map 11. The Fricourt area

early in the attack, these men were isolated and in danger of being counter-attacked. Eventually at 1.30pm an advance was made from the sunken road to Crucifix Trench, in order to reinforce the troops there; although in an extremely exposed position (German machine gun fire from nearby woods caused casualties throughout the day) the position was held. 64 Brigade was relieved that night by 62 Brigade.

The day's advance by the 21st Division, together with a similar advance to the south caused the Germans to evacuate the village of Fricourt which had become almost surrounded. Unfortunately the price was high, this was due to the failure of the 34th Division's attack to the north, and the fact that there was no direct assault on Fricourt; the 21st Division's advance was thereby, for a time, unsupported on either flank. The salient created in the German line meant that German fire was directed on the attackers from three sides during the entire day; this added to the already heavy casualties from the morning's attack meant that the War Diary of the 9th K.O.Y.L.I. initially reported their casualties as being 21 officers and 475 other ranks (including nine and 415 killed respectively); among the officer casualties, the extremely unpopular commanding officer, Lieutenant-Colonel C.W. Lynch was killed.

The 10th K.O.Y.L.I.'s War Diary reported: Killed - nine officers and 50 other ranks; Wounded - 16 officers (including the commanding officer) and 292 other ranks; Missing - 135 other ranks*.

The two Ravensthorpe men killed on 1st July were both members of the 21st Division. Fred Holmes was born in Leeds in about 1889. Educated firstly at St. Saviour's Boys' School, he later went to Wheelwright Grammar School in Dewsbury; he also attended St. Saviour's Parish Church. Before the war he worked in the pattern weaving department at Marshall, Kaye and Marshall's mill (following his father into the company), and served in the (territorial) 5th Battalion, Duke of Wellington's Regiment between 1908 and 1912. When war broke he was living with his father at 5 Beacon Street; instead of joining his old unit, he went to Dewsbury to enlist in the K.O.Y.L.I., being posted to the 9th Battalion. It is possible he chose to join the K.O.Y.L.I. because he thought he would get to see action earlier this way, or possibly the recruiting campaign developed by Lord Kitchener appealed more strongly than any sense of loyalty to his old regiment.

Fred joined up on Saturday 19th September 1914 and arrived in France almost a year later, on 11th September 1915. He survived the division's attack at Loos later that month, and his name is briefly mentioned in the Dewsbury Reporter in February 1916 as having received a parcel. The following month he is again mentioned, thanking the pupils at St. Saviour's Boys' School for the gift of another parcel; he stated that there was only one other person from Ravensthorpe in the battalion and he was in a different company. Nothing further is known of Fred Holmes; his father died within a year of Fred's death, probably the strain of Fred initially being posted as 'missing' proved too much for him.

***** *This is perhaps a good example of how the initial reporting of casualty figures, in the heat of battle, was very difficult. The 9th K.O.Y.L.I.'s true figures were substantially less than those initially reported, however the 10th K.O.Y.L.I.'s were remarkably accurate when the 'missing' figure is added to those known to be killed.*

S.D.G.W. gives the following figures for 1st July:- 9th K.O.Y.L.I. - 161 killed;
10th K.O.Y.L.I. - 155 killed.

▲ 43. Fred Holmes

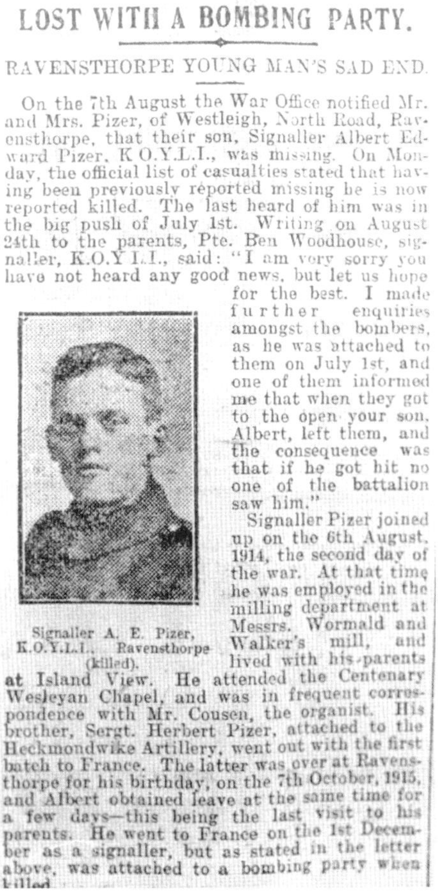

LOST WITH A BOMBING PARTY.

RAVENSTHORPE YOUNG MAN'S SAD END.

On the 7th August the War Office notified Mr. and Mrs. Pizer, of Westleigh, North Road, Ravensthorpe, that their son, Signaller Albert Edward Pizer, K.O.Y.L.I., was missing. On Monday, the official list of casualties stated that having been previously reported missing he is now reported killed. The last heard of him was in the big push of July 1st. Writing on August 24th to the parents, Pte. Ben Woodhouse, signaller, K.O.Y.L.I., said: "I am very sorry you have not heard any good news, but let us hope for the best. I made further enquiries amongst the bombers, as he was attached to them on July 1st, and one of them informed me that when they got to the open your son, Albert, left them, and the consequence was that if he got hit no one of the battalion saw him."

Signaller A. E. Pizer, K.O.Y.L.I., Ravensthorpe (killed).

Signaller Pizer joined up on the 6th August, 1914, the second day of the war. At that time he was employed in the milling department at Messrs. Wormald and Walker's mill, and lived with his parents at Island View. He attended the Centenary Wesleyan Chapel, and was in frequent correspondence with Mr. Cousen, the organist. His brother, Sergt. Herbert Pizer, attached to the Heckmondwike Artillery, went out with the first batch to France. The latter was over at Ravensthorpe for his birthday, on the 7th October, 1915, and Albert obtained leave at the same time for a few days—this being the last visit to his parents. He went to France on the 1st December as a signaller, but as stated in the letter above, was attached to a bombing party when killed.

▲ 44. Albert Pizer

Albert Pizer, the other Ravensthorpe soldier to be killed on this day served with the 10th K.O.Y.L.I. Born in Dewsbury to Arthur and Ada Pizer, Albert was just 20 years old in 1916. He had lived with his parents at Island View, Dewsbury* and worked as a cloth miller at Wormald and Walker's mill. He joined up on the second day of the war, 6th August 1914, and was on leave in October 1915 when he saw his parents and his brother Herbert (whose birthday it was, and who had managed to come home on leave from France) for the last time. It was not until 1st December 1915 that he was sent to join his battalion in France, with whom it seems he was trained as a signaller.

There is a little information about Albert's fate on 1st July; although reported as 'missing' by the War Office on 7th August, it was a letter dated 24th August that gave the clues as to his last movements. The letter was written by a Private Woodhouse to Albert's parents at 98 North Road, Ravensthorpe (they had obviously moved from Island View, Dewsbury); the letter included the following passage *"I am very sorry you have not heard any good news, but let us hope for the*

**** So named because the River Calder here was split in two, one part being used as a mill stream; the piece of land in between the two waterways resembling an island.***

best. I made further enquiries amongst the bombers, as he was attached to them on July 1st, and one of them informed me that when they got to the open your son Albert left them and the consequence was that if he got hit no one of the battalion saw him."

The only further clue to Albert's fate is in the War Diary of the 10th K.O.Y.L.I. Detailed orders for 1st July include instructions for the bombers: The officer in charge of the bombers who was to have one signaller attached to him was to be in charge of four squads of bombers who were to act as blocking parties for various trenches (to ensure that the Germans were stopped in any attempts to infiltrate down the captured trenches); they were to be attached to the Battalion's 'A' Company.

Whilst it is therefore possible that Albert became detached from the leading waves, it is equally likely that his role was to enable the officer to keep in touch with both the squads and the battalion's headquarters.

Neither Albert Pizer or Fred Holmes have a known grave and they are therefore commemorated on the Thiepval Memorial to the Missing; this is also the case for the majority of the soldiers from the 9th and 10th K.O.Y.L.I. Those that do have known graves are buried in two nearby cemeteries, Norfolk Cemetery (where Lieutenant-Colonel Lynch of the 9th K.O.Y.L.I.s is buried) and Gordon Dump Cemetery. Norfolk Cemetery is in a valley close behind where the two battalions formed up before the attack. It is possible that one of the many graves marked by 'unknown' headstones in these cemeteries contains the bodies of Fred or Albert.

Private Joseph Harris was in action quite close to Fred Holmes on 1st July; he was a member of the 10th Battalion Yorkshire Regiment, part of 62 Brigade (21st Division). Although the Brigade was in support during the 1st July, the various battalions of this brigade, including the 10th Yorkshires had to provide carrying parties for other units of the division, and were also instructed to provide detachments to assist the assaulting troops in clearing out hostile trenches. Joe Harris must have been in one of these parties, and was attached to the 4th Middlesex (a regular battalion, part of 63 Brigade*), this battalion suffered very heavily in the initial attack (a total of six machine guns seem to have been aimed at these assaulting troops). Joe wrote from 'an English hospital' about his unit's participation in the advance: *"We went over the parapet with the Middlesex Regiment and the Germans opened out with all their guns, so you can guess our lads went down fast. They swept the whole of the line with machine gun fire and that is what knocked our lads out mostly. When we got to their trenches, we soon turned the Huns out with the bayonet, they certainly don't like cold steel.....I got my wound early on in the engagement when crossing the open."*

Wounded in the back, Joe was evacuated to a hospital in Birmingham where he recovered. One of the Victoria Crosses won for heroism on 1st July was earned by an officer of Joe's battalion; Major Stewart Loudoun-Shand was fatally wounded whilst encouraging his men to attack, and is buried in the Norfolk Cemetery.

Possibly three more Ravensthorpe soldiers, Willie Kendall, Clifford Simpson and Isaac Thompson, were injured during the opening day of the Battle of the Somme, all serving with the 1st Battalion, King's Own Scottish Borderers. Clifford Simpson and Isaac Thompson had both seen service in Gallipoli when the 1st K.O.S.B. had,

**** The 21st Division's Brigades were formed up as shown on the map, with 64 Brigade on the left, 63 Brigade in the centre and 50 Brigade (on loan from 17th Division) on the right.***

along with the rest of the 29th Division, been used time and time again in attempts to break down the Turkish resistance. Although Clifford arrived at Gallipoli probably too late to see any battles, Isaac could well have taken part in the last battles of the Suvla campaign. Willie Kendall seems to have arrived in the battalion by an altogether different route.

After Gallipoli, the 29th Division was strengthened and was one of the thirteen divisions to take part in the opening day of the Battle of the Somme. The division attacked north of the River Ancre towards the village of Beaumont-Hamel. As part of the second wave of attacking troops, the 1st K.O.S.B. went over the top at 8.05am and lost heavily suffering over 500 casualties.

After the war, the area where the 1st K.O.S.B. attacked was purchased by Newfoundland (the Newfoundland Regiment lost many men here when they attacked); Newfoundland at that time was a separate colony and not part of Canada. The Newfoundland Park is now preserved on behalf of the Canadian nation and is one of the most visited parts of the Western Front.

Willie, Clifford and Isaac, like Joe Harris, recovered from their wounds only to be killed later in the war. Their stories are told in subsequent chapters.

* * *

Despite the opening day's disaster, Haig continued to press on with the attack, it was not politically possible for him to give up the first time the British army was seriously engaged in a major offensive, the French had been bearing the brunt of the fighting for over two years; although the 1st July was the first day of the Battle of the Somme, it was also the 132nd day of the Battle of Verdun.

Due to the nature of the gains made on the 1st July, the whole emphasis of the Battle changed away from the main Albert-Bapaume road, to the south where the successful attacks made by the 18th and 30th Divisions, especially, could be exploited

Apart from the success in the south, the only other part of the front where meaningful gains were made was in the area attacked by the 36th (Ulster) Division. Behind the Ulsters, in reserve, was the 49th (West Riding) Division which had been brought down from Ypres in order to take part in the Battle of the Somme. Unfortunately the gains made by the Ulster Division were unmaintainable (with an exception being a small lodgement in the German's front line trench; this became known as the 'A' Line). By the evening of the 1st July, most of the survivors of the attack were back where they started from, having been counter-attacked by the Germans. The division suffered many casualties and in the evening was relieved by the West Riding Division. Although no subsequent attempts were immediately planned for this area, the Germans were still nervous of further British attacks and they continued their barrage of the British front lines to prevent any attacks from forming up.

John Richard Hinchliffe* was a member of the 1/5th Battalion, York and Lancaster Regiment. On 1st July the battalion was in trenches in Aveluy Wood,

**** There is some inconsistency in the spelling of his surname; the majority of sources use this spelling, but the C.W.G.C. and the Medal Rolls at the Public Record Office at Kew use 'Hinchcliffe'.***

across the River Ancre, behind the Ulster Division's attack. At 1.30pm the battalion was called forward, 'A' and 'B' Companies were sent to the north side of the River Ancre and pushed into the front line trenches. 'C' and 'D' Companies proceeded through Thiepval Wood and, despite heavy shelling eventually found their way into the original front line from where, at 6.30pm they observed an enemy counter-attack dispersed by British artillery and machine gun fire. Thirteen men from this battalion were killed on 1st July.

Thiepval Wood and the immediate area plays an important part in the stories of many of Ravensthorpe's soldiers. The wood ran from the river up the steep valley to the Thiepval Ridge, on which sat the village of Thiepval; the village was the key to the German's defence in the northern half of the Somme battlefield. Thiepval was fortified and stood at the crest of the dramatic bluff which marked the northern extremity of a ridge of high ground. This high ground stretched south-eastwards past the village of Pozieres (on the Albert-Bapaume Road) to High Wood, well into the southern sector of the battlefield.

Whilst the high ground disappears into gently rolling fields to the south, the sudden ending of the ridge at Thiepval emphasizes the size of the breathtaking Memorial to the Missing which is situated in the grounds of the old Thiepval Chateau.

As described earlier, the 1/5th York and Lancasters had been pitched into the front line with two companies north of the River Ancre and two companies south of the river. On 2nd July 'A' and 'B' Companies were withdrawn from the line north of the river and joined the rest of the battalion on the edge of Thiepval Wood. It was at 11am the following morning (Monday 3rd July) after heavy artillery activity by both sides, that the battalion's War Diary records: *"A report was received that the enemy had put out a smoke barrage in front and was massing* [for an attack]. *Precautions were made to receive him."* The attack never developed. The War Diary continues:

12.30pm *Shelling on both sides died down for an hour. Estimated casualties to 12 noon - Officers: 5 wounded, 2 missing; Other Ranks: 19 killed, 150 wounded, 150 missing.*

4pm *Approx casualties O.R.. 23 killed, 200 wounded, 120 missing. Enemy shelling and rifle fire ceased altogether at 3.15pm.*

7.45pm *'B' Company sent out a party to clean up and bring dead in.*

10.40pm *Since 3.15pm the enemy had been absolutely quiet. Captain Goodall took a strong patrol of 20 volunteers to find out strength of enemy in Bosche lines. Wounded R.I.R.* [Royal Irish Rifles - of the 36th (Ulster) Division] *officer found outside wire who had been out three days. Patrol reached enemy wire and were cutting through before they were fired on. Just after party returned, enemy opened a very heavy artillery and M.G. fire which continued for about two hours.*

Although the War Diary indicates very heavy casualties during 3rd July, the figures quoted in S.D.G.W. are much lower (four killed and one died of wounds); obviously there was a great deal of confusion. Although it is not known how many men were injured on the 3rd July, John Hinchliffe was one of those who was wounded.

John was born in Mirfield on 27th August 1891. After his early education at Mirfield Parish Church School, he won a scholarship for the Mirfield Grammar School. Upon leaving the Grammar School he went to Ravensthorpe National School as an assistant teacher and subsequently moved to York for his formal teacher training. After graduating from York, John took up a position at Grimethorpe Council School, near Barnsley. He was called up into the army on 8th February 1916 and, after training, went to Southampton on 23rd June from where he was sent straight to his battalion as one of the regular drafts of reinforcements. Whilst en-route from Le Havre to the front he had time to write to a friend: *"On the way up we stayed at a farmstead. Unhappily for us there was no straw about and the rats played hide and seek with us."*

He went into the trenches for the first time on 1st July, but on the 3rd was badly wounded. The Dewsbury Reporter goes into a great deal of detail about the extent of his injuries, saying *"His wounds were on the face, shoulder and body and it is surmised that a formidable piece of shrapnel struck his face, which it grazed slightly, and proceeded downwards through the shoulder and out of the arm pit and struck his body."* He was also wounded in the foot and ankle. After being evacuated from France, he was sent to Netley Hospital near Southampton where he seemed to be making a recovery. By early August he was able to sit up in bed, however he suffered a relapse and septic poisoning set in. On Friday 11th August his parents, Mr and Mrs Albert Hinchliffe received a telegram at their home at 23 Lee Street, Ravensthorpe summoning them to the hospital. After what must have been an agonizing journey they arrived at Southampton just after midnight on Saturday 12th August. After a walk of four miles they arrived at Netley Hospital to be informed that John had died half an hour previously.

▲ 45. John Hinchliffe

▲ 46. Lewis Garside

John's body was brought home and was buried in the churchyard at St. Mary's Parish Church, Mirfield. Unfortunately his grave is no longer marked by a headstone.

Five days after Private John Hinchliffe was injured, another Ravensthorpe soldier was killed. Corporal Lewis Garside was, at 37 years of age, an experienced soldier. He had first joined the army in 1896 aged 17 and had served in the Boer War. As a reservist he would have been called up from his job at the firm of Henry Burrows and was drafted into the 1/4th K.O.Y.L.I. (the 'Dewsbury Territorials'). Arriving in France as a private on 13th April 1915, the first report of him is in an article in the Dewsbury Reporter on 11th September 1915, at which time the battalion, as part of the 49th (West Riding Division) was at Ypres. A letter from him dated 29th August 1915 was reproduced at length in the newspaper:

"We have had a decent rest out of the trenches. We had some sports and they were all right. Even a band is playing behind the firing line, so you can say they are not all dull times out here. We are once more in the trenches for a spell of about 24 days. We seem to have a bit of a bad luck as we have had two officers and two men hit in the first day in." He goes on to describe a chance meeting with an acquaintance in another regiment who *"...had just come out of the fighting line where the Germans had been using gas and liquid fire not far from where we were. You will know where we are by the last big battle* [the Germans used liquid fire at Hooge, near Ypres on 30th July 1915]. *He told me they had been burying dead on the battlefield for three nights."*

Lewis goes on to describe the flies ("there are millions") and the rain. After mentioning a letter from his brother, Harry, in the R.F.A. he attacks those "shirkers" who had not joined up. He finishes by describing how he was a member of "Ticklers Artillery". This is a reference to how, in the absence of grenades, they used empty jam tins (manufactured by the firm of Tickler) filled with explosives and converted into makeshift bombs.

On 1st July the 1/4th K.O.Y.L.I. was placed at the disposal of 96 Brigade (32nd Division) who were to the immediate right of the Ulster Division's attack. They were not called upon but nevertheless suffered 24 fatalities. By early the next morning they were holding the 'A' Line trench, the only part of the German front line to be retained by the Ulster Division. Over the next few days the battalion was used for carrying bombs and ammunition up to the front line trenches.

On 6th July, the 1/4th K.O.Y.L.I. once again took over the 'A' Line trenches. At 7.15pm two parties of bombers advanced up trenches leading to the German line and after pushing the Germans back established blocks 70 yards in advance of the original position. At 12.30am on the 7th July the Germans opened an intense bombardment which concentrated on the 'A' line. Following this bombardment, the Germans advanced towards the 'A' line both along the trenches and across the open. The War Diary describes how *"...a furious fight with bombs ensued lasting until 6.30am. Numerous casualties were incurred both from bombs and enemy snipers who were lying out in the open and who shot down our men as they fired and threw bombs out of the trench."*

At 6.30am the defenders ran out of bombs and they retired down the communication trench to the original British front line. Although the battalion had been reinforced by three companies of the 1/5th K.O.Y.L.I. who came up from Ross Street (a trench in Thiepval Wood) the position had to be abandoned. The battalion was relieved by the 1/5th Duke of Wellington's on 8th July, having sustained the previous day, according to the War Diary, 20 killed and 180 wounded. Casualties during the relief were, according to the War Diary "slight", although this is contradicted by S.D.G.W. which indicates fatalities on the 8th July as fifteen killed in action plus two died of wounds; it also confirms 20 deaths on the 7th.

Lewis Garside's obituary in the Dewsbury Reporter is only brief; the report states that *"Corporal Garside was shot through the head with an explosive bullet while working with a bombing party."* Whilst this does seem to suggest that it was during the attack on the morning of the 7th that he was killed, all sources apart from the newspaper state he was killed on the 8th. The confusion is compounded, however because as previously mentioned, the War Diary states that during relief on the 8th casualties were slight; there must therefore be some doubt as to whether the fifteen men (as stated by S.D.G.W.) were killed on this day, or whether they were in fact killed the previous day when the Germans recaptured the 'A' line trench. This is supported by the manner in which he is said to have died (ie. 'while with a bombing party').

Lewis left behind a widow and two children at home in John Street, Ravensthorpe. After the death of her husband, Sarah Garside remarried and moved to Foundry Street, Ravensthorpe. Lewis is now buried in Serre Road Cemetery Number Two, the largest British cemetery on the Somme.

Private Fred Cardwell was also in the 1/4th K.O.Y.L.I. In the period after Lewis Garside was killed, the battalion had been undergoing reorganisation in Martinsart Wood. A degree of comfort was available here as huts had been built to shelter troops at rest. On 21st July, the battalion returned to the front line, in the Leipzig Salient area, near the village of Authuille*. On 23rd July the battalion attempted to extend the British lines by attacking the Germans in the salient. The assault was not successful and the attacking troops were forced back having lost three officers and seven men killed. The battalion was relieved and went back into support trenches in the area known as the South Bluff in Authuille.

Their period in support did not last long and on Tuesday 25th July they relieved the 1/5th K.O.Y.L.I. who were holding the front line. Two companies of the battalion ('Y' and 'Z' Companies) went into the front line, 'W' Company was in reserve and 'X' Company in support in Authuille. Access to the front line from Authuille would have been principally through the communication trench known as Campbell Avenue +. Although the War Diary reports that *"the enemy were very quiet except for occasional shelling"* inevitably casualties were incurred.

According to a very detailed letter published in the Dewsbury Reporter (from a Private W. Reeves to an unnamed 'Ravensthorpe Gentleman'), Fred Cardwell, along with three others was, on the morning of Friday 28th July, *"...fetching water for their breakfasts, and to get to it they had to go to a place the Germans shell very often#. While the party were returning with the water they started shelling and they*

**** Authuille is the nearest village to the Leipzig salient. It lays adjacent to the River Ancre, at the foot of the bluff, the top of which is crowned by the Thiepval Memorial; the Leipzig Salient was a strong defensive feature which ran down towards the British front line from where the Thiepval Memorial to the Missing now stands.***

+ The present day road from Authuille to the village of Ovillers runs for the first few hundred yards on the site of Campbell Avenue.

 # Possibly Authuille village. It is likely the route they were taking was along Campbell Avenue which, as it runs up the hill towards the front line (the Leipzig Salient), would have been overlooked by the Germans on higher ground.

dropped two shells very near them. The whole lot started running and by some mishap Fred slipped and fell. While he was down another shell dropped close beside him. As he did not get up, one or two of the party went back to him. He was not wounded but was suffering from severe shell shock. They got him to a safe place and did all their limited knowledge would let them do. They at once sent for a doctor.....but I'm sorry to say he could only pronounce him dead. He was buried as decently as circumstances would permit and I am only sorry that I can't say in this letter the name of the place where he lies, but should God spare me to come home again I promise to come and let his people know. I may say that he met his death about 20 minutes past six o'clock on the morning of 28th July."

There is considerable confusion over the exact date of Fred's death, S.D.G.W. gives the date as 26th July as do the Medal Rolls at the Public Record Office; the C.W.G.C. states the 27th, but in view of the precise timing in the letter, it does seem that it probably was Tuesday 28th when Fred was killed.

Fred's parents, Mr and Mrs Sam Cardwell lived at 31 Commercial Street, Ravensthorpe. Fred was educated at St. Saviour's Boys' School and before the war worked for Jas Smith and Sons. As a pre-war territorial he was drafted into the 1/4th K.O.Y.L.I. but surprisingly was sent to France as late as May 1916.

Fred was aged just 21 when he died and is buried at Authuille Military Cemetery. The cemetery is extremely beautiful, it is on a steep slope that runs down to the River Ancre. It is not known if Private Reeves met up with Mr and Mrs Cardwell, but the chances are that he did as it seems that he survived the war.

◂ 47. Fred Cardwell

▲ 48. Authuille Military Cemetery.

The last casualty from Ravensthorpe incurred in the opening two months of the Battle of the Somme was not a member of the 49th (West Riding) Division, and for the first time since the opening day of the battle it is necessary to focus on the southern sector of the battlefield. Ernest Walker was even younger than Fred Cardwell, being just 20 years of age. Born in October 1896 at Earlsheaton near Dewsbury he joined up on 4th January 1915. Ernest lived with his parents at 17 Foundry Street, Ravensthorpe, working as a spinner at Robert Swire and Sons. After training at Basingstoke, he arrived in France with the 7th Battalion, Royal Scots Fusiliers on 10th July 1915. Some time after his arrival in France he was promoted to lance corporal.

The battalion took part in the Battle of Loos as part of the 15th (Scottish) Division, but in May 1916 was amalgamated with the 6th Royal Scots Fusiliers*, who were part of the 9th (Scottish) Division. This was part of a reshuffle to make room in the 9th Division for the newly arrived South African Brigade. The merged 6th/7th Royal Scots Fusiliers were part of the 15th Division.

Since 1st July, the Germans had been pushed back in the southern sector of the Somme battlefield as far as the village of Pozieres. The 6th/7th Royal Scots Fusiliers were brought to the Somme and marched up to Fricourt (now lying well behind the British front line) on 8th August. The battalion supplied a working party on 10th August of four officers and 200 men who were used for improving

**** The commanding officer of the 6th Royal Scots Fusiliers was none other than Winston Churchill. After falling out of favour after the Gallipoli disaster (see Chapter 5), he rejoined the army and served from December 1915 to May 1916 on the Western Front. He returned to England in May 1916 when his battalion was amalgamated.***

Butterworth Trench*. The following night a much smaller working party was detailed to carry ammunition to the front line, however on Saturday 12th August the battalion was sent 'Over the Top'.

After a short but intense artillery bombardment lasting just fifteen minutes, (the shorter bombardments gave the Germans much less notice of impending attacks) the 15th Division attacked at 10.30pm. Three battalions attacked; the 12th Highland Light Infantry was on the right, the 6th Camerons on the left and in the centre of the attack was Ernest's battalion, the 6th/7th Royal Scots Fusiliers.

The battalion had three companies ('A', 'C' and 'B') attacking in two waves. Although the left and centre of the attack was successful, and an important portion of the German Trench system known as the 'Switch Line' was captured by 11.40pm, the attack on the right had been less successful, and to compensate, the 6th/7th Royal Scots Fusiliers had to form a defensive flank along a trench known as Gloster Sap.

◀ 49. Ernest Walker

** Butterworth Trench was named after Lieutenant George Butterworth, M.C., a highly regarded composer who was killed on 5th August; he is commemorated on the Thiepval Memorial.*

▲ 50. The Thiepval Memorial to the Missing, with the Anglo-French cemetry in the foreground.

During the night the newly won trench was connected with the original British front line by digging a communication trench, no doubt the digging of this trench would have been hard work; the new communication trench was completed by 7am the next day (13th August). The War Diary gives the casualties for the attack as being 12 officers and 141 other ranks. (S.D.G.W. lists five officers and 48 men killed in the battalion on 12th August.) The battalion was relieved at 5am on 14th August, unfortunately Ernest was not amongst them.

It was not until 2nd June 1917, some ten months later, that the Dewsbury Reporter published the War Office's conclusion that as Lance Corporal Ernest Walker had been reported missing since 13th August 1916 (presumably it was on this day that a roll call was held of the survivors of the attack) they had *"been compelled to report him as killed in action."*

Ernest Walker has no known grave and is therefore commemorated on the Thiepval Memorial to the Missing. Only nine of the battalion's 53 fatal casualties have known graves.

Chapter Eight

The Somme (2) - The Pope's Nose

At the end of August, in the northern sector of the battlefield, the Germans still held most of their original trenches, only south of Authuille had the British made any progress. On the 14th July there had been a set piece attack, the first since the opening day disaster, against the German positions on the Bazentin ridge; this was in the southern sector where the largest advances had been on the 1st July. Although much smaller in scale than that on 1st July, the attack was far more successful; many lessons had been learned from the 1st July.

After the attack on the 14th July there were many smaller engagements (such as the one which cost Ernest Walker his life) and these had pushed the line back, however more of these 'line straightening' operations were required before the next set piece attack could be launched. One of these operations was to take place at Thiepval.

By 31st August, Thiepval had been surrounded on three sides but was still holding out; it had become an annoying salient jutting into the British lines. By holding onto the village, the Germans were able to prevent the British from occupying the whole of the ridge from Thiepval down to Pozieres. A renewed attempt at taking Thiepval was therefore planned for 3rd September, this was to have a serious effect on Ravensthorpe as the 49th (West Riding) Division was chosen as one of the assaulting divisions. The attack was to take place using three divisions; on the right the 25th Division was ordered to capture the Leipzig Salient, to their left was to be the 49th Division and on the extreme left, north of the River Ancre, was to be the 39th Division.

The 49th Division's front was much the same as that of the 36th (Ulster) Division's attack on the 1st July. During this first assault the Yorkshiremen had been in support suffering 105 fatal casualties; these mostly fell to the 1/6th West Yorkshires (33 casualties) and the 1/4th K.O.Y.L.I. (24 casualties). It was now the 49th (West Riding) Division's turn to make an attempt.

The division was to have two brigades making the assault - 146 Brigade's front was from the river, up Mill Road to the crown of the hill, 147 Brigade were on the right; 148 Brigade were in support. The boundary between 146 and 147 Brigades was a few yards to the west of the fork in the road that led from Thiepval to either St. Pierre Divion (right fork) or Hamel (left fork). Both brigades attacked with two battalions, each leaving one battalion in support and another battalion in reserve.

146 Brigade had the 1/8th West Yorkshire Regiment on the left of the assault and the 1/6th West Yorkshires on the right. 147 Brigade attacked with the 1/5th Duke of Wellington's Regiment on the left, and the 1/4th Duke of Wellington's on the right.

The Ravensthorpe men in the 1/5th Duke's were to attack from new trenches which had been dug in front of the original (1st July) trenches. These were named the First, Second, and Third Parallels (these were described as rough, but deep and narrow trenches). The Third Parallel ran across the Thiepval Road, to just south

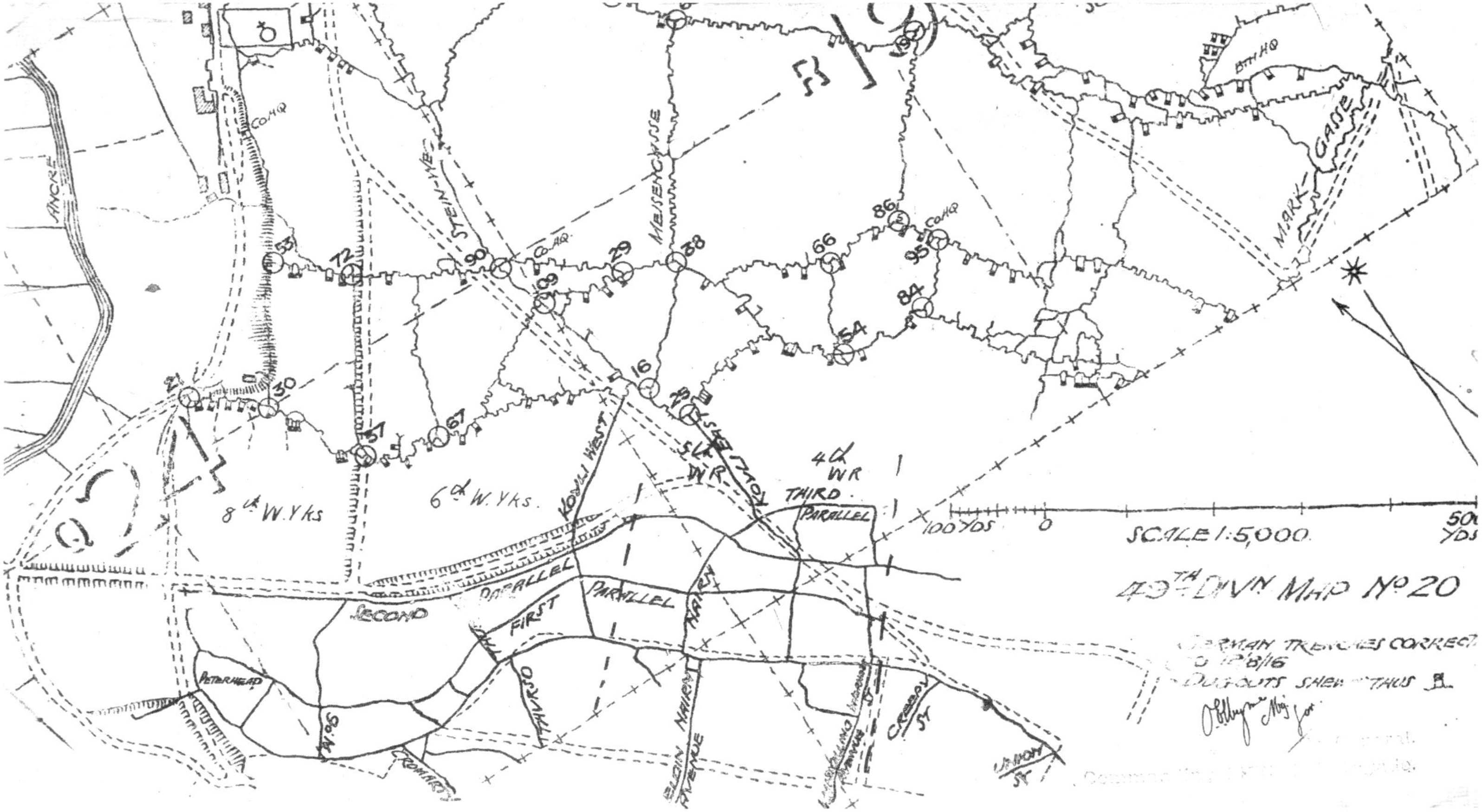

▲ Map 12. 49th Division Trench Map showing the Pope's Nose area. *Courtesy of the Public Record Office.* Reference WO 95/2796

of the fork. Two communication trenches ran perpendicular from the Second and Third Parallels, heading straight into the German front line, these were Koyli West Trench (just inside the 1/6th West Yorkshires' area) and Koyli East Trench.

It is likely that these two trenches were formerly German communication trenches from their original front line. The Brigade boundary, which separated the 1/5th Duke's and the 1/6th West Yorkshires was halfway between Koyli East and Koyli West Trenches. Koyli East Trench was to have a major bearing on the disaster which was to unfold.

Because of the way the jumping off trenches curved, some of the attacking troops of the 1/5th Duke's who were coming out of the Second Parallel on the left would, unless they corrected their alignment, be attacking into the flank of their colleagues leaving the Third Parallel. There was also a danger of a gap appearing between the battalion and the 1/6th West Yorkshires on their left. To the right, the 1/4th Duke's had, on leaving their trenches to attack half-right towards their objective, failure to do this would cause bunching between themselves and the right of the 1/5th Duke's. Such manoeuvres whilst under fire, in the featureless landscape, and in the dim first-light of dawn were going to be very difficult to perform. In the days leading up to the assault, the attack was practised (using tapes to represent trenches) near the village of Raincheval.

At 5.30pm on Saturday 2nd September the 1/5th Duke's left the village of Forceville and commenced the march to the front line; after crossing the River Ancre at Authuille they assembled ready for the assault in the Second and Third Parallels at 3.45am.

The Battalion's plan, prepared by the commanding officer, Lieutenant-Colonel H.A.J. Stanton, D.S.O. was for 'D' and 'A' Companies (on the left and right of the Battalion's front respectively) to capture the German front line between Points 16 and 54*. The German defences here were particularly strong; a German salient called the Pope's Nose was located at the top of Koyli East Trench (the apex of which was at Point 25). The German support line was to be captured by 'B' Company (between Points 38 and 66). 'C' Company was in reserve.

Meanwhile, the 1/6th West Yorkshires on the left had to tackle a strong trench system called The Triangle (this was between Points 16, 09, and 67), and the 1/4th Duke's on the right had to take the front line from Points 54 to 84 and the support line from Points 66 to 95.

The British hurricane bombardment commenced at 5.10am, dawn having broken at about 5am. A survivor said *"The whole sky seemed to light up suddenly."* At 5.13am the battalion, after hours of nervous waiting, went over the top along with the rest of the West Riding Division, for the first time in the war.

The War Diary of the 1/5th Duke's describes, in two sentences, the result of the attack: *"The whole attack failed. The 146 Brigade did not reach its objective and although the 147 Brigade reached their objective, they were unable to hold it."* The details of what actually occurred are more difficult to establish, especially as each battalion blamed its neighbour.

'D' Company of the 1/5th Duke's was to attack astride Koyli East Trench. Unfortunately one platoon, instead of assaulting on both sides of the trench managed to end up entirely on the eastern side. This left a gap in the middle of the

**** These were the last digits of map references. The exact points were R19c 1.6 and R19c 5.4***

company which was due to attack at Point 25 (the Pope's Nose). The War Diary states that *"This would not have mattered if the battalion on our left* [1/6th West Yorkshires] *had reached its objective. As it was 'D' Company had to withstand bombing attacks on its left, from its centre, and later on, from its right."*

Although half of 'D' Company did manage to occupy the front line trench between Points 16 and 25, it was impossible to bring ammunition up to them - due, according to the War Diary, to the German block at the top of Koyli East Trench. This resulted in everything having to go over No Man's Land, in the face of the ferocious enemy barrage; machine guns firing from the rear and the flanks of the attack would have added to the casualties. This inability to cross No Man's Land was to prove a source of many casualties, it also prevented orders being brought up, messages getting back, casualty evacuation and reinforcements of both men and ammunition.

The other half of 'D' Company, further to the right (east of Point 25) did receive ammunition at about 7.30am, but this had to be brought to them over the open. Further to the right, 'A' Company became mixed up with the left Company of the 1/4th Duke's, this caused a lot of bunching between Points 25 and 54. A machine gun was turned on these men, causing the company to split in two, leaving a gap near where the communication trench joins the front line approximately mid-way between these points.

'B' Company assaulted the support line but only one third of the men (and probably no officers) seem to have reached it; due to the casualties incurred and a lack of ammunition they were unable to hold onto this position. After recapturing the support line the Germans were able to come down the communication trench and, exploiting the gap that the machine gun had created, turned left and right to attack the survivors of 'A' and 'D' Companies who were holding onto the front line.

The Battalion's War Diary reports that *" 'D' Company only retired when they had no more bombs, having previously seen the troops on the right* [1/4th Duke's and 'A' Company of the 1/5th Duke's] *retire to our front parallels. They retired from the German front line about 9.30am"*.

The History of the 1/6th West Yorkshire Regiment gives details of how, during the preparations for the attack (which would not have gone unnoticed by the Germans), platoons became in a matter of days exhausted remnants of their former selves. The men had to carry stores and ammunition up the steep sides of the Ancre valley to the front line nightly from the 27th August.

This lack of rest afforded to the attacking troops would have seriously impaired their fighting capabilities. The History of the 1/6th West Yorkshire Regiment goes on to report that the Pope's Nose remained uncaptured* and that machine guns from this position were able to pour fire into the flank of the 1/6th West Yorkshires. Although the first wave of this battalion managed to cross No Man's Land, following waves were unable to do so, and this battalion's attack failed early on.

**** The History of the 1/4th Battalion Duke of Wellington's Regiment indicates that although the position was not occupied, the Germans were forced to temporarily abandon it. The War Diary of the 1/5th Dukes does not state its opinion one way or the other, although it will be remembered that it did say that the block at the top of Koyli East Trench was not cleared. Part of the confusion is probably down to the fact that at no stage has the exact boundary of the Pope's Nose been defined, it was probably the area from Point 16 to 25 and then a similar distance again (in an easterly direction towards point 54) before returning back to Point 16.***

Clearly the Pope's Nose was the key to the whole attack. What is likely to have happened is that until it was (temporarily) abandoned, machine gun fire enfiladed the 1/6th West Yorkshires, stopping their assault in its tracks. If 'D' Company of the 1/5th Duke's had advanced correctly up Koyli East Trench, it is possible that the Pope's Nose may have been subdued earlier. Unfortunately the 1/6th West Yorkshires were unable to restart their attack.

The deepest areas of penetration soon began to be counter-attacked, the Germans probably being reinforced from the garrison in the Schwaben Redoubt (this was a series of tunnels situated in the high ground a few hundred yards east of the Pope's Nose). The 1/4th and the 1/5th Duke's, running out of ammunition and down to a fraction of their original strength were unable to resist and fell back. The Pope's Nose was reoccupied and machine guns were brought to bear on the retreating troops; many were killed as they tried to get back into the parallels.

All the gains were abandoned. Virtually the only British that remained in the German lines were either dead or injured. Only seven unwounded prisoners were captured by the Germans from the 1/4th and 1/5th Battalions of the Duke of Wellington's Regiment.

Although the Battle of Loos had caused a greater loss of life to Ravensthorpe's soldiers, it is likely that because so many men from the village were serving in the 1/5th Duke of Wellington's, this attack was to cause much greater anxiety when news of it arrived back at home; many men from the village, although surviving the attack, would have been injured. The attack cost three men from Ravensthorpe their lives.

Stanley Gawthorpe, whose name had been mentioned in the Dewsbury Reporter in September 1915 when the battalion incurred casualties at Ypres (see Chapter 4), was either 17 or only just 18 when he enlisted on 28th December 1914. He lived with his parents William and Ellen Gawthorpe at 35 Tanhouse Street, Ravensthorpe and although he attended the Congregational Church and Sunday School he had expressed an interest in becoming confirmed into the Church of England. Before enlistment he worked for Armitage & Rhodes in the finishing department; in his spare time he played both cricket and football for the Congregational Church teams.

On 13th October 1916 Private Ashton of the R.A.M.C., who was an orderly at a hospital in Woolwich, wrote to Stanley's parents. A soldier called Reginald Wood whom he was looking after, on learning that Private Ashton came from Ravensthorpe, asked if he knew Stanley. It turned out that Private Wood had been in the attack with Stanley, and like Stanley was in 'A' Company; his story confirmed Mr and Mrs Gawthorpe's worst fears:-

"Stanley and I [Reginald Wood] *went over. Stanley and the rest of the company held the first line trench, whilst I and the bombing company went up the communication trench to bomb the second line. 'A' Company battalion bombers and also 'B' Company held the front line trench."* At this stage, Private Wood's account becomes slightly confusing, but it seems that although he was in 'A' Company, he became involved in 'B' Company's attack on the support line. Although they held the support line for four and a half hours they were forced to retire when they realised that the rest of the battalion had been forced back. He continues, *"We were completely surrounded so we bombed our way back again to the German front line trench and there I saw Stanley laid at the mouth of a German dugout. He had*

severe shrapnel wounds in the chest and legs and I know for certain he was quite dead."

Although aged just 19 years when he died, Stanley had risen to the rank of corporal - no mean achievement for one so young.

At 21 years of age Ernest Hinchcliffe was only a little older than Stanley. The Dewsbury News describes him as 'a pre-war reservist' (although it is more likely he was a pre-war territorial) who before the war worked for Rawdon, Briggs & Co. of Ravensthorpe. Unlike Stanley (who went to France with a later draft), Ernest arrived with the first wave of the battalion in April 1915. Promoted from corporal to sergeant some time after his arrival, he was posted as missing after the 3rd September attack. His parents, Mr and Mrs Fred Hinchcliffe of 839 Huddersfield Road, Ravensthorpe only received formal notification that he was assumed to have been killed in July 1917.

Neither Stanley nor Ernest has a known grave, indeed of the 113 officers and men of the 1/5th Battalion Duke of Wellington's Regiment killed on 3rd September, only 36 have known graves, the remainder (including Stanley Gawthorpe and Ernest Hinchcliffe) are commemorated on the Thiepval Memorial to the Missing. These 113 men listed as being killed on 3rd September do not include those who later died from their wounds. Some of these men lasted several weeks before succumbing, whilst others lasted only a short time. Walter Garfitt fell into this second category.

▲ 51. Stanley Gawthorpe

▲ 52. Ernest Hinchcliffe The third stripe is clearly an addition to the existing corporals stripes, giving further evidence of his promotion to sergeant.

Walter Garfitt was born in December 1895 to West and Sarah Garfitt. Educated at St. Saviour's Boys' School and Mirfield Grammar School, before the war he worked as a clerk at Howroyd and Oldroyd's chemical works at Tanhouse Street, Ravensthorpe. This is probably the same firm as Charles Lapish and William Hopkinson worked for (see Chapters 15 and 16), although in references to their employment, the firm is described as the Yorkshire Chemical and Dyework Company. He enlisted in January 1915, and arrived in France with the battalion in April 1915. When, in December 1915, the battalion was attacked whilst stationed on the canal bank at Ypres, Walter, although wounded in the leg by a grenade splinter, refused to leave his post until reinforcements arrived.

He wrote at the time from hospital in Leicester to his parents at 4 Dearnley Street, Ravensthorpe: *"I am wounded in the right leg but it is not anything to worry about as I don't think it shall be long before I am well again. It happened on Wednesday* [either 8th or 15th December 1915] *and I have been travelling practically all the while. The hospitals are a real treat, the nurses are fine and there is plenty of good stuff to eat. I was throwing bombs at the Germans, and of course they were throwing them back and I got a piece in the leg."*

After recovering from this wound Walter rejoined his battalion and although slightly wounded a month before the 3rd September attack, he was able to take part in it. Walter's father* received a letter from Second Lieutenant Charles Floyd dated 9th September expressing his regrets that Walter had died from his wounds on 5th September. Walter's personal effects were returned the same day by the Company Quartermaster Sergeant.

▲ 53. Walter Garfitt

▲ 54. Walter Garfitt's headstone at Forceville Communal Cemetery Extension.

* *His mother, Sarah, had died in May 1916.*

Aged 20 years, Walter was buried at Forceville, the village from which the battalion marched on 2nd September to take part in the attack. Forceville Communal Cemetery Extension was one of the first three permanent cemeteries to be constructed by the (then) Imperial War Graves Commission after the war. It contains 304 British graves.

* * *

Inevitably, after the 49th Division's failure there was an investigation into what had gone wrong. The G.O.C. of the 49th Division, Major-General Perceval reported to the II Corps:- *"I do not consider that any fault can be found with the work of the Divisional or Brigade staffs or with the arrangements or shooting of the artillery.......it is difficult to describe in detail the course of the infantry action, accounts are very conflicting. My general impression is that had the men followed their officers, the troops would have had little difficulty in gaining their objectives."*

Perceval goes on to single out the 1/6th West Yorkshire Regiment. The men failed to follow their officers and *"were the first to retire to our own lines."* Whilst he stated that the Right Brigade (ie. the 1/4th and 1/5th Duke's) reached the German support lines, this was not the case with the Left Brigade. Although Perceval acknowledged that the inability to bring up ammunition had its effect, he suggested that too many of the 3,000 bombs that the 1/4th and 1/5th Duke's had been given were expended on clearing dugouts.

His report goes on to suggest that the 1/4th Duke's rather than retiring when they ran out of bombs *"...ought to have attacked the German bombers with bayonets".* In view of the fact that the British troops were exhausted, out of ammunition, under heavy counter-attack, and being bombarded not only by German artillery, but also by British shells falling short, such a suggestion does seem unreasonable.

Although a second attack was being organised by the 146 Brigade on the left, it was not undertaken due to the retirement of the 147 Brigade. This retirement could not be prevented as the only information coming back to the battalion headquarters was from wounded soldiers. This information gave the impression that things were going well (which initially they were). Unfortunately, other information such as requests for bombs failed to get through*.

The Corps Commander (Lieutenant-General Jacob) reported to the Army Commander (General Gough), who blamed the battalion commanding officers for not going forward to see for themselves what was going on. (What this would have achieved is questionable as it was becoming virtually impossible to get across No Man's Land.) The Army Commander in turn reported to the Commander-in-Chief (Haig). The result of all this was that Brigadier-General Brereton (commanding 147 Brigade) was sacked - this is a little surprising as it was his brigade that did

**** The History of the 1/4th Duke's reports how the first official message (a request for ammunition) was received at the Battalion's headquarters at 8.40am; it had taken two hours to arrive. The last message to come arrived at midday (long after the retirement) - it had taken four hours to arrive. The information coming to the 1/5th Duke's headquarters was even slower; the War Diary indicates that the first they knew of the retirement was when the officer in charge of 'D' Company (Second Lieutenant D. A'Costa) arrived to report.***

at least take the objectives. It seems that his opposite number in 146 Brigade was spared as he did try to organise another attack which (fortunately) did not take place due to the 'early' retirement of the 147 Brigade. The 1/6th West Yorkshires were not disbanded (as the Corps Commander suggested). Perceval also survived being sent home but Haig's comments made it clear that he had to improve the standard of discipline in his division*.

Most of the survivors would have liked nothing better than to have been sent home after the battle. There were substantial numbers, however, who would never be going home. In the 1/5th Duke's, it was initially believed that six officers and 149 other ranks had been wounded and that just 19 other ranks killed, however there were another six officers and 195 men not accounted for, who were posted as 'missing'+. S.D.G.W. indicates the casualties of the 1/5th Duke's on 3rd September was six officers and 107 men killed. The casualties within the individual companies is not known, but in 'A' Company two officers were killed and one wounded (out of four); in 'B' Company, all four officers were killed. In 'D' Company, three officers went over the top, all three were injured. ('C' Company, although not in the assault, still sustained two officer casualties - both wounded.)

As previously mentioned, only 36 of the 113 officers and men killed on 3rd September in the 1/5th Duke of Wellington's have known graves. Of these 36, five are buried at Connaught Cemetery (this includes two men with 'special memorial' headstones who were originally buried at Divion Wood Cemetery Number Two, however when this cemetery came to be concentrated into Connaught Cemetery after the war, their graves could not be found). A further three of the 36 are buried at Serre Road Cemetery Number Two and 28 (including all three officers with known graves) are buried at Mill Road Cemetery.

According to 147 Brigade's War Diary, the 1/4th Duke's suffered (officers and men) 32 killed, 113 wounded and 187 missing. (S.D.G.W. indicates six officers and 147 men were killed).

Across in 146 Brigade, the 1/6th West Yorkshires incurred 18 killed, 125 wounded and 92 missing. (S.D.G.W. states three officers and 50 men.) On their left the 1/8th West Yorkshires' War Diary quotes 23 killed, 122 wounded and 157 missing. (S.D.G.W. gives four officers and 49 men.)

Casualties were not confined to the assaulting battalions, S.D.G.W. gives figures of one officer and 16 men being killed in the 1/6th Duke's and one officer and 25 men in the 1/7th Duke's. 146 Brigade's 1/5th and 1/7th West Yorkshires incurred two officers and 43 men and three officers and 16 men killed respectively.

The War Diaries state that the Reserve Brigade (148 Brigade) plus Royal Field Artillery, Divisional Engineers and the Pioneer Battalion (19th Lancashire Fusiliers) between them incurred 20 dead and 34 wounded.

* * *

Perceval was sent home in October 1917 after another poor performance in the Third Battle of Ypres.

+ These figures from 147 Brigade's War Diary tie in with the Battalion's War Diary which reports that there were 350 casualties out of the 450 who took part. (155 wounded plus 19 killed plus 201 missing is 375). The figure of 450 is substantially less than the theoretical strength of the battalion; every time a battalion went into battle it left behind in the 'Transport lines' (ie not in the trenches) a proportion of its strength. The 450 who took part is therefore 150 in each of the three assaulting companies.

▲ 55. The remains of the Pope's Nose.

▼ 56. Looking towards the Ulster Tower (in the trees) from the top of the Thiepval Memorial to the Missing.

The battlefield today is one of the most visited areas of the Western Front. The Thiepval Memorial to the Missing is close, and on the other side of the valley are the preserved trenches of the Newfoundland Memorial Park. There are two cemeteries nearby. The Connaught Cemetery now contains 1,278 burials, half of whom are 'unknown'. Mill Road Cemetery is on the edge of the Schwaben Redoubt; because of the unstable nature of the ground many of the headstones have had to be laid flat. The cemetery contains 1,304 graves, 815 (more than 60%) of them being unknown.

Precisely over the 1/5th Duke's line of attack has been built a tall memorial tower to the Ulster Division. This is one of the most famous landmarks on the Somme and until recently it has been possible to climb to the top of this tower. The front wall of the grounds of the Ulster Tower are on the approximate site of Koyli East Trench.

The Tower has been built at the fork in the road that was the boundary between 146 and 147 Brigades. The right fork to St. Pierre Divion is now just a rough track but by walking along the track you will be parallel, and slightly west of Koyli East Trench; after 130 yards on your right, a few feet into the field are the remains of a machine gun post. Whilst this is probably not the apex of the Pope's Nose, it is likely to have been part of this position, possibly the post at Point 16. The head of Koyli East Trench and the apex of the Pope's Nose is about halfway between the remains of the post and fork in the road.

None of the original front and support lines that the 1/4th and the 1/5th Duke's attacked can now be seen, however by walking up the left-hand side of the Memorial Tower grounds, at the rear of the Tower is a patch of uncultivated ground. The high ground of the Schwaben Redoubt (and the Mill Road Cemetery) is to the right; to the left the ground drops away towards the German support line, but in front of you is the approximate site of Point 54.

In front of the Tower is a small electricity substation. At this point the Third Parallel cut across the road. By standing in the road, looking towards the fork in the road, you will be facing the direction of the attack which commenced at 5.13am on 3rd September 1916, from which many men never returned.

Chapter Nine

The Somme (3) September to November

Apart from the casualties incurred on the 1st July, in the period from the opening day of the Battle of the Somme until, and including, the ill-fated attack by the 49th (West Riding) Division, there had been only one casualty incurred from Ravensthorpe in the southern half of the battlefield (Ernest Walker); all other casualties had been incurred to the north of the Albert-Bapaume road. This gives the impression that the northern sector was the one receiving the main British effort, this is quite wrong. Since the opening day of the Battle, when the gains had been made on the right wing of the attack, it had in fact been south of the Albert-Bapaume road that the main effort had been made. As briefly mentioned at the beginning of Chapter 8, it was in the southern sector on 14th July that the second 'set piece' attack had been made; this time General Rawlinson used quite different tactics from those employed on 1st July. Despite asking his soldiers to undertake a complicated night-time assault after the briefest of bombardments, the attack on the German's second line positions between Bazentin and Longueval was a resounding success. It is, however, the third set piece attack on 15th September that directly concerns Ravensthorpe.

The 15th September attack was aimed at breaking through the system of German trenches known as the Switch Line. This system ran from Pozieres on the Albert-Bapaume Road south-eastwards in front of High Wood towards Delville Wood and on to the village of Combles. By breaking through these trenches, the way would be clear for an assault on the third (and final) German trench line which stretched from Le Sars through Flers to Morval. If the third line could be breached, the trench deadlock would be over and exploitation by infantry and cavalry could be undertaken.

To assist in the attack Haig had a new secret weapon available - the tank. This had been under development in late 1915 and early 1916 as an attempt at overcoming the seemingly impenetrable trench system the Germans had constructed. Three men from Ravensthorpe took part in the first attack by the tanks, all were to survive this attack but only one survived the war.

Ewart Doodson was born in Elland in November 1898. After the deaths of his natural parents he was adopted by Mr and Mrs Tyas Wood of 453 Huddersfield Road Ravensthorpe, and he is reported to have attended the Congregational Church and Sunday School. Ewart went to work as a junior clerk at the Yorkshire Electric Power Company in Thornhill, but volunteered in October 1915 aged just 16, joining the Machine Gun Corps.

A component of the M.G.C. was the Motor Machine Gun Service. This unit was originally organised to provide mobile machine guns which were to be mounted on side-cars of motorcycles, however because of the stalemate that had developed in

France, the need for such mobile machine guns ceased. During late 1915 and early 1916 as tanks were under development, the M.M.G.S. became associated with this new weapon, changing its name to the Heavy Section, Machine Gun Corps in May 1916. (In November 1916 its name changed to the Heavy Branch, Machine Gun Corps, and in July 1917 became The Tank Corps.)

The unit had been split into six companies, 'A' to 'F' however just two of these ('C' and 'D') were ready to take part in the battle. Ewart was probably excited by his involvement with this new weapon and continued his training with the unit until August 1916 when the tanks and men of these two companies moved to France.

During the 15th September attack Ewart Doodson was part of the crew of tank D1 (probably called 'Daredevil 1'); this tank was assigned to the 14th (Light) Division and attacked a strong trench system known as The Brewery Salient to the east of Delville Wood. Ewart's tank was to go down in history as the first ever tank to go into action, starting from south of the Longueval-Ginchy road at 5.15am; Ewart's role in the tank was that of gearsman. He and another gearsman were responsible for applying brakes to the tank's gigantic tracks; it was hot, noisy work and despite the tank's size and weight (28 tons) it was vulnerable to artillery fire. Shortly after clearing out the German troops in the trenches of the Brewery Salient, Ewart's tank was hit by a shell and put out of action, he described the action in a letter to his parents:

"...We went over almost before it was first light on Friday morning, and our tank was out of action with a shell through our driving wheels within almost half an hour....It was supposed to be an exceptionally difficult position and hot too.....Fritz simply bunked and well he might to see this thing coming on him in the half light. We got through this redoubt and were well towards the German main trench when we got hit. There was plenty of flames and smoke but no one was hurt."

Ewart goes on to describe how the crew got back safely, bringing with them two wounded infantrymen. They recovered the equipment from the tank the next day; Ewart mentions that Fred Gomersall, an acquaintance from Ravensthorpe, was helping out. The last part of Ewart's letter relates how one tank crew who were also forced to abandon their tank were mistaken for Germans (due to their unusual uniform) and were held prisoner for a while by some British infantrymen. Ewart finishes his letter by thanking his parents for a parcel they had sent him.

Two weeks later on 1st October Ewart received injuries to his leg and face resulting in treatment in the Australian General Hospital in France.

Although Fred Gomersall was destined to survive the war, because his story touches that of Ewart Doodson, and he was also a member of 'D' Company, his story is briefly described. Fred Gomersall has an equally strong claim to fame to that of Ewart; as a member of the crew of D17, Fred's tank ('Dinnaken') was attached to the 41st Division. After crossing the German lines, Dinnaken was observed by a patrol of the Royal Flying Corps to be moving up the main street of Flers village, and was therefore the subject of the famous and over-optimistic report which appeared in many newspapers, describing how a *"Tank is walking up the high street of Flers with the British army cheering behind."*

The tank commander, realising that the engine was on the point of breaking down, withdrew from the village and pulled off the road, at which point the engine gave in. The crew found their way back to the British lines where they helped (according to Ewart Doodson's letter) in the salvage of parts from Ewart's tank on the edge of Delville Wood.

Gunner N. Tattersfield.

Gunner E. Doodson.

Gunner F. Gomersall.

57. Neville Tattersfield, Ewart Doodson and Fred Gomersall

Due to the fact that the third Ravensthorpe soldier to take part in this first tank attack was in 'C' Company, and this unit's War Diary for 15th September is less detailed than 'D' Company's diary, much less is known of this soldier's participation in the battle. Neville Tattersfield was born on 7th April 1892 to Moses (a flock dealer in 1877) and Louisa Tattersfield. Neville was the youngest of four sons and lived with the family at 'West Royd', Brunswick Street, Dewsbury. After attending Heckmondwike Grammar School, he joined his eldest brother, John, working in the dyeing laboratory at Jas Smith and Sons in Ravensthorpe. Tragedy was to strike the family twice in quick succession; in December 1914 Louisa died, and less than a year later, the third son, Harold also died.

On 18th August 1915, at the age of 23 Neville joined the army as a gunner in the Motor Machine Gun Service; as he owned a motorcycle it is likely he was attracted to the idea of joining a part of the army where there was a use for his hobby. His height is recorded as 5' 4½", with a maximum chest expansion of 35", he weighed just less than ten stones. As previously mentioned, however, it was not long before the M.M.G.S. became associated with the tanks.

On 1st January 1916 he was posted to the 27th Battery of the M.M.G.S., but on 1st April was transferred to the Armoured Car Section*. This Armoured Car Section seems not to have lasted a long time as within five weeks, on 4th May, he was posted to what had become, by then, the Heavy Section, Machine Gun Corps; later that month being posted to 'C' Company. On 6th June Neville attended a tank course and on 21st July went on a course to Whale Island at Portsmouth in order to learn how to use the six-pounder guns that armed some of the tanks.

Neville was sent to France with the first draft of officers and men on 16th August, arriving at Le Havre on 17th August. Some of the tanks arrived on 21st August, the second half of the company and the rest of the tanks a few days later ('D' Company arrived at the end of the month).

Training was undertaken for several weeks (occasionally watched by the Prince of Wales and Sir Douglas Haig and other high ranking officers). As previously mentioned, 'C' Company's War Diary is less detailed than 'D' Company's and it is therefore not possible to say with any certainty which tank Neville was with on 15th September. A letter from Neville published in the Dewsbury Reporter on 7th October describes how he had only *"one wash in a week and not even a shave"* he goes on *"...our 'bus' has been stuck; unfortunately our steering was wrong before we went into action but we went in and returned safely."*

Of all the tanks in 'C' Company that Neville could have been in, it is the tank of Second Lieutenant Ambrose that is the most likely candidate for Neville to have been a crew member of. This tank was attached to the Guards Division and broke down on the start line with tail problems + and engine trouble; however it seems that repairs were carried out and the tank resumed its journey only to break down again. It is not clear if the tank was recovered. It is of course equally likely that Neville was in another tank of 'C' Company but it is now impossible to be totally sure of Neville's involvement.

Tanks were used again the following day, on 16th September and again at the end of the month, some other operations were carried out in October but it is their use on 15th September that will be remembered.

The 15th September attack caused no fatal casualties to any Ravensthorpe men, however after this large attack it was necessary to undertake further line straightening operations to make the next major assault easier. All of Ravensthorpe's fatal casualties from this date until the end of the Battle of the Somme would, with the exception of one at the very end of the battle, be as a result of these operations, and (with the same exception) would all be in the southern sector of the battlefield.

The attacks after the major assault of 15th September were quite successful, and this together with the reports from Haig's Chief of Intelligence, Brigadier-General Charteris, that the Germans were on the point of breaking under the

**** Not all the M.M.G.S. personnel were allocated motorcycle and side-car combinations, there were also a few 'armoured motor batteries' equipped with converted cars.***

+ The two-wheeled tail gear was used to help steer the tank.

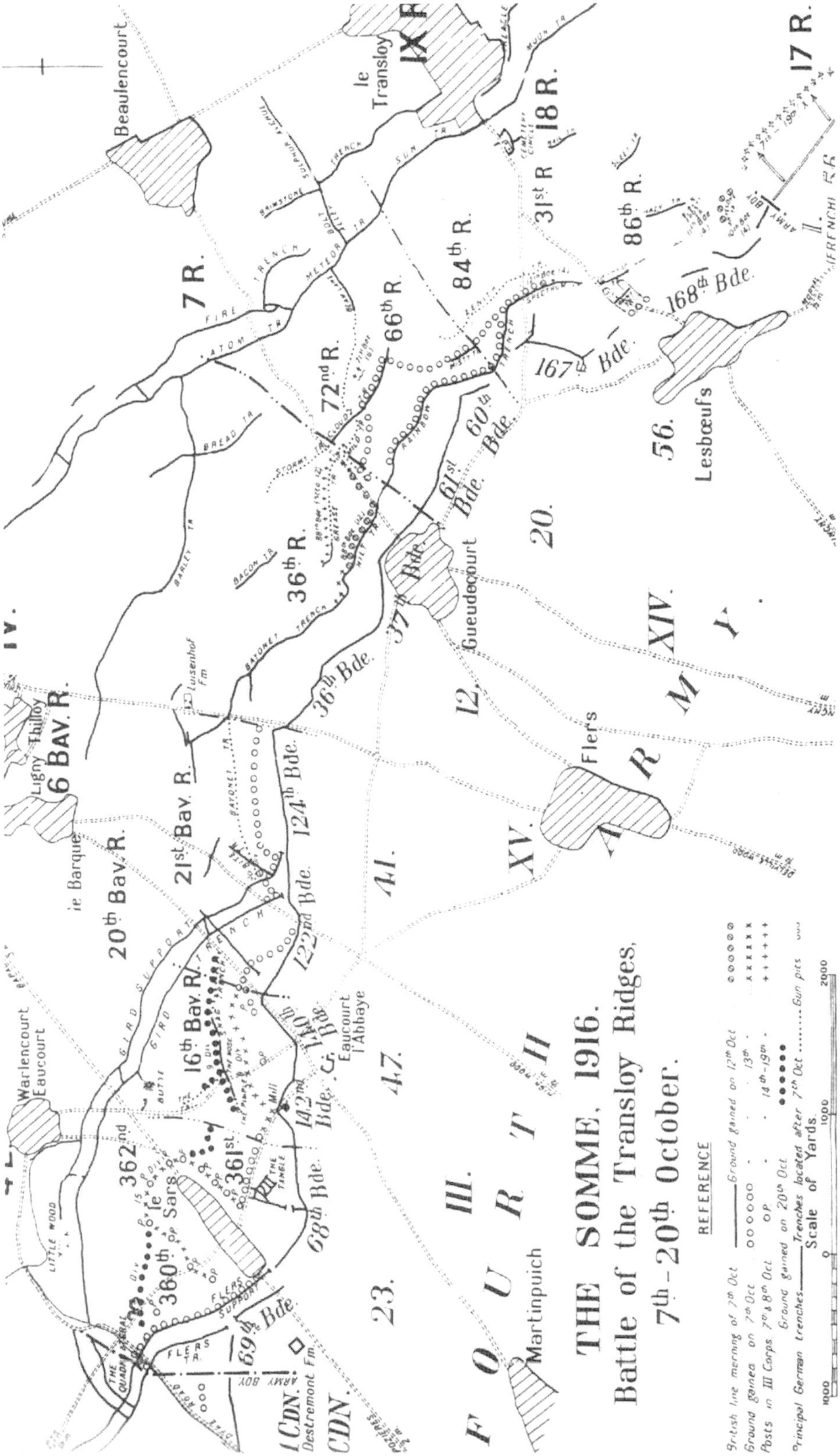

▲ Map 13. Gueudecourt

strain must have influenced Haig's decision to continue with the battle; however there was no breakthrough and the German resistance remained as resolute as ever. The 15th September attack had put the village of Flers into British hands. Immediately north-east of Flers was the village of Gueudecourt, which was captured on 26th September. Gueudecourt was at the foot of some higher ground, called Le Transloy Ridges; this higher ground was, in the opinion of Haig, a far superior position to hold over the forthcoming winter than the waterlogged valley.

* * *

After the death of Walter Garfitt, a month went by before the next casualty from Ravensthorpe was incurred. The 7th K.O.Y.L.I. was part of 61 Brigade, 20th (Light) Division. On 7th October this division was one of a total of six divisions which were to take part in a large advance. The 20th Division was ordered to attack from Gueudecourt towards the village of Le Transloy, on the extreme right of the British line (there was only one division between the 20th Division and the French).

The 7th K.O.Y.L.I. had moved up at midnight on the 6th/7th October to take over the front line trenches, but the assembly trenches behind the front line, which were required by the rear companies, could not be found. This was not particularly surprising as the landscape had, over the previous weeks, become like the surface of the moon. There were virtually no landmarks and the shell craters overlapped each other; the mud was a significant factor in the troops' daily toil. Supplies had to be manhandled to the front line, and the sheer physical exertion needed to survive drained the men; the extra effort required to fight required almost super-human strengths. The total lack of vegetation, and the obliteration of entire villages made orientation very tricky; to raise one's head above the parapet in an attempt to glimpse a landmark was to court death.

Despite the inability of the guides (supplied for the 7th K.O.Y.L.I. by the outgoing battalion) to help, the 7th K.O.Y.L.I.s had taken over the trenches allotted to them by 1.30am.

For the forthcoming attack, the battalion had two objectives. Firstly Rainbow Trench which was 200 yards away and well protected by barbed wire; a further 400 to 500 yards beyond that was Cloudy Trench, this had no barbed wire protection. At 7am the battalion complained to the artillery that the wire in front of Rainbow Trench had not been cut, a bombardment was therefore made on the barbed wire; this however provoked the German artillery into shelling the British trenches.

The attack was going to be different from many of the preceding attacks; a theory had been developed that an attack in the afternoon would enable consolidation to be undertaken in the hours of darkness. This vital consolidation would be more likely to succeed with the protection of the dark than during daylight hours, which would have been the case if the attack had been launched at the traditional time of daybreak. As a result, zero hour was set for 1.45pm and at the appointed hour, the battalion, together with three other battalions from two of the 20th Division's brigades went over the top. The first objective, Rainbow Trench, fell quickly and the battalion pressed on as soon as the artillery barrage permitted to Cloudy Trench; this being taken by 2.10pm.

Unfortunately the attack on either side of the 7th K.O.Y.L.I. had not been as successful. The 7th Somerset Light Infantry were called up to fill in a gap on the right, whilst on the left the 12th Division had failed to make headway, so a defensive flank was made from Cloudy Trench back to Rainbow Trench.

The newly won trenches were improved by the battalion until they were relieved on the night of the 8th/9th October. The War Diary reports that the operation cost ten officer casualties (one of whom was killed) and 180 other ranks; this latter figure turns out to be, according to S.D.G.W., a fairly modest 37 killed. One of these fatalities was Leonard Crane.

Leonard was born at Overton, near Wakefield in October 1880. Educated at St. Saviour's Boys' School, at the turn of the century he was working at Haigh's Pit. He later joined the army and went to South Africa seeing service in the Boer War where he was awarded the Queen Victoria Medal and the King Edward Medal. He returned home to find himself out of work due to a strike at the colliery. The Dewsbury Reporter described how he was found employment at Wormald and Walker's mill in Dewsbury by Major P.B. Walker. Over the next nine years he acted as Major Walker's orderly in the annual Territorial camps. In about 1910 he was awarded the Territorial Force Efficiency Medal in recognition of twelve years' service.

For some reason he left the mill; when the war broke out he was working as a stoker at Ingham's Coke Ovens in Thornhill. As a reservist he was called up in September 1914 and for the first twelve months of the war he served in Officers' Training Schools in Harrogate and Scarborough.

In June 1916 (after recovering from an illness which kept him in hospital in Scarborough from late 1915 to early 1916) he went to France, joining the 7th K.O.Y.L.I. It was during the attack on Rainbow and Cloudy Trenches on 7th October that he was killed by a shell.

On Sunday, 16th October, Leonard's wife (who had recently learned that her brother was missing) received a letter, at the family home at 15 George Street, Ravensthorpe, from Captain Johnstone informing her of her husband's death; the following day she received another letter, dated 12th October from one of Leonard's comrades expressing sympathy. Besides his wife, Leonard left two children*.

Although Leonard has no known grave, and is therefore listed on the Memorial to the Missing at Thiepval, his image lives on. After the Boer War, it was decided to commemorate the part played by local soldiers in that conflict, and a statue was erected in Crow Nest Park, Dewsbury. Leonard Crane was chosen as the model for the statue which was placed on top of a square plinth. The unveiling was made by none other than Robert Baden-Powell, the founder of the Scout movement, who played a significant part in the Boer War himself. The statue stands to this day in Crow Nest Park.

As previously mentioned, six British divisions took part in the attack on 7th October. One of these, the 41st Division, was the most junior of Kitchener's divisions, being raised in September 1915. Apart from two battalions, the division was raised entirely from the London area, it is therefore strange that someone from Ravensthorpe should find himself in this division.

Beaumont Wood was born in Thornhill in 1888 and before the war worked in the dyehouse at Marshall Kaye and Marshall's mill. He enlisted in November 1915 and

Jack Crane, Leonard's son was for many years the undertaker in Ravensthorpe.

▲ 58. Leonard Crane

▲ 59. Beaumont Wood

◀ 60. The Memorial to the men from Dewsbury who served in the Boer War. The statue was modelled on Leonard Crane.

found himself posted to the 26th Battalion of the Royal Fusiliers. This battalion was not recruited on geographical lines, but like many other battalions in this division was recruited amongst friends with a common interest; there was a Footballers' Battalion (23rd Battalion, Middlesex Regiment), and the 18th K.R.R.C. was subtitled 'Arts and Crafts'. The 26th Royal Fusiliers was made up largely of bank clerks and accountants from the City of London, and became known as the 'Bankers' Battalion'; what Beaumont made of this can only be imagined! Beaumont found himself posted to 'D' Company.

After arriving in France on 4th May 1916, the 41st Division took part in the previously described attack on 15th September; after this attack the division was rested. The War Diary of the Bankers' Battalion records that on 1st October the battalion was marched from Dernancourt (near Albert) up to a camp at Pommiers Redoubt, very close to the original front line of 1st July. Due to the heavy rain and muddy roads, the march was described as *"very trying"*. The battalion bivouacked for the night *"in very unfavourable conditions."* In the early hours of 3rd October, the they took over the positions of another battalion near the village of Flers*, the relief being completed at 3am. The next two days found the battalion supplying working parties to help with digging in the front line. At 6pm on the 5th October, they moved north of Flers to the Gird Trench from which the battalion was to attack towards the village of Ligny-Thilloy.

The battalion's War Diary takes up the story:

"7th October, 1.45pm: Zero Hour. Battalion in assembly trenches. 'A' and 'B' Companies in front line, 'C' and 'D' [Beaumont's company] *in support. The whole battalion went forward into the attack in good formation, the men were in good spirits. Artillery barrage very heavy, but the result of this fire, owing to a steep bank immediately to our front was unobserved. On reaching the bank our lines were subject to extremely brisk and heavy machine gun fire and the enemy had evidently managed to push several of his machine guns forward of our barrage and our infantry advancing over the crest formed a very easy target for accurate shooting. We unfortunately suffered heavy casualties but nevertheless the men continued to press forward under the very fine leadership of our officers. Our first wave managed to reach a point estimated as 50 yards from the first objective but the enemy fire proved too much of an obstacle and the men were forced to stay and dig in as best they could at a point about 350 yards from our starting point."*

The diary goes on to describe how the line reached, which was effectively just a series of shell holes, was improved and linked up with the line held by troops on the flanks and a communication trench was dug back to the original British trenches

After holding the line during the 8th, the battalion was relieved and marched back to the rear. The War Diary gives casualties as killed - three officers and 38 other ranks; missing - two officers and fifteen other ranks; wounded - seven officers and 164 other ranks. The majority of the battalion's casualties have no known grave, however ten of the men are buried at the A.I.F. Burial Ground, situated on 'Grass Lane' between the villages of Flers and Gueudecourt.

**** The Division's attack on 15th September was at Flers, so the ground would to some extent be familiar to the men.***

For some reason S.D.G.W. mistakenly states that the 38 other ranks were killed on 10th October (rather that the 7th), and it goes on to list a further three who supposedly died of wounds on this date (10th) also. It cannot be the case that these men were killed on the 10th (the battalion was out of the line), it is possible some were killed on 8th October, but the majority must have lost their lives on the 7th*. One of those who died of wounds on the 10th was Beaumont Wood.

Sister M.F. Rutherford wrote to Beaumont's parents (who lived at 34 Myrtle Avenue Ravensthorpe) at 4am on 10th October from a hospital at Etaples on the French coast: *"Dear Mr Wood, Your son, Private Beaumont Wood who was brought to us yesterday very gravely wounded has asked me just now to write to you as from himself. I am to tell you of his wound and that he has had his leg off but that he hopes, if God wills, to get over this and come home to you......He is very cheery and brave, but he is very sorely stricken. He does not realise how very bad he is. He sends his love."*

Beaumont had been wounded in both arms, both legs and his left foot. Sister Rutherford wrote again at 8.30am: *"Since writing for your son in the night time, I greatly grieve to tell you that he has died. The doctors did all they possibly could to save him but he was too badly wounded. He passed away very quietly and unconscious, believing as long as consciousness lasted that he was coming home.....almost his last words were to you and to Miss Ada Ashworth, to whom he also asked me to write."*

Private Beaumont Wood is buried at Etaples Military Cemetery which is the largest Commonwealth War Graves Commission Cemetery in France, containing about 11,000 graves.

Frank Dudley Fearnsides+ was born in February 1896 in Dewsbury, the only child of George and Betsy Fearnsides. After receiving his education at St. Saviour's Boys' School (where, according to the school records he received four strokes on the hand in 1908 for 'impertinence') he went to work as a warehouse assistant for Armitage & Rhodes. He volunteered on 11th December 1915 and joined the Duke of Wellington's Regiment on 26th January 1916. His service record still exists, and it reveals that he was 5' 2" tall, weighed 8 stone 4 lbs and had a 32" chest (34½" when fully expanded). After his training he was sent to join the 2nd Battalion on 25th May 1916. The battalion, although a regular battalion in theory, would by 1916 have many raw recruits such as Frank in its midst. The battalion was part of 12 Brigade in the 4th Division. Although present on the opening day of the Battle of the Somme, the battalion was not heavily engaged, but still suffered 50 men killed. It was not until 12th October that the 4th Division was again committed to battle when the 2nd Duke of Wellington's attacked Spectrum Trench, being north-east of the village of Lesboeufs. In this attack, the battalion lost, according to S.D.G.W., 120 men killed and died of wounds. (The battalion history has the figure slightly lower than this but indicates five officers were killed, plus two officers and 236 other ranks wounded.)

**** S.D.G.W. gives the following information for the 26th Royal Fusiliers:***
7th October: killed in action - 1, died of wounds - 1; (plus 5 officers, all killed in action)
8th & 9th October: none;
10th October: k.i.a. - 38, d.o.w. - 4; (plus 1 officer, killed in action)
11th October: k.i.a. - 1, d.o.w. - 1;
12th October: d.o.w. - 2
+ The C.W.G.C. and S.D.G.W. both incorrectly spell his name 'Fernsides'.

It seems that this attack was partially successful; however by the end of October, the division was asked to attack again, the objectives being once again Spectrum Trench, but additionally Rainy and Dewdrop Trenches. Despite the 2nd Duke of Wellington's being in brigade reserve, the battalion was asked to provide 100 men to take part in the attack - theirs' was to be, in the words of the War Diary, a *"Special Mission"*. The battalion spent the night of the 22nd/23rd October moving stores up to the front line in readiness for the attack, the tracks and trenches were very congested owing to the preparations for the attack. German shelling of these rear areas caused four men to be wounded.

12 Brigade were on the left of the Division's front, 11 Brigade were on the right; to the right of the Division was the French army. In the centre of the 4th Division's line of attack ran a sunken road. These features were common in the Somme countryside, being roads with steep banks on either side with the road being below the general level of the land; such positions were useful to both sides as they could hide troops away from observation by the enemy and away from shell and rifle fire. This sunken road was the objective of the special mission. The road itself and the dugouts that were constructed into the banks had to be cleared of Germans to prevent them firing into the flanks of the attacking troops. The attack was launched (after a postponement due to mist) at 2.30pm on Monday 23rd October; from the battalion's War Diary it seems that only one officer and seven other ranks (two of whom were wounded) managed to get into the sunken road. The War Diary states that the British artillery was falling short of its targets and this, in conjunction with the German artillery seems to have stopped the attacking infantry from getting forward. The attack was not very successful, only part of Spectrum Trench was captured. The War Diary lists the casualties as five other ranks killed, one officer and 23 other ranks wounded and nine other ranks missing. S.D.G.W. indicates that nine men from the battalion were killed on 23rd October. One of these was Frank Fearnsides.

A letter to Frank's parents who lived at 5 Cyprus Place, Jill Lane in Northorpe (part of Mirfield*) from two of Frank's comrades (who also lived in Mirfield) was published in the Dewsbury Reporter on 18th November. The letter gave no information about his death but spoke of the camaraderie there was: *"Although there is very little pleasure out here, yet we spend many happy hours together and parcels sent were always shared among us."*

On 3rd December 1916 Frank's father, George, wrote to 'The Officer in Charge of Records' in Frank's battalion asking for any of Frank's possessions to be returned. The letter seems to have been intercepted by the 'Effects Branch' who passed the query on to the battalion. The response came back that as Frank's body had not been recovered, there were no personal effects to return. This disappointing response was passed, via the 'Infantry Records Office, York', back to his father.

Some months later, however, some effects of Frank's were returned to his parents (possibly from Frank's pack which would most likely have been left with the battalion prior to the attack in which Frank was killed). The possessions which the Infantry Records Office sent out comprised of Frank's wallet, some letters,

This connection with Mirfield has led Frank to be listed on the Mirfield Parish War Memorial as well as Ravensthorpe's. The other soldiers who are commemorated on both the Mirfield and Ravensthorpe War Memorials are John Hinchliffe, Charles Lapish, Joseph Laycock and Ewart Popplewell.

cards and photographs; hopefully these gave his parents some comfort in coming to terms with the loss of their only child.

Frank, like six of his comrades who were killed on this day, has no known grave and is listed on the Thiepval Memorial to the Missing. The two men from the battalion who do have known graves are both buried in the A.I.F. Burial Ground.

John Arnold Hemingway was in the same part of the front as Frank had been when, on 5th November, his battalion (the 7th Battalion Yorkshire Regiment*) was used to assist in an attack by the 33rd Division. The division had been ordered to take a number of trenches (Boritska, Mirage and Hazy). Between the two brigades of this division that were to take part in the attack was inserted John's battalion and the 7th Battalion East Yorkshire Regiment, both part of 50 Brigade, 17th (Northern) Division.

The day's events for John's battalion are rather complicated. At 11.10am on the 5th November, a battle patrol consisting of 40 men of 'A' Company of the 7th Yorkshires attacked towards the German lines. The Germans initially fled, but on realising how few in number the attacking party were, turned round and opened fire on them. The patrol was forced to retire. It was not until dusk that 'D' Company sent forward two platoons, to either reinforce any gains that had occurred earlier or to make another attempt if the trenches were still occupied by Germans. They discovered the Germans were still in occupation so an attack was organised. The two platoons crawled forward at 10pm but were spotted and soon came under fire. Ten minutes before this attack went forward, orders had been received at Battalion Headquarters to the effect that the attack was to take place only if the trench to the right was in the hands of the 7th East Yorkshires (who had also attacked that morning). The 7th East Yorkshires did not hold the trench but it was by this time too late to stop the attack, which came to grief mainly due to fire from trenches from the right.

It is not known whether John was killed in the morning or the evening attack, but S.D.G.W. lists a total of eighteen men of the 7th Yorkshires being killed on this day, in addition the 7th East Yorkshires lost 48 men on this day. Virtually all of the 7th Yorkshires' fatalities, John Hemingway included, have no known grave - only one is buried in a known grave in the immediate area, at the Guards' Cemetery at Lesboeufs, two others being buried at Bancourt British Cemetery a little to the north.

**** The Ravensthorpe War Memorial incorrectly states that John was a member of the West Yorkshire Regiment, and for some reason also states he was a member of the 7th Battalion. Whilst he was a member of the 7th Battalion, he served, as described above, in the Yorkshire Regiment. (His is the only name on the memorial to give the battalion as well as the regiment.) It should be said that John Hemingway was not alone in being listed in the 'wrong' regiment according to the war memorial; Charles Hollingworth was also stated to have been in the West Yorkshires when, like John, he was in fact in the Yorkshire Regiment (see Chapter 15). The other example of this type of error is that of Charles Crabtree (Chapter 10) who like John Hemingway and Charles Hollingworth never served in the regiment stated on the memorial. A further two soldiers who are listed as serving in regiments from which they had previously been transferred: Joseph Laycock (Chapter 11) had transferred from the K.O.Y.L.I. to the Northumberland Fusiliers and Vivian Hickling (Chapter 22) had transferred from the Lincolnshire Regiment to the South Staffordshire Regiment.***

Not only is John Hemingway's regiment listed incorrectly on the War Memorial, there is also some jumbling of the otherwise alphabetical listing at this point on the Memorial; the casualties whose surnames commence with 'H' being listed in two stages, John's name being well out of order, coming at the very end of the 'H's', as if it had been nearly overlooked.

▲ 61. Frank Fearnsides

France stating that Pte. Hemingw... killed in action, but this was only co... the War Office about a week ago. He... dent in Ravensthorpe for about tw... and during the greater part of that ... connected with the Wesleyan Chape... day School, also being a member of th... to the time he joined H.M. Forces... up in November, 1914, in the K.O.Y... was very soon transferred to the P... Wales' Own Regiment (G... ards), and wa... ing at Darlin... nine month... overseas in 1915, to S... There he w... wounded, bu... contracted fever, and ... to hospital ... dria, Egypt, remained fo... weeks, after... ceeding to ... Glasgow, an... tained there ten weeks cl... ing upon th... granted sick visited his relatives in this district from April 6... 18th, 1916, when he returned to Richm... Darlington, and was only there a few ... fore being drafted out to France, wh... his death on Sunday, November 5th... leaves a wife and little girl age... months, and no doubt the official int... garding his death will be sad news to... friends who have known and respec... his past career. Mrs. Hemingway's... dress is 11, Ravenswharf Road, Scout...

Pte. J. A. Hemingway, Princess of Wales' Regt., Ravensthorpe (killed).

▲ 62. John Hemingway

John was born in Dewsbury in 1890, although his employment is not known it was reported in the Dewsbury Reporter that he was connected with the Wesleyan Chapel. He joined the K.O.Y.L.I. in November 1914, but was soon transferred to the Yorkshire Regiment. In August 1915 he landed at Gallipoli with the 6th Battalion Yorkshire Regiment but after being slightly wounded and contracting enteric fever he was evacuated to hospital in Alexandria, Egypt, from where, after a ten week stay, he was sent to Glasgow. A similar length of time was spent in Glasgow after which he was granted home leave of six weeks which he spent with his wife, Ethel, in Ravensthorpe; a short period with the regimental depot in Richmond followed, before he was sent to the 7th Battalion in France.

Although Ethel Hemingway received a letter from one of John's comrades on 27th November stating that John had been killed, it was not until February 1917 that the War Office confirmed this. Little else is known of John, although after her husband's death Ethel moved from 11 Ravenswharf Road, Scout Hill (just outside Ravensthorpe's boundary, being situated in Dewsbury) to 19 Tanhouse Street Ravensthorpe. Besides a widow, John left behind an 18 month old baby girl. John is commemorated on the Thiepval Memorial to the Missing.

Charles Blamires* was killed at the end of the Battle of the Somme. Once again little is known about him, indeed even his age is not known. Before the war, Charles worked at Kilner Brothers, a firm of glass bottle manufacturers, in Thornhill Lees. Leaving his wife and child at 35 Albion Street, Ravensthorpe he joined up, probably in 1915, first of all into the Duke of Wellington's Regiment. He was transferred to the South Staffordshire Regiment, serving in the 1/5th Battalion, which was part of the 46th (North Midland) Division. It is likely he was injured and after recovering was transferred again, this time to the Gloucestershire Regiment. It was in the 8th Battalion of this regiment that Charles found himself in November 1916 as part of 57 Brigade, 19th (Western) Division.

Since the opening day of the Battle of the Somme, when the British attacked on a line from Serre in the north to Carnoy in the south, headway had been made, particularly in the south, along much of the line. Thiepval had been taken, but the Germans were still tenaciously holding onto their original front line trenches north of the River Ancre. An operation to push them back was therefore organised to be undertaken by divisions forming part of General Hubert Gough's Fifth Army. (The Reserve Army had been renamed the Fifth Army in October and had taken responsibility for the northern part of the battlefield, with Rawlinson's Fourth Army's responsibility being in the south where the initial gains had been made.)

These Fifth Army divisions, on what was to be the last 'set piece' attack of the Battle of the Somme, were (from north to south) the 31st, 3rd, 2nd, 51st (Highland), 63rd (Royal Naval), and 19th (Western) Divisions. The attack was launched on 13th November. Charles Blamires' 8th Gloucesters did not take part in the opening day of this battle.

Like so many of the other offensives attempted during the Battle of the Somme, it was again only a partial success; the village of Beaumont-Hamel was at last taken by the 51st (Highland) Division, and on 14th November, the 63rd (Royal Naval) Division took the village of Beaucourt. The attack ground to a halt, and in a last attempt to push on to the original objectives another assault was planned for the 18th November. This was to be the final attack of the Battle of the Somme, and once again the 19th (Western) Division was to take part, but this time with 57 Brigade taking a leading role. The 8th Gloucester's War Diary describes how the battalion spent the final days before the assault in 'Cromwell Huts' near Aveluy+.

The attack was launched at 6.10am on Saturday 18th November. Snow had fallen overnight, which caused great difficulties to the attacking troops in keeping orientated. 57 Brigade (on the right of the division) attacked alongside 56 Brigade in an approximately northerly direction down a valley towards the village of

Both the Ravensthorpe War Memorial and the large Dewsbury Borough War Memorial spell his name Blamires; however the C.W.G.C., S.D.G.W. and the records at the Public Record Office use Blaymire. As the newspapers also use Blamires, I have adopted this version.

+The commanding officer of the 8th Gloucesters had been injured in late October. Lieutenant-Colonel Carton de Wiart was one of the most colourful characters to come out of the First World War; the son of a Belgian lawyer, de Wiart served in the Boer War, being wounded twice. Remaining in the army he lost an eye in Switzerland. When the First World War broke out he was soon wounded, resulting in him having his left hand amputated. He was awarded the V.C. on 3rd July 1916. Wounded again he returned to his battalion, only to be wounded as mentioned above in October. Promoted to Brigadier-General he survived the war (having been wounded twice more). In the Second World War he was captured by the Italians. He lived to the age of 83.

◂ 63. Charles Blamires wearing a hat with what seems to be the Duke of Wellington's badge.

▾ 64. The Thiepval Memorial to the Missing.

Grandcourt. Sleet was falling which, due to the swirling wind made visibility virtually nil. Despite these problems, the attack was pressed home. Unfortunately, although the first objective was reached, the attack ground to a halt. Casualties were heavy. The 8th Gloucester's War Diary records twelve officers and 283 other ranks being killed and wounded. The following day the troops were forced to fall back slightly due to German counter-attacks.

It was during this attack on the 18th that Charles Blamires was killed. According to S.D.G.W., a total of 78 men plus at least five officers from the 8th Gloucesters were killed on the 18th (another eight men died of wounds on the 18th and 19th). Over half of the casualties, Charles included, have no known graves and their names therefore appear on the Thiepval Memorial to the Missing. Of those with known graves, nine are buried at Grandcourt Road Cemetery and 21 at Connaught Cemetery.

Chapter Ten

The Retreat to the Hindenburg Line

Although the Battle of the Somme officially ended on Sunday 19th November 1916, this fact was not immediately obvious to the men with the unenviable task of holding the front line trenches. In front of them, across a desolate No Man's Land were the Germans, still likely to bombard them unexpectedly with artillery or even attack with a sudden raid. Behind the British front line was an equally desolate devastated zone across which the army had attacked during the previous four months. The sheer physical exertion required to arrive at the front line trenches was bad enough, it was then a matter of trying to keep warm in the grip of winter. The troops sheltered in trenches that were alternatively sheet ice in which it was impossible to dig, or when a thaw set in, oozing with clinging mud. In a rare departure from its usual unemotive narrative the Official History describes the conditions in graphic terms:

Here in a wilderness of mud, holding water logged trenches or a shell hole post, accessible only by night, the infantry abode in conditions which might be likened to those of earthworms rather than of human kind. Our vocabulary is not adapted to describe such an existence because it is outside the experience for which words are normally required. Mud, for the men in the line, was no mere inorganic nuisance and obstacle. It took on an aggressive, wolf-like guise, and like a wolf could pull down and swallow the lonely wanderer in the darkness.

It was a desperate existence made worse by the need, via orders coming from high command, to dominate No Man's Land. The British, unlike the French, did not allow a 'live and let live' state of affairs to exist.

It was in these truly appalling conditions that Percy Boothroyd found himself in December 1916. Percy had been sent to France in mid-October, joining the 9th Battalion, West Yorkshire Regiment (32 Brigade, 11th (Northern) Division) and had therefore missed his battalion's latest action in September.

Percy was born on 16th October 1889; he had an elder brother and a sister and attended the Primitive Methodist Chapel in Ravensthorpe. After being educated at Ravensthorpe St. Saviour's Boys' School he became an errand boy for a local grocer. He later worked for the Lion Stores in Thornhill Lees and later still was a grocer's assistant at the Cooperative Society's Ravensthorpe store. It was whilst working for the Co-op in Doncaster that he enlisted, being sent to France on his 27th Birthday, 16th October 1916.

At the end of November the battalion was ordered to leave its billets in the village of Englebelmer and proceed to the front line where they were to relieve the 6th Battalion, Border Regiment (33 Brigade, 11th Division). The relief was completed by 6pm on Tuesday 28th November, the battalion occupying reserve trenches a little to the west of Beaucourt railway station, the village having been taken a few days previously by the 63rd (Royal Naval) Division.

Percy wrote to his mother at 107 Sackville Street, Ravensthorpe on Wednesday 29th November indicating that they were having a three day march to the fighting

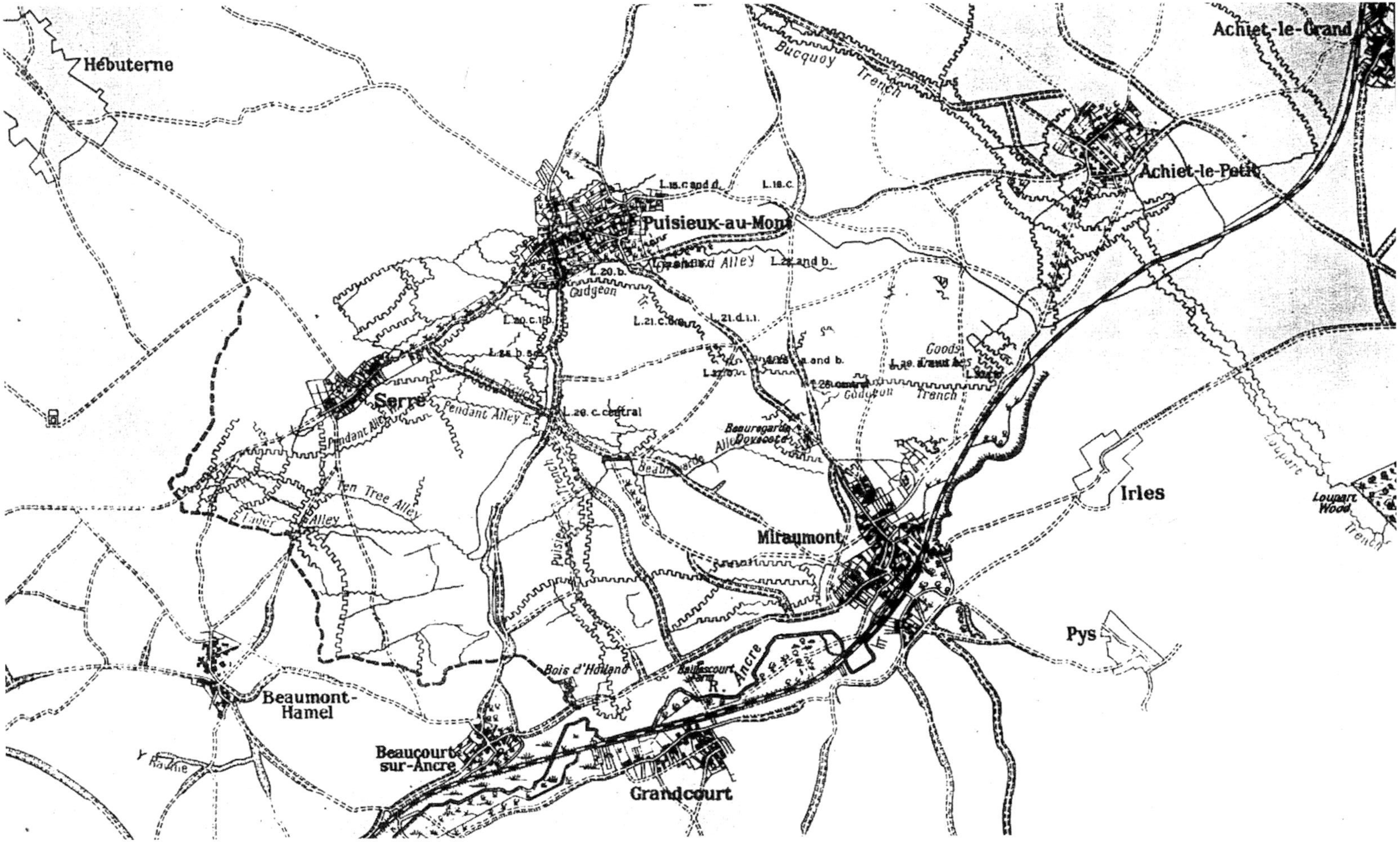

▲ Map 14. Beaucourt

line (he probably meant to say that they were expecting to be in the reserve trenches for three days before going to the front line. Certainly, even in the awful conditions that they found themselves, it would not take three days to move from the reserve trenches to the front line.)

Whatever Percy meant to say, on the same day as the letter was written, the battalion's War Diary records: *"Trenches shelled at 10pm, four men killed and four wounded."* (S.D.G.W. states 4 killed in action and 1 died of wounds, but confusingly gives the date as 30th November.) It does not seem that Percy ever made it to the front line trench (the battalion moved up on 2nd December); it is more than likely that one of the soldiers injured in this incident was Percy Boothroyd.

Sometime during the course of the next few days, a postcard arrived at Percy's mother's home to say that Percy had been injured. Another postcard soon followed, arriving on Thursday 7th December, to say that whilst he was wounded he was *"going on nicely"*.

Unfortunately, on the same day as Mrs Boothroyd received the second card, reassuring her of her son's condition, Percy died. According to the matron in charge of the 12th General Hospital in Rouen (to where Percy had been evacuated), Percy passed away at 2.30 in the afternoon, she wrote further that Percy *"had a severe haemorrhage and died quite suddenly....he did not know he was so ill."*

▲ 65. Percy Boothroyd

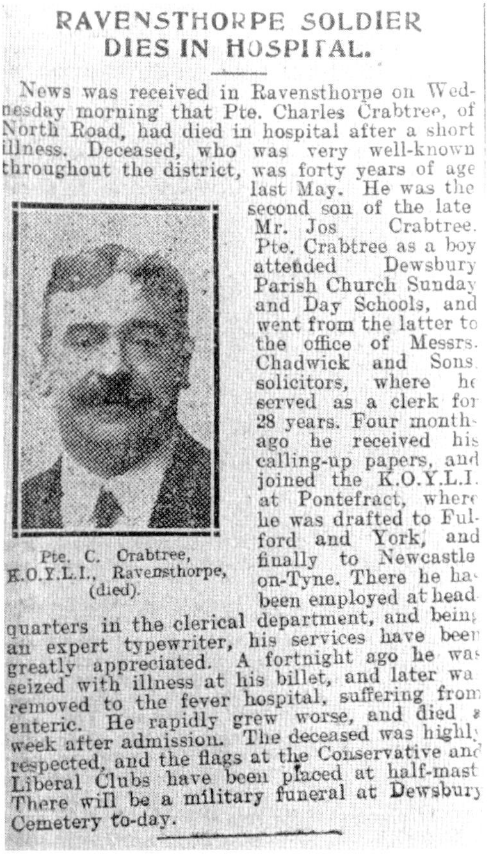

RAVENSTHORPE SOLDIER DIES IN HOSPITAL.

News was received in Ravensthorpe on Wednesday morning that Pte. Charles Crabtree, of North Road, had died in hospital after a short illness. Deceased, who was very well-known throughout the district, was forty years of age last May. He was the second son of the late Mr. Jos Crabtree. Pte. Crabtree as a boy attended Dewsbury Parish Church Sunday and Day Schools, and went from the latter to the office of Messrs. Chadwick and Sons, solicitors, where he served as a clerk for 28 years. Four months ago he received his calling-up papers, and joined the K.O.Y.L.I. at Pontefract, where he was drafted to Fulford and York, and finally to Newcastle-on-Tyne. There he has been employed at headquarters in the clerical department, and being an expert typewriter, his services have been greatly appreciated. A fortnight ago he was seized with illness at his billet, and later was removed to the fever hospital, suffering from enteric. He rapidly grew worse, and died a week after admission. The deceased was highly respected, and the flags at the Conservative and Liberal Clubs have been placed at half-mast. There will be a military funeral at Dewsbury Cemetery to-day.

Pte. C. Crabtree, K.O.Y.L.I., Ravensthorpe, (died).

▲ 66. Charles Crabtree

Percy was buried the next day, Friday 8th December in the St. Sever Cemetery Extension, Rouen. His name appears not only on the Ravensthorpe Parish Church War Memorial, but also on the Roll of Honour of the Primitive Methodist Church, which Percy attended with his family.

Charles Crabtree, according to the War Memorial served with the Northumberland Fusiliers. This is actually quite wrong. Charles was born in Dewsbury in May 1876; after attending Dewsbury Parish Church School, he served as a clerk at Chadwick, Son and Nicholson solicitors for many years until, in August 1916, he was called up into the army, joining the K.O.Y.L.I. It is likely that he was passed as being not sufficiently fit for overseas service and he was sent instead to Newcastle (this may be the reason for the Northumberland Fusiliers reference on the Memorial) where, according to the Dewsbury Reporter *"...he has been employed at Headquarters in the clerical department, and being an expert typewriter, his services have been greatly appreciated."* In late November he became ill with enteric fever and after a week in hospital died on 7th December (the same day as Percy Boothroyd).

His body was brought by train back to Dewsbury. The mourners had met at his house at 124 North Road at 2.30pm on Saturday 9th December, but owing to delays en route, it was not until 3.50pm (much later than scheduled) that the train arrived. The burial took place at Dewsbury Cemetery by lantern light later that night.

The last casualty of 1916 was Fred Mellor. Although there is no evidence that Fred is related to Willie Mellor (see Chapter 6), the photographs of the two men indicates a family resemblance. Fred was born on 23rd January 1877; there is no information about his early life, but after the death of his father, Fred gave up his business (he was a butcher) and took over his father's pub, the New Albion Inn, Ravensthorpe. The only extra information about him is that he attended Ravensthorpe Parish Church and was a member of the Liberal Club. After being called up on 8th August 1916, Fred (like Charles Crabtree) was not passed fit for front line duties, being categorised B(1); this meant that he was, however, fit for garrison duty overseas. He was therefore sent to the 12th (Labour) Battalion, Lincolnshire Regiment, proceeding overseas just twelve days after his call up.

The battalion, as a labour unit, was not intended to be involved in any fighting. It was despatched to France on 20th August (Fred was one of the original contingent), arriving at Le Havre from where it was sent up the coast to Dieppe. Although the town of Dieppe was not as large as Le Havre or Boulogne, it was still important as a port for the importation of the enormous quantities of supplies that the British army needed. The battalion's work seems to have revolved around assisting in the railway yard at Roux Mesnil which had a large ammunition dump alongside it.

In mid-December Fred's wife, Gertrude, received a telegram at their home at 2 Charles Street, Ravensthorpe informing her that Fred was dangerously ill in the hospital at Dieppe. Permission was granted for her to travel to see him and Gertrude Mellor, together with her sister set off at once, arriving in Dieppe on Thursday 14th December. Unfortunately Fred had already died earlier that day. Stopping for his funeral on Saturday (the 16th), Gertrude and her sister returned home on Tuesday 19th December.

Fred died just short of his 40th birthday and is buried at Janval Cemetery, Dieppe, in a small Commonwealth War Graves Commission plot within a much larger civilian cemetery.

▲ 67. Fred Mellor

▲ 68. Tom Chapman

The stories of two of the Chapman brothers, Philip and James (Jim) have already been told in Chapter 3. Thomas Chapman (who was older than Philip and Jim) was born in Norwich in 1878, where at least three of the five brothers were born. The family were well connected with the army, their father William was an old soldier and Philip, Jim and Thomas were all either reservists or pre-war territorials. Thomas, like his brothers was called up as a reservist in the first days of the war, but unlike his two brothers did not immediately go out to France. There is little information about the family in the newspapers, but it seems that Tom (as he was known) joined the Army in 1899 and after serving his time as a regular, became a reservist. Before the outbreak of the Great War he worked as a stoker for the Mirfield Gas Company.

Because of his seventeen years in the army, first as a regular and then as a reservist, Tom was entitled to be discharged in June 1916, however it would only have been a matter of time before he would have been conscripted back into the army; he therefore signed back on 'for the duration'. It is possible that it was in the middle of 1916, after signing on, that Tom was sent to France, possibly joining the ammunition column of XIV Brigade, Royal Horse Artillery. Until May 1916, XIV Brigade R.H.A. (part of the 7th Division) had its own ammunition column, but following changes in ammunition supply arrangements, from May, these units were absorbed into divisional ammunition columns. After XIV Brigade's ammunition column was disbanded, it is likely that Tom served either with 7th Division's ammunition column or with the guns of XIV Brigade, R.H.A.

Commencing at the beginning of 1917, there was a reorganisation of artillery units within the B.E.F. when some of the artillery brigades were removed from the

69. Tom Chapman's headstone in Bray Military Cemetery.

70. John Street, Ravensthorpe. *Photograph courtesy of Kirklees Community History Service.*

control of divisions and placed under the command of the various armies*. These units (which included XIV Brigade, R.H.A.) had their ammunition columns restored; this restoration taking place from January 1917 onwards. It seems that in January 1917, XIV Brigade R.H.A. was still part of the 7th Division.

It has not been possible to ascertain what happened to Tom. He died of wounds on 14th January 1917, possibly incurred during an attack made on Munich Trench, just south of Serre, by 91 Infantry Brigade (part of 7th Division). The artillery of the 7th Division, including XIV Brigade, would have been supporting this attack, and there is no doubt that the German artillery would have been keen to silence the British guns. It was possibly as part of this German counter-artillery barrage that Tom received his fatal injuries.

Tom now lies buried at Bray Military Cemetery, in the village of Bray-sur-Somme, the cemetery contains nearly 900 graves. These graves are made up of men who died from wounds at the three Casualty Clearing Stations that were located in the village in 1917 and from concentrations of 200 graves from the surrounding battlefields that took place just after the war until as late as 1924. It is not known whether Tom died at one of the Casualty Clearing Stations, or whether his was one of the 'concentration' burials.

Tom's wife, Flora, who lived at 23 John Street, Ravensthorpe, received a communication (probably a telegram) from the War Office on Friday 26th January 1917 telling her that her husband had died at a dressing station. He left behind two boys aged 8 and 10.

Like Leonard Crane whose story was told in Chapter 9, Harry Ellam was a member of the 7th K.O.Y.L.I., however Harry would not have served with Leonard as, after being called up in September 1916, he joined the battalion in France at around Christmas later that year, which was after Leonard's death. Harry was born in Dewsbury in 1894 but brought up in Hopton, near Mirfield, where he attended the Hopton Congregational Day School. Before the war he worked as a piecer for Henry Hamer and Sons. On 17th February 1917, Harry's name was mentioned in the Dewsbury Reporter as having received a parcel from the committee of the 'Ravensthorpe and Northorpe Soldiers and Sailors Christmas Parcel Fund'; this fund having been set up to supply local soldiers with parcels for Christmas. Unfortunately, Harry was already dead when this was published.

In early March, Harry's mother received two letters at the family home at 19 Raven Street, Ravensthorpe from his officers. Lieutenant E.H. Hanson wrote to express his sympathy as Harry's platoon commander. He stated that he "*.....was not in the trenches on the particular day* [that Harry was killed] *but the officer who saw the shell burst tells me that death must have been instantaneous.....his death occurred at 12.15pm on 12th February in the front line trench.*"

The next letter was presumably from the other officer that Lieutenant Hanson mentioned. Second Lieutenant A.W.L. Stewart wrote that Harry and another soldier were killed by a shell. (According to S.D.G.W., no other soldier was killed in the 7th K.O.Y.L.I. on this day although one man from the battalion was killed on the following day.) Second Lieutenant Stewart went on to say that Harry's grave

After being detached from divisional control, the artillery brigades were liable to serve wherever they were needed.

A further reorganisation of artillery brigades took place in 1918 - see explanation in Chapter 19.

had been marked and although he was not a religious man he had said a few prayers with some of his comrades.

The War Diary of the 7th K.O.Y.L.I. describes how the battalion moved on 11th February from Carnoy up to the front line at Morval (which is due south of Lesboeufs). Although about six miles as the crow flies, the journey would have been long and difficult. Only 425 men of the battalion went into the trenches, as 250 were left behind at the camp at Carnoy*. Possibly due to the lack of numbers (the battalion was well below strength due to the casualties it had incurred during the Battle of the Somme) or possibly due to the condition of the ground, the front line trench ('Bosnia Salient') was not manned continuously, gaps were covered by Lewis guns (light machine guns). The battalion was unable to work on the trenches due to the frozen state of the ground. The War Diary describes how *"During the tour it was difficult to get hot drinks to the men and also to use screw picquets for putting out* [barbed] *wire because the ground was so hard."*

It is difficult to see how a grave could be dug in these circumstances, it is possible Harry's body was placed in a convenient shell hole, covered and marked. Whatever happened, after the war, Harry's body was not found and the name of Harry Ellam therefore appears on the Thiepval Memorial to the Missing.

▲ 71. Harry Ellam

▲ 72. Allen Oldroyd

**** This was normal routine. Battalions never went into the line with every man in the unit, a proportion was kept behind in the 'transport lines'; the primary reason for this being if the battalion suffered heavy casualties there would always be a cadre left, around which the battalion could be re-formed.***

Moving briefly away from the Somme, the 23rd Division was, in the early part of 1917, in the Ypres salient. One of the battalions in the division was the 8th K.O.Y.L.I.; Private Allen Oldroyd of 4 West Vale, Dewsbury was a member of this battalion. He was admitted to hospital in Boulogne in early December 1916 suffering from trench foot. This condition was a common problem in the waterlogged trenches of the Western Front. With no opportunity to dry their feet, the soldiers stood in water and mud for hours, and sometimes days at a time. As a result their feet often became swollen and bloated and in extreme cases hospital treatment was required. It seems complications must have set in, as on 16th February 1917 Allen Oldroyd died of bronchitis and pneumonia.

Before the war Allen worked for the Standard Patent Glazing Company (this is one of the few companies for which the men on the Memorial worked still to be trading today). He was educated at Dewsbury Moor Council School and attended St. John's Church, Dewsbury Moor. After the war his widow moved to Scout Hill, just on Ravensthorpe's boundary with Dewsbury, it is likely that this is the reason that his name was included on the Ravensthorpe War Memorial.

Allen died aged 32 and is buried in Boulogne Eastern Cemetery. Due to the sandy nature of the ground, the headstones in this cemetery are not in the usual vertical position, but are laid flat on the ground similar to those at the nearby Wimereux Communal Cemetery where Willie Beckett is buried (see Chapter 4).

* * *

It will be recalled from Chapter 2 that when the 49th Division left for France in April 1915, steps were immediately taken to create replacement battalions. These second line territorial battalions were formed into divisions and trained in order to be sent to France. The 62nd (2nd West Riding) Division was kept back in Britain for coastal defence duties until the end of December 1916, when orders were received to proceed overseas. The division arrived in France in mid-January 1917, disembarking at Le Havre, and concentrating at the town of Frevent which is between St. Pol and Doullens. The battalions of the division then marched to Beauval (just south of Doullens) and from there to Bus-les-Artois where they arrived on the evening of 23rd January. As with the 49th Division in April 1915, parties of officers and men were sent to the front line for instruction by the troops already there, the 19th (Western) and 32nd Divisions performing this role.

The first of the 62nd Division's casualties was incurred during one of these periods of instruction when a private in the 2/6th West Yorkshires was killed in action on 27th January*. There was some illness in the units due to the extreme cold - a hard frost had set in which was soon covered by snow - many men were living in tents; the comfortable life in England of just a few weeks previously must have seemed a long way away!

Apart from the instruction in the trenches and the specialist courses that were being run (such as for Lewis gunners and bombers) much hard manual labour was required to be done behind the lines, this involved railway construction, road repairs, maintenance of ammunition dumps and the burying of cables. This work

**** James Capewell is commemorated on the Thiepval Memorial to the Missing.***

continued until the end of January. In early February, the division was told to make itself ready for taking over trenches in the Beaumont-Hamel area of the Somme. The History of the 62nd (West Riding) Division describes the conditions:

"Trenches as such did not exist, for they had been obliterated by the concentrated fire of the guns......The front line was held by a series of posts and dugouts which somewhat resembled islands in a sea of mud. Shell holes pock-marked the ground, often overlapping one another and where pathways existed between them they were but a few inches wide. The holes were full of water and more than one man lost his life through slipping off the narrow pathway into the slimy mass which engulfed him".

These conditions were as a direct result of the Battle of the Somme which had been at its height six months earlier; indeed during August 1916, realising that they were losing too many troops, the Chief of Staff of the German Army, General Erich von Falkenhayn* was replaced by Field-Marshal Paul von Hindenburg. Hindenburg together with his deputy, General Erich Ludendorff + realised that von Falkenhayn's rigid defensive tactics and immediate counter-attacks to regain any lost ground were costing them heavily, and they therefore set about changing the German army's defensive tactics to a more flexible approach. Rather than heavily manning the front line trench, a 'defence in depth' scheme was used instead, whereby the defence was spread over a deep zone; this would be easier to defend, cost the Germans less in terms of casualties, but cost the British more.

In order to take full advantage of these new tactics, a whole new trench system would be required and in September 1916 a site for this was selected about 25 miles behind the present front line. The line would consist of an Outpost Zone, 600 yards deep containing a few troops and a series of concrete dugouts in order to slow down any advance. Next would be a Battle Zone, about 2,500 yards deep, this would contain several trench lines, masses of barbed wire and a network of concrete machine gun emplacements. Immediately behind this would be stationed troops ready to counter-attack should the Battle Zone be captured. It was thought that the attackers would have suffered so many casualties that they would be unable to resist a strong counter-attack.

This new line, called the Siegfried Line by the Germans but known to the British as the Hindenburg Line, was 90 miles long and had the added advantage to the Germans of saving about 25 miles of front line, which would not therefore have to be manned. This saving of manpower (about thirteen divisions would be freed) was sorely needed by the Germans who had suffered enormous casualties both on the Somme and at Verdun. Initially it was intended that the line would only be occupied if the British broke through the existing front line, but on 4th February 1917 the order was given by the German High Command to prepare for the withdrawal. During the withdrawal the Germans were to implement a 'scorched earth' policy whereby nothing of possible use to the Allies was to be left standing. Houses were destroyed, road junctions were mined, wells were filled in (some may even have been poisoned), even fruit trees were cut down to prevent them being used as a source of food. The Germans also left behind hundreds of booby traps,

**** The Kaiser was the Commander-in-Chief, but control of military policy was effectively in the hands of the Chief of Staff.***

+ As the war progressed, von Ludendorff was to become the more dominant of these two men. By the end of the war he had become effectively the political as well as military head of the German nation.

from simple pieces of duckboarding in trenches which, when stepped on, would set off a grenade, to a huge delayed-action mine under the Bapaume Town Hall; this went off on 25th March, several days after the British occupied the town causing many casualties to the troops that were sheltering in the building.

The first sign that the Germans had started to abandon their position was made on 22nd February when a patrol by members of the 7th Royal West Kents of the 18th Division discovered that there were no Germans on the crest south of the village of Petit Miramont*. It is probable that this early withdrawal from the Ancre valley was made due to the fact that an attack had been made on 17th and 18th February by the 63rd (Royal Naval), 18th (Eastern), and 2nd Divisions on the northern and southern sides of the River Ancre. This had made the German's hold on the villages of Pys and Miramont very tenuous. Despite this, the Allies were surprised by the German withdrawal and gave orders for the Germans to be harried during their retirement; however the Germans were determined to give up the ground at their own pace and left behind stubborn rearguards who caused casualties to the following troops who happened to be from the 62nd (West Riding) Division.

The 62nd Division had taken over part of the front line on the night of the 13th/14th February, the relief being completed the following night. During the night of the 20th/21st February, 187 Brigade moved up into the front line, relieving the troops who had been there the previous week. The 2/4th York and Lancaster Regiment held the front line with other battalions of the brigade in support and reserve. Conditions, as previously described, were awful, the 2/5th K.O.Y.L.I. reported 43 men with trench foot on 23rd February. The following day, Saturday 24th February, the 2/4th York and Lancasters were ordered, at 3.15pm, to move forward in pursuit of the Germans; at 4pm an advance was made but due to the state of the ground progress was very slow. After only 500 yards, with darkness having fallen, a halt was made. That night (24th/25th February), the 2/4th K.O.Y.L.I. relieved the 2/4th York and Lancasters.

At 8am on 25th February the 2/5th K.O.Y.L.I. passed through the positions the 2/4th K.O.Y.L.I. were holding, and continued the advance. The War Diary of the 2/5th K.O.Y.L.I. gives further details of its part in the pursuit of the Germans, the battalion was in the Beaumont-Hamel - Miramont area:

24th February: *In support at Beaumont-Hamel.*

25th February: *Ordered at 2am to move up to front line and continue the advance made by the 2/4th Y&L the day previous. Deployed at 8.10am on either side of Puiseux Road* [the road out of Beaucourt leading north to Puiseux]....... *morning very misty and ground in a bad state....... Advance continued under fairly heavy shell fire until 1.15pm......Gained touch with the 2/4th K.O.Y.L.I. in the Wuntwerk* [also known as the Lozenge]. *Casualties six killed and nine wounded.*

One of the day's casualties was a soldier from Ravensthorpe.

Herbert Gamble was born in 1897 to Mr and Mrs Fred Gamble. Before the war he worked for G.H. Hirst & Co. of Queen Street, attending the Primitive Methodist

**** This was just a preliminary withdrawal. The main withdrawal was made between 14th March and 5th April.***

▲ 73. Herbert Gamble

▲ 74. Fred Watson

Chapel. Herbert enlisted into the K.O.Y.L.I. on 6 March 1916, and after training left for France with the rest of the 62nd Division on 9th January 1917.

In early March a letter was published in the Dewsbury Reporter from Second Lieutenant John Atkin to Herbert's parents saying that Herbert was killed on the 26th (of February) *"...just as he was going up to the trenches. He suffered no pain, but was killed instantly along with another poor lad."* It is likely that Second Lieutenant Atkin was mistaken as all other sources indicate it was on Sunday 25th February that most of the battalion's casualties were incurred. After the death in action of the first member of the 2/5th K.O.Y.L.I. on the 21st February*, six soldiers (including Herbert) were killed in action on the 25th (another one died of wounds on this day), all seven have no known graves and their names therefore appear on the Thiepval Memorial to the Missing. (As far as Second Lieutenant Atkin's letter is concerned, on the 26th two soldiers lost their lives; one was killed in action and is also commemorated at Thiepval, the other died of wounds and is buried at Aveluy Wood (Lancashire Dump) Cemetery.)

It was about this time that the most decorated soldier on the Ravensthorpe War Memorial earned the first of his gallantry medals. Frederick William Watson was born in Leeds on 8th November 1878 to David and Jinnie; he enlisted in the K.O.Y.L.I. on 27th February 1897, aged just over 18 years, giving his trade as 'mechanic'. There is some doubt as to his real name, as the documents from his

**** Joshua Smith who is buried at Beaumont-Hamel British Cemetery.***

enlistment indicate that he gave his name as Frederick Wilson, the Wilson later being changed to Watson. He was 5' 3½" tall with a chest expansion of 33½" (when fully expanded 34") and weighed 8 stones 8 lbs. It was also noted that besides a circular scar on his left buttock, he had the letters 'FW' tattooed on his right fore-arm. Fred signed on for seven years 'with the colours', with a further five years to be served as a reservist.

He was awarded a Good Conduct Badge on 27th February 1899 (the second anniversary of his enlistment), little more than two months later, on 6th May, he was promoted to lance corporal. On the fourth anniversary of his enlistment, in 1901 he was awarded a second Good Conduct Badge and was promoted to corporal on 4th April of that year. In December he was posted from the 1st to the 2nd Battalion of the K.O.Y.L.I. and sent to South Africa where the British were fighting the Boer farmers.

It was in South Africa that he first got himself into trouble when, on 4th May 1902, he was given a severe reprimand for *"Neglect of Duty whilst in charge of a Block House"**. Despite this, three months later, on 14th August, he was promoted to sergeant. He continued to serve in South Africa for a further four months until October 1902 when he was posted, with the rest of the battalion to Malta. Whilst in Malta his terms of service were amended so that he was to serve the full twelve years 'with the colours'.

In March 1904 the battalion was transferred to Crete, where it stayed a further year until coming back home in March 1905. On 21st July 1906 Fred found himself in trouble again, being given a further severe reprimand when caught *"Gambling in camp* [at Bisley] *about 9.45pm."*

Despite these misdemeanours, it seems that Fred was a good soldier as on 18th January 1908, a month short of the eleventh anniversary of his enlistment, and with still over a year of his engagement to run, he was signed on to serve a total of twenty one years. There is no doubt that his volunteering for this extended service was connected with him being medically examined a month earlier, when he was found fit for service in West Africa. Fred was seconded to the Northern Nigeria Regiment, part of the West Africa Frontier Force, leaving the United Kingdom on 15th February 1908. He served in west Africa for a year, returning home in April 1909; later that year, on 9th June, he married Ada Ellen Taylor in Ravensthorpe Parish Church.

Returning to the 2nd Battalion, he served part of the next period of his service in Ireland; it was in Cork where on 2nd February he was to receive a *"Reprimand* [for] *neglect of duty when in charge of a fatigue party (allowing men to fall out)."* It seems that rather than keeping the men working, he allowed them to rest, but was found out by his sergeant-major.

On 24th May 1912 he was posted to the 5th (territorial) Battalion, which recruited one of its companies in Goole, where he would have worked as a sergeant drill instructor (several regulars were employed in each of the territorial battalions). It was in this town that his three sons, George, Morris and Jack were born, (George being born in September 1912).

When war broke out he was a likely candidate to go to France with the 2nd Battalion, K.O.Y.L.I., however regular troops were desperately required to train

**** Chains of fortified posts had been constructed in an attempt at keeping the Boers confined to certain areas.***

the new recruits who were flooding into the army and threatening to overwhelm the system. As a result he was promoted to Company Sergeant Major and kept back as a drill instructor.

Rather than being posted to one of the Kitchener 'service' battalions, he remained with the 5th Battalion, and could therefore have expected to have been posted to France in April 1915 when the 49th Division (which included the 1/5th K.O.Y.L.I.) was despatched; however it was again decided that he was more useful being kept back in order to help train the second line battalion that was being formed. It was therefore not until January 1917 that Fred went to France as a Company Sergeant Major with the 2/5th K.O.Y.L.I., 62nd Division.

In early March the 2/5th K.O.Y.L.I. was in reserve at Beaumont-Hamel, on the 6th, the battalion moved up into support at Bois d'Holland (on the eastern edge of Beaucourt) and the next day moved up to the front line which was at that time between the villages of Miramont and Achiet-le-Petit. On the right of the battalion was the 10th Essex (part of 18th (Eastern) Division). The War Diary of the 2/5th K.O.Y.L.I. for 8th March describes how Second Lieutenant Atkin (the same officer who had written to Herbert Gamble's parents) led a daylight patrol, an action for which he earned the Military Cross. The diary goes on *"CSM F.W. Watson established a post in Resurrection Trench to assist the 10th Essex to carry out a bombing attack. A previous attempt had failed. CSM Watson awarded the D.C.M."*

The Dewsbury Reporter, clearly quoting from an official communique adds a little extra information saying that the action was on the night of the 8th/9th March and that the *"...previous attempt had been made without success owing to the enemy's resistance. As it was of great importance to the success of the operation that this post was established, CSM Watson volunteered to carry it out and was completely successful."*

The 10th Essex was at this time preparing for an attack on the village of Irles as part of the continued push on the Germans during their retirement. The Germans were, however, not yet ready to go and resisted all probes by the 10th Essex. Part of the preparations for the attack on Irles by the Essex was the requirement of pushing the Germans back in Resurrection Trench so as to allow the battalion to form up correctly for the impending attack.

The final patrol by the 10th Essex before the attack was in the early hours of 9th March and was, after failures on previous nights, finally successful. The Essex launched their attack at 5.15am on 10th March*.

Fred Watson's citation for the D.C.M. reads "For conspicuous gallantry and devotion to duty. He succeeded in establishing a post at a critical time under the most trying conditions. He has at all times set a splendid example of courage and determination."

On 7th April a letter was published in the Dewsbury Reporter from Fred to his wife (who was living at 3 William Street, Ravensthorpe) telling her he had won the Distinguished Conduct Medal.

* * *

**** S.D.G.W. gives casualties for the period as:***

2/5th K.O.Y.L.I. :- 8th March - 1 killed in action; 9th March - 1 k.i.a. and 1 died of wounds; 10th March - 1 d.o.w.

10th Essex :- 8th March - 5 k.i.a. and 1 d.o.w.; 9th March - 2 k.i.a. and 2 d.o.w.; 10th March - 6 k.i.a. and 4 d.o.w. plus at least one officer k.i.a.

As mentioned in Chapter 2, during the middle of 1915 it had become evident that the number of men volunteering for the army was falling away, and that steps would have to be taken to ensure that the army was kept supplied with men. The National Registration Act of 1915 compelled everyone in the country to register certain details, such as their age, sex and occupation. The information was collated, and by September it was obvious that there were large numbers of men, not engaged in vital war work such as munitions, who had yet to volunteer for the armed forces. The names of those men aged between 18 and 41 were forwarded to recruiting offices so that they could be encouraged to enlist.

Lord Derby, the chairman of the West Lancashire Territorial Association and a prominent politician was appointed Director-General of Recruiting in October 1915. He moved swiftly to implement a plan, which became known as the 'Derby Scheme', to give men the final opportunity to volunteer; this last chance ran for just two months and ended on 15th December 1915. Under his scheme, two and a half million men attested their willingness to serve if called upon; these men also had the opportunity to state in which Regiment or Corps they wished to serve.

Unfortunately for the Government insufficient single men attested, and it was politically impossible to call up the married men until all the available single men had been enlisted. In January 1916, therefore, the Military Service Act was introduced, in which, for the first time in Britain, men were conscripted into the army. All unmarried men between 18 and 41 were called up, although a high number of these were categorised medically unfit or given exemptions because of their employment. Conscription was not, however, introduced in Ireland because of the political situation there.

The call up papers for the single men were despatched in March 1916; however it soon became evident that this would not produce sufficient recruits, so conscription was extended to married men in May.

Unless the service record exists, it is almost impossible to tell, for men who served later in the war, whether they were pre-war territorials, early volunteers, volunteers under the Derby Scheme or conscripts. Several of the Ravensthorpe soldiers whose service records exist were 'Derby volunteers' - examples include Frank Fearnsides (Chapter 9), Ralph Crawshaw (Chapter 12), Friend Whitwam (Chapter 15) and Harry Campbell (see below).

* * *

Harry Campbell was the next Ravensthorpe casualty, his death occurred to the north of the Somme area where Fred Watson was serving. Harry was born in Luckenvada, Germany in September 1884 to Ralph and Emily Campbell. There is no record of how he came to be born overseas, nor any details of his early life. He went to work at Marshall, Kaye and Marshall's mill immediately on leaving school. Harry was heavily involved with St. Saviour's Parish Church, being a member of the Men's Bible Class, his family were also well known at the church. He married Louisa Livsey at St. Saviour's on 10th August 1912.

Harry volunteered under the Derby Scheme on 6th December 1915, and was placed on the army reserve until called up, this occurring on 25th July 1916. Leaving Louisa behind at their home at 13 Lee Street Ravensthorpe he was sent from the recruiting depot at Pontefract to join the Royal Garrison Artillery at Great Yarmouth. From there, on 5th August, he was posted to the 221st Siege Battery which was being formed at Dunoon (west of Glasgow); the battery forming part of the River Clyde defences. On 10th January 1917 the battery went to France as a four gun (8 inch) howitzer battery, joining the 33rd Heavy Artillery Group* which was part of the Third Army.

In March 1917 the 221st Siege Battery was located in Arras and was, on most days, used for routine bombardment of the German trench lines and rear areas. On 20th March it is likely that the German artillery somehow located the battery's position and bombarded it. There were five injuries plus one man killed. Gunner Harry Campbell was the fatal casualty. Second Lieutenant L.W. Johnstone wrote to Louisa Campbell : *"This morning whilst carrying out his duties, your husband was killed instantaneously by a shell which fell within a foot of him. His death has cast a gloom over the battery, with all of whom he was a favourite. I personally feel his loss very keenly as he has acted as my 'batman' since I joined the battery three months ago. He was always a keen worker and nothing was too much for him. He was always looking forward to the day when this awful war would end and he could return home to Yorkshire.....Your husband was laid to rest in the British Cemetery just outside the city."*

Louisa also received a letter from Mr Bentley, Managing Director of Marshall, Kaye and Marshall's mill. The Liberal Club, where Harry was a member, lowered their flag to half-mast. Later that year Louisa received a letter informing her that she would, with effect from 8th October, receive a weekly pension of 13s 9d from the Government.

Harry is buried in the Faubourg d'Amiens British Cemetery in Arras which contains over 2,500 graves; the cemetery has the Arras Memorial to the Missing built along one side of it.

* * *

The 49th (West Riding) Division had, since its mauling on the Somme in September 1916, moved north to the Neuve Chapelle area (where the division had been introduced to the Western Front in April 1915). John Ellis was a member of the 1/5th Battalion, York and Lancaster Regiment within this division. John was born on 28th April 1892 in Lowmoor, Bradford to Mr and Mrs William Ellis. The family moved to Ravensthorpe where he attended the Primitive Methodist Church and was a teacher in the Sunday School. He was a member of the Christian Endeavour Society and on the committee of Band of Hope. John worked as a strap maker for Hartley Brothers Ltd, who were leather curriers in Ravensthorpe, until he joined up on 25th October 1915.

He initially joined the Queen's Own Yorkshire Dragoons+ but it was with the

**** Each Army Corps had two (later four) Heavy Artillery Groups. The Groups usually contained five batteries.***

+ John was probably in the 2/1st Regiment, which was the second line unit to this Regiment. The 2/1st were stationed in the United Kingdom throughout the war, being converted to a cyclist role in November 1916, which is probably when men were posted away from the regiment and were sent to infantry battalions in France. It seems that the majority of these men went to the 8th Y&L, although many others went to the 1/5th Y&L (John included) and others to the 1/4th K.O.Y.L.I. (see George Sutcliffe, Chapter 13).

▲ 75. Harry Campbell

▲ 76. John Ellis. The date of death is wrong on the photograph; John died in 1917, not 1916.

York and Lancaster Regiment that John went to France, being sent at Christmas 1916.

During March 1917 the 1/5th York and Lancasters were holding trenches at Neuve Chapelle. On 23rd March the battalion took over the front line trenches from the 1/5th K.O.Y.L.I. Just in front of them, in No Man's Land, was a position known as the Duck's Bill Crater. On the night of the 28th/29th March a raid was organised by the 147 Brigade, to the right of the battalion's position. It is possible that John was killed during the German artillery retaliation for the raid on the morning of Thursday 29th March, (the War Diary states there was *"...a certain amount of retaliation..."*) however according to a letter written to John's parents at 79 Garden Street Ravensthorpe by Corporal F. Johnson, John was shot through the jaw whilst 'on patrol' (this may have been a patrol of No Man's Land during the hours of darkness). The letter went on to say that John did not live long, he died whilst Corporal Johnson and others carried him away. He was buried the next day *"...in a pretty little British cemetery, the service being conducted by the chaplain."*

The War Diary states there were two fatal casualties on the 29th, the other being Private Walter Muir. The battalion was relieved later on the 29th by the 1/5th K.O.Y.L.I. and moved back to Pont-du-Hem.

It is in the Pont-du-Hem Military Cemetery that John Ellis and Walter Muir lie, side by side. Strangely the C.W.G.C. have incorrectly marked John's headstone with the date 29th May (Walter Muir's has the correct date of 29th March). The photograph of John also compounds the confusion by giving his year of death as 1916 rather than 1917

The original burials (which numbered 350) now form plots 1,2,3 and part of plot 4. As John is buried in plot 3 it seems that his grave was part of the original cemetery, which was begun in an apple orchard in July 1915.

Chapter Eleven

Mesopotamia

As with Gallipoli, the campaign fought in Mesopotamia (now Iraq) was, as far as the Western Front generals were concerned, an unnecessary drain on the country's resources. They believed, with some justification, that the war could only be won in France and Belgium and sending troops to other theatres was a waste of effort. Unlike the thought process that brought about the Gallipoli campaign, the Mesopotamian plan (if it can be called that) came about as a result of early successes of a very limited nature against a weak enemy.

Oil driven ships (that formed part of the Royal Navy's strength) depended on their fuel coming from the Anglo-Persian Oil Company whose pipeline ran down to the Persian Gulf at Basra. The British Government, before the war, had secured a controlling interest in this company and this, together with the fact that Britain had colonial obligations (a protectorate over the local Sultanate of Kuwait) meant the Government had sufficient motivation for sending troops to the area.

Whilst protection of the pipeline through Persia (now Iran) would be almost impossible, it was felt that a victory against the Turks (who were known to be preparing an offensive against Basra) would ensure that the local Arabs, sensing it would be in their best interests to help the victors, came onto the British side and would therefore give protection to the vital oil pipeline.

In October 1914 the British Cabinet requested the Indian Government to send two brigades of infantry to Basra (each brigade contained three battalions of Indian troops plus one British battalion). Oil installations on Abadan Island were captured and Basra was occupied on 22nd November 1914 with very little effort; the Turkish troops went into a disorderly retreat.

At this point the objectives of the operation had been achieved and there was no need to continue offensive operations, however the ease with which victory had been won led senior officers and local politicians to believe that an advance up the River Tigris to Baghdad would be easy. No thought seems to have been given as to why this should be undertaken. Even if successful, little damage would have been caused to Turkey, and the risks due to the extreme heat and numerous diseases would be great. Nevertheless another brigade was sent from India, and this, together with the two brigades already in Mesopotamia formed the 6th Indian Division.

The town of Qurna was occupied at the end of 1914; by March 1915 optimism had overcome the caution that should, with hindsight, have been applied and troops were gathered under the Commander-in-Chief in Mesopotamia, General Sir John Nixon, in preparation for an advance on Baghdad. In mid-April, before setting out, they first of all had to beat off an attack on Basra. This attack was made by the Turks but supported by many Arabs who also damaged the pipeline 100 miles to the north-east as it made its way into Persia. These local difficulties with the Arabs did not dampen the enthusiasm for the forthcoming advance. The advance was to be made by Major-General Sir George Gorringe up the River

▲ Map 15. Mesopotamia

Euphrates, but the main effort was to be by Major-General Sir Charles Townshend up the Tigris towards Baghdad.

The first advances up these rivers were relatively straightforward, Townshend easily captured the town of Amara (100 miles up river from Basra) on 31st May. Meanwhile on the Euphrates, Gorringe was having more difficulty but took the town of Nasiriya by 22nd July; despite the relatively small number of casualties incurred in capturing this town, a severe strain was put on the limited medical facilities which already had their hands full coping with sunstroke and disease.

The river boats (known as 'Townshend's Regatta') that supplied the two columns were coming under ever increasing strain to keep the troops supplied the further the advances were made. Despite the obvious supply difficulties, General Nixon decided to press on; only the town of Kut lay in the way of Baghdad. Kut was taken by Townshend's troops on 28th September 1915 when he routed the Turkish defenders who lost between 3,000 and 5,000 men and all their artillery (both sides had started with about 11,000 men each). Unfortunately, due to a fall in the water level, he was unable to prevent the escape of the bulk of the Turkish force who fell back to Ctesiphon, 16 miles from Baghdad.

Nixon now pressed the British Cabinet for permission to advance on Baghdad, whose capture it was said (without any justification) would be as important as the capture of Constantinople. In order to gain the permission he sought, Nixon claimed he could take Baghdad with the troops he currently had (Townshend's force was a little over one infantry division, and he had told Nixon he required two divisions). Nixon also stated that he faced just 10,000 Turkish troops (Townshend had estimated 20,000). Finally Nixon claimed his transport difficulties had been resolved; this was untrue. The British Cabinet, needing a victory (the Suvla landings at Gallipoli had just failed and in France the Battle of Loos had not achieved the breakthrough that had been hoped for) gave permission. Nixon ordered Townshend to attack without waiting for the reinforcements that the War Office promised. Townshend's force of 14,000 men advanced against the Turks (who had been reinforced and numbered about 30,000) at Ctesiphon. These Turkish reinforcements were spotted by a British aeroplane, but before this vital information could be relayed to Townshend, the aeroplane was shot down.

Townshend's troops (the 6th Indian Division) attacked the Turkish left and, as at Kut, the Turks retreated despite being in possession of heavily fortified defences. Rather than the retreat turning into a rout, the Turks reinforced their second line and despite all attempts, this could not be taken. At the end of the first day (Monday 22nd November 1915) the British had sustained 4,500 casualties, the Turks about twice that number. Enemy counter-attacks were repulsed the next day, the Turks sustaining so many casualties in these attacks that they were forced to pull even further back to a new defensive position.

On Wednesday 24th, after assessing the situation, Townshend decided to withdraw his division back to Kut, this commenced the next day. The British and Indian troops retreated without difficulty, and reached Kut on 3rd December where, critically, Townshend decided to make a stand. There were a number of reasons for this decision; Townshend stated that his troops were exhausted (although they could have been rested as the Turks took a further three days to reach Kut in force), also the town had become a major base for the British in southern Mesopotamia. Finally, by holding this town, the Turks would be prevented from advancing further down the Tigris.

The lack of medical resources started to have an impact on the wounded British and Indian troops; Nixon had relied on Baghdad being taken, and the wounded being treated in the city. Townshend's chief medical officer described Kut as *"The most insanitary place the British had occupied in Mesopotamia."*

Townshend, despite being surrounded by the Turks failed to arrange for a proper search for food to be made, and did not take steps to reduce the troops' rations for nearly ten weeks. The Turks launched an attack at Christmas which was repulsed, thereafter the Turks were content simply to blockade the British.

Messages were sent from Townshend to Nixon indicating he could only hold out for two months. In view of this, a relieving force made up of two Indian Divisions newly arrived from France was despatched in January 1916, but before it was properly equipped. This relieving force managed to get to within twenty or thirty miles of Kut before it was defeated by the Turks.

Townshend, who had failed to make any attempt to help the relieving force by attacking the Turks, then announced he could hold out for a further three months.

British reinforcements began arriving at Basra, only to become bogged down in an organisational bottleneck. This was made worse by the rain, floods and mud that also prevented the easy launching of further attempts to reach the besieged garrison.

Meanwhile after the fighting had stopped in Gallipoli, the Turks started sending troops on the long overland journey from the Dardanelles to Mesopotamia.

A further attempt to relieve Townshend was made on 8th March, this force was defeated by the Turks when only seven miles from Kut. A final attempt under Major-General Gorringe (who had been commanding the column advancing up the Euphrates) was made in April; although it broke through the Turkish lines twenty miles south of Kut, it was unable to make any further progress mainly due to the Tigris being in a state of flood (due to the melting of snow in the mountains many miles to the north). Despite these conditions Townshend's force managed to beat off Turkish attacks but the situation was now desperate. The troops were on the edge of starvation, and although horse meat was available, many of the Indian troops refused to eat this on religious grounds. On 29th April 1916, Townshend was forced to surrender; between 8,000 and 10,000 British and Indian troops went into captivity. The men were herded across the desert, being flogged, murdered and tortured en route; disease also took its toll. Nearly two thirds of the men were to die in captivity before the end of the war. Townshend was taken to Constantinople where he was held in comfort by the Turks for the rest of the war.

Although no Ravensthorpe soldiers were killed during Townshend's campaign, at least one from the village arrived in Mesopotamia just after the surrender at Kut.

Harry Harris was born in Old Swinford, Worcestershire, in 1891 or 1892 to Joseph and Lizzie Harris; within two or three years the family moved to Ravensthorpe where Harry's younger brother (named Joseph after his father) was born.

After leaving school, Harry went to work at Oldroyd's mill in Ravensthorpe; he volunteered for the army in July 1915, joining the Miners' Battalion*, which was then being recruited by the West Riding Coal Owners' Association. For some

As described in Chapter 2, this became the 12th Battalion, K.O.Y.L.I.

reason, however, Harry did not stay in this unit for long; although he was not one of the last recruits to the battalion (his original regimental number is lower than other - later arrivals - who remained with the battalion) he was transferred to the East Lancashire Regiment. It is likely that he was part of a large draft that was transferred between the 12th K.O.Y.L.I. and the East Lancashires.

Originally joining the 3rd Battalion of the regiment (which was just a holding unit) he was transferred to the 6th East Lancashires, probably in May 1916 (some months earlier in December 1915 Harry married Miss Jane Abbott of Batley).

In June 1915 (just before Harry had joined the K.O.Y.L.I.) the 6th East Lancashires had been sent to Gallipoli as part of the 13th (Western) Division; after the evacuation of the peninsular the division was sent via Egypt to Mesopotamia where they took part in the April attempt at relieving the Kut garrison. The relieving force suffered 23,000 casualties in its abortive attempt to get through. Although Harry was sent as a reinforcement in May 1916, it is unclear when he actually arrived in Mesopotamia, the evidence points to him being with a draft of one officer and 94 other ranks who arrived on 4th July 1916.

After Harry's arrival, there was little activity, the major enemy being the almost unbelievable heat. The 6th East Lancashire's War Diary states the conditions in May were 'improving', with the water supply being complimented as 'efficient'. In late June the diary describes the battalion carrying out routine guard and convoy escorting duties in temperatures of 115°F (46°C) which, towards the end of July had increased to an incredible 125°F (52°C).

The battalion's casualties (according to S.D.G.W.) indicate that the deaths due to heat and disease were almost as great as the daily toll of a battalion on the Western Front. In June ten men died, but in July this rose to 26 (none of the deaths being due to enemy action). It can only be speculated as to the cause of these deaths, some would probably be as a direct result of the heat, but water-borne diseases such as enteric fever (typhoid), dysentery and cholera were prevalent. These diseases were attributable to the Rivers Euphrates and Tigris being, in effect, open sewers from Baghdad and every town that lay on their banks.

Unfortunately one of these monthly statistics included the death of Private Harry Harris from Ravensthorpe who died on 20th July 1916 aged 24. His last letter home was reproduced in the Dewsbury News:-

"Just a line to let you know that I and my pals are living comfortably in the land of the dust. I have done nothing else but guard so far, and was only with my battalion four days after landing, being one of 25 chosen to do guard duty for the East Herts Yeomanry [sic: Hertfordshire Yeomanry - 'C' Squadron of the Regiment being attached to the 13th (Western) Division from early July 1916]. *We don't get to know anything going on out here, but we manage to get a bit of news regarding France, though its nothing at all. I don't know how Fred or Joe* are going on but I hope they get a cooler climate to do their fighting in. When we had left the ship and were marching up to camp, many were overcome and fell through heat."*

Harry is buried in Basra War Cemetery in Iraq, the cemetery contains over 2,500 war graves. For understandable reasons the current state of repair of the cemetery is not known.

**** Joe was Harry's younger brother and, unknown to Harry, had been wounded a few days before the letter was written on the opening day of the Battle of the Somme - see Chapter 7. Presumably Fred was another brother, but it has not been possible to trace him.***

Towards the end of the siege at Kut, General Sir John Nixon resigned his command of the Mesopotamian forces due to health problems, he was replaced in August by Sir Stanley Maude, a relatively junior Major-General who had previously commanded the 13th Division. Under Maude, the British troops were gradually reinforced at Basra for the remainder of 1916. On 13th December 1916 Maude, with 50,000 men under his command, started to advance up the Tigris; progress was slow but steady. The Turks, heavily outnumbered, were defeated at Kut on 24th February 1917. Like the earlier campaign, the advance was centred on the River Tigris, the British using naval gunboats which pursued the retreating Turks. Many Turkish troops were 'captured' by these gunboats, being observed from the decks of the boats, standing on the river banks with their hands held up in surrender. It is not recorded how the gunboats dealt with their 'prisoners'.

A successful manoeuvre on 5th March at the Diyala River, ten miles south of Baghdad, by part of the advancing troops caused the Turks to evacuate the area. Baghdad was occupied without opposition on 11th March 1917, Maude being promoted to Lieutenant-General. A pause of six months then ensued, in order to wait for cooler weather in September.

The Turkish garrison at Ramadi, sixty miles north-west of Baghdad was attacked and surrendered at the end of September, further actions were fought at Daur and Tikrit on 1st to 4th November. Later in November, Sir Stanley was guest of honour at an event organised by the Jewish School in Baghdad. Coffee was handed out, but only Sir Stanley took any milk with the coffee; the following morning he was struck down by cholera and died shortly afterwards*.

ONE KILLED; ANOTHER DIES IN MESOPOTAMIA.

Mrs. Abbott and her family, of Baines Street, Dark Lane, Batley, have suffered heavily through the war. In November a son, Pte. Willie Abbott, who was in the Territorials, was killed by a German sniper, and now Mrs. Abbott's daughter has received news that her husband, Pte. Harry Harris, has died from the effects of the heat in Mesopotamia. Deep sympathy will be felt by all local people with the relatives of these two soldiers who have given their lives in the service of King and country.

Pte. H. Harris, East Lancs., Ravensthorpe and Batley (died from illness).

The news regarding Pte. Harris is official, and it states that he died on July 20th. A very sad circumstance is that he and his wife were only married in December. The late soldier is the eldest son of Mrs. Harris, of Ravens Street, Ravensthorpe. He enlisted in the K.O.Y.L.I. in July, 1915, but later was transferred into the East Lancashire Regiment. His brother, Pte. Joseph Harris, of the Yorkshire Regiment, has been wounded in the recent heavy fighting, as previously reported in our columns. Pte. Harris, before joining the Army, worked for Messrs. R. Swire and Sons, of Ravensthorpe. He was 24 years of age, and formerly played with the Ravensthorpe Albion football team.

◂ 77. Harry Harris

** Sir Stanley Maude died on 18th November 1917. He was the only Commander-in-Chief of British forces in any of the theatres of war to die whilst carrying out his duties in the Great War. He is buried in Baghdad (North Gate) War Cemetery.*

* * *

Only a little information exists about the second Ravensthorpe soldier who died in Mesopotamia. Joseph Laycock was born in Batley on 18th September 1894 and as a boy attended the Wesleyan Sunday School. He volunteered aged 19 in August 1914, leaving his job at G. & J. Stubleys in Batley, joining the K.O.Y.L.I. and being posted to the 6th Battalion. Joe arrived in France in May 1915 with his battalion as part of the 14th (Light) Division. He was seriously wounded at Hooge, near Ypres, in early August 1915; one of his letters describes the German's use of liquid fire, which was used by them at Hooge on 30th July 1915 (see Chapter 7).

After recovering from his wounds in England, Joseph was more than likely reclassified as being not fit for active service in France, but would however have been passed fit for garrison duty overseas, and was therefore sent to India in September 1916, probably as part of the 1st (Garrison) Battalion East Yorkshire Regiment*. In September 1917 Joseph was sent to Mesopotamia, joining the 2nd (Garrison) Battalion, Northumberland Fusiliers.

In mid-September 1918, his parents, Richard and Elizabeth Laycock received a letter from Joseph at their home in Eastfield Road, Northorpe, saying that he had never been in better health. Shortly after writing this he fell ill whilst in Baghdad and was, according to the Dewsbury Reporter, transferred to Basra where he died on 15th September 1918. It is not clear, however, if he was actually transferred to Basra as the Commonwealth War Graves Commission's records show him being buried in Baghdad (North Gate) War Cemetery. It is possible that he was due to be transferred to Basra, but died before starting the journey. The cemetery contains nearly 6,000 burials, and like the cemetery at Basra its current state of repair is not known.

Joseph Laycock was one of the many thousands of men who fell victim to disease whilst serving in this most inhospitable of climates. He died just three days short of his 24th birthday.

* * *

Towards the end of 1918, and despite the imminent surrender of Turkey, it was decided to continue the campaign in order to eliminate all Turkish influence from the area. Sir Stanley Maude's successor, Sir William Marshall, resumed the attacks against the Turks, moving onto the Mosul oilfields.

Leaving Baghdad on 23rd October 1918, the Anglo-Indian force reached the Little Zab River, 77 miles north of Baghdad in less than two days. The surprised Turkish troops fell back to Sharqat, sixty miles away, where after a day's fighting the disillusioned Turks surrendered, bringing an end to the campaign in Mesopotamia.

** This was not a regular battalion; as its 'Garrison' designation suggests, it was made up of soldiers not fit enough for active service but who could be sent to parts of the Empire in order to ensure there were no uprisings. They were effectively undertaking the type of Empire policing operation that the Regular Army did before 1914.*

◂ 78. Joseph Laycock.

▾ 79. Baghdad (North Gate) War Cemetery. *Photograph courtesy of the Commonwealth War Graves Commission.*

Chapter Twelve

The Battle of Arras

As described in Chapter 10, the German withdrawal to the Hindenburg Line in March 1917 came as a surprise to the Allies* and effectively ruined the Allied plans for the year; these plans had been formulated by a new French Commander-in-Chief and agreed by a new British Prime Minister.

On 12th December 1916 the French had replaced 'Papa' Joffre as Commander-in-Chief with the eloquent and flamboyant Robert Nivelle. Nivelle (whose mother was English) had attacked the Germans superbly at Verdun and done much to regain French pride. He persuaded not only the French Government that he had found the key to breaking the deadlock of trench warfare, but also, using his near-perfect English, managed to bring David Lloyd George, the new British Prime Minister round to his point of view.

Lloyd George who succeeded Asquith as Prime Minister of the Coalition Government on 7th December 1916 had, until this point, been firmly of the opinion that the best way of bringing about Germany's downfall was to attack her allies such as Turkey in the east, and then advance through the Balkans. This strategy, he believed, would be much less costly than frontal attacks against the seemingly impregnable trenches on the Western Front. It is likely that Lloyd George was hedging his bets; if Nivelle succeeded he would share in the credit for backing Nivelle's new tactics, but if he failed it would strengthen his case for moving the emphasis of Britain's war effort to other theatres.

The new Prime Minister had a very low opinion of the British generals and aimed to curb the power of Haig (whose promotion to Field-Marshal became effective on 1st January 1917) and the C.I.G.S., General 'Wully' Robertson (who was the military advisor to the Cabinet and the link between Downing Street and G.H.Q. in France). He therefore used a conference at Calais on the 26th and 27th February 1917, which was ostensibly organised to discuss improvements to the French railway system in order to improve supplies to the B.E.F., to try and place the B.E.F. under the control of the French army. Not surprisingly Haig and Robertson were furious+ and pressure from the Cabinet enabled the proposal to be amended so that Haig was only to be subordinate to Nivelle for the period of the forthcoming offensive. In addition Haig's own idea for an attack in Belgian Flanders was forced to be postponed.

** The Germans were in the habit of making unexpected moves in the early part of each year - in April 1915 they launched the gas attack at Ypres; in February 1916 they had attacked at Verdun thus dislocating the Allied Somme offensive; the withdrawal of March 1917 had been totally unexpected, and as will be described later, March 1918 was the turning point of the war.*

+ Even so many years on from these events it seems astounding that a politician should consider putting almost the entire British army under the control of a foreign Commander-in-Chief whose line of responsibility lay solely to his own Government.

Nivelle's plan was for his own armies, strengthened by the B.E.F. taking over yet more of the front line, to attack on the Aisne behind an extremely violent artillery bombardment. The infantry would follow up and a breakthrough achieved within forty-eight hours. Nivelle required the B.E.F. to take part in a diversionary battle around the town of Arras, where British troops had been holding the front line since March 1916 when they had relieved the French Tenth Army.

The British assault was planned by General Sir Edmund Allenby whose Third Army was to attack along with General Horne's First Army on the left and General Gough's Fifth Army on the right*.

The plan was upset however by the German withdrawal to the Hindenburg Line. Although this withdrawal was mainly in the sectors of the Fourth and Fifth Armies, some ground was given up by the Germans on the right of Allenby's Third Army. The plan had therefore to be amended to incorporate an attack on part of the deep defences of the Hindenburg Line; the assault was scheduled for 8th April, although it was put back by twenty-four hours (at the request of Nivelle) to 9th April, Easter Monday.

Nivelle's plans meanwhile had also been spoilt by the German's withdrawal. Instead of adapting his plans, Nivelle refused to believe that the Germans had fallen back to a new line and at first insisted there should be no change to the plan. This would have resulted in his armies in the north attacking into a void. He eventually realised that the Germans had, in fact, retreated and ordered his left wing to follow up the German withdrawal, however this order came too late and the Germans fell back without French interference.

Worse was soon to follow; the Germans launched a raid on some French trenches on 4th April and one of the prisoners they brought back was found to have in his possession orders detailing the forthcoming French offensive which was due to start on 16th April. The Germans therefore discovered the exact timings and frontage that was to be assaulted by the French and made arrangements to meet the attack.

On 6th April, as a result of the German policy of unrestricted submarine warfare, the U.S.A. declared war on Germany. It would however take many months for the Americans to make their presence felt on the Western Front.

After a five day preparatory bombardment, the British troops went over the top on 9th April at 5.30am. The Third Army, in the centre, attacked on a frontage of just less than ten miles, from Bullecourt in the south to Roclincourt in the north. A total of ten divisions (plus two in reserve) made the assault. To the left of the Third Army, protecting the northern flank, was the Canadian Corps of Horne's First Army. The Canadian Corps, consisting of four infantry divisions, was commanded by Lieutenant-General Sir Julian Byng. The Canadian's task, together with the British 24th Division, was the capture of the vitally important Vimy Ridge. Unsuccessfully attacked by the French in 1915, the ridge rose gradually in front of the British trenches, however at its crest it fell away, plunging dramatically two hundred feet onto the Douai plain. From the east (the German perspective) it appeared as a mighty cliff, dominating the land for miles around.

**** Allenby had taken over command of the Third Army when Monro was sent to Gallipoli (see Chapter 3). Sir Henry Horne was promoted to command the First Army in the autumn of 1916 when Monro was once again despatched from the Western Front, this time being sent to India. (Horne had commanded XV Corps on the Somme in 1916 and had previously, in 1915, been G.O.C. 2nd Division.)***

It is with the Canadian Corps that Ravensthorpe's interest lies on Easter Monday 1917, the opening day of the Battle of Arras, which is officially known as The First Battle of the Scarpe.

* * *

Herbert Nicholls was born in Belfast on 24th March 1897 to George and Emma Nicholls. It is not clear when he emigrated to Canada, or even whether he or his family went straight to Canada or via England. All that is known is that on Wednesday 15th December 1915, Herbert walked into a recruiting office in Toronto and enlisted. His attestation papers, which are available in Canada, indicate that he was 5' 9" tall and he had a scar on his right shin and scald marks on his right shoulder. He gave his address as 62 Muriel Avenue, Toronto and his next of kin as his sister, Mrs Emma Barber of 16 Endean Avenue, Toronto.

Other details from his attestation papers indicate Herbert had brown hair, blue eyes and declared himself to be a member of the Church of England. He stated his occupation as a farmer and upon being examined was passed fit for the Canadian Overseas Expeditionary Force ('C.E.F.') and was posted to the 123rd Battalion, aged 18 years and nine months. Herbert was by no means alone in the C.E.F. in being born in the United Kingdom; as at 15th February 1916 the Canadian Corps was comprised of just 30% of native born Canadians, with 62% of its strength coming from soldiers born in the U.K. A further 8% were classified as 'other', many being U.S. citizens.

After undergoing training for the next eight months, Herbert embarked for England at Halifax, Nova Scotia on the S.S. Cameronia on 8th August 1916, arriving in Liverpool ten days later. A further period of training ensued in England until, on 5 December 1916, nearly a year after volunteering, he was sent to the Western Front, transferring to the 60th (Victoria Rifles of Canada) Battalion C.E.F. which was part of the 3rd Canadian Division; this division was made up of 7, 8 and 9 Brigades, the 60th Battalion being in 9 Brigade.

After just four months in France, Herbert's battalion took part in the attack on Vimy Ridge, but fortunately for Herbert and the rest of his battalion they were not in the first waves of the attack, instead they were in support, moving into the old front line trenches at 11.15am. The battalion's headquarters were located in the Goodman Tunnel, which was one of a series of tunnels dug to assist the Canadian attack, these enabled the troops to be discharged rapidly and safely into the front line trenches from where they launched their attack.

On 10th April the battalion was still in the old front line, being in support of 8 Brigade (this brigade was made up of battalions of Canadian Mounted Rifles - cavalry who had been converted into the infantry role). The 60th Battalion took over the front line trenches 'freshly dug on Vimy Ridge' the next day, the War Diary describing the trenches as being 'in a terrible condition'. Patrols were sent out on 12th April to reconnoitre the trench system west of the village of Vimy, and on 13th April a patrol entered Petit Vimy. Casualties during this period being seven other ranks killed and one officer and sixty other ranks wounded.

By the end of the month the battalion was back in the old front line, providing working parties in the Grange Tunnel area; however there was a shock in store for the men. For several months the battalion had been hearing rumours that it was to be disbanded (as recently as March they had been told they were not to be broken up *"at least for the present"*) however on 29th April the commanding officer, Lieutenant-Colonel F.A. Gascoigne gathered the battalion together to tell them they were to be disbanded.

The battalion's War Diary recorded the feelings of Lieutenant-Colonel Gascoigne: *"Disbanding a force of 828 fighting men (all ranks), well trained with a perfect organisation for political reasons seems most unjust and shows little feeling or respect for officers, N.C.O.s and men who have been in the trenches for fourteen months and those who have made the supreme sacrifice with their lives and who rest in named and un-named graves throughout France and Belgium. If tried and efficient battalions are broken up like this in the midst of a great war and on the very battlefields, it will surely be more discouraging than encouraging to further recruitment in Canada."*

The War Diary then went on to give the text of his address to the battalion:

"....[The] *Provinces of Quebec and British Columbia were too ambitious and put into the field a greater proportion of battalions than they were entitled to and more than they could support with reinforcements.* [Other] *provinces then demanded representation in the field on the basis of recruiting and the Canadian authorities selected the 60th and 73rd Battalions as the two Province of Quebec battalions to be withdrawn, to make room for Ontario's Battalion and one from Nova Scotia. There is no reason why the 60th should have been selected except it is junior to four purely mounted battalions to be sent to France and Montreal was not providing its quota of reinforcements....."*

A letter was read out from Sir Julian Byng and the battalion moved off. Eleven officers, 'C' Company, the band and one-third of the specialists went to the 5th Canadian Mounted Rifles, whilst twenty officers, two-thirds of the specialists, and 'A', 'B' and 'D' Companies (together with Herbert) went to the 87th (Canadian Grenadier Guards) Battalion who were part of 11 Brigade, 4th Canadian Division.

* * *

It will be remembered how the seventeen year old Ewart Doodson had taken part in the first tank assault ever made on 15th September 1916. In the analysis of this first experiment, the High Command decided that the tanks had been a success, but that many more than the 49 that had been available would be needed for any impact to be made on the war. By April 1917 some new tanks had arrived but due to production difficulties, in the six months since their first use the number of tanks had only risen to sixty. For the Battle of Arras, of these 60 tanks, just eight were allocated to the Canadian Corps, all of these being given to the 2nd Canadian Division. These eight tanks were from 12 Company, 'D' Battalion*. Once again Ewart Doodson was destined to be in the thick of the fighting. The eight tanks of

**** A reorganisation had resulted in 'D' Company becoming 'D' Battalion; three Companies (10, 11 and 12) forming the battalion.***

12 Company moved to Mont St. Eloi at the end of March and from there moved forward on the night of 7th/8th April to a sunken road called Elbe Trench, north of the village of Neuville St.Vaast. At 5.30am on 9th April - zero hour - four of the tanks moved forward with Canadian troops (6 Brigade, 2nd Canadian Division) and four with 13 Brigade (a British brigade which was on loan from the 5th Division.)

Due to the speed of the assault, the tanks were left far behind by the infantry, whose advance captured the German trenches and a position known as Hill 135 at relatively low cost. The terrain after the bombardment proved to be too difficult for the tanks and it was not until 7.15am that they managed to reach the German front line. The War Diary of 'D' Battalion describes how *"...the ground proved utterly impossible for tanks, all tank commanders got out and led their tanks on foot, but despite this precaution all tanks became ditched between the German second and third line. There they remained until dug out by their crews on succeeding days."* Four of the tanks had become stuck in a sunken track called Blenpense Ditch, the others in trenches.

Unfortunately Ewart was not one of the soldiers who was to return to dig the tanks out. Despite not engaging German troops there were some casualties to 'D' Battalion, the War Diary stating two officers and eight other ranks being killed with nearly forty men wounded. Ewart was one of those who lost their lives.

A letter was published in the Dewsbury Reporter on 27th April from one of Ewart's comrades. The letter, from James Anderson, was dated 18th April and describes how three of the crew of the tank had *"...got outside to make a necessary adjustment and were working together when a shell dropped a yard behind us. Ewart and the sergeant were immediately unconscious. The sergeant died in a few minutes and Ewart lived for about half an hour but never regained consciousness and had no pain whatever....The wound was in his skull. I was with him till the end with his head on my knee. Every possible aid was given....I have his wristlet watch and some of his private things and will send them...."*

Neither Ewart Doodson nor the sergeant who was probably Charles McNamee have a known grave and both are commemorated on the Arras Memorial to the Missing. The Memorial stands in front of the Faubourg d'Amiens British Cemetery and commemorates some 36,000 men who fell in the Arras area between 1916 and 1918 and who have no known grave; the majority of the names are from the 1917 Battle of Arras.

*   *   *

After the assault on Vimy Ridge on 9th April when their front was overrun, the Germans realised that it would be impossible to retake the ridge and did not mount any counter-attack (mainly because the local commander had mistakenly placed his reserves too far back). Further south, the opening day's attack was also successful even against the Hindenburg Line trenches, although the penetrations were not as deep as to the north where advances of up to 3½ miles were achieved.

On 10th April, Haig together with Allenby and Horne, issued orders for the continuation of the offensive. Their plans were foiled partly by the weather (snow

RAVENSTHORPE "TANK" MAN.

KILLED BY A SHELL.

"WOULD HAVE GIVEN MY LIFE."

Gnr. Ewart Doodson, Heavy Section, Machine-Gun Corps (adopted son of Mr. and Mrs. T. Wood, 453, Huddersfield Road, Ravensthorpe), one of the first crews of the armoured cars known as the "Tanks," has been killed by a shell. The following letter describing the sad occurrence has been received from his friend, who hails from John O'Groats:—" B.E.F., 18th April, 1917.—Dear Mr. Wood,—It is with a heavy heart that I am writing this letter to you to-day. I will not postpone the subject of it, because I know you are strong enough to bear such news which it is my duty to convey to you. We are once more in action, and Ewart has passed away at his post. He was struck by a piece of shell, and died shortly afterwards without the slightest pain. I was in the same crew as he, and was beside him at the time, being by his side when he fell. I have been his most intimate friend ever since he joined the Army, and the shock has been terrible to me; his friendship was such as I have never known before. I have lost my best friend in the world. It is part of my duty to tell you exactly how it happened, but it is very difficult for me to make myself lucid, and I must ask you to pardon the disjointed state of this letter. Three of us—the sergeant, Ewart, and myself—had got outside to make a necessary adjustment, and were working together when a shell dropped about a yard behind us. Ewart and the ser-

Gunner E Doodson (of the Tanks), Ravensthorpe, (Killed).

◂ 80. Ewart Doodson

▾ 81. The Arras Memorial to the Missing which stands on one side of the Faubourg d'Amiens British Cemetery.

began to fall heavily) and partly by the prompt arrival of German reserves. The result was, as often happened, a fleeting opportunity of a breakthrough being snatched away. The German defenders recovered and the battle over the next few days and weeks degenerated into one of attrition, culminating in another set-piece battle on 23rd April. This attack (on 23rd/24th April) was, after the war, to be named the Second Battle of the Scarpe.

There were a number of reasons for the battle being continued (Haig, it will be remembered, had his eyes on an offensive in Belgium and only reluctantly took part in the Arras offensive): Firstly, the French had suffered a major defeat when their attack was launched on 16th April. Despite Nivelle's reassurance of victory within forty-eight hours, backed up by a promise to discontinue the offensive if a breakthrough was not achieved within that timescale, he continued sending his troops forward who were slaughtered in their thousands on the Chemin des Dames ridge. Nivelle was discredited in the eyes of the French Government and was removed as Commander-in-Chief on 15th May. Secondly, and to make matters worse, the French army began to mutiny, the first signs of this becoming apparent on 17th April.

Over the course of the following weeks the mutiny spread throughout the French army. Although prepared to defend their trenches, there was widespread refusal by the French soldiers to go over the top. Haig was not initially informed of the mutiny although he did become aware that something was amiss.

With the French effectively out of the war for the moment and with the Americans still many months away from arriving in force, Haig was forced to continue the battle in order to prevent the Germans going all out to attack the French and delivering a knock-out blow against them. It is against this background that the next two men from Ravensthorpe were to lose their lives, both on 25th April.

Ralph Crawshaw was born in Ravensthorpe to Harry and Jane Crawshaw in November 1884. He was educated at Ravensthorpe St. Saviour's Boys' School and attended Ravensthorpe Congregational Church, being a member of the church cricket team. Ralph married Mary Ellen Fearnley at St. Mary's Parish Church, Mirfield on 14th May 1910, and lived with his wife at Spring Place Cottages, Dark Lane, Northorpe. He worked as a case maker for Newsome Brothers who were piano manufacturers in Ravensthorpe, and was a member of the Northorpe and Ravensthorpe Conservative Club and Mirfield Parish Cricket Club.

Ralph attested on 9th December 1915, and was sent home until September the following year. On 2nd September 1916 he was called up, joining the Duke of Wellington's Regiment. There seems to have been some doubts as to his medical condition as he received two medical examinations, the first on 21st September, and a second on 29th December. These reports tell us that Ralph was 5' 5½" tall, with a 40½" chest (when expanded). After basic training at Tynemouth he was posted to France on 9th January 1917, arriving at the 34th Infantry Base Depot the following day. He was to stay at this depot, no doubt receiving further training, for over a month until, on 23rd February he joined the 9th Battalion, Duke of Wellington's Regiment (part of 52 Brigade, 17th (Northern) Division).

Ralph's battalion did not take part in the opening day of the Battle of Arras, as the 17th (Northern) Division was in reserve on that day. In late April the 9th Duke of Wellington's were in billets in the centre of Arras near the Grand Place. Following an inspection by their commanding officer, Lieutenant-Colonel French,

◀ 82. Ralph Crawshaw was aged 32, not 33 as indicated on this photograph.

on 21st April the battalion was warned to be prepared to proceed to the trenches. The order came on 23rd April and the battalion marched towards the support trenches at Orange Hill. After moving through Monchy and Monchy Wood on 24th April, the battalion arrived at Orange Hill. At 8.30pm orders were received to move forward to a sunken road near Monchy in order to make an attack on Rifle Trench, which lay just outside Monchy.

The battalion attacked at 3.20am on Wednesday 25th April. Riflemen and bombers led the assault with Lewis gunners and rifle bombers following. The War Diary describes how, despite German fire "*....the advance still went on steadily until about 100 yards from the enemy trench when whistles were blown and the machine gun and rifle fire grew even worse and our men were forced to retire back to our trench where they were reorganised and sent over again, but met with the same reception. Again, for the third time, they went over but had to retire. Then two platoons of 'C' Company, our reserve, went out to strengthen them and they went over for the fourth time but failed to reach the trench except for on the right of the line where they found the opposition was not so heavy. Sixteen men got in at this point and held the trench all day by throwing out bombing stops* [barricades in the

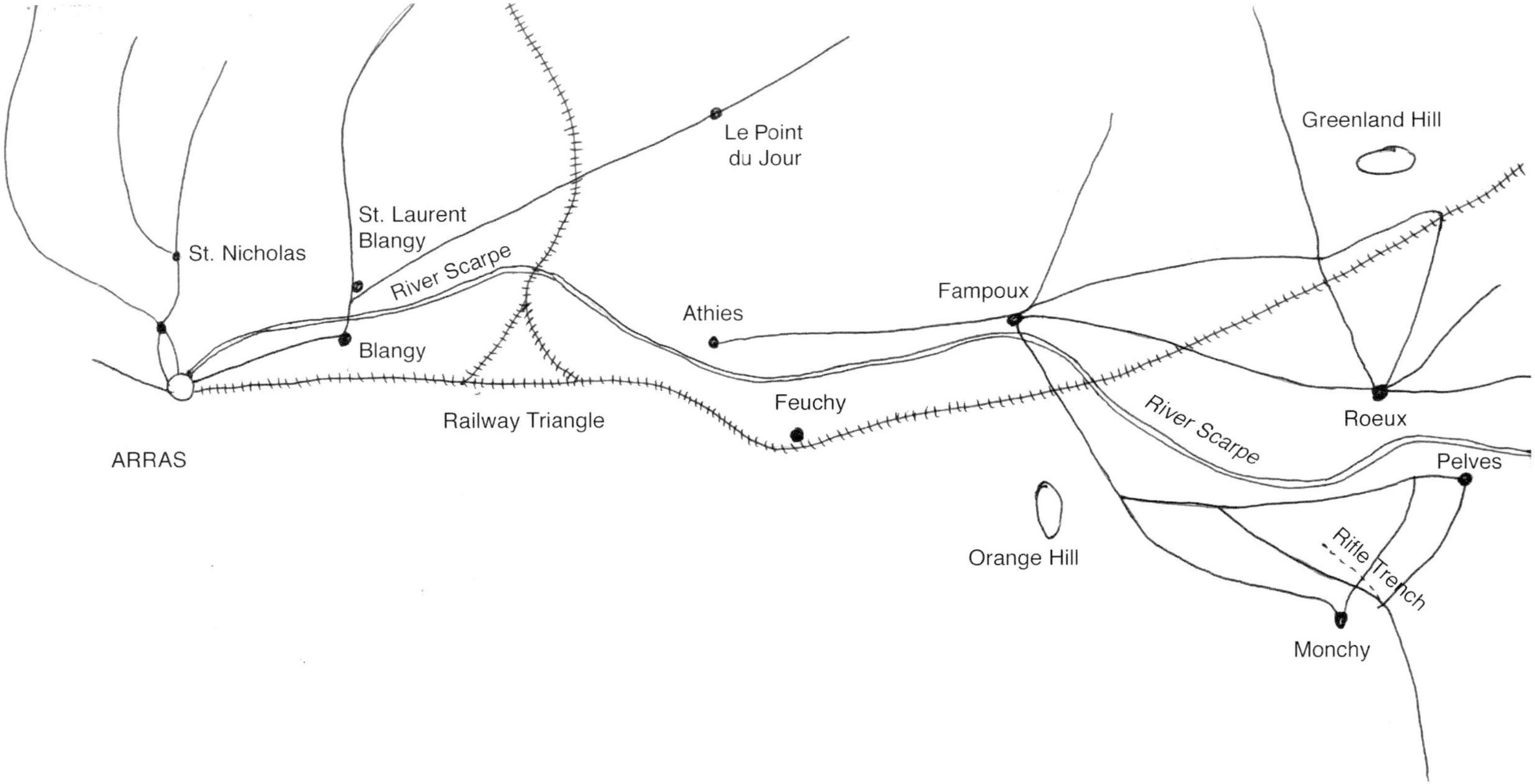

▲ Map 16. Arras/Monchy including Rifle Trench

trenches to stop enemy soldiers throwing hand grenades ('bombs') at the British troops]. *They had to retire at night....*"

The battalion's casualties during the day, according to the War Diary, were over two hundred men killed, missing and wounded.

The battalion was relieved that night and returned to Arras, however Ralph Crawshaw was not one of those who marched back to Arras, he was one of the 75 men (plus one officer) who, according to S.D.G.W., were killed on 25th April (nine more men were to die of their wounds over the next two days). Ralph has no known grave and is commemorated on the Arras Memorial to the Missing.

To the north of Monchy, on the opposite side of the River Scarpe are the villages of Fampoux and Roeux. Fampoux had been captured on 9th April however Roeux, to the east of Fampoux, with its fortified dye factory, known as the Chemical Works, had not fallen (the factory, which was to be the scene of some bitter fighting, was not to be captured until 11th May). The Chemical Works straddled the Arras-Douai railway line, to the south of which was Roeux village itself.

The 51st (Highland) Division attacked the Chemical Works on 23rd April; to the left of the railway line was 153 Brigade, this brigade secured positions to the north of the Chemical Works and up to the edge of Greenland Hill, including Clover Trench. (Clover Trench was the main road from Roeux to the village of Gavrelle to the north.) In the mean time 154 Brigade attacked south of the railway line. Both the Chemical Works and the village were taken by the Highlanders, but due to the strength of the defences (tunnels between the village and the Chemical Works enabled the Germans to reinforce their positions) and counter-attacks, the Highlanders were forced out. The only success was to the north of the railway line; reinforcements were urgently requested, and these arrived in the form of two battalions from the 34th Division - the 26th and 27th Battalions, Northumberland Fusiliers; the 27th Battalion contained a soldier from Ravensthorpe.

After arriving at Arras on 22nd April, the 34th Division was ordered to move up in support of the 51st (Highland) Division's attack on the Chemical Works on 23rd April, 103 Brigade of 34th Division coming under the orders of the G.O.C. 51st Division. At 11.40pm the 27th Battalion, Northumberland Fusiliers was ordered to go into the trenches north of Fampoux where they came under the orders of 153 Brigade, and they were instructed to relieve battalions on the left of 153 Brigade's front. The intention had been for the two battalions of Northumberland Fusiliers to support 153 Brigade in an attempt to recapture the Chemical Works, but by 8pm with the two Northumberland Fusiliers battalions not having arrived, the attack was launched by the 6th Seaforth Highlanders without their support.

The attack was beaten off by the Germans, and all the Seaforth Highlanders could do was dig a new trench to the north of the railway. It was into this area that the 27th Northumberland Fusiliers moved. Two companies of the battalion were ordered into Cadiz Trench, but another two companies went into a most exposed position running from Clover Trench down to the railway cutting east of the Chemical Works (north of the railway line); these positions were occupied by the 27th Northumberland Fusiliers from 25th to 27th April.

With the Chemical Works now surrounded on three sides and with the only communication by the Germans into the Chemical Works being via the tunnels, the Germans would have been keen to bombard the troops holding the newly taken trenches. These trenches were held under extremely difficult circumstances and continuous bombardment (the War Diary of the 27th Northumberland Fusiliers describes the situation - with considerable understatement - as 'obscure').

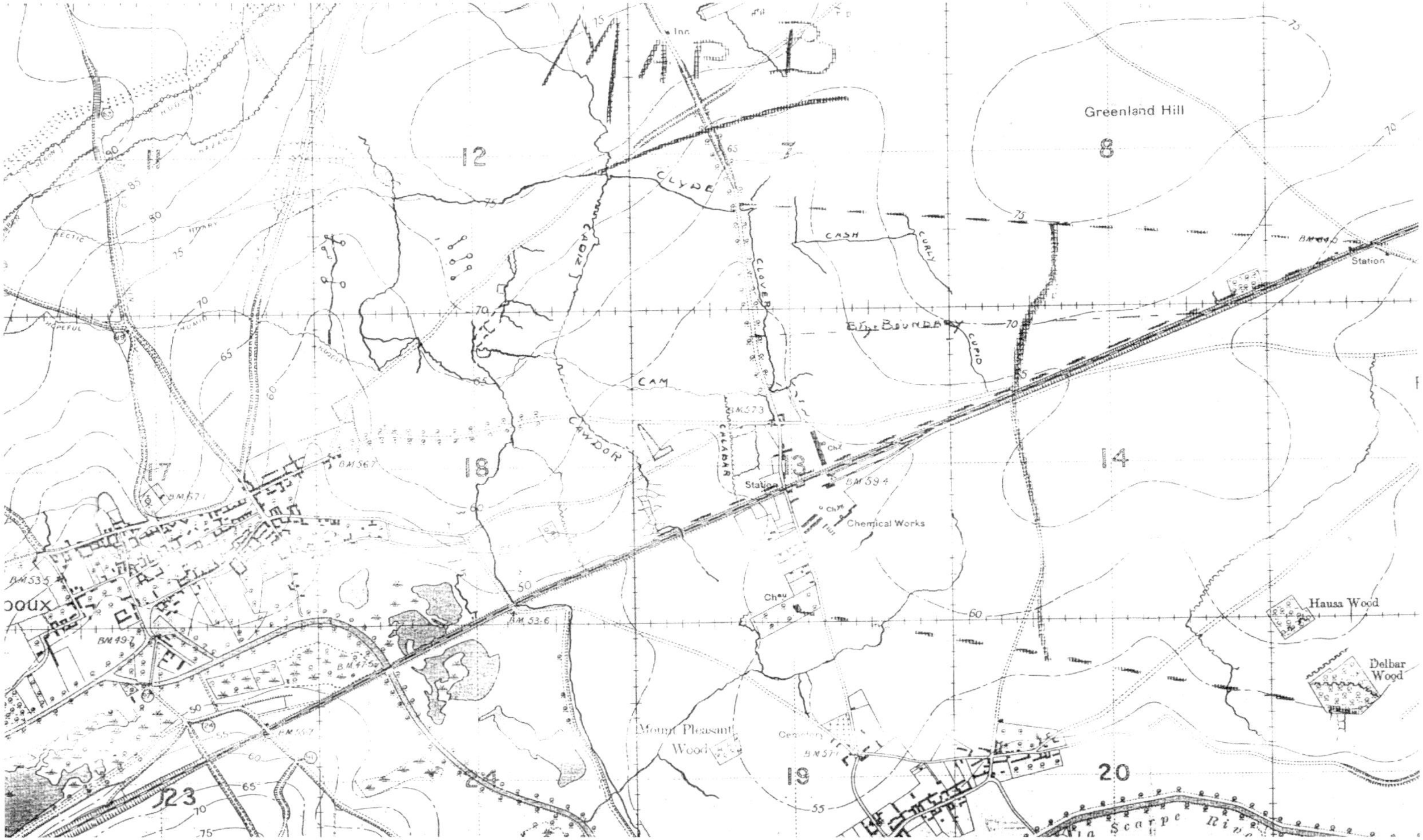

▲ Map 17. Trench Map of Roeux. *Courtesy of the Public Record Office.* Reference WO 95/2464.

◂ 83. Taken prior to his transfer to the Northumberland Fusiliers, Willie Cawthorne wearing a hat with a West Yorkshire Regiment badge.

▾ 84. Queen Street, Ravensthorpe.
Photograph courtesy of Kirklees Community History Service

After being relieved on 27th April the 27th Northumberland Fusilier's War Diary gave the battalion's casualties for the period 24th to 27th April as one officer and 74 men killed plus two officers and 157 men wounded (S.D.G.W. states one officer and 28 men killed).

One of these casualties was William Cawthorne. Willie, as he was known, was born on 24th April 1896; his early life was spent in Thornhill Lees where he lived with his family, attending the Holy Innocents' Church School. The family moved down the road to Ravensthorpe in about 1912 (it is likely his father died sometime before the outbreak of the war). Willie worked as a piecer (repairer of broken threads on a loom) for G.H. Hirst & Co. in Ravensthorpe until joining the 16th Battalion, West Yorkshire Regiment (1st Bradford Pals). He was declared unfit to serve abroad so underwent an operation to enable him to be passed fit. It is likely that following this operation he was transferred to the Northumberland Fusiliers, and was sent to France at the end of July 1916, joining the 27th Battalion. The 27th Battalion was a 'pals' battalion known as the 4th Tyneside Irish who had suffered massive losses on the opening day of the Battle of the Somme and needed many reinforcements to bring it back up to strength - in the process of which the battalion would have lost much of its local character.

It was not until early June that Willie's mother received word at 66 Queen Street that he was missing. At the beginning of July she received another letter stating that Willie had been killed in action on 25th April, the day after his 21st birthday. Private Willie Cawthorne has no known grave and is commemorated on the Memorial to the Missing at Arras, along with many of the battalion's other casualties. Just three of the thirteen men from the 27th Northumberland Fusiliers who died on 25th April have known graves, being buried in Brown's Copse Cemetery.

*　*　*

Since the advance from Beaumont-Hamel at the end of February (following the retreat of the Germans to the Hindenburg Line) the 62nd (West Riding) Division had remained in the Achiet-le-Grand and Achiet-le-Petit area north of Bapaume, where they were employed in repairing roads and other damage caused by the Germans (this was made necessary as a result of the deliberate 'scorched earth' policy of the Germans during their withdrawal). The division took over the line in front of the village of Bullecourt on the night of 4th/5th April. Bullecourt (which was in German hands and part of the Hindenburg Line defences) formed a salient which jutted towards the British lines. It was defended on its three sides by strong trenches which lay on the west, south and east of the village. The trenches were protected by three belts of barbed wire, each ten to fifteen yards wide. Machine gun emplacements also formed part of the village's defences, these had excellent fields of fire.

In order to support the assault to the north (which commenced on 9th April), an attack was organised by General Gough's Fifth Army which was positioned at the southern end of the Arras front. The initial attack by the 62nd Division (which was adjacent to the extreme right of the Third Army front) and the 4th Australian Division on their right was originally planned for 9th April, however this was cancelled and was instead scheduled to commence at 4.30 am on 10th April.

In accordance with the plan for this 10th April attack, strong patrols were pushed out by the 2/7th and 2/8th Battalions, West Yorkshire Regiment. These patrols could not see any sign of the tanks which were supposed to be joining in the attack, nor was there any movement from the Australians. Due to heavy machine gun fire the patrols were withdrawn, only to find that because of the non-arrival of the tanks, the attack had been cancelled; notice of the cancellation had only been received after the patrols had set out.

Undeterred by the failed attack, Gough ordered another attempt the following day and in the early hours of 11th April, this time supported by tanks, the Australians attacked Bullecourt. Although they managed to penetrate the barbed wire and enter Bullecourt the Germans counter-attacked, their artillery cutting off the escape route. Many prisoners were taken by the Germans. Bitterly disappointed, the Australians blamed the tanks and the 62nd (West Riding) Division for failing to help. The 62nd Division's 2/6th and 2/8th West Yorkshires had only been intended to support the attack (due to their losses in the failed assault of the previous day, the 2/7th West Yorkshires did not take part in this second attack), and once again the tanks failed to appear at the West Yorkshires' start line; this time the battalions did not push forward - this decision is understandable due to the previous morning's mix up.

This First Battle of Bullecourt did not involve any soldier from Ravensthorpe becoming a casualty and is told slightly out of chronology with the rest of the chapter in order to set the scene for the Second Battle of Bullecourt which was to take place some weeks later.

The Battle of Arras (officially named the First, Second and Third Battles of the Scarpe) had been fought for much longer than Sir Douglas Haig had wanted. In order to consolidate the gains made so far and end the battle on a line suitable for defence, a final attack was planned for the Third Army, this was to be supported by the First Army to the north and the Fifth Army to the south.

This last attack, which was planned for Thursday 3rd May, was to become known as the Third Battle of the Scarpe. Once again the Fifth Army was to assault Bullecourt; this aspect of the battle (the Second Battle of Bullecourt) was to have a disastrous effect on Ravensthorpe.

In the period since 11th April, artillery had been shelling Bullecourt which gradually disintegrated into little more than a pile of brick dust. Orders received by the 62nd (West Riding) Division indicated that the division was not only to assist with the capture of Bullecourt (primarily the responsibility of the 2nd Australian Division) but press on and take the village of Hendecourt which lay behind Bullecourt. In the days leading up to 3rd May the division (which was to use all three brigades in the assault) practised the attack behind the lines.

The plan was for 185 Brigade (comprising of four battalions of the West Yorkshire Regiment) to attack on the right (next to the 2nd Australian Division) and help take Bullecourt. On the left 187 Brigade (which was made up of two battalions of K.O.Y.L.I. and two battalions of the York and Lancaster Regiment) would form a defensive flank facing towards the Third Army's area. In the centre 186 Brigade (four battalions of the Duke of Wellington's Regiment) would take the Hindenburg Line trenches north of Bullecourt and then press on to Hendecourt. It is the attack of the 186 Brigade, and particularly the 2/5th Battalion, Duke of Wellington's Regiment that concerned Ravensthorpe.

Leading the assault of 186 Brigade would be the 2/5th Duke of Wellington's on the right and the 2/6th Duke of Wellington's on the left. Behind these battalions

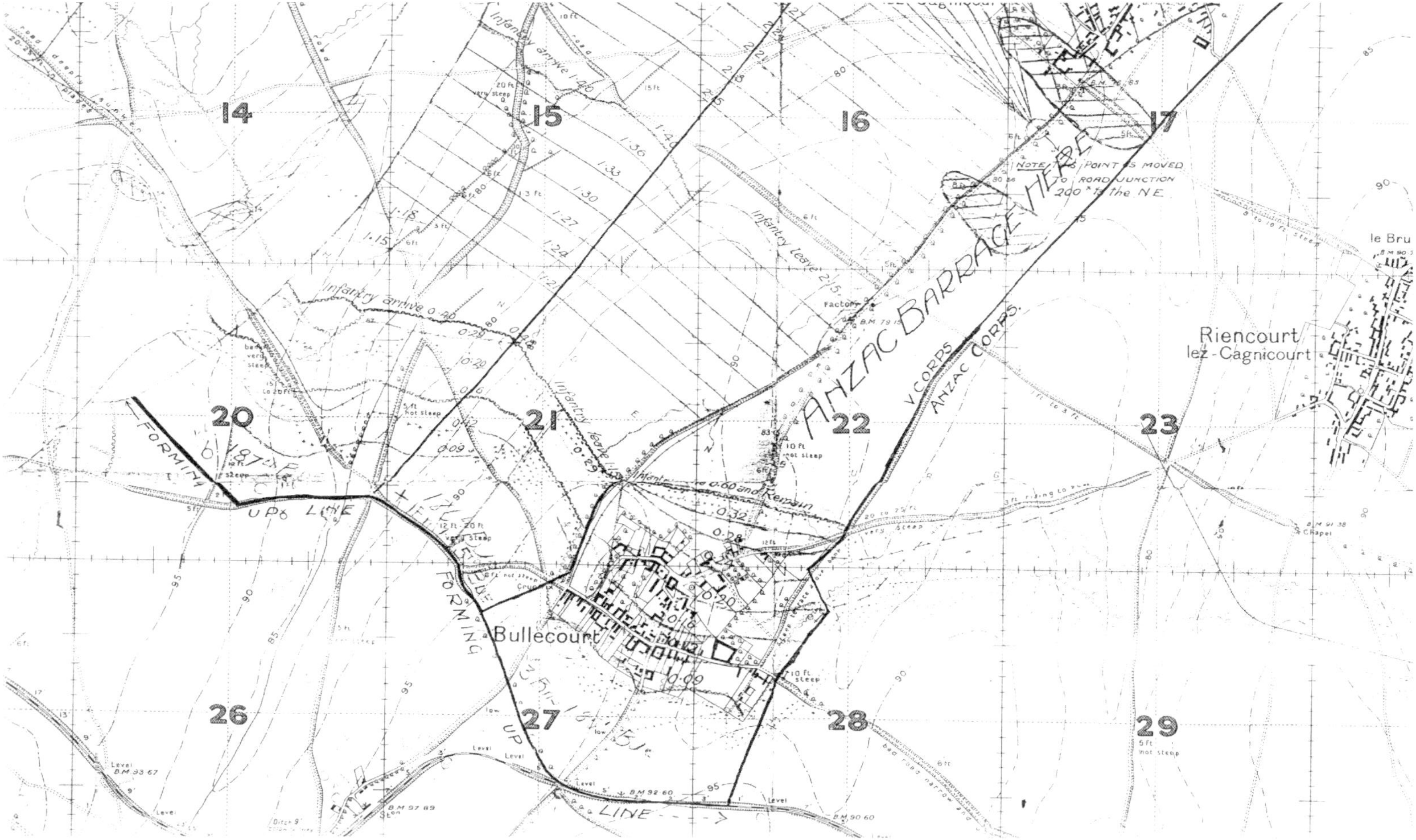

▲ Map 18. Trench Map of Bullecourt. *Courtesy of the Public Record Office*. Reference WO 95/3084.

were the 2/7th and 2/4th Duke's respectively. At dusk on 2nd May (which had been a hot, clear day) tapes were laid out to guide the troops to their assembly positions. Last minute problems had arisen due to German artillery cutting telephone lines but these were repaired and communications re-established. The troops filed into the trenches and were in place by 3.30am, fifteen minutes before zero hour.

The night was dark (the moon became obscured at 2am) but despite this the Germans must have suspected something was taking place as shortly before zero, they started shelling the British front line. At 3.45am the British artillery opened up and immediately German S.O.S. rockets could be seen requesting their own artillery to lay down a protective barrage. This resulted in the Germans bombarding the sunken road from which the Duke's attack was to be launched; this was clearly a predetermined course of action on behalf of the Germans who were obviously aware of the sunken road's existence and its likely use as a jumping off point.

The British 'creeping' barrage moved slowly forwards at a rate of 100 yards every three minutes. The infantry followed the wall of shells as closely as possible* despite being burdened with the usual paraphernalia (such as mats which were being carried to be laid across the belts of barbed wire).

The Germans also responded to the S.O.S. rockets by shelling No Man's Land, however it was the German machine gun barrage which the War Diaries describe as being *"very efficient"*.

At this point an unexpected problem arose. Due to the dry weather of the preceding days, the British barrage was causing dust clouds to rise up. This, together with the smoke from the shells was blown towards the British lines. The dust and smoke along with the dark, moonless night caused the British troops to lose direction, it also prevented observation of progress from headquarters in the rear (numerous battalion and brigade headquarters were sited on the line of the railway embankment on the northern edge of Ecoust village).

The attack was initially thought by Brigade headquarters to be *"progressing favourably"* (4.15am); then *"partially successful"* (5.30am); but growing realisation of failure caused *"...the artillery* [to be] *brought back to the second objective.....to allow our troops to consolidate, if possible, on the first objective"* (9am).

By 1pm 186 Brigade's War Diary acknowledged *"Attack unsuccessful, our troops having been unable to consolidate even in enemy's first line on account of heavy machine gun fire."* The brigade's War Diary has a detailed report on the battle which indicates that despite heavy enfilade machine gun fire from both flanks, the 2/5th Duke's with the 2/7th Duke's in support (being on the right of the brigade front) together with the 2/8th West Yorkshires obtained a footing in the first objective for several hours. The troops held on here until being bombed out, when they retired to shell holes and the sunken road. Despite this failure to push through, it seems that a party was observed by an aeroplane *"in the vicinity of the*

***** *The creeping barrage had been developed to assist assaulting troops in gaining entry to the German trenches. By keeping close to the line of the barrage, there would be no time between the barrage passing over the German trench and the arrival of the attacking soldiers. The Germans would therefore be trapped in their dugouts (where they had been forced to shelter from the bombardment). The pause that occurred in the old style bombardments between the barrage lifting and the arrival of the troops was often the main reason for the failure of attacks, the Germans having vital moments to prepare themselves and their weapons for the arrival of the attacking infantry.***

factory"; these were probably men from the 2/7th or 2/8th West Yorkshire Regiment.

The attack on the left of the brigade front was even less successful, the wire was not as well cut and proved to be almost impossible to get through. The 2/4th and 2/6th Duke's were forced to occupy shell holes in front of the barbed wire. After reorganising on the railway embankment a second attempt was made by these two battalions but once again it failed, all that could be done was to occupy the line of the sunken road.

Little information is supplied in the War Diary of the 2/5th Battalion, Duke of Wellington's Regiment, although it does claim that the battalion's 'A' Company held their objective until 4pm, at which point they were forced back to the railway embankment; it also states that 'B', 'C' and 'D' Companies *"...came under heavy shell, rifle and machine gun fire and were held up in front of the enemy front line trench, small parties holding out in shell holes until after dusk when they returned to the embankment."*

The battalion's War Diary gives casualties as:

Killed - *Captain T. Bentley*, Lieutenant O. Walker +.*

Missing, believed killed - *Second Lieutenant Jacobs #.*

Missing - *Captain G.Glover #, Lieutenant G.Ridley #, Second Lieutenants Darwent #, Heaton +, Hutton #, and E.T. Sykes +.*

Wounded - *Captain W. Shaw, Second Lieutenants Fisher and Simmons plus two with shell shock.*

Other Ranks - *Killed 2; Missing 123; Wounded 275.*

As will become apparent these figures in the immediate aftermath of the battle were inaccurate.

The 3rd May 1917 was the first time that the 2/5th Battalion, Duke of Wellington's Regiment had gone 'over the top'. Like the battle precisely eight months earlier when the 1/5th Duke of Wellington's had gone into an attack for the first time, the resulting casualties were very obvious to the communities of Mirfield and Ravensthorpe (from where the battalions drew many of their recruits).

The Dewsbury News and Dewsbury Reporter both carried some news of the casualties in their editions of Saturday 12th May, but it was not until a week later, 19th May, that the newspapers caught up with the shocking results of the attack. The headline on the front page of the Dewsbury News read *"The Duke of Wellingtons in Action - Mirfield, Ravensthorpe and Northorpe men Missing."* Although not a lurid headline by today's standards, it was certainly stronger than the normal style of headline it printed, and the lists it supplied, mainly of men still missing, both in the edition of 19th May and in the subsequent week's edition made it clear that there had been a major battle involving a local battalion.

**** Captain Tom Bentley died of wounds the following day. Although not named on the Ravensthorpe War Memorial he did have strong connections with the village; Tom was a designer whose father was the Managing Director at Marshall, Kaye and Marshall's mill who had written to the widow of Harry Campbell when her husband had been killed (see Chapter 10).***

+ Killed.

 # Survived.

A total of four Ravensthorpe soldiers were killed on this day, all from the 2/5th Battalion Duke of Wellington's, making this (along with 26th September 1915) the worst day of the war for Ravensthorpe*.

Frederick Eddison Eastwood was born in Ossett; it is not clear exactly how old he was as although both local newspapers give his age as 22, the C.W.G.C. give his age as 20 and as can be seen from the photograph, his age here is given as 21. He lived with his parents (Frederick and Emma) together with his four older brothers at 28 Duke Street Ravensthorpe. All five brothers joined the army, Fred (regimental number 240715) enlisted in Mirfield with his brother Harry (regimental number 240719) in the Duke of Wellington's Regiment probably on the same day, Monday 9th November, 1914.

Fred, who had attended St. Saviour's Boys' School, was, before the war, a member of the choir at St. Saviour's Parish Church and a member of the Church Institute. Away from the church Fred and Harry were members of Ravensthorpe Cycling Club (in 1915 Fred was listed as one of the Vice Presidents of the club); until joining up Fred worked as a cloth finisher at Wormald and Walker's mill. Both brothers went to France with the 62nd Division in early January 1917. On 20th January 1917 a brief mention of Fred was made in the Dewsbury News when lists of men who had received parcels was published; in acknowledging his parcel, he went on to say: *"We are moving from here today. I think they must have been saving us to give the Germans the knock out blow, and I hope we bring it to an end as I am getting tired of it."* Clearly the bitterly cold weather of January was affecting his morale.

It was left to Harry to break the news to their parents that Fred had not returned from the attack. He wrote on 3rd May to say that Fred was missing and wounded after the shell hole in which Fred and three others were sheltering received a direct hit from another shell. Two of the soldiers were killed outright and Fred and another were wounded. Harry went on to say that he had heard that Fred had been taken prisoner.

Two days later Harry wrote again, although having received little further information, he said that he understood that none of the men who were with Fred had got back (whether he meant those that were with Fred in the shell hole or those that were with Fred during the advance, is unclear). A discrepancy now crept into the story; Harry quoted from a platoon sergeant who *"...had said that Fred was wounded in the trench which the Boches made too hot for our lads to hold, since then the trench has been recaptured."* Harry therefore speculated (possibly to try and comfort his parents) that Fred had been taken prisoner. Harry added in his letter that Arthur Kershaw was also wounded and taken prisoner.

Little is known about Arthur Kershaw. Aged 24 his parents were named as Mr and Mrs Ben Lister of Gladys Street, Liversedge. Although the C.W.G.C. state he was a private, both the War Memorial and S.D.G.W. give his rank as lance corporal. Presumably he was a friend of the Eastwoods, possibly joining up with them as his Regimental number (240720) is immediately after Harry Eastwood's.

**** The four casualties for 26th September 1915 (Battle of Loos) are described in Chapter 3, but were from three different battalions. The 3rd September 1916 attack on the Pope's Nose during the Battle of the Somme described in Chapter 8 involved the deaths of two men from Ravensthorpe plus fatal injuries to a third - all three being in the 1/5th Dukes of Wellington's.***

▲ 85. Fred Eastwood clearly showing off his Lewis gunners badge on his lower left sleeve.

▲ 86. Arthur Kershaw. The badge above his right breast pocket was worn by territorials in the early part of the war to show they had volunteered for service overseas.

Harry Webster was the oldest of the Ravensthorpe casualties from the 3rd May battle, aged 29 (according to the C.W.G.C.) or 30 (according to the newspapers). Harry like so many others was educated at St. Saviour's Boys' School. He was the youngest son of Mrs Hannah Webster who, according to the Dewsbury Reporter *"had lived in Mirfield for 40 years* [but] *now resided at 20 Charles Street, Ravensthorpe."*

A pre-war territorial (he had joined the Duke of Wellington's in 1911) before the war Harry was employed by J. & J. Wilkinson, oil extractors, of Mirfield. The first his mother knew that Harry was missing was when she received a letter which was subsequently printed in the Dewsbury Reporter. Dated 8th May the letter read:

"Dear Friend, according to a promise made between me and your son Harry, I regret to write that when we came out of action he was reported missing. I have made a lot of enquiries about him, but all is in vain. No one seems to know anything about him, but if there is any news, I will let you know as soon as possible. I trust that no harm has come to him as he was a good lad and a good soldier. We are all sorry in our platoon that he is missing but we hope that he will turn up all right. Yours faithfully, Private A. Quarmby, 19th Platoon, 'D' Company."

▲ 87. Harry Webster. The five pointed star on his right sleeve is the Territorial Force proficiency star. The stripe on his left sleeve is a long service stripe signifying two years' service.

▲ 88. Fred Sykes

Harry who was due home on leave at Whitsuntide (27th May), was officially reported as presumed killed in April 1918.

Frederick Sykes was the final Ravensthorpe fatality on this day. Fred, who was a cousin of Willie Cawthorne (who had died on 25th April 1917 - see story earlier in this chapter) was 22 years old and the son of Mr J.H. and Mrs E. Sykes of 36 Woodbine Street Dewsbury. Before the war Fred attended Ravensthorpe Day and Sunday Schools, later working as a hurrier for his father at Crawshaw and Warburton's Colliery. (This would have been a physically demanding job, hurriers being the men engaged in moving the baskets or wagons of coal from the coal face to the bottom of the shaft.)

Joining up in December 1914, Fred, according to the Dewsbury Reporter *"wore a medal he had gained as a first class shot and he was a 'master machine gunner'."* He was promoted to lance corporal following the battalion's arrival in France.

Fred was wounded during the attack at Bullecourt but failed to survive the end of the day. He is the only Ravensthorpe casualty from the 3rd May with a known grave, being buried at Achiet-le-Grand Communal Cemetery Extension*. Besides his parents, Fred left behind a brother, at least two sisters and a fiancee called Doris.

**** Achiet-le-Grand was a British railhead and the site of two Casualty Clearing Stations (45th C.C.S. and 49th C.C.S.). Also buried here is Captain Tom Bentley.***

As previously related the 2/5th Duke's War Diary initially gave casualty figures as:

Killed - *2 officers, 2 other ranks,*
Missing - *7 officers, 123 other ranks,*
Wounded - *3 officers, 275 other ranks.*

The actual casualty figures, according to S.D.G.W. are 4 officers and 172 other ranks killed or died of wounds between 3rd and 5th May (including 3 officers and 168 men who lost their lives on 3rd May).

Only two officers and eight other ranks have known graves (of these ten men, the one officer and four other ranks who died on 4th and 5th May all have known graves). The one officer and four other ranks who died on 3rd May and who have known graves, are buried at Bailleul Road East Cemetery (Captain E.T. Sykes* and one other rank); Achiet-le-Grand Communal Cemetery Extension (Fred Sykes); and at Croiselles British Cemetery and Tilloy British Cemetery (one burial in each).

Of the five who died on 4th and 5th May, three (including Captain Bentley) are buried at Achiet-le-Grand Communal Cemetery Extension, and two are buried at Sauchy-Lestree Communal Cemetery.

The remaining two officers and 164 other ranks, including the three men from Ravensthorpe who have no known graves, are commemorated on the Arras Memorial to the Missing.

Casualties in other units of the 62nd (West Riding) Division were not as severe. The 2/6th Duke's who attacked alongside the 2/5th lost (according to S.D.G.W.) four officers and 89 other ranks. The two battalions in support were the 2/7th (who lost three officers and 77 other ranks) and the 2/4th Duke's (three officers and 69 other ranks).

The 2/8th West Yorkshires (who attacked with the 2/5th and 2/6th Duke's) lost 27 other ranks. To the right, 185 Brigade's attack was led by the 2/6th West Yorkshires who lost five officers and 105 other ranks. The 2/5th West Yorkshires and 2/7th West Yorkshires lost two officers and 49 men, and five men respectively.

On the left of the division's attack was 187 Brigade. Its battalions lost:

2/4th K.O.Y.L.I. - 1 officer and 24 men,
2/5th K.O.Y.L.I. - 3 officers+ and 77 men,
2/4th Y&L - 5 officers and 81 men,
2/5th Y&L - 4 officers and 72 men.

The 62nd (West Riding) Division, in infantry alone (ignoring the divisional troops and artillery) lost 34 officers and 847 other ranks.

Although the Second Battle of Bullecourt continued for a further two weeks, this attack was effectively the end of the Arras offensive. Designed as a diversionary attack to Nivelle's main thrust further south, because of the failure of the French attack, and the resulting mutinies in the French army, the British offensive had to

Although the War Diary has him as a Second Lieutenant, both S.D.G.W. and the C.W.G.C. indicate the 22 year old from Huddersfield held the rank of Captain.

+ Including the commanding officer, Lieutenant-Colonel W. Watson, who is commemorated on the Arras Memorial to the Missing.

be continued. As previously mentioned, General Nivelle was sacked and was replaced by General Petain who managed, over time, to restore the morale of the French army.

For different reasons, General Allenby was recalled to London on 5th June and replaced as commander of the Third Army by Julian Byng, who had until that point been commanding the Canadian Corps.

Sir Douglas Haig, who had been forced to conform to the French plan in 1916 when Joffre chose the Somme as the front to be attacked and again in 1917 when he had to conform to Nivelle's ill-fated attack, was now free to pursue his long preferred option of attacking out of the Ypres salient.

Chapter Thirteen

Preliminaries to Third Ypres

Following the closing down of the Battle of Arras, Sir Douglas Haig was released at last from having to conform to French strategy, and was now able to develop his plans to break out of the Ypres salient between the River Lys and the North Sea in Belgian Flanders. There were several reasons behind Haig's wish to attack from Ypres. Firstly, the salient that was formed in 1914 (when the British, against all odds, stopped the German advance) and narrowed in 1915 (when the Germans attacked at the junction of the French and Canadians, using poisoned gas) had become a death trap for the soldiers defending it. A high daily rate of casualties was being incurred just by simply holding the lines, the Germans effectively surrounded the British troops on three sides. If the bulge in the line could be flattened, many lives would be saved as the Germans would have a much less effective field of fire.

The second reason for an attack here was directly due to the Germans being so close to the Channel Ports. Although the Germans were on the defensive, there was always a possibility that they might attack, and if they did, and they made a small advance there would be a threat not only to the B.E.F.'s line of supply but also their line of retreat.

Admiral Jellicoe, the First Sea Lord, thought that most of the German submarines that had been operating an unrestricted campaign against Allied shipping since February 1917, were based on the Belgian coast (although this was not, in fact, the case). Because of this belief, Jellicoe was keen to have the Belgian coast cleared of German occupation, therefore denying the use of the ports to German submarines. This would inevitably result in a decrease in the submarine menace.

The fourth and possibly main reason for an attack in this sector was the fact that an advance here would have the strategic benefit of cutting the Germans off from their supplies - a major railway line ran through Roulers, twelve miles north-east of Ypres.

Haig's plan for the Flanders offensive was for an attack in two stages. Firstly the Messines Ridge, which runs south of Ypres towards the Belgian-French border, was to be captured. This would have the result of securing the right flank and prevent the Germans from having observation over the main thrust out of Ypres. The second stage was the actual attack from Ypres, this would have the aim of capturing the high ground east of the town, and following the breakthrough would enable the railway junction at Roulers to be taken. Simultaneous to this breakthrough, there would be an amphibious landing on the Belgian coast which would free the ports of Zeebrugge and Ostend.

The term 'high ground' in Flanders is of course only a relative term as the area is very flat; the high ground that was to be the subject of the second stage of the attack was a barely noticeable ridge of low hills that surround the saucer-like dip

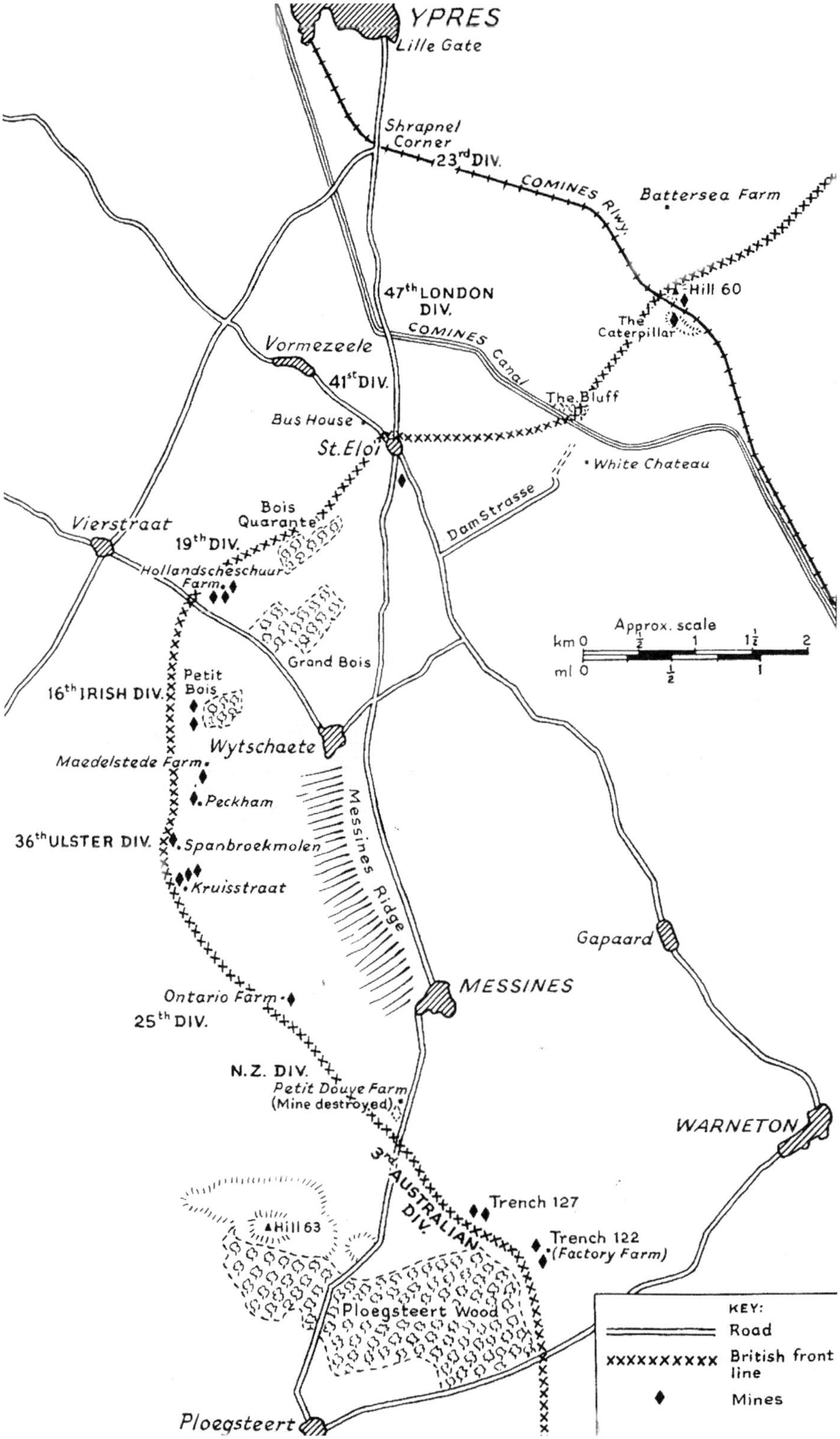

▲ Map 19. Messines Ridge

in which Ypres lays. This high ground was a major advantage to the Germans who could look down on the British positions.

The Messines operation was entrusted to the Second Army under General Sir Herbert Plumer. Known as 'Daddy' Plumer to the troops, he was rather fat, with white hair and a large white moustache which hid his puffed out cheeks. Plumer, despite his comical appearance had an unrivalled knowledge of the Ypres salient, and was very methodical and careful when attacking, keeping casualties down to a minimum. Plumer, with his Chief of Staff, Major-General Charles Harrington, made a formidable team. Their plans were carefully made, with 72 of the new Mark IV tanks, and nearly 2,300 artillery pieces being made available. A scientific barrage and counter-battery plan was drawn up for the guns, taking into account the German tactics for defence. In addition a huge model of the Messines Ridge was made in order to brief the attacking troops as to their roles. All of these factors were overshadowed, however, by one overriding feature that was to set this attack apart from all others before and after it.

The main feature of Plumer's plan for the attack on the Messines Ridge was the use of a number of mines which had been dug out from the British lines under No Man's Land and made ready for detonation under the German trenches and strong points. The task of digging the shafts and tunnels for these mines was enormous and had been underway since the end of 1915; some of the mines were up to 2,000 feet long, at a depth of up to 100 feet. Specialist tunnelling companies of Royal Engineers were formed, with former miners being asked to volunteer for these units, many of these men transferring from the Miners' Battalion, the 12th K.O.Y.L.I.

The Germans were not unaware of what was going on, and they undertook anti-mining activity of their own. Under the soil of Belgium, there developed a different type of warfare to that which was been fought out on the surface. Each side listened for evidence of their opponents driving tunnels towards their own trenches or tunnels. If the sound of digging abruptly stopped, there was every chance that the enemy was about to blow a mine with the intention of destroying trenches or the tunnels being dug, thus killing or trapping the miners underground. Occasionally, tunnellers accidentally broke into the enemy's workings, and vicious sub-terranean fights broke out. It required a great deal of nerve to go underground with these sorts of dangers added to the usual dangers associated with 'normal' mining.

The intention had originally been to detonate the mines as part of a diversionary attack for the opening day of the Battle of the Somme, but this did not take place, principally because a large amount of explosives were destroyed by a German air raid before it could be used for these mines. As it turned out, this was a stroke of good fortune for the British as it allowed the tunnels, that had been so labouriously dug, to be put to a much better use than that of a diversion.

As previously mentioned, Plumer's plan also called for a massive artillery bombardment which opened up on 21st May; this concentrated on destroying the German artillery. At 3.10am on Thursday, 7th June, nineteen of the mines were detonated*; almost one million pounds of high explosive tore through the German

Of the 24 mines dug, two were lost to German counter-mining. Three of the remaining 22 were not detonated (later in the war they were dismantled), but of the 19 detonated, two failed to blow up. The positions of the two unexploded mines were lost. One blew up during a thunder storm in 1955, the other remains undiscovered to this day.

lines (the shock of the explosion, it was said, could be felt in London, 130 miles away).

Nine divisions of Plumer's Second Army advanced, meeting almost no resistance; by 9am the crest of the ridge had been taken with very light casualties, any strongpoints left intact were bypassed to be cleared by mopping up parties. Although advances later in the day and on subsequent days did incur some casualties, the operation was an unqualified success. British casualties, by First World War standards were light at 17,000. The Germans by contrast lost around 25,000 men, 10,000 of whom were killed with 7,000 men being taken prisoner.

No casualties were incurred from Ravensthorpe during this attack, although the War Memorial records the name of one Ravensthorpe soldier who died on this day.

* * *

George Jackson had previously served as a regular soldier earning medals for his service in India in 1888 and the Victoria Medal for his participation in the Boer War. At the outbreak of the First World War, George was working at the Thornhill Carbine Works, and because he had already served his time after leaving the army as a reservist, he was not liable for further call up. Despite this he volunteered, and until he was accepted back into the army, took part in the recruiting drive in

▲ 89. George Jackson

▲ 90. Recruiting outside Dewsbury town hall. The slogan on the side of the town hall is urging men to join up so as to avoid the need for conscription. *Photograph courtesy of Kirklees Community History Service.*

Dewsbury. After rejoining, he was given the rank of Pioneer-Sergeant and was sent, as a drill instructor, to various camps, where his services would have been desperately needed to train the raw recruits that were flooding through the recruiting offices.

George was posted to the 14th Battalion, Manchester Regiment. The Battalion was not to become a fighting unit; it was initially part of the original Fourth New Army that Kitchener raised. However, as described in Chapter 2, the original Fourth New Army was broken up in April 1915 to provide reserves for the first three new armies. In the resulting reorganisation the battalion became a reserve battalion (a training unit), part of the 3rd Reserve Infantry Brigade. In August 1916, in order to manage the training of the recruits in a better manner, a new corps was formed called the 'Training Reserve', to be made up of reserve battalions such as the 14th Manchesters. The battalions of the Training Reserve abandoned their regimental associations and became simply consecutively numbered battalions from 1 to 112. The 14th Manchesters became, coincidentally, the 14th Training Reserve Battalion, part of the 3rd Training Reserve Brigade*.

On 13th January 1917, a letter from George appeared in the Dewsbury News in which he described how he was in hospital in Stafford with head injuries caused by a fall on frozen ground. He had received a postal order (possibly from the Ravensthorpe and Northorpe Soldiers and Sailors Christmas Parcel Fund) which he stated was *"...specially welcome for the purpose of buying nourishing food; I am unable to take solid food at present."*

Seemingly recovered from his injuries, he was home on leave in May but on 9th June a further article appeared in the newspapers stating that on Thursday 7th June, Hannah Jackson had received a telegram at 40 Crawshaw Street informing her that her husband was seriously ill in a military hospital near Rugeley (the site of a large camp) in Staffordshire. Although setting off straightaway, Mrs Jackson was too late to see her husband before he died.

George Jackson was brought back home and was buried on Monday 11th June in St. Mary's Parish Churchyard, Mirfield. Brockton Camp (presumably where George was employed as an instructor) was represented at the service by four sergeants. A number of other soldiers also attended the funeral (being recruits and others recovering from wounds) and they provided a firing party over the grave; two buglers played the Last Post. Aged 45, George left a widow and eight children.

*   *   *

After the success of the Messines operation, Haig made a crucial mistake; instead of using Plumer to command the attack at Ypres, he instead handed over responsibility for this battle to the more ambitious General Hubert Gough. At 47 years of age, Gough was younger than many divisional commanders. A protégé of Haig, he had been promoted rapidly in the early part of the war. Like Haig, he was a cavalryman, and his more 'thrusting' outlook made Haig believe he was more likely to achieve a breakthrough than the cautious Plumer. As a result of handing over the command of the battle to Gough, there was a seven week delay between

**** Hence the number '3' on the shoulder patch of the photograph.***

the end of the Messines operation and the commencement of the main battle at Ypres. This delay was to prove costly.

In the meantime, General Rawlinson and his Fourth Army headquarters was ordered from its position on the southern end of the British sector on the Western Front on the Somme, and moved to the extreme north of the front line. From here it was to make secret preparations for an amphibious landing on the Belgian coast. This landing was planned to link up with Gough's breakout from the Ypres salient.

The plan was certainly ambitious; a total of 14,000 troops had been earmarked, and techniques were devised which were similar to those for the D-Day operation 27 years later. Pontoons 560 feet long were to be used to mount the sea wall (they were to be put in place by two monitors tied together) and specially adapted tanks were built, with ramps attached to help them to climb the steep slope of the artificial barriers behind the beach. The 1st Division was chosen to lead this attack.

Unfortunately, despite all precautions, the Germans got wind of the plan and, on 10th July, launched a pre-emptive bombardment and attack across the Yser Canal at Nieuport, gaining positions which would cause difficulties to the plan.

The 2nd Battalion, Royal Munster Fusiliers was part of 3 Brigade, 1st Division and, according to their War Diary moved in early July from the village of Coxyde to Champermont Camp from where working parties were despatched. The War Diary describes how, on 10th July, German shell fire fell on the camp, cutting communications with brigade headquarters; most of the huts were damaged. Losses included not only the kits of ten officers but also the headquarters mess accounts. Around midday the dressing station was badly damaged and the battalion's Medical Officer established a new one. That evening, shortly after receiving orders to move, a staff officer arrived cancelling the previous order, explaining that due to the Germans having attacked and gained ground, the battalion had to stay where they were. The battalion was placed under the orders of 2 Brigade, with two companies ('B' and 'C') being sent forward to support troops nearer the front line.

The War Diary very unusually lists the fatalities for the day by name, indicating four officers were slightly wounded, plus six other ranks killed, one other rank died of wounds and 37 other ranks wounded (S.D.G.W. indicates 7 men killed in action plus 3 died of wounds). One of the men listed was Lance Corporal Samuel Brierley.

Sam was born in Delph in about 1891 to John and Eliza Brierley. In 1909 or 1910 the family moved from Delph, no doubt due to the Armitage & Rhodes factory in this village having burned down; as mentioned in the Prologue, the factory was rebuilt in Ravensthorpe. Sam was employed by the company as a weaver; little other information is known about him, apart from the fact that he was a member of Ravensthorpe Working Men's Club, and that he played the clarinet. Sam joined the K.O.Y.L.I. in Dewsbury on 4th September 1914, but was transferred (as many men were) to fill out the Irish Regiments, for whom recruiting had not been as brisk. Joining the Royal Munster Fusiliers, Sam was stationed in Ireland until September 1916 when it seems that he was sent as one of the drafts to reinforce the 2nd Battalion in France. It is likely that he joined the battalion in November.

Sam's wife, Hilda Brierley, besides receiving the usual official telegram also received a letter of condolence from a pal of Sam's, Private H. Key. As well as a wife, Sam left behind three children, the oldest of whom was five years old.

Sam is buried at Coxyde Military Cemetery in Belgium, as are all the men of the battalion who were killed during this attack.

Following the German assault, it was decided to withdraw the 1st Division south-west of Dunkirk where a fenced-off training ground was built. In great secrecy, the preparations for the amphibious operation continued, but this was to be in vain as the operation never took place; following the failure to break out of the Ypres salient, the plan was at first postponed and then cancelled.

Replacing the 1st Division on the extreme left of the Western Front was the 49th (West Riding) Division.

The 49th (West Riding) Division, it will be remembered had, following the Battle of the Somme, moved to the Neuve Chapelle area; the division stayed in this sector until 13th July when it was ordered to proceed to Bethune railway station. After de-training at Dunkirk, the division moved up the coast, taking over the coastal defences at Nieuport on 18th July.

The 1/5th K.O.Y.L.I. took over part of the front line with the 1/4th K.O.Y.L.I. in support of them. The K.O.Y.L.I.s soon discovered that this was not a quiet sector, the Germans were still active following their attack on the 1st Division. On 19th July the Germans launched another attack but were beaten off; enemy artillery heavily bombarded the British positions on 20th July and again on the night of the 21st/22nd July, using a new type of gas shell. This gas, called mustard gas, caused blistering both externally and internally and because it was colourless and virtually odourless gave little warning of its presence. The only sign of the gas was a faint smell of garlic or mustard which was to give the gas its name. Upon coming into contact with it, there would be a slight irritation of the nose and throat

▲ 91. Sam Brierley

▲ 92. George Sutcliffe

followed by sneezing and vomiting; eyes became inflamed and painful, leading to temporary blindness. Coughing continued in survivors for a week.

The immediate effect of the bombardment of the 21st/22nd July in the 1/4th K.O.Y.L.I. was seven men killed and nine men wounded, however this does not include those who had become poisoned by gas; nine officers and 413 men having been affected. The following day, there were a further three officers and 73 men who became affected by the lingering gas. (Casualties in the 1/5th K.O.Y.L.I., although bad, were not as high as the 1/4th K.O.Y.L.I.'s.)

With casualties as heavy as these the 1/4th K.O.Y.L.I. were withdrawn, however the full results of the gas attack only became apparent over the next few days. One man died of gas poisoning on 22nd July and two on the 23rd. Over the course of the next five days, 82 men died of the effects of the gas; the rate at which the men died then began to diminish, with 20 men succumbing over the subsequent four days.

One of the early gas casualties was a Ravensthorpe soldier.

George Clement Sutcliffe was born in Mirfield on 18th March 1884 to Mr and Mrs James Sutcliffe. Educated at Mirfield Parish Day School he followed in his father's footsteps by becoming a waterman, being employed by Sam Schofield of Lower Hopton to carry coal by barge between Brighouse and Wakefield. George was married with three children, living at 751 Huddersfield Road, Ravensthorpe and was a member of the Wesleyan Chapel in Ravensthorpe. Before the war George had joined the territorials (possibly the Duke of Wellington's) but in January 1914 transferred to the Yorkshire Dragoons (a Yeomanry Regiment based in Wakefield); the reason for him arranging this transfer is possibly due to his barge run terminating in Wakefield.

The newspapers describe George as *"..not being of robust constitution.."* which is the likely reason for him not being sent to France until December 1916, despite his volunteering four times. This posting to France necessitated another transfer*, this time to the K.O.Y.L.I. After having a few days home leave and ten days training, George joined the locally raised 1/4th Battalion.

Amy Sutcliffe, George's wife, received a telegram on Tuesday 31st July informing her that George had died of gas poisoning on Monday 23rd July; George is buried in Adinkerke Churchyard Extension, on the Belgian coast. Two British Casualty Clearing Stations were here in July 1917, and the graves from these two stations, which number just 70, were made at the rear of a Belgian military cemetery.

Another Ravensthorpe soldier in the Yorkshire Dragoons had been transferred to the infantry at this time - see John Ellis; Chapter 10.

Chapter Fourteen

Third Ypres (1) Pilckem Ridge and Langemarck

Following the success of the Messines operation, everything was now ready for the battle that was to allow the British army to break out of the Ypres salient. Haig believed that by launching a major assault in this sector, there would be a greater chance of delivering a telling victory against the Germans. As has been mentioned in the previous chapter, Haig ordered General Gough to take over the planning of this operation from the more cautious General Plumer.

Haig wanted a breakthrough, but was aware that the depth of the German defences would necessitate a wearing-out fight; this contradiction was never resolved. The situation was exacerbated by Haig's appointment of General Gough whose Fifth Army would take charge of the battle. Haig believed that Gough's cavalryman's attitude and reputation for being a 'thruster' was more likely to result in a breakthrough than General Plumer's step by step tactics.

In drawing up his plans, Gough failed to pay sufficient attention to the capture of the Gheluvelt Plateau, the key to the German positions at Ypres. His plan was for the first attack to capture the first, second and third lines of defences, the last of which lay 6,000 yards (nearly four miles) behind the start line. Here Gough expected to have to halt in front of the village of Passchendaele while a further bombardment would take place followed by another assault. This would then result in a breach in the German lines and enable a breakthrough by the cavalry to take place towards the Belgian coast in conjunction with the planned amphibious assault and also enable the railway centre of Roulers to be captured.

Although an ambitious plan, Gough's troops would be far more skilled than those that had been available to General Rawlinson the year previously on the Somme. Rather than attacking as a battalion (or company) in a long line, platoons were now divided into four specialist sections, of riflemen, bombers, rifle-bombers, and Lewis gunners which were capable of fire and movement tactics, designed to give each other mutual support.

German tactics, meanwhile had also evolved and behind the thinly held outpost line was a deep 'Battle Zone' containing, instead of trenches (which could not be built and kept dry due to the high water table), dozens of blockhouses or pillboxes. The fields of fire of each of these covered others, so that any attackers would be caught in a lethal cross-fire.

For ten days prior to the attack, the artillery had bombarded the German lines and pillboxes. This had the unfortunate side effect of destroying the delicate system of dykes and drainage ditches which prevented the low-lying land from flooding.

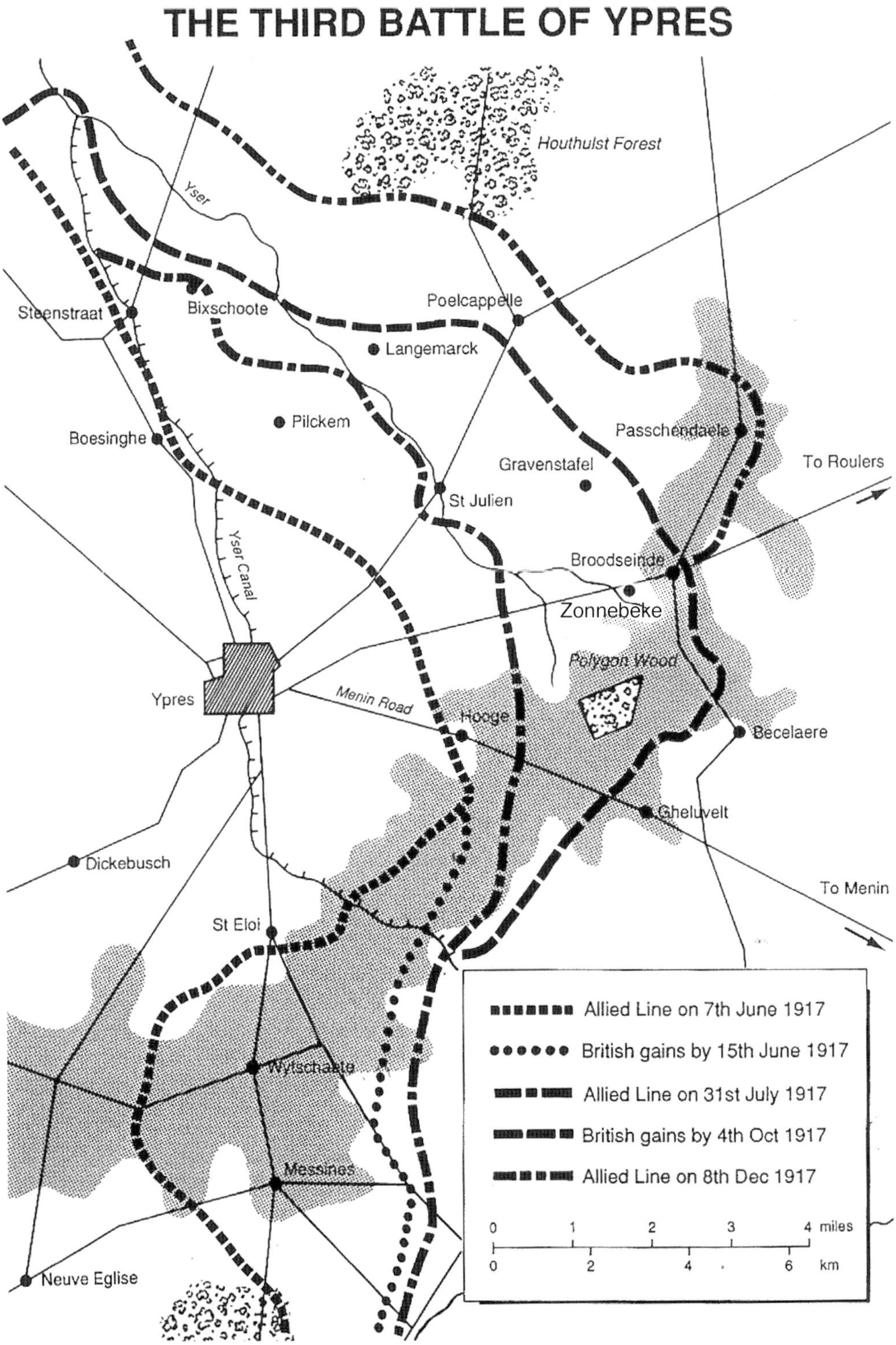

▲ Map 20. The Third Battle of Ypres

The British infantry on the ten mile front went over the top at 3.50am on Tuesday 31st July. Gough had ten divisions assigned to his seven mile front; on his right was Plumer's Second Army which attacked with five divisions and to Gough's left was the French First Army which attacked in conjunction with the British. Although the men reached their first objectives in most places (although, significantly, little progress was made in the direction of Gheluvelt), this was in part attributable to the thinly held nature of the outpost line. After a mile, German resistance increased significantly and the troops found the advance becoming much more difficult. The German tactics had worked; attacking troops had become disorganised by the outpost line and once up to the main line of resistance, they were cut down by the overlapping fields of fire from machine guns in the blockhouses.

These blockhouses should have been destroyed either by artillery fire or by tanks. Unfortunately, due to bad weather in the days before the attack the R.F.C.'s reconnaissance aeroplanes were grounded and were unable to help in pinpointing the artillery's targets. The slow moving tanks had been left behind by the infantry's dash through the outpost line, and those that did reach the blockhouses were often destroyed by enemy fire before they could attack the strongpoints.

The attack slowed down and at 1pm drizzle started falling which, by 4pm, developed into heavy rain. For the first time in the Third Battle of Ypres, the weather was to have a significant outcome on the result of the fighting. With the drainage ditches destroyed, the rain had nowhere to go and simply stayed on the surface. The battlefield became a swamp and all forward movement stopped. Any surviving tanks became irretrievably bogged down. The artillery barrage however crept relentlessly forward at 25 yards a minute, leaving the infantry far behind and unprotected. To compound this, rearward communication broke down as telephone lines were cut by German artillery and the only messages that could be sent were via runners (who often became casualties themselves) or by carrier pigeon.

At about 9.30am the first of the German counter-attacks began; these increased in ferocity during the day. The attacks were launched by specially trained German counter-attack divisions which drove back the British troops in some places.

The first day's battle (known as the Battle of Pilckem Ridge) involved the loss of one Ravensthorpe soldier.

Arnold Nelson Tompkins was born in October 1896 to Clarence and Emily Tompkins, being the youngest of five brothers. Apart from the fact that the family moved from Heckmondwike to Ravensthorpe, little is known about his early life.

Arnold went into partnership with his brother Edward, running a hair dressing business from the family home at 126 North Road, Ravensthorpe. He was a member of the Ravensthorpe and Northorpe Conservative Club and attended Staincliffe Wesleyan Chapel. Arnold was called up in October 1916, aged 20 and was enlisted in Dewsbury, joining the Royal Scots Fusiliers.

After receiving training Arnold was posted to France in May 1917, joining the 6th/7th Battalion (the same battalion as Ernest Walker had been in when he lost his life in August 1916) part of 45 Brigade, 15th (Scottish) Division. On 31st July the division attacked astride the Ypres-Zonnebeke road towards the village of Frezenberg, 45 Brigade being in support of the other two brigades of the division.

Arnold's battalion were on the right of 45 Brigade and moved up from Erie Camp at 3.30am using 'F' Track towards the front line. The 6th/7th Royal Scots Fusiliers

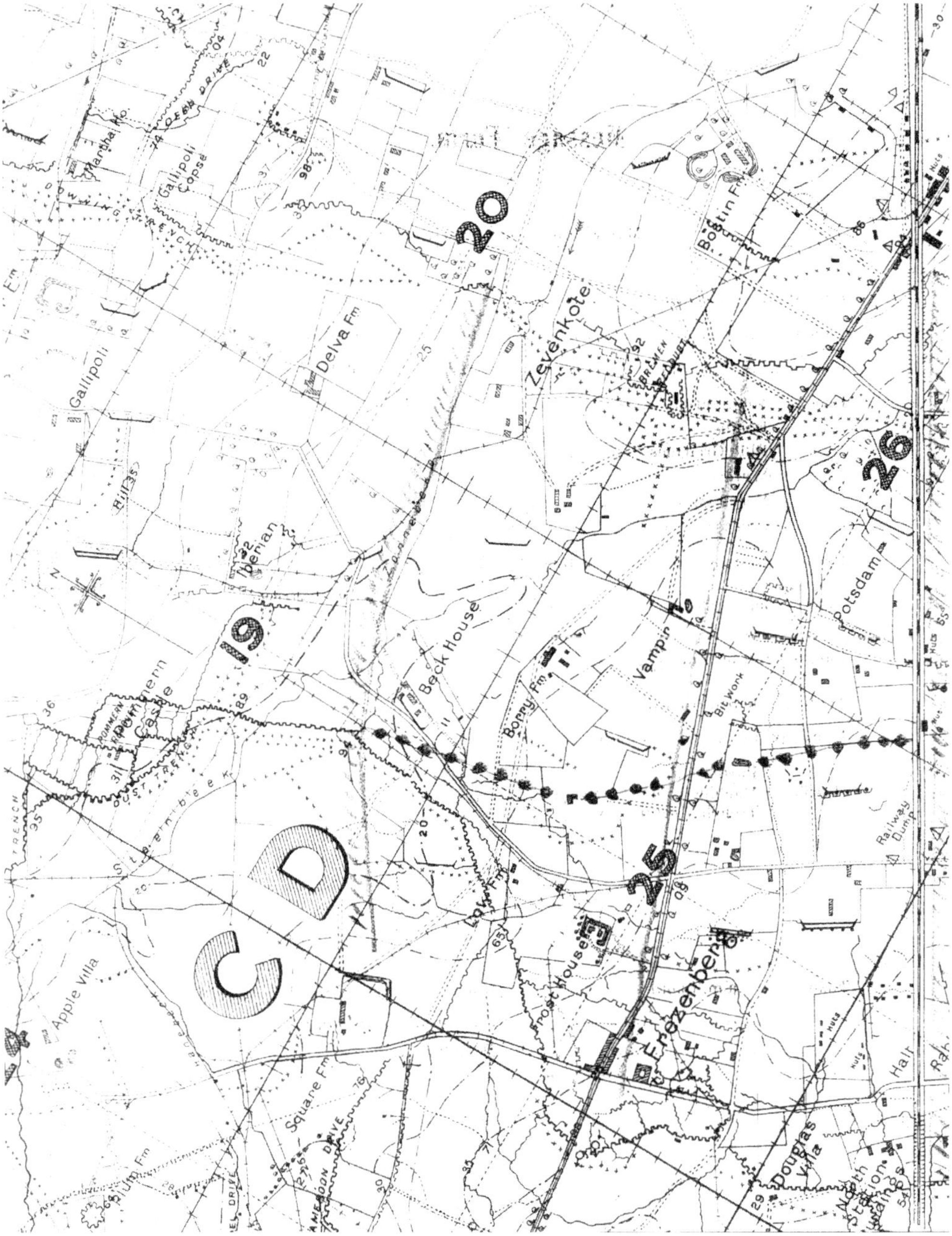

▲ Map 21. Trench Map of Frezenberg/Potsdam. *Courtesy of The Public Record Office.* Reference WO 95/1943.

with the 6th Cameron Highlanders on their left and the other two battalions of the brigade behind (the 11th Argyll and Sutherland Highlanders and the 13th Royal Scots) were in position in the old German front line (possibly Ice Trench - which they had raided a few days earlier) at 7.30am.

The plan was for the battalions of 45 Brigade to pass through the positions already taken, and to press on to objectives known as the Green Line. At 10.18am the battalions moved forward behind a creeping barrage; whilst the 6th Cameron Highlanders on the left managed to make some progress, the 6th/7th Royal Scots Fusiliers encountered problems. On the right of the Fusiliers was the 8th Division who had failed to advance as far as anticipated; because of this, when the Fusiliers advanced, they were caught by enfilade fire from uncaptured German positions south of the Ypres-Roulers railway line. As they moved forward, Arnold's battalion found themselves being shot at from the rear, from these uncaptured positions. It was now 11.30am and heavy casualties were being sustained, including the battalion's company commanders.

Between 1.30pm and 2pm, German counter-attacks were launched against the brigade; these were repeated at 4.25pm. The attacks forced the 6th Cameron Highlanders to fall back (they had advanced further than the 6th/7th Royal Scots Fusiliers), but when British artillery shells started falling amongst a company of the Fusiliers who were in a position, north of the railway line, known as 'Potsdam', they too fell back. The brigade's War Diary ends its detailed account of the day's events: *"Throughout the day the greatest difficulty was experienced in finding out where the front line was, and the artillery was very much handicapped by this."* The experience of the company of Royal Scots Fusiliers at Potsdam certainly reinforces this statement!

The 6th/7th Royal Scots Fusiliers lost 72 men on this day, one of whom was Arnold Tompkins. Arnold is buried at Tyne Cot Cemetery, the largest Commonwealth War Graves Commission cemetery on the Western Front, containing nearly 12,000 burials. It is named after a barn called Tyne Cot (or Tyne Cottage) which stood in the centre of a number of pillboxes near the village of Passchendaele*. The original cemetery had only 300 burials, it was not until after the war that the thousands of other graves (Arnold's included) were concentrated into the cemetery. Of the casualties in Arnold's battalion, 59 have no known grave and are commemorated on the Menin Gate Memorial to the Missing in Ypres, the remaining men are buried in six different cemeteries, Tyne Cot Cemetery having, with four graves, the highest number of known burials from the battalion's attack.

Following the opening day's assault and German counter-attack, certain line straightening operations were attempted over the following days, but the swamp-like nature of the battleground and the difficulty in transporting supplies over duckboard tracks which had to be laid (and which immediately became the target of German artillery) caused immense difficulties for the troops in the most advanced positions.

It was the task of the Royal Engineers (assisted by troops who, not being in the front line were technically 'at rest' - although the rest they received was very little indeed) to make and maintain these duckboard tracks. Each infantry division had on its strength three 'Field Companies' of Royal Engineers, each company being about 200 men strong.

The village was captured at the end of the battle - see Chapter 15.

▲ 93. Arnold Tompkins

▲ 94. George Pickles

After the attack on 31st July, many divisions were replaced by fresher ones, this included the 8th Division (who had attacked on the right of Arnold Tompkins' division) who were replaced by the 25th Division in the Hooge area.

One of the companies of Royal Engineers forming part of the 25th Division was the 106th Field Company; George Arthur Pickles, from Ravensthorpe, was a member of this Field Company.

George was born in Briestfield near Thornhill in March 1884, the only son amongst three children. After attending Whitley Day School and Whitley Church (being a member of the choir) he worked as a joiner for a number of years at Ingham's Colliery at Thornhill until going to work for Morton Son & Co., engineers, of Brooklyn Mills, Ravensthorpe. He became a member of Ravensthorpe Working Men's Club.

It is not known when his connection with Ravensthorpe came about, but he possibly moved to the village when he married, residing with his wife at 47 John Street, Ravensthorpe. George volunteered for the army, enlisting in Dewsbury on 12th July 1915, joining the Royal Engineers. It seems that he served in France until early August 1916 when he was invalided home with trench foot and gas poisoning. After being treated in Royds Hospital, Huddersfield for a number of months he returned to a base in Newark, and was sent back to the front on 22nd April 1917, being posted to the 106th Field Company.

It was this unit which on the 4th and 5th August was ordered to lay, according to the War Diary "... *a double duckboard track starting from Birr Cross Roads* [behind the original British front line near Hooge] *forwards. Over 800 yards was laid on these two days."* The task was not completed without casualties, four men of the 106th Field Company being killed on 5th August, one of whom was Sapper George Pickles.

George's wife received a letter from Major W.F. Fitzpatrick, who was in command of the company describing George as being, despite only a recent addition to the company, *"...very popular and his death has been a great blow."* He goes on to state that George had been killed instantaneously by a splinter from a German shell which had caught George whilst he was on the way up to do *"an important piece of work"*.

Of the four men from the 106th Field Company, R.E. who were killed on this day, two are buried at Belgian Battery Corner Cemetery and another at Birr Cross Roads Cemetery, however George has no known grave, and is therefore commemorated on the Menin Gate Memorial to the Missing in Ypres. The Memorial was intended to be inscribed with the names of the missing who died in the Ypres salient during the whole of the war, however during the building of the memorial it was realised that there would be insufficient room for all of the names to be listed. The decision was therefore taken that this memorial would cover the period up to midnight on 15th/16th August 1917; any men killed after that date who had no known grave would be commemorated elsewhere. The Menin Gate Memorial contains the names of about 55,000 men with no known grave. The Tyne Cot Memorial, built at the rear of Tyne Cot Cemetery in Passchendaele village, covers the period of 16th August onwards and has engraved on its panels the names of a further 34,000 men, being those men whose names could not be accommodated on the Menin Gate Memorial.

Due to the state of the ground and the difficulty of movement, no further attack was possible until 10th August when the 18th and 25th Divisions captured the village of Westhoek. Whilst the troops were floundering through the Ypres mud, the Canadian Corps were making preparations in the south to launch an attack in the hope of drawing German troops away from Ypres (or at the very least preventing fresh reinforcements being sent to the salient).

Several weeks earlier, on 7th July, Haig had concluded that an attack well away from Ypres would divert German attention; as a result Lieutenant-General Sir Arthur Currie's* Canadian Corps was ordered to make an attack on the town of Lens.

Lens, and more particularly the village of Loos, had been the scene of a major battle in 1915 (see Chapter 3); the ground had been considered unfavourable for this first battle, and matters had not improved in the intervening period.

Following the receipt of his orders, Currie went out onto some high ground overlooking Lens and realised that an assault on the town would be difficult and costly. Behind and between Loos and Lens was Hill 70; the hill had been captured temporarily by the 15th (Scottish) Division during the Battle of Loos in September 1915. He considered that an attack on this hill would be easier for his troops, and still have the desired effect of tying down German reserves. Currie therefore took the extremely unusual step of questioning his orders with the commander of the First Army, General Horne. Field-Marshal Haig was brought into the discussion

**** Currie had taken over command of the Canadian Corps from Sir Julian Byng when Byng was promoted to command the Third Army. (Byng was promoted due to Allenby being sent to command the British forces in Palestine in June 1917 - see Chapter 17).***

and agreed that Hill 70 could be the target rather than the town of Lens, although in agreeing to the alteration, Haig warned Currie that the Germans would not give up Hill 70 easily.

This area of France, like Belgian Flanders where the Third Battle of Ypres was being fought, is very flat; there were numerous slag heaps, and the only dominant feature apart from these was Hill 70. Clustered around the town of Lens and on a spur of relatively high ground were a number of small villages, such as Cite St. Laurent, Cite St. Emile and Cite Ste. Elisabeth. These were 'company villages' occupied by the mine workers before the war and were ugly, sprawling eyesores; there was now little to mark their presence other than heaps of rubble. It was in one of these villages that the 87th (Canadian Grenadier Guards) Battalion, C.E.F. found itself.

The 87th Battalion, which had Herbert Nicholls in its ranks was part of 11 Brigade, 4th Canadian Division. (The first part of Herbert's story has been told in Chapter 12.) Although it was not to take part in the attack on Lens, the division was up in the front line. Unfortunately the Germans had realised that an attack was about to be launched, although as the attack was a diversion it is likely that the British High Command would have not been too upset that the Germans knew of the attack, as this would have the desired result of drawing extra German troops to the area.

The 87th Battalion was intended to divert German troops away from the fronts of the 1st and 2nd Canadian Divisions, as it was these divisions which would be making the attack on 15th August; the battalion moved up to trenches around Cite St. Theodore, due west of Lens and astride the Lens to Bethune railway line on 10th August. 'B' Company was in the front line from Absolom Trench to Crocodile Trench; also in the front line, and to their left (in Cite St. Theodore itself) was 'D' Company; 'A' and 'C' Companies were in support.

The battalion's War Diary for 12th August describes how the already heavy shelling was now continuous, the Germans paying particular attention to Fosse 9. On 13th August, the battalion pushed patrols out with the intention of establishing posts in the German's front line. Although this was temporarily achieved, the Canadians were forced out.

On 14th August, the War Diary describes 'considerable' artillery activity on Cite St. Theodore and Fosse 9. It goes on *"In the afternoon the Brick Kiln was heavily shelled with 5.9's* and armour piercing shells and we suffered about 15 casualties, and also had a large number of men buried, forcing the vacation of this point by 'A' Company......about 7.20pm orders received from brigade that in addition to patrols and party attacking Great Peter Street* [a German trench] *we would send one platoon to attack trench leading southerly from Culvert in N13c, this was detailed to Lt. Meyrick of 'D' Company with number 14 platoon."*

It was on this day, 14th August (the day before the attack on Lens) that Herbert Nicholls was killed. It is not known what exactly happened to him, and no obituary seems to have appeared in the Dewsbury newspapers, however further detail appears in the 87th Battalion's War Diary which enables us to speculate how Herbert was killed. The War Diary includes the text of messages which had been sent from the various companies to the battalion's headquarters, one of these from 'A' Company reads: *"Enemy heavy shelling Brick Kiln has knocked front of it in, we*

**** Size of German artillery piece - not actually 5.9 inch but 150mm.***

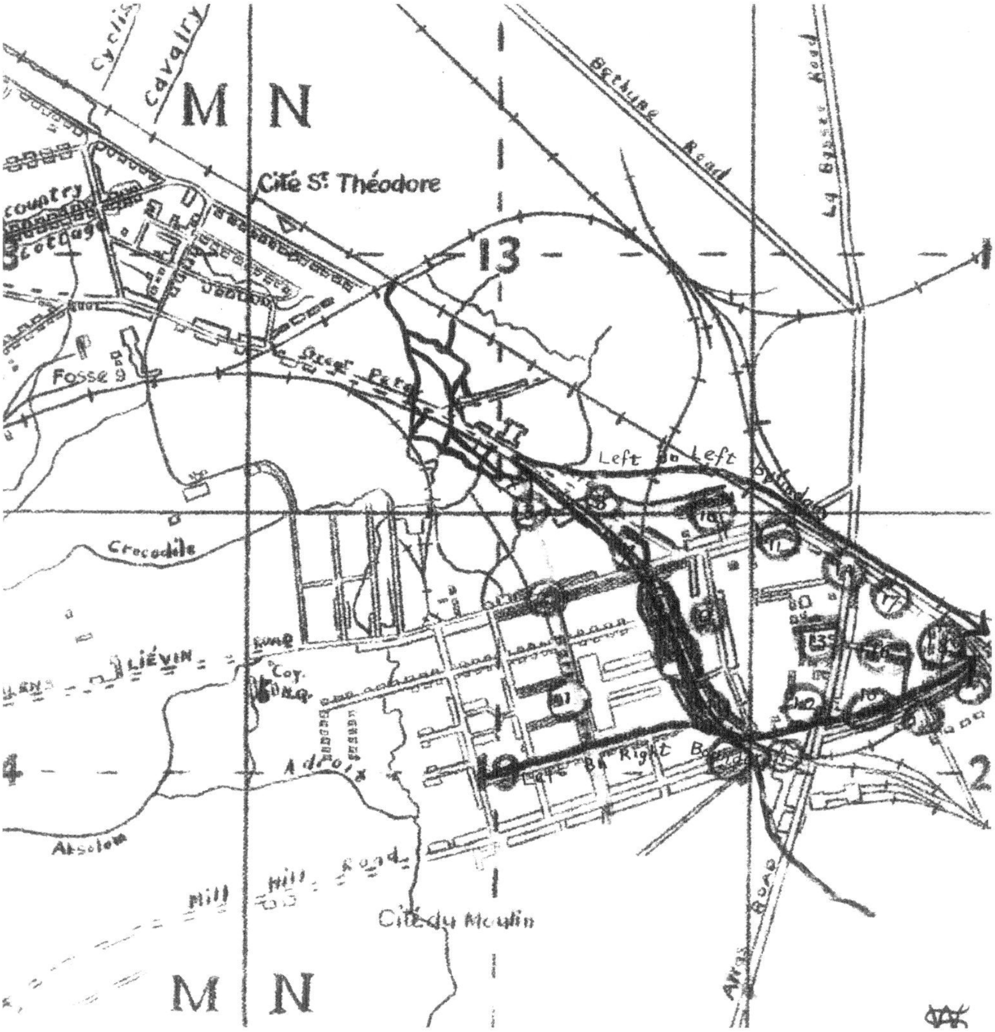

▲ Map 22. Trench Map of Lens. *Courtesy of the Public Record Office.* Reference WO 95/3904

have had quite a few casualties there ie. men buried. I am getting men out of it as soon as dark as it is a death trap now as Hun is using armour-piercing shells on it. Can I use men from 'D' Company Platoon carrying for us to fill up my sections? This is most urgent as we could not carry on otherwise.....[signed] *G.E.Jaques, Captain, O.C. 'A' Company."*

Clearly the heavy shelling may have resulted in Herbert's death although the patrol undertaken by Lieutenant Meyrick's platoon may equally have caused Herbert to lose his life.

As previously mentioned, as no obituary can be found for Herbert Nicholls his story remains largely incomplete, indeed there is nothing to connect him with Ravensthorpe apart from his name on the War Memorial*. What is known is that on 15th August the 1st and 2nd Canadian Divisions assaulted Hill 70. Although, as predicted, the Germans were holding the position in strength, the Canadians managed to take the hill and then fought off several German counter-attacks. Although five German divisions were tied down as a result of this attack, their high command was not deceived; it was realised that Ypres was still the main focus of the British army.

Herbert is commemorated on the Vimy Memorial to the Missing. This names over 11,000 Canadian soldiers who were killed in the First World War and have no known graves. A further 7,000 are commemorated on the Menin Gate Memorial in Ypres.

* * *

On 16th August, the day after the diversionary attack at Hill 70, a further attack was launched by General Gough's Fifth Army at Ypres. Although not on the same scale as the opening day's attack on 31st July, this assault by eight divisions was aimed at taking the village of Langemarck. Despite the village being taken by the 20th Division, the attack was expensive in terms of casualties and generally unsuccessful, with only a few hundred yards of ground being captured in the centre.

One of the casualties of this attack was Clifford Simpson. Clifford was born in Accrington, Lancashire in about 1894. Nothing is known about when or why his family moved to Ravensthorpe, all that is recorded in the Dewsbury News is that Clifford was living with his parents at 141 Sackville Street, Ravensthorpe and working as a beamer (arranger of yarn on the beam of a loom) at Rawdon, Briggs & Co. in Ravensthorpe+. Clifford must have been an early volunteer for the army as, after receiving his training, he was sent as a reinforcement to the Dardanelles, joining the 1st King's Own Scottish Borderers (29th Division) in Gallipoli. He then took part and was injured in the opening day of the Battle of the Somme (see Chapter 7). After recovering from his chest injury he was posted to the 7th/8th Battalion K.O.S.B.#, part of the 15th (Scottish) Division.

**** There was a family called Nicholls who resided in Ravensthorpe, living at 1 School Street, before and during the First World War but it has so far proved impossible to link Herbert to this family.***

+ This is contradicted by the Dewsbury Reporter which states that he was employed at Hartley Brothers who were leather curriers.

 # The 7th and 8th Battalions had merged in May 1916.

It seems that he was injured again, probably in February 1917 and after recovering returned to the 1st K.O.S.B., having been promoted to lance corporal.

For the Battle of Langemarck, the 29th Division (containing the 1st K.O.S.B.) attacked to the north of Langemarck. The 29th Division was the most northerly British division in the attack (to the left was the French army), two brigades of the division went into the attack. The 1st K.O.S.B., being in 87 Brigade, had on their left the 2nd Battalion, South Wales Borderers, also part of 87 Brigade; on the K.O.S.B.'s right was the 1st Battalion, Newfoundland Regiment of 88 Brigade.

Attacking at 4.45am, the battalion's War Diary describes how the first objective *"...was taken and consolidated without much trouble"* but subsequent advances became more difficult. The 1st K.O.S.B. lost one officer and 34 men in this attack on 16th August.

At first Clifford's parents were told that their son was wounded and missing, a few days later a letter came saying that he had been killed, followed by another communication repeating that Clifford had been injured. According to the Dewsbury News, Thomas Simpson, Clifford's father, then made enquiries which resulted in the confirmation of his son's death.

Clifford has no known grave and is therefore commemorated on the Tyne Cot Memorial to the Missing, as are 22 of the 34 men from this battalion killed on this day; of the remainder of the battalion's fatal casualties on this day, seven are buried in Dozinghem Military Cemetery*.

After the failure of the Battle of Langemarck on 16th August, Haig decided to hand day to day control of the battle to General Plumer's Second Army, whose area of responsibility was extended northwards. Gough's Fifth Army meanwhile still had responsibility for the northern end of the battlefield, but would now fulfil a secondary role and conform to Plumer's orders. Plumer requested a three week pause in order to make arrangements for the continuation of the battle. Haig readily agreed to this proposal and Plumer's staff set about drawing up plans for attacks of a more limited nature. Before Plumer's plans could be put into effect, there were a further three casualties amongst Ravensthorpe's soldiers, two of these being killed in the Ypres salient.

William Ridley was born in Dewsbury in about 1896. After attending St. Saviour's Boys' School (where he received two strokes on the hand in March 1908 for 'inattention') he worked at Jas Smith and Sons, dyers and dry cleaners. Joining up in Heckmondwike at the age of 19, he was sent to join the 8th Battalion, Duke of Wellington's Regiment (11th (Northern) Division) in October 1916. Four months later in February 1917 he was reported in the Dewsbury News acknowledging a parcel from the Ravensthorpe and Northorpe Soldiers and Sailors Christmas Parcel Fund.

The next time his name appeared was in the Dewsbury Reporter of 15th September 1917 when it was mentioned that his father who lived at 8 Spen Valley Road in Ravensthorpe had received a letter from Sergeant R.C. Bradshaw to say that William had been killed by a sniper on Monday 27th August *"...when*

**** Three casualty clearing stations were positioned close to one another, these were named by the British soldiers, with typical humour, Dosing'em, Bandage'em and Mendin'em. These names have now been adopted into the titles of the now permanent cemeteries that were built adjacent to these casualty clearing stations. The cemeteries are Dozinghem Military Cemetery, Haringhe (Bandaghem) Military Cemetery, and Mendinghem British Cemetery.***

▲ 95. The Vimy Memorial to the Missing.

◄ 96. The entrance to Tyne Cot Cemetery, at the rear of this cemetery stands the Tyne Cot Memorial to the Missing.

attempting to capture some strong German forts, and death was instantaneous." Sergeant Bradshaw returned William's letters, wallet, identification disc and other personal belongings.

Whilst not involved in a major assault, William's battalion had been taking part in an attack on Pheasant Trench, south-east of Langemarck, the trench being south of Pheasant Farm.

The battalion's War Diary states that the left hand side of the attack was successful, but the right was held up by heavy machine gun fire. This fire came from the roof of Pheasant Farm, and the right side of the battalion was forced to dig in just 60 yards from the original position. The left side of the battalion's attack managed to reach Pheasant Trench. The attack cost the battalion three officers and 38 other ranks. William, like 34 of the men killed on the day has no known grave and is commemorated on the Tyne Cot Memorial to the Missing; four of the others are buried in Poelcapelle British Cemetery.

Little is known about George Fieldhouse, who was 23 years old and was born in Dewsbury to Mr and Mrs Charles Fieldhouse. Enlisting in February 1916 (after working for Critchley, Sharpe and Tetlow in Cleckheaton) he was posted to the 4th Battalion Grenadier Guards in November 1916, later transferring to the 2nd Battalion; George was killed on Sunday 2nd September 1917.

The circumstances surrounding his death are unclear; the battalion had been providing working parties up until 30th August. The battalion's War Diary mentions that three men from the 3rd Battalion Coldstream Guards were killed that evening (30th August) when a German shell hit the Coldstream battalion's

RAVENSTHORPE SOLDIER SHOT BY A SNIPER.

On Tuesday morning last Mr. Wrigley, Spen alley Road, Ravensthorpe, received a letter ·om Sergt. R. C. Bradshaw that his son, Pte. William Wrigley, Duke of Wellington's Regiment, was shot by a sniper on August 27th when attempting to capture some strong German forts, and death was instantaneous. At the same time he forwarded deceased's letters, wallet, identification disc, and other personal belongings. Pte. Wrigley had just been eleven months in France, and had taken part in heavy fighting. He joined up at the age of 19, and was in his 21st year. He was formerly employed by lessrs. Jas. Smith and Sons, dyers and dry eaners. Another of Mr. Wrigley's sons is in ie Royal Engineers.

Pte. W. Wrigley, West Yorks., Ravensthorpe (killed).

▲ 97. The caption naming William 'Wrigley' instead of Ridley is an error by The Dewsbury Reporter. The obituary was corrected in the following week's edition.

▲ 98. George Fieldhouse

cookers, the 2nd Grenadier Guards being nearby but suffering no casualties. Later that same evening one man from the 2nd Grenadier Guards was wounded by a shell.

The following day the Grenadiers were relieved and moved back about a mile, where they stayed until 4th September. In this period, the War Diary reports that just one man was wounded (possibly from bombs dropped by German aircraft, or long range shelling). The battalion moved back to the front line on 5th September. No mention is made of fatal casualties, and the only conclusion is that George was one of the men who were injured. This is to a certain extent confirmed by inspecting S.D.G.W. which indicates that George was the battalion's first fatal casualty since early August although there is still some area of doubt here as in such circumstances as these (a soldier dying after receiving wounds in the area behind the front line), one would expect that S.D.G.W. would state 'died of wounds' rather than 'killed in action' and that the soldier would have a known grave.

Private George Fieldhouse has no known grave and is commemorated on the Tyne Cot Memorial to the Missing.

* * *

It is now necessary to break the narrative of the Third Battle of Ypres. Away from the scene of the bitter fighting around Ypres, normal trench holding operations continued. The vast majority of a soldier's experience of front line duty consisted of a daily routine which varied little throughout the war. The large battles such as the Somme, Arras and Third Ypres were very much out of the ordinary course of events. The day to day routine of trench warfare consisted of periods in reserve (at rest), in support (immediately behind the front line), and in the front line itself.

The front line routine started just before day break when there was the morning 'stand to'. This involved being ready to receive a surprise attack by the enemy (the period just before dawn was the favourite time for launching an attack). After this had passed off uneventfully, breakfast was prepared, which usually consisted of trying to fry bacon over a home made cooker. This was followed by an inspection of kit and equipment by the officers, together with men being given tasks for the day, such as mending a parapet or improving a communication trench.

After an evening 'stand to', small patrols would be organised with instructions to undertake such nightly activities as mending the barbed wire in front of the British trenches, patrolling No Man's Land, and otherwise (using the phraseology of the generals) 'Dominating No Man's Land.' Those men not involved in these activities would try to snatch some sleep in the shallow dug-outs scraped into the side of the trenches. This would not be easy with men constantly passing along and inadvertently kicking or knocking the sleepers. The occasional crack of a sniper's rifle, glare cast down from a soaring flare or brief chatter of a machine gun would occur as either one side or the other saw (or thought they saw) enemy soldiers.

It was in routine operations such as these that Bertie Howroyd was killed. Bertie was born in Ravensthorpe in about 1898. Living with his parents, Ephraim and Ellen Howroyd at 93 Clarkson Street Ravensthorpe, he attended the Wesleyan Church and Sunday School and worked as a percher for Pickering Greaves and Co.

(A perch is a frame on which cloth is placed for inspection; a percher is the person who inspects the cloth.) Bertie was called up in about April or May 1917 and after just three months training (part of which he spent in hospital) was sent to France, joining the 10th Battalion, West Yorkshire Regiment (17th (Northern) Division), who were positioned north of Roeux, near Arras (see Chapter 12).

The battalion's War Diary reads:

5th September: *Battalion proceeded to relieve the 6th Dorsets in front line. Relief complete about 12 midnight.*

6th September: *Quiet day with very little shelling. Some slight enemy trench mortar activity.....Every man available employed in improving the trenches. Active patrolling carried out at night.*

Although no mention is made of any casualties, S.D.G.W. indicates that three men from the battalion were killed at this time, two on 6th September and one on 7th September. Bertie was one of those killed on 6th September; he was just 19 years old.

The news of his death came to his parents via Bertie's aunt who lived at 7 Myrtle Road, Ravensthorpe; Bertie had on him at the time of his death a letter from her, and it was therefore to that relative that Colour Sergeant Major W. Joyce wrote to say that Bertie had died. He said that he had been killed *"...straight out and did not suffer one minute"*.

Bertie is buried alongside his two comrades from the 10th West Yorkshires in Brown's Copse Cemetery at Roeux.

99. The cap badge on Bertie's hat is misleading, showing the South Staffordshire Regiment, rather than the West Yorkshire Regiment.

▲ 100. Mrytle Road, Ravensthorpe. *Photograph courtesy of Kirklees Community History Service*

▼ 101. Brown's Copse Cemetery.

Chapter Fifteen

Third Ypres (2)
Menin Road Ridge, Polygon Wood, Broodseinde, Poelcapelle, 1st & 2nd Passchendaele

It will be remembered how, following the failure of General Gough to achieve a breakthrough at the Battle of Langemarck on 16th August, Haig transferred responsibility for the Third Battle of Ypres over to Sir Herbert Plumer's Second Army. Plumer, instead of repeating Gough's failed 'breakthrough' tactics would instead use 'bite and hold' techniques. This would involve only a limited amount of ground being seized, which would then be prepared for defence in order to meet the inevitable German counter-attacks. The German's tactics would be used to the British troops' advantage - by taking the lightly defended ground, thus incurring only slight casualties, the British troops would be more able to withstand the German counter-attacks using their own fire power and also using prearranged artillery and machine gun barrage fire from the rear.

General Plumer first used these tactics in the Third Battle of Ypres on 20th September, in the Battle of the Menin Road Ridge; this limited advance was to be repeated several times with pauses of about a week between each assault. Plumer was planning to take, in approximately a month, the ground that Gough had hoped to seize on the first day.

Plumer also abandoned for the time being the use of tanks, which had proved to be totally unsuitable in the waterlogged and pock-marked ground; instead he would rely on artillery of even greater strength to subdue the defences. In the build up to the infantry assault in the Battle of the Menin Road Ridge the artillery frequently paused its bombardment, giving the impression of an imminent attack; these tactics were designed to confuse the Germans when the time came for the real assault.

After a seven day bombardment, the British troops from eleven divisions went into action at 5.40am on 20th September; the assault was an outstanding success. The attack against the Gheluvelt Plateau was made by four divisions and one of these, the 23rd Division, advanced down the remains of the main road towards Gheluvelt itself. The only area where the British failed to take their objectives was about a mile west of the village of Gheluvelt, at a place named Tower Hamlets.

The barrage that protected the advancing British troops was extraordinarily heavy, not only was artillery of all calibres used, but also massed machine gun fire played on the area behind the German front.

The Machine Gun Corps had been formed in October 1915 when it had been decided that the control of the Vickers machine guns should be removed from battalion level and given to a higher level of command. The Machine Gun Corps was formed into companies, each company being given a number corresponding to the infantry brigade to which it belonged. It was with the 23rd Division's 68 Brigade, and in particular with the 68th Company, M.G.C. that Ravensthorpe's interest lies for the Battle of the Menin Road Ridge.

Ernest Ledgard was born in Mirfield in May 1880 to Frank and Mary Ledgard. For seventeen years before the war he had worked as the wharf manager for Mr Sheard Thornton, coal merchant, but then moved on to be the manager at the coal depot at the Lancashire and Yorkshire Railway for James Wilby Ltd.

Ernest was called up in January 1917 and after undergoing initial training at Blyth in Northumberland, went on to Clipstone Camp in Nottinghamshire for machine gun training. Posted to France on 6th May, he joined the 68th Company, M.G.C.

The unit's War Diary describes how, in early September, the company was in the Dickebusch area. After a period of training, on 18th and 19th September the company (which was split into four sections) moved up to Tor Top Tunnel in Armagh Wood, which is at the southern end of Sanctuary Wood. A total of four M.G.C. companies were employed in providing a protective barrage of fire for the 23rd Division's attack; in addition to this barrage, three of the four sections of the 68th Company, M.G.C. were placed under the orders of the three battalions of 68 Brigade that were making the assault. Number 1 section was in reserve, whilst numbers 2, 3 and 4 sections were allocated to the 13th Durham Light Infantry, 10th Northumberland Fusiliers and 11th Northumberland Fusiliers respectively. Each section was ordered to go forward with the infantry, the battalions attacking from positions near the eastern end of Sanctuary Wood. It would not have been an easy operation for the machine gunners as these were heavy weapons and each gun required a team of six men to operate it.

It has not been possible to determine with which section (and therefore with which battalion) Ernest attacked; the division's attack was generally successful, the 10th and 11th Northumberland Fusiliers taking the first and second objectives (the Red and Blue Lines) and the 13th D.L.I. pressed on towards the northern end of the Tower Hamlets position. Due, however, to the lack of progress by the division on their right (the 41st Division), the 13th D.L.I. had to throw back their southern flank to keep in touch with the 41st Division who had not quite taken all their objectives at Tower Hamlets.

The British army was now firmly established on the Gheluvelt Plateau and in a position to repulse the German counter-attacks. The 23rd Division's casualties were light by First World War standards, the three battalions of infantry taking part in 68 Brigade's attack losing just 171 men killed. The War Diary of the 68th Company, M.G.C. gave casualty figures of one officer and nine other ranks killed, plus two officers and sixteen other ranks wounded. One of the men killed was Private Ernest Ledgard.

A letter was received by Ernest's wife at their home at 285 Ravenswharf Hill, Dewsbury on Tuesday 2nd October, telling her that her husband had been killed on 20th September by a German shell. The letter, from Second Lieutenant L.N. Vizard, stated that Ernest had been killed together with the officer who was with

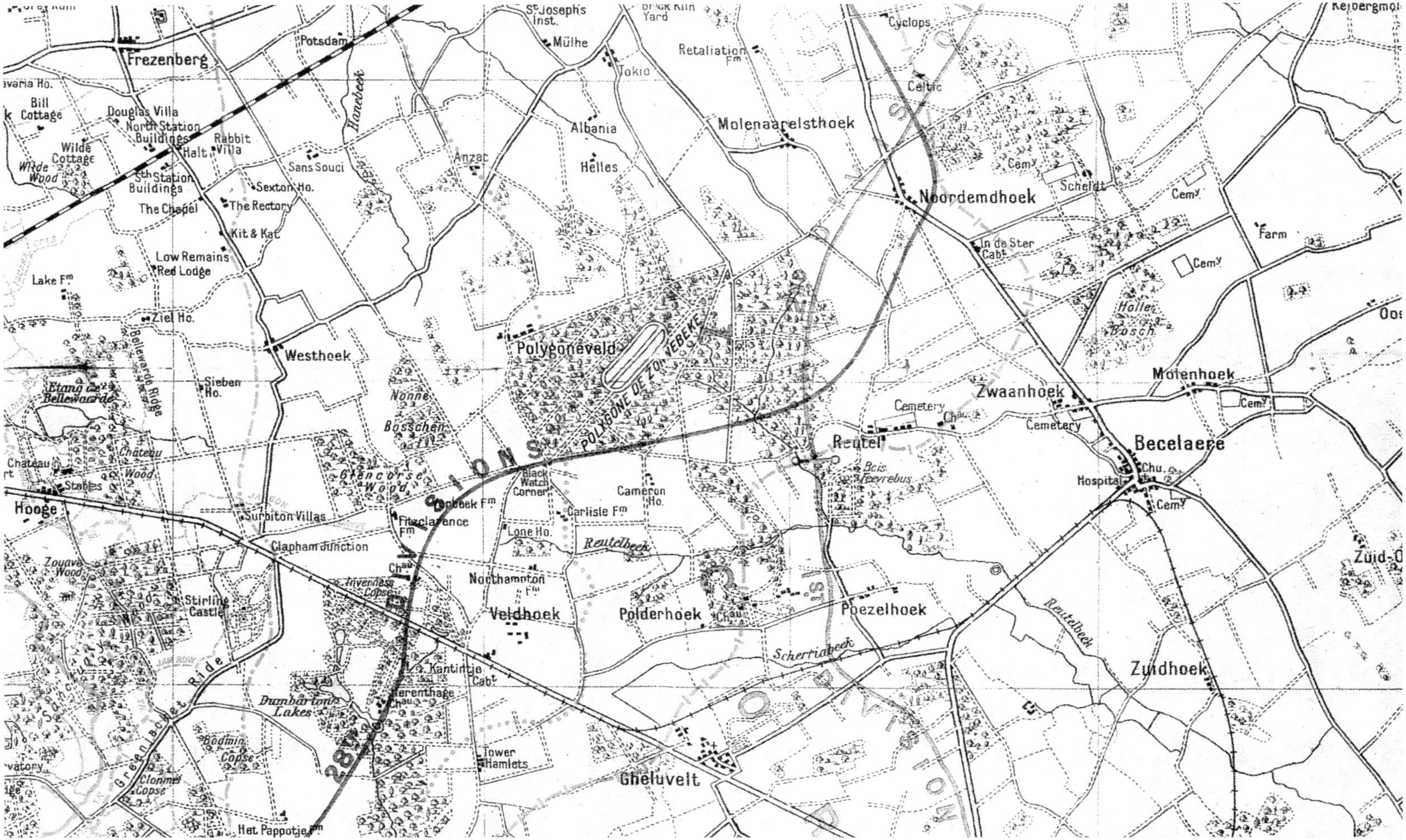

▲ Map 23. The Tower Hamlets area

him* and goes on to describe Ernest as *"....a man to be proud of, always willing, always cheerful and ready to undertake any task which fell to his lot"*. Ernest, who was 37 years old, besides his widowed mother living at Craven Street, Ravensthorpe, left a wife and young child. The Liberal Club, of which he was a member, flew its flag at half mast as a sign of respect.

Ernest's name is commemorated on the Tyne Cot Memorial to the Missing.

Despite the success of the Battle of the Menin Road Ridge, Haig was forced, on 23rd September, to abandon the plans for the amphibious operation on the coast. The headquarters of Rawlinson's Fourth Army (which was to have undertaken the amphibious attack) was now not needed, and its operations were suspended. Rawlinson himself went to a liaison role in Paris until 1918 (see Chapter 18). The B.E.F. operated with just four armies (First, Second, Third and Fifth) for the remainder of the year.

Less than a week after the Battle of the Menin Road Ridge, a follow up attack was made by Plumer's Second Army in an action that became known as the Battle of Polygon Wood.

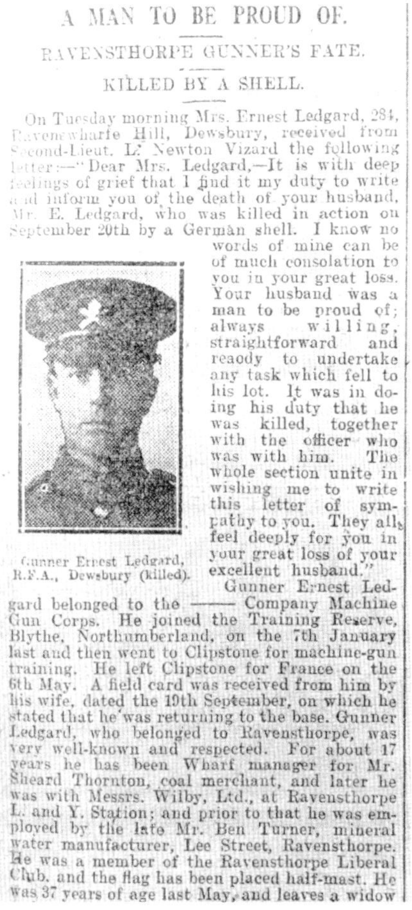

A MAN TO BE PROUD OF.

RAVENSTHORPE GUNNER'S FATE.

KILLED BY A SHELL.

On Tuesday morning Mrs. Ernest Ledgard, 284, Ravenswharfe Hill, Dewsbury, received from Second-Lieut. L. Newton Vizard the following letter:—"Dear Mrs. Ledgard,—It is with deep feelings of grief that I find it my duty to write and inform you of the death of your husband, Mr. E. Ledgard, who was killed in action on September 20th by a German shell. I know no words of mine can be of much consolation to you in your great loss. Your husband was a man to be proud of; always willing, straightforward and reaody to undertake any task which fell to his lot. It was in doing his duty that he was killed, together with the officer who was with him. The whole section unite in wishing me to write this letter of sympathy to you. They all feel deeply for you in your great loss of your excellent husband."

Gunner Ernest Ledgard, R.F.A., Dewsbury (killed).

Gunner Ernest Ledgard belonged to the —— Company Machine Gun Corps. He joined the Training Reserve, Blythe, Northumberland, on the 7th January last and then went to Clipstone for machine-gun training. He left Clipstone for France on the 6th May. A field card was received from him by his wife, dated the 19th September, on which he stated that he was returning to the base. Gunner Ledgard, who belonged to Ravensthorpe, was very well-known and respected. For about 17 years he has been Wharf manager for Mr. Sheard Thornton, coal merchant, and later he was with Messrs. Wilby, Ltd., at Ravensthorpe L. and Y. Station; and prior to that he was employed by the late Mr. Ben Turner, mineral water manufacturer, Lee Street, Ravensthorpe. He was a member of the Ravensthorpe Liberal Club, and the flag has been placed half-mast. He was 37 years of age last May, and leaves a widow

▲ 102. Ernest Ledgard

▲ 103. John Gledhill

** Probably Second Lieutenant R.F. Smith, who is commemorated on the Tyne Cot Memorial to the Missing.*

On Wednesday, 26th September, seven divisions attacked Polygon Wood and the village of Zonnebeke in weather not usually associated with Third Ypres. The day was hot (68°F / 20°C) and dry (over the previous week there had been no rain) and with temperatures having reached 75°F (24°C), the battlefield had largely dried out. A light drizzle had fallen in the last two days before the attack but this had not altered the ground conditions. On the morning of the attack there was a little mist which served to hinder the Germans in the forthcoming battle.

One of the divisions which attacked in the Battle of Polygon Wood was the 3rd Division. The division attacked with its 8 Brigade on the left of the Ypres to Roulers railway line* and 76 Brigade on the right. The 76 Brigade had two battalions (2nd Suffolks and 10th Royal Welsh Fusiliers) leading the attack with the 1st Gordon Highlanders and 8th King's Own (Royal Lancaster Regiment) in support. The division attacked from a line, the centre of which was near a position called Potsdam, which had been an objective of the 6th/7th Royal Scots Fusiliers on 31st July (see Chapter 14).

The War Diary of the 8th King's Own states that following the launch of the attack at 5.30am, a note from 'B' Company was received at battalion headquarters at 7.10am, indicating that all was going well and that casualties were light. The situation deteriorated in the afternoon when the Germans started launching their counter-attacks. A request from 'A' Company (received at headquarters at 2.15pm) to retire due to heavy German shelling was refused - the order to hold on 'at all costs' was given. German counter-attacks were broken up by British artillery. Again, as with the Battle of the Menin Road Ridge, ground had been gained and the German counter-attacks totally repulsed.

The battalion ended the day holding a line from St. Joseph's Institute (a school building in Zonnebeke village) to a position called Tokio (being south-east of the institute); this line was slightly behind the positions held by the 2nd Suffolks. The casualties suffered (according to S.D.G.W.) by the 8th King's Own were 58 killed plus two died of wounds; unfortunately, these statistics included Private John Gledhill.

John Gledhill, aged 35, was born in Ravensthorpe and after attending school went into apprenticeship at Newsome Brothers, piano manufacturers, in Ravensthorpe, working for the firm for over 20 years (also working for this firm was Ralph Crawshaw whose story has been told in Chapter 12). In his spare time John played for Ravensthorpe Clarence football team and was a member of Mirfield's 2nd XI cricket team; he was also a member of both the Liberal Club and Church Institute. John was called up on 1st August 1916, initially joining the R.F.A. and trained at Ripon and Whitchurch until being transferred into the King's Own (Royal Lancaster Regiment). After being allowed home leave at Christmas 1916, John was posted to the 8th Battalion in France on 6th January 1917.

Nothing is known about how John was killed, his wife received a letter at their home at 39 Clarkson Street, Ravensthorpe, dated 12th October stating that John had been killed 'between 26th and 29th September', although all sources agree he was killed on 26th September. John has no known grave and is commemorated on the Tyne Cot Memorial to the Missing.

* * *

** Now a road.*

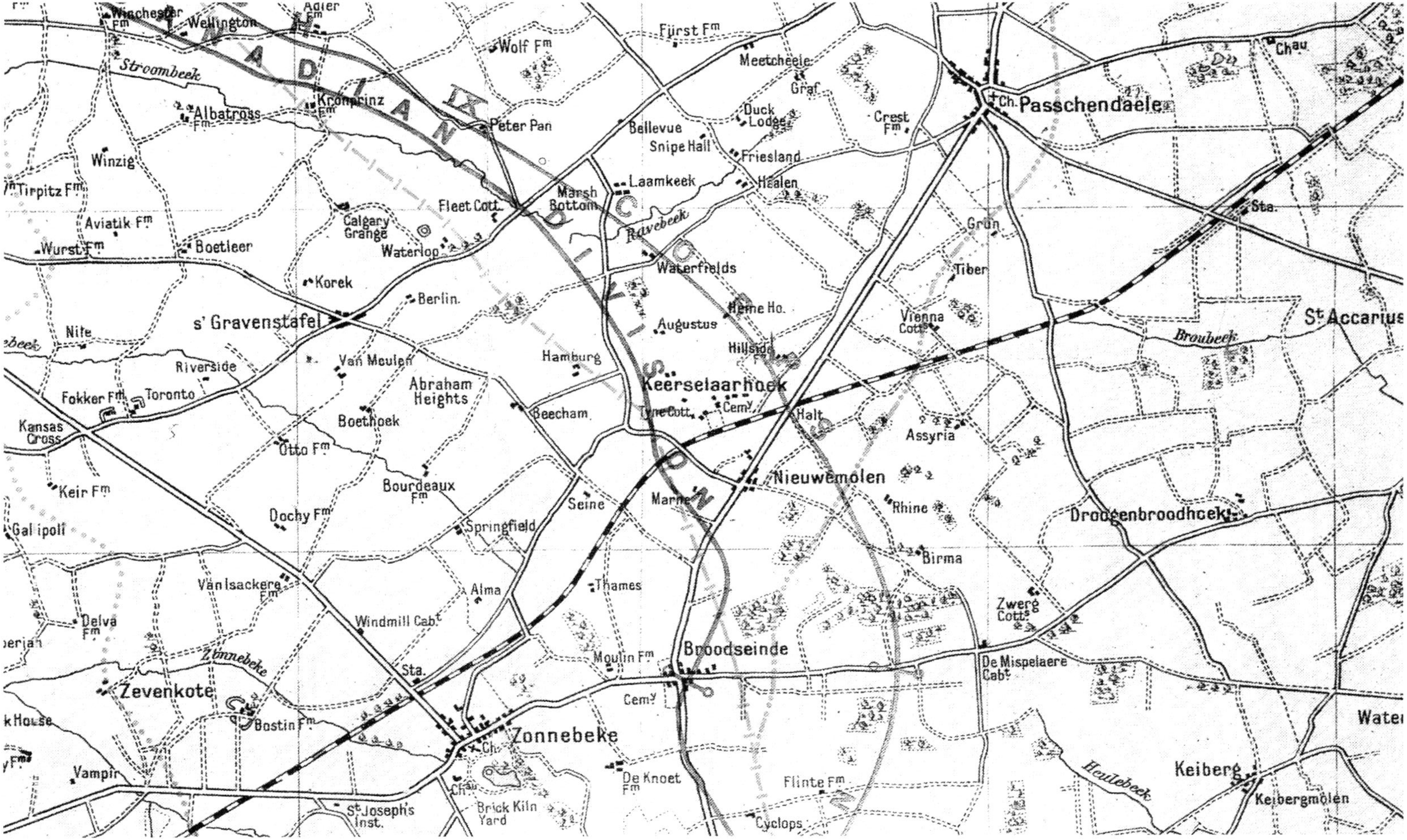

▲ Map 24. The Zonnebeke/Passchendaele area

Following the realisation that their elastic defence tactics were not working, the Germans launched a series of desperate counter-attacks at the end of September and early October; once again these were smashed by British artillery and machine gun fire.

The third of Plumer's assaults took place on Thursday 4th October 1917. Twelve divisions were used in the Battle of Broodseinde in which tanks were used for the first time in Plumer's attacks. Although disrupted and inconvenienced by rain (showers had started on 2nd October, becoming heavy on the day of the assault), the attack - which was intended to take the Broodseinde Ridge and the eastern end of the Gheluvelt Plateau - was again successful.

The Germans had decided to amend their tactics slightly and instead of counter-attacking the British at the earliest opportunity, they decided to mount these assaults a day later, thus giving themselves more time to organise the attacks; this however meant that their front lines had to be held by more men, who simply became casualties of the initial British bombardment and assault. The change in tactics failed to work and the counter-attacks were still broken up by British artillery. Believing the Germans now to be on the point of collapse, Haig ordered the cavalry to be moved up in readiness to exploit any breakthrough that might come about. Unfortunately this did not occur.

Nobody from Ravensthorpe was killed in the Battle of Broodseinde, but the village's luck did not hold out for the next of Plumer's attacks

Preparations for the next blow, scheduled for 9th October were seriously hampered by the rain which started to fall extremely heavily on 7th October. Additionally the Germans had improved the deployment of their barbed wire in front of their positions. The previous problem for the British, of movement across the barren moon-scape of a battlefield that had been fought across over the previous weeks now reoccurred; long meandering plank roadways were constructed that with the cold rain and clinging mud, became treacherous. Anyone straying from these was likely to be sucked under and consumed by the mud which stretched as far as the eye could see. Shattered tree stumps showed where woods had once stood, a small pile of bricks marked the remains of a village. Casualty evacuation became a marathon with relays of up to sixteen men being required for each stretcher case. The front line was held by pockets of men spread out in water-filled shell holes. Inter-unit relief was almost impossible.

Despite these problems, the high ground of the final ridge seemed, to G.H.Q., a target which could be achieved with one final push. If the German line could not be broken, by taking the final ridge, the troops would at least be on higher ground which, whilst not dry, would be less wet than the ground currently occupied. It is against this background that an attack was ordered against the village of Poelcapelle and the surrounding area; if successful, this attack would pave the way for an assault on the final ridge at Passchendaele.

At 5.20am on Tuesday 9th October, the Battle of Poelcapelle commenced. One of the eleven divisions attacking was the 49th (West Riding) Division which was being used for the first time in the Third Battle of Ypres. The 49th Division and the 66th (2nd East Lancashire) Division to their right were expected to advance along two parallel spurs of high ground in the direction of the village of Passchendaele; the 49th Division was to attack along the Bellevue Spur. Between the two divisions lay the valley of the Ravebeek, normally a stream but now inundated, and described by an intelligence summary as *"Saturated ground. Quite impassable. Should be avoided by all troops at all times."*

The 49th (West Riding) Division started approaching the front line from the town of Ypres (approximately two miles away) at 7pm on 8th October. It was thought that the division would be able to easily cover this distance in five hours and be at the jumping off positions at midnight, giving the troops five hours rest before the attack at 5.20am; unfortunately it proved to be impossible to be in position by midnight. The duckboard tracks were coated with slime or submerged and seemed to be shattered every few yards (the Royal Engineers had not had sufficient time to make repairs). The men, being heavily laden (each man carried 60 lbs of equipment) slipped and collided and fell off the tracks into water-filled craters, their comrades stopped in an attempt to rescue them; the columns of men halted, lurched forward and then halted again. Both the 49th and 66th Divisions only just made it to their jumping off positions on time. The men, covered from head to foot in mud and slime, had covered barely 400 yards per hour.

Meanwhile the artillery was attempting to lay a barrage on the German positions; this too was proving to be virtually impossible. The gun platforms were continually sinking into the mud and, being unstable, made accurate aiming impossible. The guns themselves were up to their axles in mud, making adjustments and manouvering a nightmare. The ammunition had to be brought to the gun lines on pack mules, these animals encountering the same difficulties on the duckboard tracks as the men. Each journey took eleven hours, and when the shells arrived at the guns, each round had to be cleaned individually to make it fit for firing. These difficulties were the cause of what was described as a 'feeble' barrage.

The 49th (West Riding) Division attacked at 5.20am with their 146 and 148 Brigades, the troops came to the Ravebeek which was by now a swamp, 150 feet wide, the water being waist deep in the centre. Only 146 Brigade (containing four battalions of the West Yorkshire Regiment) got across; on the right 148 Brigade were unable to cross the morass and in a desperate attempt to advance, the three battalions making the attack (the 1/4th and 1/5th York and Lancasters and the 1/5th K.O.Y.L.I.) attempted to move up the remains of the Gravenstafel to Meetcheele road. The battalions, being in one column, came under machine gun and shrapnel fire from the Germans and despite the introduction of the 1/4th K.O.Y.L.I., the attack failed. The German barbed wire was intact and the troops had virtually no chance of reaching their objectives.

The division suffered 2,585 casualties (S.D.G.W. gives 654 men killed in the division's infantry battalions on 9th October), primarily amongst its two attacking brigades, however 147 Brigade, made up of battalions of the Duke of Wellington's Regiment did not escape without casualties, its four battalions losing 41 killed on this day. Other casualties were inevitably incurred, with numerous soldiers being wounded; it was probably on this day that Private Fred Hey sustained his injuries.

Fred was born in about 1889 to Job and Susan Hey, although there is some confusion about his age as the C.W.G.C. state he was 29 in 1917, but the newspapers gave his age as 28. Nothing is known of his early life; it seems that before the war he was living with his sister at 16 Bradbury Street, Ravensthorpe. Associated with the Primitive Methodist Church in Thornhill Lees, where he taught in the Sunday School, Fred had worked as a tenterer for Marshall, Kaye and Marshall but just prior to enlisting in 1915 he was working in Huddersfield.

(A tenterer is the person who stretches cloth on a tenter (a frame) in order to ensure the cloth does not lose its shape whilst it is drying.) It was in Huddersfield that he joined the Duke of Wellington's Regiment, being posted to the 1/5th Battalion in France in February 1916.

Fred was wounded twice during the Battle of the Somme, firstly in the leg on July 14th, from which he quickly recovered, only to be injured during the attack on the Pope's Nose (see Chapter 8), receiving a wound to his back and having three ribs fractured. Recovering from these wounds, he was home on leave at Christmas, but according to the Dewsbury Reporter, was not to rejoin his battalion until 17th July 1917.

The War Diary for the 1/5th Duke of Wellington's states that the battalion was heavily shelled on the evening of 9th October; it was probably during this bombardment that Fred was injured. Fred was evacuated from the front line, through the casualty clearing station and arrived at one of the base hospitals on the coast on Wednesday 10th October. It was from the hospital in Wimereux (north of Boulogne) that one of the matrons wrote to Fred's sister, Mrs Heaton, to say that Fred had arrived badly injured, with wounds in his shoulders and legs, his left leg being so badly damaged that it had been amputated at the casualty clearing station. The letter said Fred *"sent his love to her* [his sister] *and he would write when he was able."* Fred died from his injuries four days later on Sunday 14th October and is buried in Wimereux Communal Cemetery.

RAVENSTHORPE SOLDIER DIES FROM WOUNDS.

The matron of the London General Hospital, Boulogne, wrote to Mrs. Arthur Heaton, Bradbury Street, Ravensthorpe, regretting to inform her of the serious illness of her brother, Pte. Fred Hey, who was admitted on October 10th suffering from severe wounds to shoulders and legs. His left leg was so badly wounded that it had to be amputated at the casualty clearing-station. He sent his love to her, and said he would write when he was able. The matron assured Mrs. Heaton that everything possible was being done for him, and he had every care. On Wednesday a telegram was received from the hospital stating that he had died on October 13th from gas gangrene and amputation of the left leg. Pte. Hey enlisted in the Duke of Wellington's at Huddersfield in 1915. In February, 1916, he went out to France, and was wounded in the leg on July 14th. He returned to the fighting line, and on September 3rd, 1916, was again wounded in the back and had three ribs fractured. He was home on leave at the beginning of December last and at Christmas. On July 17th this year he rejoined at Ripon, and then went to Clipstone and France. He was 28 years of age, and his father, Mr. Job Hey, now of Thornhill Lees, worked for many years for the District Council. Pte. Hey was formerly a tenterer at Messrs. Marshall, Kaye, and Marshall's, but when he enlisted was working at

Pte. Fred Hey. Duke of Wellington's, Ravensthorpe (died of wounds).

▲ 104. Fred Hey

▲ 105. Charles Hollingworth

Fred Hey was not the only Ravensthorpe soldier to become a casualty on 9th October. Charles Henry Hollingworth was born in 1893 to Mr and Mrs Henry Hollingworth. In his youth, Charles attended St. Saviour's Church (going to St. Saviour's Boys' School) and was a member of the Boys Brigade; he later went to work as a cloth fuller for Henry Wheatley and Sons at Hopton Mills. After being called up into the army on 6th October 1916, he was posted to France with the Royal Field Artillery on 27th December, but was later transferred to the infantry, joining the 6th Battalion, Yorkshire Regiment. It was with this unit, in the 11th (Northern) Division that Charles was involved in the attack on 9th October.

The 11th Division was in the line a little to the north of the 49th (West Riding) Division, and like the West Riding Division, their approach to the front line was fraught with difficulties, taking fourteen hours to complete. The 11th Division attacked to the north of the village of Poelcapelle at 5.20am with the 6th Yorkshires and 9th West Yorkshires leading the assault.

During the attack Charles received a gunshot wound to the right arm, resulting in a fracture, plus bullet wounds in his back. He sent a field post card to his mother which arrived at 775 Kiln Terrace, Huddersfield Road, Ravensthorpe on Wednesday 17th October to say he was wounded and in a French hospital. After his condition stabilised he was evacuated to England, arriving at the Hartley University War Hospital in Southampton on Sunday 28th October. The following day, the hospital chaplain wrote to his parents to say Charles had arrived and was *"going on well"*. Suddenly, Charles' condition deteriorated and he died on Tuesday 30th October.

An inquest into his death was held, which was heard on the afternoon of Thursday 1st November. The family were represented by Charles' mother and sister. After the evidence of identification was heard, the inquest was told how Mrs Hollingworth had last seen her son alive on Christmas Day 1916, when he had set off for France. The proceedings then heard how Charles had been admitted to hospital on Sunday 28th. On Tuesday, the wound had started to bleed and it was felt that the only chance of saving him was to perform an operation. Although this was successful in stopping the bleeding, Charles died later from loss of blood. The jury returned a verdict of 'death due to loss of blood, the result of a wound received in battle.'

The chaplain who had previously written to Charles' parents wrote again describing how *"Charles had talked to* [him] *in the most cheerful way about Dewsbury, Thornhill and Mirfield....although I knew he was very seriously wounded, I expected his ultimate recovery."*

Charles was buried in the grounds of St. Mary's Parish Church in Mirfield on Saturday 3rd November, the service being conducted by the vicar of Ravensthorpe, the Reverend R.H. Sutch. Amongst the mourners was Charles' fiancee, Lizzie Thornton. Charles was 24 years of age.

After the Battle of Poelcapelle, in which Fred Hey and Charles Hollingworth received their fatal wounds, a period of just four days elapsed before the next Ravensthorpe soldier was killed.

Clifford Haley was born in Gomersal in 1898 to Mr and Mrs Charles Haley. After attending St. Saviour's Boys' School and the Ravensthorpe Congregational Church Sunday School, Clifford joined his father in working at Hartley Brothers, curriers, in Ravensthorpe. In his spare time Clifford played the cornet in the Dewsbury Borough Brass Band, of which his father was conductor.

Enlisting on 18th February 1917, after his training Clifford was sent to France on 18th August, joining the 6th Battalion, K.O.Y.L.I. in the 14th (Light) Division. The battalion's War Diary tells how they were ordered to occupy the front line south-east of Polygon Wood. The conditions were grim: *"The position consisted chiefly of shell holes, but some much damaged trenches were also used* [two] *streams had become practically impassable; marsh and waterlogged shell holes for a width of about thirty yards formed very safe flanks. Our front was also covered by a marsh formed by the junction of the two streams. Only one passable place was found in the Reutel to Ypres Road."* The diary goes on to describe how the whole position was overlooked by the Germans which *"...caused some trouble with sniping and machine gun fire. The battalion was shelled almost every night and a good deal during the day."*

On Saturday 13th October* Clifford lost his life; it was raining and Corporal N. Murray had (according to an article appearing in the Dewsbury Reporter) made way for Clifford in *"...a little shelter in the trench...when a shell burst on the top..."* the explosion caused Corporal Murray, Clifford and another soldier to be buried. Whilst Corporal Murray managed to extricate himself, he found that the other two had been killed +.

Clifford's family received a letter at their home at 65 Sackville Street from Second Lieutenant Cyril A. Taylor and Corporal Murray in which they and the Company Commander expressed sympathy in the family's bereavement.

▲ 106. Clifford Haley

▲ 107. William Haldenby

***** *The newspapers indicate the day was 12th October and the photograph gives 11th October.*

+ S.D.G.W.: - 1 killed on 11th October; 7 killed on 12th October; 5 killed plus 1 died of wounds on 13th October. Of the six fatalities on 13th October, three are commemorated on the Tyne Cot Memorial to the Missing and two are buried in Tyne Cot Cemetery.

Clifford has no known grave and is commemorated on the Tyne Cot Memorial to the Missing.

Whilst Clifford was killed in the front line, Private* William Haldenby would have expected to be safe when, on 14th October he was returning to Dulwich Camp, near Elverdinghe after his battalion had been sent to get cleaned up at the baths at Elverdinghe Chateau. The battalion (1st Battalion, Scots Guards) had just taken part with the rest of the Guards Division in the Battle of Poelcapelle, the battalion having come out of the front line on 13th October.

Upon returning to Dulwich Camp, dinner was served probably from the large, mobile cookers that battalions had as part of their equipment (these cookers followed the battalion about, except of course into the front lines). The serving of the meal was being completed when the battalion was caught in a raid by a German aeroplane which dropped five bombs. These bombs killed six men outright and wounded twelve others, a further six of the wounded succumbed to their wounds later that day or on the following day.

According to a letter written to his wife at 109 Sackville Street, Ravensthorpe, William was a short distance away from one of these bombs and although no wounds were found on him, he *"died instantaneously from shock."*

William, who was 36, was born and lived in Leeds until moving to Ravensthorpe where he worked as a case fitter at Cottam's Victoria Piano Works in Ravensthorpe for eleven years (it is possible that this was the same firm as John Gledhill and Ralph Crawshaw worked for, as the name Newsome Brothers and 'Cottam's' seems to have been interchangeable). He joined up on 1st July 1916, going to France in February 1917. He left a widow and three young children.

The six men, including William, who were killed outright, all lie side by side at Bleuet Farm Cemetery, near Elverdinghe.

*   *   *

Prior to the Battle of Poelcapelle, in view of the deteriorating weather conditions, both Gough and Plumer recommended to Haig that the battle be brought to an end, however Haig insisted that the attacks should continue. Even the nightmarish conditions of the Battle of Poelcapelle did not persuade G.H.Q. to call a halt; instead preparations were ordered for an assault on the village of Passchendaele which was attacked just three days later on 12th October. Eight divisions were involved in this attack which was a failure due to the mud preventing an accurate or heavy barrage to be fired; the infantry crawled forward but were stopped from advancing by uncut barbed wire and fire from the German pill boxes.

The final two soldiers from Ravensthorpe to be killed in the Third Battle of Ypres lost their lives shortly after this First Battle of Passchendaele.

Friend Whitwam was, at 42, the oldest soldier named on the Ravensthorpe War Memorial to die on active service+. Nothing is known about his childhood or youth,

**** Both of Ravensthorpe's soldiers who served in Guards Battalions held the rank of Private; the rank of Guardsman, which replaced it was not introduced until 1923.***

+ George Jackson (see Chapter 13) at 45 years of age, was older than Friend Whitwam but not sent abroad. The ages of a further three of the men on the War Memorial are not known (Charles Blamires - Chapter 9, Robert Ouldridge - Chapter 20 and Charles Matthews - Appendix 1).

although it is known he was born in Mirfield in May 1876. He married Annie Newhill on 2nd November 1901 at Wellington Road Chapel, Dewsbury and they lived at 11 William Street, Ravensthorpe. Friend was a regular attender at the Primitive Methodist Chapel, where he had been a member of the choir for twenty years.

Volunteering on 11th December 1915, his papers indicate that he was 5' 9" tall and weighed just less than 10 stones with a chest measurement of 37" fully expanded; he stated his occupation as being a yeast dealer. Friend was called up on 12th September 1916 and was at first sent to the 2/4th Battalion Northumberland Fusiliers, a training battalion based at York, although the battalion moved in November 1916 to Clevedon in Somerset.

On 16th June 1917 Friend arrived in France and was sent to the training camp at Etaples. On 1st July 1917 he was ordered to join the 13th Battalion Durham Light Infantry (68 Brigade, 23rd Division). He arrived at the battalion's headquarters on 4th July and was posted to 'A' Company; it is likely that he took part in the Battle of the Menin Road Ridge on 20th September.

On 18th October, the 13th D.L.I. was ordered from the camp at Railway Dugouts (south of Ypres) to the front line at Reutel, east of Polygon Wood. The battalion's War Diary for 21st October indicates that although it was fairly quiet during the day, in the evening the Germans shelled the positions quiet heavily, the casualties being thirteen men killed plus a further thirteen wounded. One of those killed was Friend Whitwam.

Annie Whitwam received a telegram on Saturday 3rd November informing her of her husband's death. A letter came a few days later from an army chaplain in which Annie was told that Friend had been killed by a shell and had died without suffering, being buried about five miles east of Ypres.

If Friend was indeed buried, his grave was not found after the war and he is now commemorated on the Tyne Cot Memorial to the Missing along with twelve of the thirteen men who were killed on 21st October.

Charles Lapish was killed two days later on 23rd October. Born in Asselby, near Goole, in 1888 to George and Mary Ann Lapish, he was educated at Mirfield National School and Heckmondwike Higher Grade School. Leaving school he went to work for the Yorkshire Chemical and Dyework Company in Tanhouse Street, Ravensthorpe, as an analytical chemist.

In his spare time, Charles was heavily involved in church work, being a member of St. Saviour's Parish Church Choir, the Men's Bible Class and secretary of the Church Institute; he was also a member of 'PADS' the Parish Amateur Dramatic Society. Leaving his family and his fiancee, Grace Gledhill, he joined the army in February 1916, training at Hedon, Hornsea and Withensea on the East Yorkshire coast, before being posted to the 10th Battalion K.O.Y.L.I. (21st Division) in December 1916.

Charles was wounded in the neck on 3rd May 1917 during the latter stages of the Battle of Arras; not being badly wounded he was not sent back home. He was wounded again in September, a letter appeared in the Dewsbury News on 29th September in which he was reported to have written that once again he was only lightly wounded and therefore *"...not one of the lucky ones for 'Blighty' – having recovered too quickly."* The letter goes on to say that he had at last met someone he knew, although he did not state who that was.

▲ 108. Friend Whitwam

▲ 109. Charles Lapish

In mid-October the 10th K.O.Y.L.I. passed through Brewery Camp, east of Dickebusch, the battalion's War Diary describing it as fifty tents *"floating in a sea of mud"*; the battalion spent just one night at Brewery Camp before moving on to the camp at Railway Dugouts. From here, on Tuesday 23rd October, the battalion was ordered to the front line near Reutel (the same area in which Friend Whitwam had been killed). It seems that Charles never completed the journey; on the way up to the line, near Hooge, the German shelling became heavy, with one shell falling in the middle of 'B' Company; the resulting casualties, according to the battalion's War Diary were 'about 20'. It is easy to imagine the confusion of the moment with wounded men laying about, orders being shouted, company and platoon officers trying to find who was injured and who was not, medical orderlies giving rudimentary first aid. All the time crashes of more artillery making everyone duck, and the sudden glare of a Very light. The battalion's officers would have been keen to proceed from this unhealthy spot.

Later, when the day's events were recorded in the War Diary the casualty figure was amended to two officers and twelve other ranks wounded plus two other ranks killed (S.D.G.W. indicates 4 men killed plus another who died of wounds). One of those killed was Charles Lapish.

Charles' widowed mother heard in early November that Charles had been killed. This seems to have come from the parents of Arnold Tompkins; Arnold (who had been killed on 31st July - see Chapter 14) had a brother, Aubrey, who had written to his parents to say that he had seen Charles Lapish the previous day (25th October), killed by a shell. Although this report gives a date two days later than the official date (23rd October), it must be presumed the information was genuine (possibly Aubrey had been told on the 25th that Charles had been killed). It was not until Friday 16th November that Charles' mother received official confirmation at the family home at 36 Clarkson Street that Charles had been killed.

Charles is commemorated on the Tyne Cot Memorial to the Missing.

* * *

The failure on 12th October of the First Battle of Passchendaele led to the final hope of strategic victory in Third Ypres being abandoned, however the high ground of the Passchendaele Ridge was still a tempting target, if only to allow the British troops the benefit of dryer ground on which to spend the winter. Haig therefore ordered a final assault to be prepared. This, the Second Battle of Passchendaele, was scheduled for 26th October.

Two days before the attack was due to take place, and hundreds of miles away from the Flanders plain, the Austrians (reinforced by six German divisions) attacked and threw back the Italian army from their mountain-top positions on the Italian - Austrian front line in the Alps. Although the Italians were forced to retreat a full seventy miles they managed to hold the Germans and Austrians on the line of the River Piave. Reinforcements were requested by the Italian Commander-in-Chief and Lloyd George, seeing an opportunity to weaken Haig, readily agreed, sending General Plumer plus five divisions; the French Government sent a further six divisions. (See Chapter 22 for further details of the war in Italy.)

In a final all-out effort to ensure the Third Battle of Ypres ended on a high note, Haig, for the first time in the battle sent the Canadian Corps into action. Despite all previous problems, somehow the Canadians, reinforcing their reputation as amongst the best troops available to Haig, managed to advance and got to within 500 yards of Passchendaele village. This attack, on 26th October, although the last major assault of the Third Battle of Ypres was not the end of the battle, further small scale attacks were made until 6th November when the village was finally taken*.

The Third Battle of Ypres officially ended on 10th November 1917, having cost in the region of 300,000 Allied casualties +. Although less costly than the Somme (400,000 casualties) the conditions in which the battle was fought has given it a reputation for sheer awfulness that will probably never be extinguished.

* * *

After Charles Lapish was killed, the next soldier from Ravensthorpe to lose his life was Wilfred Arthur Hirst. Wilfred was the son of George and Clara Hirst of 26

**** The Third Battle of Ypres is now more commonly (but inaccurately) known as the Battle of Passchendaele. The (two) Battles of Passchendaele forming only a relatively small part of the overall battle.***

+ The cost to Ravensthorpe was thirteen soldiers killed, which is just less than the Battle of the Somme, in which fifteen men from the village were killed.

Dearnley Street, Ravensthorpe. Born in Mirfield in August 1893, Wilfred worked at Kershaw Brothers, cabinet makers, in Ravensthorpe until joining the Royal Engineers March 1917. He was posted to the 426 Field Company, a third line (or depot) territorial unit which was formed on 1st January 1917 and was used for sending drafts to the first and second lines of the company. The field company was, in peace time, the 2nd (West Lancashire) Field Company R.E. Like the infantry units, when the company went to France, it replicated itself, the original unit becoming the 1/2nd Company, the new one the 2/2nd; ultimately the 2/2nd was sent to France, and the third line unit (to which Wilfred was drafted) was created, this being the 3/2nd (West Lancashire) Field Company.

Whilst undergoing his training at Caernarvon (where the company was based), Wilfred received some inoculations which seem to have made him unwell. He was home on leave in mid-October for his sister's wedding, but after returning to his unit became worse, and was admitted to Bangor Hospital on Thursday 25th October suffering from a septic arm and bleeding from the mouth. He deteriorated rapidly, vomiting blood on Friday morning and shortly afterwards became unconscious; he died later that day at the age of 24.

Wilfred was buried on Monday 29th October at Mirfield Parish Church; a large attendance included representatives from Kershaw Brothers, Ravensthorpe Parish Football Club (with whom he was a player) and the Bible Class (of which he was a member).

The last two soldiers from Ravensthorpe who became casualties in the Ypres salient in 1917 were both members of the 49th (West Riding) Division. Since the Battle of Poelcapelle, the division had lost its commander, Major-General Perceval

▲ 110. Wilfred Hirst

▲ 111. Wilfred Hirst's headstone in St. Mary's Parish Churchyard, Mirfield.

who was sent home on 18th October. Perceval's replacement was Brigadier-General Neville Cameron who was promoted from command of 151 Infantry Brigade (50th (Northumbrian) Division).

All of this would have been of very little concern to Private Luke Leadbeater. Luke was born in Newcastle-upon-Tyne in 1898. After his father, also called Luke, died his mother remarried; it may have been at this time that the family moved to Ravensthorpe, where they lived at 636 Huddersfield Road. A member of Ravensthorpe United Methodist Church and Sunday School, Luke worked at Jas Smith and Sons until, on 14th February 1917, shortly after his 18th birthday, he joined the Duke of Wellington's Regiment. After receiving the usual period of training he was posted to the 1/5th Battalion on 11th October. It was to be less than six weeks after joining the battalion that Luke was killed.

On 19th November, the battalion moved up to the Broodseinde Ridge, north of Becelaere. The battalion's War Diary describes the sight that met the battalion during the move to the front line:

"The enemy persistently shelled the whole area whilst the relief was going on. The whole of the country between Ypres and the new forward line was one mass of shell holes and when one looked back from the different ridges it is a marvel how ever the original front line was held for so long in front of Ypres and still more of a marvel how the ground was afterwards taken. Duckboard paths and plank roads were made across the mass of shell holes for the infantry, and there were separate tracks for mules."

The diary entry for 22nd November (the day Luke was killed) is brief, indicating heavy shelling by the Germans at intervals throughout the day.

Second Lieutenant R.B. Atkinson, wrote a letter to Sarah Rowbottom, Luke's mother, but it was a letter from Lance Corporal Arthur Sheard to Luke's fiancee

▲ 112. Luke Leadbeater

▲ 113. William Greaves

that gave the details surrounding Luke's death; it seems that Luke had been sheltering in a dug-out in the trenches on Thursday 22nd November when a shell came over, killing Luke and another soldier and wounding a third.

Luke Clegg Leadbeater is buried in Aeroplane Cemetery; in the adjoining grave is Private John Wiseman who was the other soldier from the battalion to be killed on this day.

A month after Luke was killed, William Greaves was injured. William, at 21, was two years older than Luke, and had been sent to France in January 1917. William was born and went to school in Ravensthorpe (playing in the St. Saviour's Boys' School football team); he also attended the Parish Church where he sang in the choir. After leaving school he worked for Rawdon, Briggs & Co. in Ravensthorpe until September 1916 when he was conscripted into the army, joining the K.O.Y.L.I. After being sent overseas he joined the 1/5th Battalion, being wounded in the right leg in May 1917. After recovering from this injury, in August he was wounded again, this time in the face and left knee. Again he recovered and writing what would be his last letter home on 8th December, William told his mother not to worry: *"I shall be home at Christmas if they are giving leave when I get back to my battalion."*

William was wounded for the final time on either 14th or 16th December, other than the wound being in his right thigh, no details survive about the incident. The battalion was providing working parties at this time in the Ypres salient, and it can only be assumed that William was on one of these when wounded. He was evacuated to hospital at Etaples, on the French coast, from where a chaplain wrote to his parents to say that their son was receiving the best of care. A few days later Sister R. Hervey wrote to say that he might be able to write himself in a few days time, but it would be a while before he was fit enough to travel to England. Unfortunately, this was not to be the case, as William developed pneumonia and died on 16th January 1918.

William's parents, Joseph and Sarah Greaves who lived at 7 Day Street, Ravensthorpe, received the information from the War Office a few days later.

William is buried at Etaples Military Cemetery.

Chapter Sixteen

Cambrai: Lessons Learned?

During much of the Third Battle of Ypres, the condition of the battlefield was such that it was impossible for the tanks to have much affect on the outcome of the battle. Within days of the opening of the battle, it became clear that the terrain was unsuitable for tanks. Frustrated at the lack of opportunities, Lieutenant-Colonel J.F.C. Fuller, the Chief Staff Officer of the Tank Corps sought an area of the Western Front that was suitable for exploitation; what was needed was an area which was dry and was not already devastated by artillery fire, because swampy or heavily pock-marked ground invariably reduced the effectiveness of the tanks.

The lines in front of the German held town of Cambrai were recognised as a suitable spot and Fuller drew up a plan for a large raid on the German trenches to be undertaken by the Tank Corps.

Brigadier-General Hugh Elles (a Royal Engineers officer commanding the Tank Corps) was enthusiastic about the plan, especially as there was to be no preliminary bombardment. This would therefore avoid the Germans being warned about the attack and would also avoid the terrain being turned into a mass of shell holes.

As G.H.Q. was fully occupied at this time with the Third Battle of Ypres, the plan was put before General Byng, on the front of whose Third Army lay the town of Cambrai.

Some time before Fuller's plan was drafted, Brigadier-General Hugh Tudor, who commanded the artillery in the 9th (Scottish) Division had been looking at how to avoid the necessity of each artillery piece having to register prior to a bombardment. This registration invariably alerted the Germans to an imminent attack. Instead of the registration, Tudor worked out that an accurate bombardment could be brought down on the enemy by using a technique called predicted shooting - mathematics would avoid the need for registration. (Each gun was unique in the way it fired, once each barrel was calibrated, calculations based on the range to the target and the weather conditions could be made, giving the gunners accurate data to enable them to hit targets without having to fire ranging shots.)

This discovery meant that instead of the usual artillery fire lasting several days, the guns could open up a hurricane bombardment just as the troops attacked.

When Fuller's plan came to Third Army Headquarters, Byng invited the Tank Corps to comment on Tudor's scheme, the result of which was the formulation of a much larger idea, involving a major infantry attack on the Hindenburg Line, rather than just a raid by the Tank Corps. A breach would be made in the line and the cavalry would pass through to exploit the open ground behind.

The battle was to be unique in several ways besides in the use of the artillery. Instead of using tanks in small numbers, an overwhelming force was mustered in a relatively small area (six miles of front was to be attacked) and infantry / tank cooperation was worked out so that each would give the other close support during the attack.

In view of the expansion of the plan from a raid into an attempt to punch a hole in the Hindenburg Line, a total of five divisions were selected to take part in the attack. Originally the main weight of the attack was to be in the south, however the topography of the area soon made it obvious that Bourlon Wood was the key to the plan. Bourlon Wood dominated the approaches to Cambrai, sitting on high ground south-west of the town.

As mentioned in Chapter 10, the Hindenburg Line was incredibly strong; as well as a heavily wired outpost line (the barbed wire being hundreds of yards deep), there was also a further wide and strongly wired fire trench behind. There were numerous machine gun posts with excellent fields of fire. A support trench was sited two hundred yards behind, equally well protected and wide (the width of the trenches was intended to prevent tanks from crossing). The whole system was repeated a mile to the rear, with another (incomplete) system further back. In order to overcome this formidable obstacle, the plan for the tanks had to be very carefully thought out; in addition to the 378 fighting tanks, a further 54 tanks were to be fitted with sledges in order to transport ammunition forward to the attacking troops (the supply of which had always been a problem). Grapnels were to be fitted to 32 other tanks so as to enable them to drag to one side the thick belts of barbed wire. Nine tanks were equipped with wireless equipment in the hope that the ever present problem of communication may be overcome, and two were given bridging material (there were two canals crossing the proposed battlefield); one tank was even given telephone cable to lay.

In addition each tank carried a tightly rolled fascine of brushwood which, when dropped into the wide trenches, would allow tanks to cross.

At 6.20am on Tuesday 20th November, five divisions from Byng's Third Army attacked. The surprise of the attack together with devastating artillery fire and the appearance of the tanks totally overwhelmed the 2½ German divisions who were holding the front. The infantry divisions used in the attack were, from south to north, 12th (Eastern), 20th (Light), 6th, 51st (Highland), and 62nd (West Riding). In addition, to the north (ie. the left) of the West Riding Division, the 36th (Ulster) Division was to be used to secure the left flank of the attack, their assault to be made shortly after that of the other divisions. The Ulsters were to attack to the north of the Canal du Nord, which had not been completed when war broke out and was still effectively a large, dry ditch. One of the division's objectives was a large spoil heap which had been made by the French before the war when they were digging out the canal. This spoil heap was an important feature as it dominated the immediate area.

As can be seen from the map, these divisions faced the Germans in a rough semi-circle. As will be mentioned later, the 62nd (West Riding) Division's objective was towards Bourlon Wood, taking the villages of Havrincourt, Graincourt and Anneux in the process. To their left, the 36th (Ulster) Division was to guard the flank of the attack by taking Moeuvres, whilst on the right the 51st (Highland) Division were to capture Flesquieres village and ridge, and the 6th Division the village of Ribecourt.

The 20th (Light) Division had been ordered to take Welsh Ridge and La Vacquerie whilst on the extreme right the 12th (Eastern) Division were to capture Lateau Wood and the village of Les Rues des Vignes. There were ten vital bridges over the second canal in the area, the St. Quentin Canal (or Canal de l'Escault); this canal, unlike the Canal du Nord, was complete. These bridges were in the

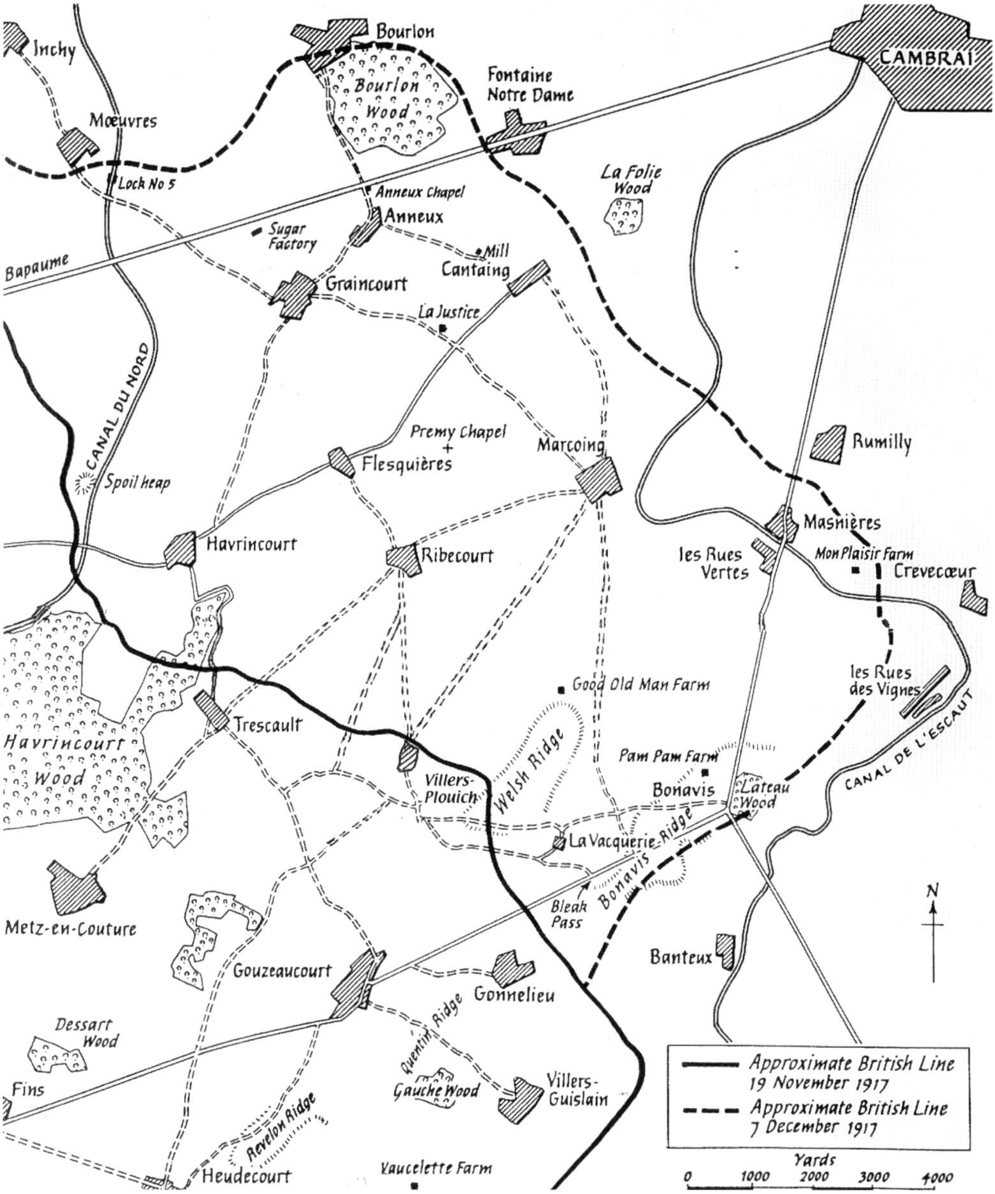

▲ Map 25. Cambrai

vicinity of the villages of Marcoing and Masnieres and were the objectives of the 29th Division. This division was to attack approximately four hours after the main assault, passing through the hole that was to be punched in the Hindenburg Line by the 20th Division.

The 20th (Light) Division contained a soldier from Ravensthorpe; William Hopkinson was serving with the 7th K.O.Y.L.I., part of 61 Brigade.

The 20th Division's most difficult objective was anticipated to be La Vacquerie. This was a hamlet built on a small hill and was part of the so-called 'Blue Line'. La Vacquerie stood in front of the main Hindenburg Line defences but was connected to them by deep trenches. The attack was to be over open ground with 61 Brigade's 7th Duke of Cornwall's Light Infantry and 12th King's Liverpool Regiment leading the assault; whilst the 7th Somerset Light Infantry were to make for the centre of La Vacquerie. The 7th D.C.L.I. and 12th King's were to assault the main Hindenburg Line to the east of the village.

Although the attack went surprisingly well at first, German resistance started to increase as the advance went further into the Hindenburg Line system, with eleven of the supporting tanks being knocked out by artillery firing over open sights.

The 7th K.O.Y.L.I.'s War Diary describes the day's action for the battalion; unsurprisingly there is no clue as to William Hopkinson's exact involvement. The battalion was not in the first wave of the attack, instead it was to follow the 7th D.C.L.I. and advance, along with the three tanks they had been allocated, to the Brown Line.

The 7th K.O.Y.L.I. left its assembly point at 'Fifteen Ravine' one mile west of La Vacquerie at 3am on 20th November and formed up ready for the attack behind the tanks, 'A' and 'B' companies leading with 'C' and 'D' companies behind. The first waves went in at zero hour (6.20am), the 7th K.O.Y.L.I. expecting to move off at 6.30am. At 6.35, while still waiting to advance, the German artillery opened up, but was, according to the battalion's War Diary *"weak"*. At last, at 6.45am the battalion moved off, suffering only a few casualties from the German artillery.

The War Diary describes *"At about 8.10am casualties were becoming heavy from machine gun fire. Owing to the late start....the battalion was now too far behind our barrage to derive much benefit from it. By the time the Hindenburg Support Line had been captured and pockets of the enemy mopped up the battalion was somewhat disorganised."*

The War Diary continues: *"Captain Hargreave was ordered to advance with a portion of his company and men belonging to 'B' and 'C' companies to the final objective. The tanks had pushed on following the barrage and were about 1000 yards* [just over ½ mile] *ahead, but the machine gun fire was very heavy... casualties were very heavy during this stage and Captain F. Hargreave was killed."*

The battalion's fatal casualties on 20th November were Captains F.P. Hargreave and H.R. Prust plus seventeen other ranks killed. One of these was William Hopkinson.

There is only a small amount of information available about William Hopkinson, and some of this is contradictory. William was born in Nottingham in 1885. He left his job at the Yorkshire Chemical and Dyework Company in Ravensthorpe and enlisted in Leeds. William had, according to the Dewsbury Reporter, only been at the front for three weeks when he was killed whilst serving with the 7th K.O.Y.L.I. It is, however, possible that this was his second spell in France as, according to the

RAVENSTHORPE MOTOR DRIVER KILLED IN FRANCE.

Mrs. Hopkinson, of Beacon Street, Ravensthorpe, but now residing with her parents at Altofts, has received information that her husband, Pte. William Hopkinson, of the K.O.Y.L.I., was killed on November 20th in the great battle near Cambrai. He had been at the Front only three weeks. Pte. Hopkinson was 32 years of age, and was employed at the Yorkshire Chemical and Dyeware Works, Ravensthorpe, as a motor-lorry driver. He leaves a widow and infant child.

Pte. William Hopkinson, K.O.Y.L.I., Ravensthorpe (killed).

◂ 114. William Hopkinson

▾ 115. The Cambrai Memorial to the Missing.

Medal Roll at the Public Record Office in Kew, he originally served in the 10th K.O.Y.L.I. (21st Division).

Upon William joining the army, his wife seems to have left their home at 20 Beacon Street, Ravensthorpe and, together with their child, returned to her parents who lived in Altofts. It was while she was living in Altofts that she learned of her husband's death.

William, like both of the officers and the sixteen other men from the battalion who were killed in action on 20th November* has no known grave and is therefore commemorated on the Cambrai Memorial to the Missing. The Memorial, containing the names of just over 7,000 men adjoins Louvernal Military Cemetery at Doignes, a few miles to the west of Cambrai alongside the main Bapaume to Cambrai road.

* * *

As described earlier, the key to the Battle of Cambrai were the heights of Bourlon Wood. It was at this northern end of the front that the 62nd (West Riding) Division was located; the division was making exceptional progress. The G.O.C., Major-General Walter Braithwaite gambled on throwing his entire division into the battle and attacked using all battalions within its three infantry brigades. Two brigades were to break into the Hindenburg system (187 Brigade was on the left, with 185 Brigade on the right), whilst the third (186) Brigade was in reserve and ready to 'leapfrog' the other two brigades in order to take the division's final objectives, being the villages of Graincourt and Anneux. (A detachment was then to gain the high ground to the west of Bourlon Wood, and there link up with the 1st Cavalry Division who were to be advancing from the north-east.) The division was arranged:

187		**185**	
2/5th K.O.Y.L.I.	2/4th K.O.Y.L.I.	2/6th West Yorks	2/8th West Yorks
2/4th Y&L	2/5th Y&L	2/5th West Yorks	2/7th West Yorks

▲

186	
2/5th Duke of Wellington's	2/6th Duke of Wellington's
2/7th Duke of Wellington's	2/4th Duke of Wellington's

The first objective (the Blue Line) was the Hindenburg main front line defences. This was to be taken by the first wave. The second objective, the Brown Line (the Hindenburg Support Line), was to be taken by the second wave. This second objective lay on the Flesquieres to Hermies road.

* ***One of the soldiers in this statistic is Private W. Walker. See Appendix 1.***

It was nearly five miles from 186 Brigade's start line in Havrincourt Wood to Anneux on the Cambrai Road; the high ground was another mile away. A lot was being asked of the division.

The 2/4th K.O.Y.L.I., it will be remembered, was a battalion that recruited one of its companies from Dewsbury (see Chapter 4). The battalion's War Diary describes how, on 20th November, they attacked with 'A' and 'B' companies leading the assault and 'C' and 'D' companies supporting. Eleven tanks (three of which were wire crushers) were allotted to the battalion. The battalion's objectives were firstly the front line trench running from Vesuvius (a large crater) to Oxford Road (to be taken by 'A' and 'B' companies) and secondly a line running westerly from the north-west corner of Havrincourt village (the objective of 'C' and 'D' companies).

Unfortunately, by 6.20am the tanks had not arrived; notwithstanding this, the battalion attacked, quickly overrunning the outpost line. The tanks caught up with the infantry and assisted in overcoming opposition from Boggart Hole, where a trench mortar and two machine guns were captured. A tank had been detailed to deal with a crater named Etna*, but it failed to arrive, so a platoon from the 2/4th K.O.Y.L.I., together with two platoons from the 2/5th K.O.Y.L.I. were detailed to capture the strongpoint. Casualties were being incurred on the battalion's right in the area of Havrincourt Park and Chateau Wood; the park and the wood were also dealt with, and a total of 70 prisoners and two machine guns were captured in Chateau Wood.

The battalion's 'C' and 'D' companies now pressed on to capture Havrincourt village, which was taken in conjunction with troops from the 2/6th West Yorkshires. Snipers who were firing from first floor windows were swiftly dealt with, as was a machine gunner who had set up his gun in the square in the centre of the village.

The Blue Line was reached at 9am and consolidation took place. The battalion had captured 200 prisoners, ten machine guns and three trench mortars for a cost of 47 men killed (plus 14 others who died of wounds on 20th November and over the next three days). Two of these fatal casualties were from Ravensthorpe.

Percy Bennett was born in Ravensthorpe in 1893 to Albert and Mary Alice Bennett. After attending St. Saviour's Boys' School he became a cloth miller at Marshall, Kaye and Marshall's mill. In his spare time he was connected with St. Saviour's Church and was also captain of Ravensthorpe Intermediate Club team. Percy joined up on 26th June 1917; he was home on leave in October (his last home leave before being posted overseas) and married Lillian Whitehead of Crawshaw Street, Ravensthorpe. Ten days later he was sent to France.

Nothing is known about how Percy died, his parents receiving notification in mid-December at their home at 40 Granny Avenue, Churwell in Leeds (they had moved there from 32 Netherfield Road, Ravensthorpe). After the war Lillian remarried and moved to 55 Garden Terrace, Ravensthorpe.

Cyril Glover, at 24, was the same age as Percy Bennett and had also been born in Ravensthorpe; his parents were Mr and Mrs W.H. Glover. After attending St. Saviour's Boys' School, he went to work for Bell Brothers, engineers, in Ravensthorpe with whom he was employed for nine years; in his spare time he played football for the St. Saviour's football team. Cyril joined the K.O.Y.L.I. on 5th

**** Vesuvius and Etna were craters blown by the Germans during their spring retirement. Both had subsequently been fortified.***

▲ 116. Percy Bennett

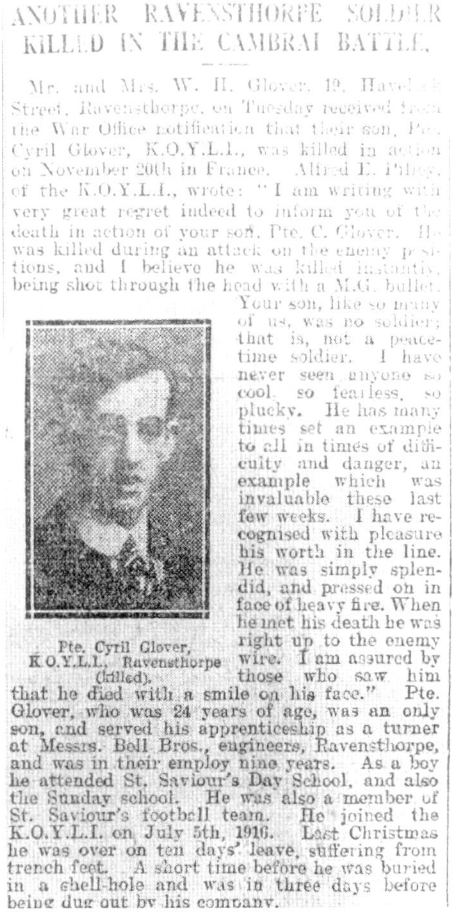

ANOTHER RAVENSTHORPE SOLDIER KILLED IN THE CAMBRAI BATTLE.

Mr. and Mrs. W. H. Glover, 19, Havelock Street, Ravensthorpe, on Tuesday received from the War Office notification that their son, Pte. Cyril Glover, K.O.Y.L.I., was killed in action on November 20th in France. Alfred E. Pilley, of the K.O.Y.L.I., wrote: "I am writing with very great regret indeed to inform you of the death in action of your son, Pte. C. Glover. He was killed during an attack on the enemy positions, and I believe he was killed instantly, being shot through the head with a M.G. bullet. Your son, like so many of us, was no soldier; that is, not a peace-time soldier. I have never seen anyone so cool, so fearless, so plucky. He has many times set an example to all in times of difficulty and danger, an example which was invaluable these last few weeks. I have recognised with pleasure his worth in the line. He was simply splendid, and pressed on in face of heavy fire. When he met his death he was right up to the enemy wire. I am assured by those who saw him that he died with a smile on his face." Pte. Glover, who was 24 years of age, was an only son, and served his apprenticeship as a turner at Messrs. Bell Bros., engineers, Ravensthorpe, and was in their employ nine years. As a boy he attended St. Saviour's Day School, and also the Sunday school. He was also a member of St. Saviour's football team. He joined the K.O.Y.L.I. on July 5th, 1916. Last Christmas he was over on ten days' leave, suffering from trench feet. A short time before he was buried in a shell-hole and was in three days before being dug out by his company.

Pte. Cyril Glover, K.O.Y.L.I., Ravensthorpe (killed).

▲ 117. Cyril Glover

▼ 118. A works trip from Bell Brothers engineers, 1912. *Photograph courtesy of Kirklees Community History Service.*

July 1916 and was subsequently sent to France, joining the 2nd Battalion He served in this unit until December 1916, when he was buried alive for three days in a shell hole until being dug out. Probably as a result of this incident, he was home on leave at Christmas 1916 (suffering from a wound to the face and trench foot). Upon recovering Cyril returned to France joining the 2/4th K.O.Y.L.I. in early 1917.

His parents received a letter at their home at 19 Havelock Street written by Private Arthur Pilley, in which he described how Cyril was killed instantly *"...being shot through the head by a machine gun bullet."*

He went on to describe how he *"...had never seen anyone so cool, so fearless, so plucky. He has at many times set an example to us all in times of difficulty and danger....when he met his death he was right up to the enemy wire. I am assured by those who saw him that he died with a smile on his face."*

Both Cyril Glover and Percy Bennett are buried at Hermies Hill British Cemetery.

* * *

On the extreme right of the 62nd Division's attack was the 2/8th Battalion, West Yorkshire Regiment. The battalion encountered little resistance at first, the Germans being totally cowed by the hurricane bombardment and the arrival of the tanks. German resistance steadily increased, but the battalion was able to capture its objective of Chapel Trench (north-east of Havrincourt) after overcoming 'considerable resistance'. Part of the battalion's difficulty may have been due to the inability of the 51st (Highland) Division on the battalion's right to move forward as quickly as the 62nd Division. The battalion consolidated in Chapel Trench having lost, according to S.D.G.W., thirteen men killed (nine of these are buried in Grand Ravine British Cemetery). One of the men from the battalion was a soldier from Ravensthorpe named George Arthur Ledgard; George survived this day's battle without injury but before detailing George's story, it is necessary to follow the day's action for the rest of the 62nd Division.

In order to avoid any unnecessary delays, Brigadier-General R.B. Bradford (commanding 186 Infantry Brigade) ordered his brigade to follow the advance of the 185 and 187 Brigades, so that when the moment came to take over the attack they would be able to do so immediately. Aged just 25, Bradford was the youngest ever general in the British army and had been awarded the V.C. the previous year on the Somme whilst commanding the 9th Battalion, Durham Light Infantry.

186 Brigade moved forward with the 2/6th Duke of Wellington's on the right and the 2/5th Duke of Wellington's on the left; warnings were issued that pockets of Germans were still about and likely to be met with.

Despite this warning, casualties were incurred; it was between the Blue and Brown Lines (first and second objectives for the division) that the commanding officer of the 2/5th Duke of Wellington's (Lieutenant-Colonel T.A.D. Best) was killed. The battalion was moving down Oxford Road (the road from Havrincourt Wood to Havrincourt village), and approaching Chateau Wood and Havrincourt village when they came under machine gun and rifle fire from a strong point that had not been mopped up. Lieutenant-Colonel Best and Lieutenant Bodker were both killed*, other casualties included two other officers wounded and 26 casualties to other ranks. 'D' Company was sent forward and took the enemy strongpoint. Besides capturing one officer and 58 German soldiers, they also rescued a Corps intelligence officer and a K.O.Y.L.I. sergeant who had been taken prisoner by the Germans earlier in the day.

The 2/5th Duke of Wellington's continued their advance, during which they came across a ditched tank, the crew of which were fighting off a number of Germans. The tank crew, who were defending the tank from the outside, were rescued and the Germans beaten off. With the assistance of other tanks, the battalion, with 'D' Company still leading, attacked a German trench called Kangaroo Alley. Little resistance was encountered and the battalion moved on to Anneux Chapel on the Bapaume to Cambrai road.

It had been planned that the 62nd Division would proceed to take the high ground to the west of Bourlon Wood, but because of the failure of the 51st (Highland) Division to take the village of Flesquieres on their right, the 62nd Division was already in an exposed position. Major-General Braithwaite offered to assist the 51st Division by attacking Flesquieres from the rear; an alternative suggestion was made to allow the 51st Division to pass through ground taken by the West Riding Division, thereby bypassing the village. Neither of these options were taken up. The decision was therefore taken to halt at Anneux Chapel in order to allow the 51st Division to catch up the next day; this hold up at Flesquieres was to have serious consequences.

The 2/5th Battalion, Duke of Wellington's Regiment took 350 prisoners and captured 15 machine guns during the day at a cost of three officers and ten other ranks killed, two officers and 55 other ranks wounded and four other ranks missing. S.D.G.W. gives casualties amongst the 'other ranks' for this day at just 19. This battalion suffered the most heavily of the four battalions in 186 Brigade, although by far the worst battalion casualties for the division were suffered by the 2/4th K.O.Y.L.I. (55 other ranks). Altogether the division suffered just 217 fatalities on 20th November amongst its rank and file - a very small number indeed for the ground gained.

No soldier from Ravensthorpe was killed whilst attacking with the 2/5th Duke of Wellington's on 20th November, although several would have been involved in the battle; one Ravensthorpe soldier was decorated for his part in the day's events.

Harry Eastwood, it will be recalled from Chapter 12, had joined up with his brother Fred. After the attack on Bullecourt on 3rd May 1917, Fred had been reported missing; in the months following the attack Harry had been promoted to sergeant. For his part in the attack at Cambrai, Harry was awarded the Military Medal, being presented with the ribbon a month later.

A letter from Harry to his parents was published in the Dewsbury Reporter in mid-January 1918. In the letter Harry is reported as saying that they *"...had given old Fritz the shake up of his life...*[they had] *soon made short work of the Hindenburg Line, and the Germans were only too pleased to be made prisoners....their division had made a name for itself that would carry for years. It advanced the furthest of all the first day and their brigade* [186] *went furthest in the division and their battalion went furthest in the brigade and they were*

**** Both officers are buried side by side at Ruyaulcourt Military Cemetery.***

territorials so the regulars might put that in their pipe and smoke it!...it was terribly hard work. Their casualties were extraordinarily light, in his company they had only about three killed and twenty wounded, the majority [of the wounds] *being slight...*"

The advance of 4½ miles in one day under battle conditions was a record that was not to be beaten by the rest of the British army during the remainder of the war.

Although Harry Eastwood did not mention this, the advance he describes was undertaken by men carrying more than 60 lbs of equipment.

* * *

The following day's battle, 21st November, saw 186 Brigade again make an advance of more than a mile, but without taking the vital Bourlon Wood. 186 Brigade alone had, in two days, advanced six miles, capturing eight officers 1,130 other ranks, 34 field guns and 38 machine guns, but problems were beginning to mount up. Flesquieres not being taken on the first day had disrupted the planned timetable; many of the tanks had been damaged or had suffered mechanical breakdowns and were in need of repair; the cavalry had abjectly failed to perform due to its inability to get across one of the canals (it had been expected that squadrons of cavalry would be raiding deep into the German rear, causing panic and confusion). Additionally, many of the troops were exhausted after two days constant fighting (there were few reserves available due to the losses at Third Ypres earlier in the year). Most significantly, there was increasing German resistance, fresh divisions were being identified by the British; these were being rushed into the area by a very worried German High Command.

At the northern end of the battlefield, the artillery had difficulty in getting through the bottleneck of Havrincourt and the 62nd Division, with no reserves (all of its battalions having being committed in the fighting of the last two days), was in need of relief.

Haig's original concept for the Battle of Cambrai was to attack for just two days, however after forty-eight hours of fighting, the vital high ground of Bourlon and Bourlon Wood had not been taken; Haig had therefore to decide whether to stop the attacks as German reinforcements were now arriving, and the element of surprise had been lost. The alternative was to continue the attack in the hope that the breakthrough could be achieved (after all an amazing success had already occurred) or, at the very least the continued attack would enable the high ground at Bourlon Wood to be taken. If this high ground was not taken, the British troops would be in a dangerously exposed position, and would be able to be dominated from the German positions in the wood; this would make the current British line untenable, and a withdrawal would be necessary. In view of this, Haig decided to continue the battle; this would only be able to be accomplished if the exhausted divisions were withdrawn and replaced with fresh ones, this was scheduled for the 22nd/23rd November.

* * *

It is now appropriate to return to the story of George Ledgard. It will be remembered how the attack by the 2/8th West Yorkshires early on the 20th November had been successful, incurring very few casualties; the battalion had not been in action on the 21st. On the evening of 21st November, 185 Brigade moved up and took over the front line trenches from the Duke of Wellington's battalions of 186 Brigade. George, as a member of the 2/8th Battalion, West Yorkshire Regiment would have been one of those men who marched into the front line that night. The relief was completed by 2am on Thursday, 22nd November.

The 2/8th West Yorkshires had taken over a stretch of sunken road which led in a north-westerly direction from Anneux Chapel on the main Bapaume to Cambrai Road; this sunken road was on ground that sloped up towards Bourlon Wood. To the battalion's right were the 2/7th West Yorkshires, and to their left were the 2/6th West Yorkshires. During the relief, there had been some confusion as to the exact position this last battalion should be taking over; although it seems that the battalion did in fact get into the correct position, it had done so only just before dawn, and there were gaps in the line held by this battalion and the 2/8th West Yorkshires. It is unfortunate that it was in this area that the Germans chose to launch a small but fierce counter-attack.

The German bombardment started at 7.05am on 22nd November, with an infantry attack following shortly afterwards. Despite firing flares to ask for artillery support, no British guns opened up. As a result, the 2/6th West Yorkshires were forced to give ground and by 9am were back at the factory on the Bapaume

119. George Ledgard

to Cambrai road, where they dug in. The 2/8th West Yorkshires, although also heavily attacked, did not fall back so far. Reinforcements arrived and the 2/6th West Yorkshires (with the assistance of the 2/5th West Yorkshires) and the 2/8th West Yorkshires (with the assistance of the 2/4th Battalion, York and Lancaster Regiment) counter-attacked and drove the Germans back. The War Diary of the 2/8th West Yorkshires indicates casualties of three officers and 68 other ranks *.

That evening, as planned, the 62nd Division was relieved by the 40th Division, however there were nineteen men of the 2/8th West Yorkshire Regiment who had been killed during the 22nd November who would not be marching out of the line. One of those was George Arthur Ledgard.

George was born in Ravensthorpe in 1898 to Mr and Mrs John Ledgard. The Dewsbury Reporter of 8th December 1917 gives a little information about George, but misleadingly links his death to that of Luke Leadbeater+. The two had been life-long pals, attending Ravensthorpe United Methodist Church and Sunday School together, and both being employed by Jas Smith and Sons. George joined up on 18th November 1916 and was sent to France in February 1917.

In the article about the two friends, the Dewsbury Reporter briefly mentions George's last letter dated 17th November addressed to his parents at their home at 569 Poplar Terrace, Huddersfield Road, Ravensthorpe. The letter mentioned that he was preparing to go to the front line again, and that he was an officer's servant. The article goes on to give the date of George's death as being 21st November, however on this day the battalion was not in action. (This date, 21st November, is supported by information contained in the Medal Roll at the Public Record Office in Kew.)

A further two dates are given as the ones on which George was killed. Both the C.W.G.C. and S.D.G.W. give the date as 23rd November, although once again the battalion was not in action on this day, having been relieved on the evening of the 22nd November. (Apart from two men who died of wounds, no one from the battalion was killed on 23rd November.) Finally, in November 1918 an 'In Memoriam' notice was placed in the Dewsbury Reporter. This indicated that the family believed George was killed on 20th November.

It is likely that all three of these dates are wrong; the only date not mentioned was 22nd November, the day of the German counter-attack, it is probable that George was killed on this day, the same day as his life-long pal, Luke Leadbeater.

Rifleman# George Ledgard, aged just 19 years old, has no known grave and is therefore commemorated on the Cambrai Memorial to the Missing; the vast majority of the fatal casualties of the 2/8th West Yorkshire for this day are commemorated here, although three of the men are buried at Rocquigny-Equancourt Road British Cemetery.

* * *

S.D.G.W. - 2/6th West Yorkshires - 30 men plus five officers killed.
- 2/8th West Yorkshires - 18 men plus one officer killed.

+ See Chapter 15. Luke Leadbeater had been killed at Ypres whilst serving with the 49th (West Riding) Division.

 # The 8th Battalion, West Yorkshire Regiment was, along with the 7th Battalion West Yorkshires, the pre-war (territorial) 'Leeds Rifles'; the Leeds Rifles adopted this rank instead of Private.

With Haig having made the decision to continue the battle, the 40th Division was ordered to take the vital position of Bourlon Wood. Supported by 100 tanks plus a heavy artillery bombardment, the division attacked the wood on 23rd November. Over the course of the next few days, Bourlon village and wood were to be the scenes of bitter fighting.

Due to the attrition at Ypres earlier in the year, the British had few reserves, and as a result, after just two days resting, the 62nd (West Riding) Division again found itself, on 24th November, being ordered to the front line to relieve the hard-hit 40th Division; the relief taking place the following day.

On 27th November the 62nd Division launched an attack from Bourlon Wood (which was partially in British hands) towards Bourlon village. In the tangle of dense undergrowth, with snipers and machine gun nests dotted around, some progress was made on the right, however little or no progress was able to be made on the left. A German counter-attack at 4.30pm forced the right of the division back to the centre of the wood, to a point near that from which they had launched their attack earlier in the day. The following day there was little activity by either side, and on the night of the 28th/29th November the 62nd Division was again relieved.

The Germans were however planning a massive counter-attack against the whole of the Cambrai salient. The British now held a large area of land which bulged into the German line; this was going to be difficult for the British to hold. Although the Germans had some tanks of their own* they decided against using these and instead developed a plan which made use of a short but intense artillery bombardment using a high proportion of gas shells. Infiltration tactics had been developed by their infantry, and these methods, undertaken by specially selected and trained 'storm troopers' were to be the basis of the German counter-attack on 30th November against the tired British troops who were sitting in a narrow, exposed salient.

The Germans assaulted the British lines both in the south, in the area where the 20th (Light) Division had attacked ten days earlier, and in the north at Bourlon Wood. The British troops were caught unawares on the right and although they managed to inflict heavy losses on the Germans, they were forced to fall back. The arrival of reinforcements helped to stabilise the line, but much of the gains of 20th November had been lost, indeed the Germans managed to gain some totally new ground in the extreme south. In the area of Bourlon Wood, the German attack failed.

Although the 62nd (West Riding) Division was not involved in the German counter-attack, they did suffer a high profile casualty when Brigadier-General R.B. Bradford was killed by a long range German shell outside his Brigade Headquarters near the village of Graincourt. He is buried at Hermies British Cemetery, just opposite Hermies Hill British Cemetery, where Percy Bennett and Cyril Glover are buried.

The battle died down, but it was realised that many of the British positions were unsustainable, and further withdrawals to a more suitable defensive line were ordered reluctantly by Haig.

***A heavy German tank had been developed which was fairly ineffective; the Germans were not averse to repairing captured British machines and using these against their former owners.**

Because the successes of 20th November had been hailed in Britain as a major victory (for the first time since the beginning of the war church bells had been rung up and down the country as a sign of the achievement) the German counter-attack caused Haig some discomfort. Some politicians, led by the Prime Minister, Lloyd George sought to embarrass the Commander-in- Chief, with questions being asked in Parliament and an official inquiry being launched. Haig weathered the storm although he was forced to replace both his head of intelligence (Brigadier-General Charteris) and his Chief of Staff (Lieutenant-General Sir Lancelot Kiggell) - a move which would have suited Lloyd George as he had been hoping to weaken Haig's position for some time. In addition, three Corps commanders were relieved of their commands: Pulteney (III Corps) and Haldane (IV Corps) being sent home, with a third (Snow of VII Corps) also being replaced, but on health grounds.

British casualties for the period 20th November to 8th December were about 45,000 of whom 20,000 were killed.

Both the British and Germans were to learn vital lessons from the Battle of Cambrai. For the first time on the Western Front, the opposing trench lines had been broken. The British had achieved this through the use of massed tanks and a predicted artillery bombardment. On the other side the Germans had achieved their success by a devastating artillery bombardment, including gas shells, and the use of specially selected and trained troops who were under orders to infiltrate between strongpoints and exploit the areas behind rather than attacking strongpoints frontally.

Although neither side achieved the long aspired for breakthrough, clearly the key to unlocking more than three years of trench deadlock was close at hand. Both sides would have the winter months to reflect on the battle and draw conclusions. It was merely a question of which side would have the first opportunity of putting into practice the lessons they had learned.

Chapter Seventeen

Palestine - War in the Holy Land

The 100 mile long Suez Canal which links the eastern Mediterranean with the Red Sea was, in the early 1900's, considered to be one of the vital arteries of the British Empire. It cut thousands of miles and many weeks off the journey from the British Isles to India; was a vital supply route in peacetime, and even more vital in times of war. After the evacuation from Gallipoli in January 1916 it was feared that the canal would be the target of a Turkish advance from their bases in Palestine. Such an advance would cut the canal to British shipping and leave India dangerously vulnerable.

An attack on the canal by the Turks on 3rd February 1915 was beaten off by Indian troops; this attack made the British aware of the dangers of leaving the canal inadequately defended, and troops needed for France were sent to Egypt; many of these eventually finding themselves involved in the Gallipoli campaign.

Whilst one of the ostensible reasons for the eventual evacuation from Gallipoli was the need to reinforce the B.E.F. on the Western Front, initially most of the divisions which had been involved in the Gallipoli campaign were sent to Egypt rather than France, only the 10th (Irish) Division did not go to Egypt, being sent instead to Salonika. The primary reason for the divisions being sent to Egypt was to allow them to recover from the ordeal on the peninsular and absorb reinforcements, but also it was deemed necessary to reinforce the garrison in Egypt as the Turks, after their success on Gallipoli may now, it was felt, return to attack the Suez canal. The existing garrison in Egypt (comprising of the 10th and 11th Indian Divisions, together with Indian Cavalry units and the newly formed 31st Division) was therefore reinforced with fourteen divisions from Gallipoli*.

This rather large garrison did not stay intact for long, by June the Anzacs, the Royal Naval Division, the 11th, 29th and 31st Divisions were all sent to France and the 13th Division went to Mesopotamia.

At the start of 1916 the Commander-in-Chief in Egypt, Lieutenant-General Maxwell was joined by General Sir Archibald Murray + and the two shared responsibilities until March when Maxwell returned to Britain, Murray taking sole charge of the Egyptian Expeditionary Force (E.E.F.).

The second attack on the canal took place on 4th August 1916 (although there had been a number of earlier raids). Supported by Germans, the attack at Romani,

**** These were - five Anzac Divisions plus the Royal Naval Division, 11th (Northern), 13th (Western), 29th, 42nd (East Lancashire), 52nd (Lowland), 53rd (Welsh), 54th (East Anglian) and 2nd Mounted Division. (The Mounted Division was a division made up of (dismounted) Yeomanry, but was broken up as a division in Egypt.)***

+ Murray had been Sir John French's Chief of Staff in 1914. Doubts were raised about his stamina and in January 1915 he became Deputy C.I.G.S. In September 1915 he was promoted and replaced his near namesake, General Sir James Wolfe-Murray as C.I.G.S. until the end of the year when Sir William Robertson took over (see Chapter 1), resulting in Murray being sent to Egypt.

20 miles south-east of Port Said, was launched against positions held by Australian troops; although the Australians were forced to give some ground, the Turks had to disengage and started to fall back across the Sinai Desert. This was the last time the canal was threatened; the troops of the E.E.F. went onto the offensive and started to probe the Turkish lines, although there were few successful raids as the Turks were often warned in advance by local Arabs who were friendly to the Turks.

It was realised that a strong supply line would be needed from Egypt if the Turks were to be pushed back, and the only way of this being possible was across the Sinai Desert. A pipeline and railway were started, using local labour formed into the Egyptian Labour Corps; during 1916 this pipeline snaked its way slowly across the desert.

Meanwhile the Turkish rule to the south-east of Suez, in Arabia, was coming under threat, not by direct British military intervention but through rebellion. The Arabs had been governed by the Ottoman Empire for several centuries, and now saw their chance of gaining independence from Turkish rule. During the course of 1916, an Arab revolt was planned with British assistance. This flared up into open rebellion in June 1916; British seaplanes supported the Arabs in the overthrow of the Turkish garrison at Jeddah, a town on the Red Sea coast near Mecca. Other garrison towns were overrun by the Arabs, but the Turks were not totally overwhelmed; a strong force held out at Medina, and the revolt came near to collapsing.

In Cairo, a group of British experts had been formed to analyse the information coming out of Arabia, one of its junior members was Thomas E. Lawrence who was to become known as Lawrence of Arabia. The diminutive Lawrence (he was just 5'3" tall) had studied the subject of the Crusades whilst at Oxford, and had then spent several years participating in archaeological digs in Arabia. In October 1916 Lawrence talked his way onto a mission to Jeddah, and whilst there, he detached himself from the official party to do some scouting for General Murray's G.H.Q. to inform them of local conditions. After returning to Cairo, Lawrence was sent back to Arabia, where, in conjunction with Arab leaders he raided Turkish positions and blew up railway lines for several months, gaining immortal fame in the process.

Back in the north, just before Christmas 1916, a British column, advancing with the aid of the pipeline and railway across the desert, took the village of El Arish, and came across the first green patches of cultivation in Palestine; the British troops were now on the threshold of crossing into enemy held territory, and would soon be embarking on massive advances which would reinforce the views of politicians at home that success away from the Western Front could be achieved at a very small cost.

In early 1917, just as Murray's E.E.F. had gained this toehold in Palestine, his force was reduced when the 42nd (East Lancashire) Division was sent to the Western Front, although this was partially offset by organising into one (infantry) division the various regiments of yeomanry that had been operating with the E.E.F. This division became the 74th (Yeomanry) Division.

The invasion force, after defeating several outposts had, by the end of February, crossed the border into Palestine and commenced Lloyd George's strategy - that of knocking out Germany's allies. This was to be the start of a long haul; despite low Turkish morale, there was no immediate collapse of the Turkish army.

The first major obstacle in the invasion of Palestine was the strongly defended town of Gaza. On 26th March, the British forces attacked the town; although

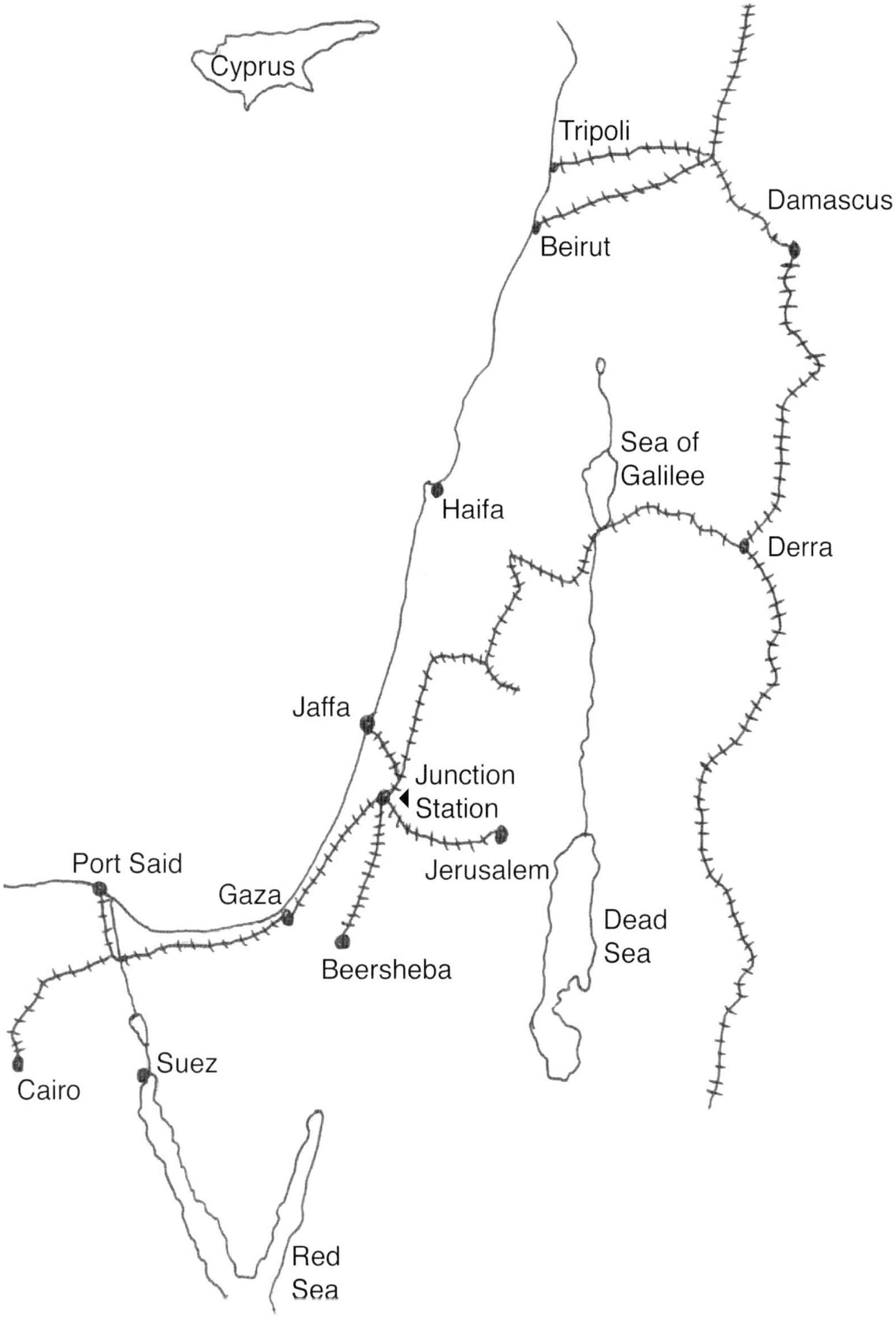

▲ Map 26. Palestine

assisted by a dense fog, the British troops were unable to defeat the Turks and the British fell back four miles to Wadi Ghazi. Despite the defeat, Murray sent an optimistic report to London indicating that had it not been for some bad luck the attack would have succeeded. The War Cabinet, in view of the recent success in Mesopotamia (Baghdad having fallen on 11th March 1917 - see Chapter 11) and misled by Murray's report, ordered Murray to attack again, with Jerusalem as the ultimate objective. Lloyd George needed a morale boosting victory, as the Western Front was turning into an expensive blood bath (the Battle of the Somme had finished four months previously).

Both the Turks and the British received reinforcements, the British obtaining eight tanks, previously used for training purposes at home. The scene was set for the Second Battle of Gaza which took place on 19th April 1917. Again the British were unable to break through the Turkish lines who had taken up excellent defensive positions, using features such as impenetrable hedges of cacti which worked as well as any barbed wire.

From May until June, further reinforcements arrived in the shape of a division from Macedonia (Salonika) being the 60th (2nd/2nd London) Division; in addition a further 'new' division was formed (the 75th) from British and Indian battalions. The situation had all the makings of a second Gallipoli, the Turks in strong positions and the British sending more reinforcements which were sorely needed on the Western Front.

In June, before he could renew the offensive, Murray was recalled to London. Lloyd George at first wanted General Smuts, a South African of Dutch extraction who had fought against the British in the Boer War at the turn of the century, to take over from Murray (Smuts had until recently been campaigning against the Germans in Africa, but had been brought to London to sit on the War Cabinet). Smuts, however declined the invitation and Robertson, the C.I.G.S., therefore suggested General Allenby* as a suitable candidate. Lloyd George emphasised to Allenby that he was not being sent to a 'sideshow', and that after France, Palestine was the most important theatre of the war. He told Allenby that he wanted Jerusalem to be captured as a Christmas present for the British people.

Asking for reinforcements, Allenby received the 10th (Irish) Division from Salonika. His command now amounted to seven infantry divisions, and three mounted divisions +.

Even though Murray had failed to break through at Gaza, he had laid the groundwork for the forthcoming campaign, the most important of these was the completion of the pipeline and railway across the Sinai Desert.

Allenby, when war broke out was G.O.C. Cavalry Division; when the second Cavalry Division was formed he took over command of the Cavalry Corps, and later took charge of V Corps. In October 1915 he was appointed to command the Third Army. When transferred to Palestine he felt at first this was a criticism of his handling of the Battle of Arras (see Chapter 10), this was not the case; as a 'Cavalry' general, he was well equipped to deal with the hoped for breakthrough and subsequent mobile war. Additionally, Haig did not hinder his appointment as the two did not get on well together and had clashed over the tactics to be used at the Battle of Arras.

+ The seven infantry divisions were the 10th (Irish), 52nd (Lowland), 53rd (Welsh), 54th (East Anglian), 60th (2nd/2nd London), 74th (Yeomanry) and 75th. The mounted divisions were the Anzac Mounted Division, Australian Mounted Division, and the Yeomanry Mounted Division. In addition to these was the Imperial Camel Corps, various Royal Flying Corps squadrons, 'E' Company Tank Corps, plus formations of Armoured Cars.

The Turks had also been reinforced; German troops arrived, and General Erich von Falkenhayn (previously commander of German forces on the Western Front) was transferred to Palestine to take charge of the Turkish and German forces.

On 27th October, the British started a bombardment of Gaza. The Turks had been fed reports indicating that a third frontal attack on Gaza was imminent, but on 31st October, an attack was launched on Beersheba, twenty miles south-east of Gaza. The lightly defended town fell to a daring cavalry charge made by regiments from the 4th Light Horse Brigade of the Australian Mounted Division. As expected, the Turks moved units to defend the area from the successful attack, weakening Gaza's defences.

The fall of Beersheba enabled a successful attack to be made on Tel es Sheria (half way between Beersheba and Gaza); the position, being on high ground, was vital to the Turkish line. This attack was also successful. A third attack was made on Gaza itself, this attack, rather than being directed through the cactus-hedged suburbs was made from the coast and was the final straw for the Turks, they fell back from the Gaza defences, and for virtually the first time in the war there was a gap that could be exploited by cavalry.

Whilst the infantry advanced through picturesque orange groves into the town of Gaza on 6th November the three mounted divisions were ordered to cut the Turks off by driving in a north-westerly direction for the sea. There were several opportunities for cavalry charges, one of these at the village of Huj on 8th November was made by 1½ squadrons of Warwickshire Yeomanry and 1½ squadrons of Worcestershire Yeomanry. This small band of horsemen (part of the Australian Mounted Division), charged at a much stronger Turkish position, without any covering fire from artillery or machine guns. Turkish artillery was turned and fired point blank at the onrushing yeomanry but the momentum of the charge was too much and in a few minutes the Turks fled, leaving behind many of their dead, seventy prisoners and numerous artillery pieces.

Due to stiff rearguard actions, many being less easy to overcome than the position at Huj, the majority of the Turkish troops managed to escape the encircling movement; however the Turks were totally disorganised by the British advance and fell back in almost complete disorder.

The pursuit by the British infantry and cavalry inevitably slackened over the next few days. In the line of the cavalry's advance was the village of Junction Station. This marked the point where the railway line running west out of Jerusalem met the north-south railway. If the village was captured, Jerusalem would be cut off from the sea, and the route to the Mediterranean would be open for the mounted troops.

Before Junction Station could be taken, however, two villages had to be taken that stood in the way – Katrah and El Mughar.

It is at this point that the one Ravensthorpe soldier to die whilst serving in Allenby's Palestine campaign was killed.

Isaac Walker Thompson was born in Pudsey in 1886 to George and Harriet Thompson; he had at least three brothers all of whom were to serve in the war. After the family moved to Ravensthorpe (51 Garden Terrace), Isaac worked at the Ravensthorpe works of Dewsbury Corporation's sewage department, and along with his brother John, was a member of Ravensthorpe Liberal Club. Isaac enlisted in Dewsbury on 8th May 1915, joining the King's Own Scottish Borderers; after eleven weeks training he went to Gallipoli, joining the 1st Battalion (29th

Division) on 18th August. Following the evacuation, the 29th Division went to France, taking part in the first day of the Battle of the Somme, Isaac being wounded on this day, receiving a gunshot wound to his left leg (see Chapter 7); Isaac's brother, John Alfred Thompson was injured on the same day, whilst serving with the 10th Battalion, Yorkshire Regiment.

Isaac spent some time in hospital in Torquay, and after some home leave and further training in Edinburgh was posted to the 1/5th Battalion of the K.O.S.B., part of the 52nd (Lowland) Division, joining the battalion in February 1917.

During the Palestine campaign, Isaac (or 'Ike' as he seems to have been known) was wounded twice, being in hospital at one stage with septic poisoning. It is not clear when he received these wounds, but it is likely to have been during the earlier battles at Gaza. Clearly recovered from his wounds he was with his battalion when, on 13th November, it was ordered to assist the 1/4th K.O.S.B. in an attack on El Mughar.

The two K.O.S.B. battalions had marched into position on the reverse side of a hill in the early hours of the morning. After spending a cold night without blankets and breakfasting on half rations, the battalions advanced over the brow of the hill where the village of El Mughar - their objective - was pointed out lying amongst groves of cypress trees on a small hill at the end of a ridge. Below the ridge was a flat plain; it was likely to be difficult ground to attack over if the Turks put up resistance.

120. Isaac Thompson

▲ 121. The Jerusalem Memorial to the Missing, to the rear of the Jerusalem War Cemetery. *Photograph courtesy of the Commonwealth War Graves Commission.*

Although disorganised by the sudden advance, the Turks had placed machine guns behind the cacti hedges, and their artillery had taken up positions on an adjoining ridge, giving them a clear field of observation over any attack. The neighbouring village of Katrah (approximately a mile away) was to be attacked by two battalions of Royal Scots Fusiliers*.

The 1/4th K.O.S.B. advanced under a hail of machine gun and shrapnel fire. About 400 yards from the edge of the village, the troops came across a dry river bed from which they returned the Turkish fire. Realising that the advance on El Mughar was stalling, the 1/5th K.O.S.B. was ordered forward to assist, unsurprisingly they too were met with intense fire and joined the 1/4th Battalion under cover in the river bed. Meanwhile, the attack on Katrah was also held up.

The Brigadier-General in charge of 155 Brigade (Brigadier-General Pollock McCall) had joined the K.O.S.B. in the river bed and due to the problems encountered was contemplating calling for artillery support to suppress the Turkish fire. It was now early afternoon, since the advance was ordered at 7.45am and the battalions had come under fire at 10am, little had been achieved; however help was at hand. To the left of the infantry were the yeomanry of the 6th Mounted Brigade (comprising 1/1st Berkshire Yeomanry, 1/1st Buckinghamshire Yeomanry and 1/1st Dorset Yeomanry) being part of the Yeomanry Mounted Division. At 3pm they moved forward, using the cover of a dip known as Wadi Jamus and approached to within two miles of the Mughar Ridge. The yeomanry advanced first

Like the 1/4th and 1/5th K.O.S.B., the 1/4th and 1/5th Royal Scots Fusiliers were part of 155 Brigade, 52nd (Lowland) Division.

at a trot, then to a canter, and when within 100 yards charged into the Turkish positions to the north of the village.

Seizing the opportunity Brigadier-General McCall grabbed a rifle and personally led the two battalions of Kings Own Scottish Borderers in a charge to the Turkish positions. The War Diary of the 1/4th K.O.S.B. describes how, at 4pm, the battalion *"...made a final rush, driving the enemy from all his positions, in the gardens and cactus hedges, and forcing him into the open behind the village..."*

After a few minutes of hand to hand fighting, the Turkish troops realised that discretion was the better part of valour and threw their weapons to one side and surrendered.

The Yeomanry had cut off the Turkish retreat, and over a thousand prisoners were taken; the Royal Scots Fusiliers had also taken their objective of Katrah, however the real success was the fact that the way was now clear for an advance on Junction Station, this was taken early the next morning, 14th November by a brigade from the 75th Division with support from armoured cars; there was no Turkish opposition.

The day's casualties for the 1/5th K.O.S.B. were one officer and 18 other ranks killed, plus a further two officers and 110 other ranks wounded. The 1/4 K.O.S.B. lost slightly more heavily, having three officers and 26 other ranks killed, plus nine officers and 138 other ranks wounded. The 1/4th and 1/5th Royal Scots Fusiliers between them suffered fatal casualties of one officer and 26 other ranks; the three regiments of yeomanry had one officer and 15 other ranks killed on 13th November.

One of the casualties of the 1/5th K.O.S.B. was Isaac Thompson. Isaac's wife received a letter of condolence at 35 Bradbury Street from Private Joseph Shore, who had been 'Isaac's chum since coming out to Palestine'. The letter described how *"...Ike did not suffer, death being instantaneous. Some of his chums and myself attended the funeral. He was buried with every respect. All of the boys in the company send you their deepest sympathy."*

Although the letter relates how Isaac's comrades attended his funeral, Isaac unfortunately does not have a known grave. All the other casualties of the 1/5th K.O.S.B.'s action on 13th November are buried at Ramleh War Cemetery, about five miles north of Junction Station, in the modern state of Israel. Isaac is commemorated on the Jerusalem Memorial to the Missing, which lists the names of over 3,000 men who were killed in Palestine and Egypt who have no known graves.

After the capture of Junction Station, Allenby's forces continued their advance; unlike on the Western Front, much progress had been possible. Since the breakthrough at Gaza, fifty miles had been covered, with about 10,000 prisoners and 100 artillery pieces being taken (this represented about one third of Turkey's troops in the region and a half of its artillery). Despite these impressive statistics, Jerusalem still had to be taken. Allenby received instructions from London not to advance beyond his means, but despite this he decided to press on to Jerusalem.

By now, the wet season had started, and the roads and tracks that crossed the Judean hills, which stood in the way of an advance on Jerusalem, had become virtually impassable; in these conditions the advance ground to a halt. The Turks chose at this point to launch a counter-attack, which was halted after some desperate fighting. Despite the conditions, the British somehow managed to advance again. These advances were made against a demoralised enemy who soon melted away when attacked. On 9th December, it was discovered that the Turks had withdrawn, and that Jerusalem was undefended.

Allenby entered Jerusalem through the Jaffa gate at noon on 11th December. Symbolically, and out of religious respect, he entered the city on foot*, with other officers following behind; one of these officers was Major T.E. Lawrence.

Allenby's name was added to the long list of conquerors of Jerusalem, stretching back from stories told in the Old Testament, through to the Crusades. Over 400 years of Ottoman rule was ended, however in order to placate Jerusalem's inhabitants of all religious persuasions, a carefully worded proclamation was drafted stating that all places of prayer would be maintained and protected.

*   *   *

The retreating Turkish army was harried on its way by the Royal Flying Corps who bombed the enemy columns; due to the weather, however, it proved impossible for troops to follow the Turkish retirement.

In early 1918, Allenby's plans were dislocated by a massive German offensive on the Western Front (see Chapter 18) which resulted in two complete divisions, the 52nd (Lowland) and the 74th (Yeomanry) being sent to France as well as numerous other infantry battalions and yeomanry regiments. This loss was partially compensated by the arrival of two Indian Army divisions from Mesopotamia and further reinforcements which eventually arrived from India.

Due to the upheaval and reorganisation that was required following the withdrawal of these units, there was little activity for several months. Conditions in the Turkish army continued to deteriorate, and desertions grew to epidemic proportions.

The last phase of the Palestinian campaign commenced after the weather had cooled in September. Starting on 19th September, 1918, Allenby's E.E.F. broke through the Turkish lines near the coast and assisted by a Lawrence-inspired Arab uprising, routed the Turks. By 30th September advanced units of Australian Light Horse were at the gates of Damascus. Here, Allenby's troops, exhausted and suffering from many diseases (including an influenza epidemic) were rested. A small detachment moved north, but the armistice that was signed by the Turks on 31st October prevented any further bloodshed.

In this last few weeks of campaigning 75,000 prisoners were taken; in addition to this figure are those Turkish troops who were killed or wounded, and those who deserted. This was at a cost of just 853 Allied soldiers killed. The front was pushed back 350 miles, with some units covering 600 miles.

Although Turkey was defeated, it is difficult to see how Lloyd George's strategy of knocking Germany's allies out would, by 1917, have shortened the war. The plan for the Dardanelles of 1914 and 1915 may theoretically have seriously weakened Germany's ability to fight the war at that time, but by 1917, with Russia on her

**** Allenby was respected for this act. It did him no harm that in Arabic 'Alla-nebi' means 'The Prophet of God'. There was also a prophecy that ran 'When the waters of the Nile come to Palestine, Jerusalem will be retaken from the Turks'. This of course came true when the pipeline was constructed across the Sinai Desert!***

knees and about to sign an armistice (and the Bolshevik Revolution releasing many German troops back to the west) the 'Easterner' strategy was irrelevant.

The war could only be decided in the west, and it was in the west that Germany was to launch a massive blow against the British. This was the decisive moment of the First World War.

Chapter Eighteen

The Kaiser's Battle

Following the death of William Greaves in hospital at Etaples on the French coast, on 16th January 1918, there was no further addition to Ravensthorpe's growing Roll of Honour for two months. The next two men whose names appear on the War Memorial did not even serve abroad.

Charles Buckley was born in Stockport to John and Louisa Buckley in 1898 or 1899. It is not known when or why Charles came to Ravensthorpe, but before enlisting he lodged with his married sister, Mrs Thorpe at 57 Clarkson Street, Ravensthorpe. Whilst working as a miner for the Mirfield Colliery Company, he received his call up papers and on Wednesday 27th February 1918 reported to the barracks at Pontefract, from where he was sent to the Royal Field Artillery depot at Newcastle-upon-Tyne. One week later, on Wednesday 6th March Charles was undergoing training when he was thrown from a mule and kicked by the animal. He was examined by a R.A.M.C. officer (Captain James MacRae) who must have believed the injury not to be too severe. Charles was again seen that evening whilst in bed, and his injury seemed to be easier. The following morning (Thursday 7th March) it was realised that Charles was badly hurt and he was sent to Newcastle Infirmary, being admitted at 12.45pm. The injury was diagnosed as a ruptured intestine, and it could not be operated on. Charles died later that day aged just 19.

Charles was buried in Mirfield Parish Churchyard on Wednesday 13th March. An inquest into his death was held at Newcastle, the coroner being mildly critical of the fact that Charles had not been examined between Wednesday evening and Thursday morning. According to a report in the Dewsbury Reporter the coroner said: *"It was rather extraordinary that Buckley had not been examined by a doctor during the night...*[if this had occurred]*...developments in* [Charles'] *condition would have been noticed and an earlier removal to the infirmary might have been made..."*

Arnold Sheard was born in Dewsbury in December 1897. He lived with his parents at 2 Field Street Ravensthorpe, working as a finisher at Armitage and Rhodes until being called into the army. It is likely that upon being given his medical examination, he was passed as unfit to serve overseas; as a result he was transferred from the Northumberland Fusiliers and posted to the Royal Defence Corps. This corps was formed in August 1917; made up of eighteen battalions they were for home service only, being kept in static positions within Britain. The members of the corps were mainly employed in guarding prisoners of war.

On Monday 11th March 1918, Arnold was admitted to the Military Hospital at Newcastle, suffering from double pneumonia. He died three days later on Thursday 14th March, aged 20. Like Charles Buckley, Arnold is buried at St. Mary's Parish Church, Mirfield.

*   *   *

▲ 122. Charles Buckley's headstone in St. Mary's Parish Churchyard, Mirfield.

▲ 123. Arnold Sheard

The attritional battles of 1917, especially that of Third Ypres had weakened the army, and to make matters worse, the Prime Minister, Lloyd George had lost confidence in Sir Douglas Haig and was determined to stop him killing more men in further (as he saw it) wasteful attacks on the Germans. Despite wishing to dismiss Haig, Lloyd George did not have the political strength to do this. Instead he chose to restrict Haig by keeping him short of reinforcements, of which there were plenty in the British Isles. (Following the introduction of the Military Service Act in 1916, there was at the end of 1917 over 600,000 trained recruits at home ready for drafting to units abroad.) Another of Lloyd George's manoeuvres was that of forcing the resignation, in February 1918, of Haig's chief ally in London, the C.I.G.S., General Sir William Robertson.

In order to overcome this manpower shortage, Haig was forced in the first two months of 1918 to undertake a massive reorganisation within the B.E.F. Naturally enough he wanted to bring the battalions of infantry (and other units) up to full strength, but could only do this by disbanding a large number of battalions, using these men to swell the numbers in the under-strength battalions. Whilst this could have been achieved by reducing the number of divisions under his control, he decided against this, and instead reduced the number of battalions in each brigade from four to three. Until this time, infantry divisions had comprised of three brigades, each made up of four battalions, each battalion having a theoretical strength of about 1,000 officers and men. The reduction of battalions in each brigade did not, however, extend to the Canadians, nor to the Australians and New

Zealanders who retained the four battalion brigade until the end of the war. The reorganisation resulted in a total of 115 Battalions being totally disbanded, with a further 38 battalions being merged to make 19 battalions.

The resulting difficulties, as drafts of men were taken into battalions, and with every brigade shedding a battalion (and with some battalions being moved from one division to another) was, within a few weeks, going to have serious consequences.

Following the poor performance of Gough's Fifth Army* at Ypres, the headquaters of the Fifth Army was moved south and was posted to the right of the British line. It was unfortunate for Gough that he took over not just British trenches, but was also asked to take responsibility for part of the line formerly held by French troops. Lloyd George had been asked, and had agreed, to relieve the French of a further 25 miles of their front line. This extra portion of the line (taken over in January 1918) meant that the British now held 126 miles of the front. Not only did this spread the troops even more thinly on the ground +, but the trenches the British troops took over were found to be poorly constructed and in need of a lot of work to bring them up to a suitable state of repair. There was, of course, insufficient labour available for this amount of work.

Although the B.E.F. was under severe manpower pressure at the start of 1918, the opposite was true for the Germans.

In Russia, there had been two revolutions; the first in March 1917 brought a Liberal Government to power in place of the Tsar. This Provisional Government, under Alexander Kerensky, attempted to keep Russia in the war, but this only led to an acceleration in the collapse of Russia's armies. The second revolution, in November 1917, saw the Bolsheviks under Lenin seize control of the country and resulted in a separate peace treaty being signed between Germany and Russia. This, the Treaty of Brest-Litovsk, enabled the Germans to withdraw their divisions from the eastern front and transfer them to France in readiness for a final knockout blow against the Allies.

The Germans recognised that at this stage in the war, the only effective force that was opposing them was Britain and its Empire. The French army had been brought to its knees by the mutinies of April and May 1917. Although many of the problems that caused the mutinies had been overcome, it was still the British army which continued to take the war to the Germans. The United States of America had of course entered the war in April 1917, but with only a tiny pre-war army it was taking a long time to build up its forces in France.

Following the resignation (engineered by Ludendorff) of the German Chancellor, Bethmann Hollweg in July 1917, Ludendorff had effectively become the political as well as military head of Germany. He hoped that by attacking in the spring of 1918, Germany could knock Britain out of the war before America could bring its huge resources to bear. The attack would be a huge gamble, if it failed, defeat would be inevitable, but victory would ensure a peace, with Germany able to dictate much

---

It must be remembered that this did not consist of a permanent force. The Fifth Army was effectively a high level command, into whose control were rotated corps and divisions. The Fifth Army, like the other armies in the B.E.F., had as virtually its only permanent personnel the 'staff' who formulated plans for the corps and divisions under its control.

+ The despatch to Italy of five British Divisions under General Plumer in November 1917 had of course already led to a thinning out of the troops in the front line - see Chapters 15 and 22.

of its terms. The battle when it came would therefore have to be pressed with all the force the German army could muster. The code name for the concept of this spring offensive would be *Kaiserschlacht*, or The Kaiser's Battle.

With the temporary superiority in numbers, Ludendorff had to decide where on the Western Front to strike. Three plans emerged from the discussions Ludendorff held. One, codenamed *'George'* was to attack the British in northern France, adjacent to the Belgian border near the town of Armentieres; an alternative plan (named *'Mars'*) was for an arrack at Arras. It was, however, the third plan (operation *'Michael'*) that was chosen.

Operation *Michael* was a plan for an attack on the southern end of the British line, where it joined with the French. By separating the French and British armies, Ludendorff expected to be able, once he had broken through the trench lines, to turn north, forcing the British back towards the Channel Ports.

Haig was aware of the importance of the Channel Ports, without which he could not hope to keep the B.E.F. supplied. Behind the British line in the north, there was very little countryside through which the B.E.F. could fall back before the English Channel was at their backs. The situation to the south, the part of the line that Gough's Fifth Army held, was entirely different. In the event of German attacks forcing the army to fall back here, there was plenty of strategically unimportant ground that could be given up. In view of this, Haig ensured that the Second, First and Third Armies in the north and centre, and covering between them 84 miles of front with 40 divisions, had more divisions per mile than the Fifth Army. With 42 miles of front to hold, Gough's Fifth Army had just twelve infantry and three cavalry divisions (the strength of a cavalry division was substantially less than that of an infantry division).

Realising that if attacked, Gough would be in serious difficulties, Haig gave Gough permission that he could, if necessary, withdraw to a line further back. This in itself was a significant concession as in the war so far, every yard of ground was regarded as precious and not to be given up lightly. The other factor which justified the weakening of the southern sector was the promise, given by General Petain, the French Commander-in-Chief, that in the event of the British being attacked, the French would send troops to give support to the British.

Meanwhile German divisions were being rushed back from the Eastern Front. These, and the divisions which had previously been on the Western Front were re-equipped and retrained in preparation for the forthcoming offensive. In addition, there was a reorganisation within the German army, the best troops were creamed off and became storm troopers who would probe for, and exploit, any weaknesses in the British line. The divisions were also given designations, the better ones would be 'attack divisions' whilst the remainder became 'trench holding' divisions. The storm troopers and attack divisions, besides containing the best troops, also had the pick of the equipment which included a new type of light machine gun.

Finally, and most importantly, was the planned contribution of the artillery. Under a relatively junior officer, Colonel Bruchmuller, a fire plan had been drawn up which it was hoped would totally subdue the British infantry prior to the attack. This would involve a high proportion of gas shells. Much of this plan had been practised in the German counter-attack at Cambrai in November 1917.

Gough, holding the southern sector of the front with its poorly constructed trenches, could do little to prepare for the attack. His tired troops dug trenches as best they could, both in the front line and to the rear, in the so-called 'Battle Zone' where it was hoped any German attack would founder.

It was virtually impossible for the front lines to be fully manned, and as a result whilst redoubts (usually on higher ground) were adequately garrisoned and defended with barbed wire, there were tracts of land between the redoubts which would be difficult to defend. It was anticipated that the British troops, having good observation over this land, and with excellent fields of fire from their redoubts would be able to decimate any German attack that broke through the front line.

Until mid-March the British were unaware on which part of their front the attack would fall. It was clear that a German attack was imminent, but the Germans managed to carry out sufficient deception operations to keep the British guessing almost to the final moment.

At 4.40am on Thursday 21st March a terrific bombardment commenced on Gough's Fifth Army front, extending into the southern part of the front held by Byng's Third Army. At 9.40am the Germans attacked using 62 divisions. Facing them were just 14 divisions of Byng's Third Army and 15 divisions (including three Cavalry) of Gough's Fifth Army.

One final piece of luck befell the Germans. It was vital that their troops, particularly the storm troops, forced a passage between the British redoubts. They were assisted greatly in this by a dense fog which came down. Blinded by the fog and gas which became intermingled with it, the British infantry had no chance of preventing the Germans infiltrating between, and then surrounding their redoubts. In such conditions and with all communications cut, they felt abandoned. The artillery they had expected to come to their aid was blinded by the fog and did not receive reports due to the telephone wires being cut in the initial German bombardment. Many British batteries had, in any case, been silenced by the German guns.

The British redoubts were seldom attacked by the German storm troops, they passed on leaving the mopping up of these positions to following troops. One by one the redoubts fell. In a few areas, where the fog had lifted, the British were able to pour heavy fire on the Germans who in these places lost heavily.

It is difficult to estimate the significance of British morale (or lack of it) at this time. The recent reorganisation and disbandment of numerous battalions must have had a negative effect on the British troops.

The Germans advanced four miles on the first day of the attack, taking over 100 square miles of British-held ground, this was about the same amount of land taken by the British during the entire Battle of the Somme in 1916. A significant part of the reason for this massive success compared to the British attempts to break through over the previous 3½ years of the war was the fact that this was probably the first time an attacking force was not faced with a well manned front line entrenched on well prepared positions. The Germans victory was not without cost, they suffered 40,000 casualties with British losses being comparable, including 21,000 men who were taken prisoner.

The German success, spectacular as it was, was within their expectations only on the southern sector of their front. It was here, on the poorly defended line of Gough's Fifth Army that the Germans broke through the Battle Zone, forcing Gough to order a retirement to the Crozat Canal. Elsewhere on Gough's front, and further north in the Third Army sector, the Germans were held within the Battle Zone.

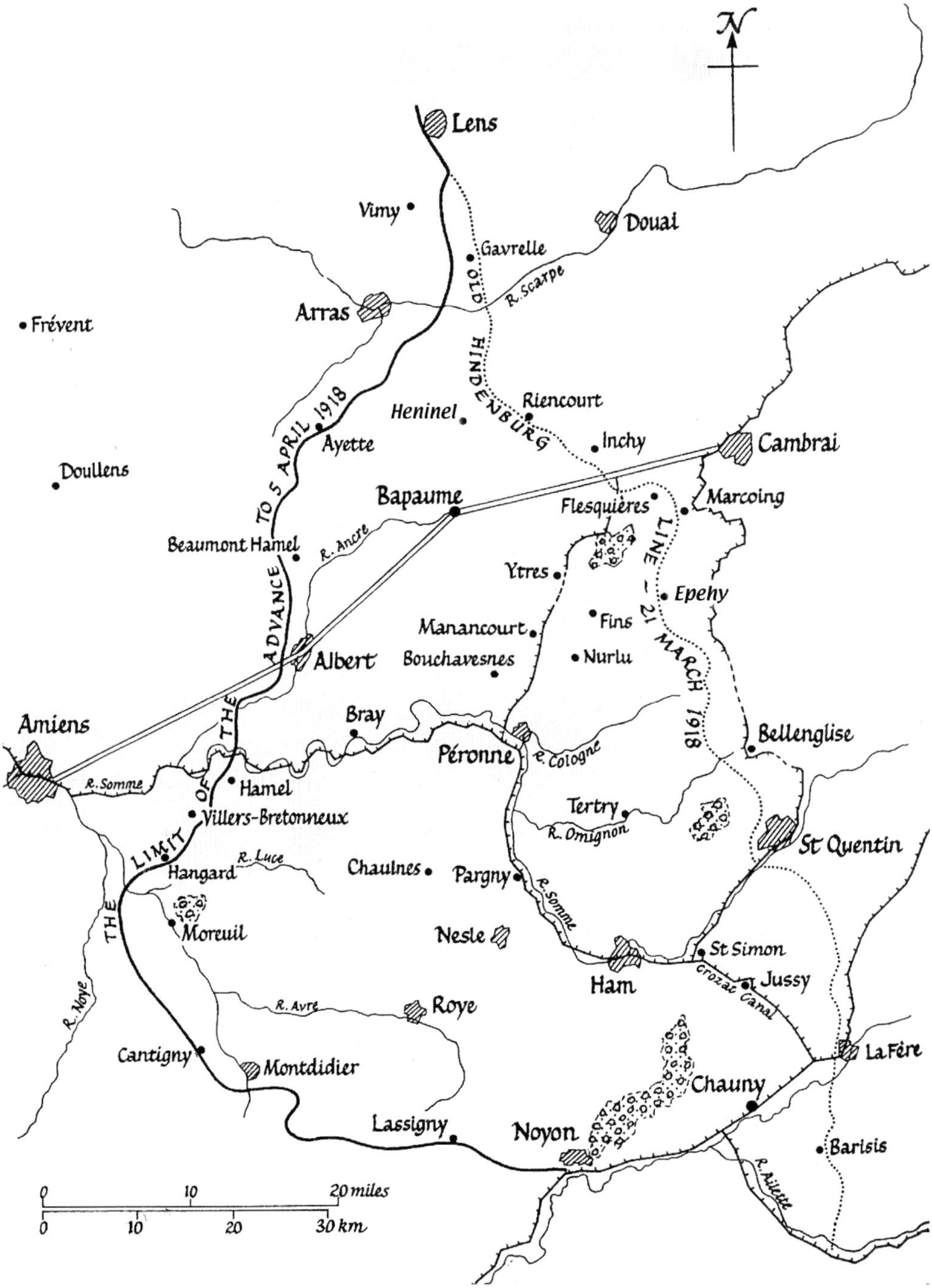

▲ Map 27. Operation *Michael*

The German assault continued into the second day. Again assisted by fog, the Germans attacked. Although stubborn resistance was put up in many places, including a counter-attack by 25 tanks of the 2nd Battalion, Tank Corps, the Germans continued their advance, forcing their way over the Crozat Canal. Further withdrawals were ordered by Gough which in turn forced a small retirement to be ordered by Byng to the north.

* * *

It will be recalled that the Battle of Cambrai in 1917 had created a salient in the German lines. The plan for Operation *Michael* did not include a frontal attack on this, the Flesquieres Salient, instead the salient would be heavily shelled with gas shells, and attacks launched from the north and the south aimed at surrounding the salient and capturing the three divisions of troops within it. To the south of the Flesquieres Salient was the boundary between the Fifth and Third Armies.

The 21st Division, part of Gough's Fifth Army, was holding nearly three miles of front line. It was through this division that the Germans were planning the southerly attack of their pincer movement on the Flesquieres Salient.

One soldier from Ravensthorpe was to be killed on the second day of the Kaiser's Battle in this area.

John William Roberts, born in Bolton, was just 19 years old, and part of 'D' Company, 2nd Battalion, Lincolnshire Regiment. On 21st March at 5.45am, an hour after the German barrage had opened up, the battalion was ordered to man its battle positions. These would have been in the vicinity of Chapel Hill, one of the British redoubts; Chapel Hill itself was garrisoned by the 1st Lincolns who, like the 2nd Lincolns, were part of 62 Brigade, 21st Division.

Another strong position, a little to the south was the village of Epehy. This was held by the 6th, 7th and 8th Battalions of the Leicestershire Regiment, which formed 110 Brigade, also part of 21st Division.

The 2nd Lincolnshire's War Diary describes how the battalion had difficulty in finding their battle positions due to the thick fog and enemy gas. Nevertheless, the positions were manned *"...soon after 7am* [on the 21st]*, although stragglers continued to report until 10am. The positions were maintained all day against repeated attacks by the enemy. About 12 noon a party of the enemy succeeded in getting round the left flank under cover of a sunken road. This party was engaged* [by a machine gun]. *A number were killed and the remainder, about 50, surrendered."*

The War Diary for the following day, 22nd March, describes how orders to retire to the village of Heudicourt were received about 12 noon. This was because the Germans had *"...penetrated the British line at Epehy and were threatening the line of retirement. 'A' and 'D' Companies losing heavily in getting clear."* It is likely that it was during this retirement that John was killed.

A further retirement from Heudicourt was made at 5pm and a rearguard action was fought.

Nothing is known about the fate of Private John Roberts. His parents, William and Mary of 26 Lee Street, Ravensthorpe held out hope for several months that he

◂ 124. John Roberts

▾ 125. The Pozieres Memorial to the Missing, which surrounds the Pozieres British Cemetery.

may have been taken prisoner as in January 1919 appeals for information were made in the local newspapers in which it was stated that he was *"...thought by his officers to be a prisoner of war."*

Of the 44 men killed on the 21st March and 24 men who lost their lives on 22nd March only eight have known graves; John, like many of his comrades has no known grave and is therefore commemorated on the Pozieres Memorial to the Missing. The memorial surrounds Pozieres British Cemetery on the Albert to Bapaume Road and lists the names of over 14,600 men, most of whom were killed between 21st March and 5th April 1918. Although in the heart of the 1916 Somme battlefield, the Memorial commemorates those men from the Fifth Army who were killed during the German Spring Offensive of 1918 and who have no known grave. Ironically the Memorial stands within the sector held by the Third Army in 1918. (The men killed at this time whilst serving with the Third Army and who have no known grave are commemorated on the Arras Memorial to the Missing.)

The defence of Chapel Hill and Epehy was unusual in terms of the battle that raged on 21st and 22nd March in that the troops withstood the German onslaught much longer than did men in other redoubts. Although the Germans did penetrate between the two positions in the vicinity of Vaucelette Farm, which was held by the 12th/13th Northumberland Fusiliers (also part of 61 Brigade, 21st Division), once the fog lifted the garrisons on Chapel Hill and in Epehy poured fire on the Germans who were then forced to halt their advance.

Although the troops of the 21st Division were forced to fall back, actions such as these took the sting out of the German attack here in the northern part of the Fifth Army front. Despite these heroic actions, by 23rd March the Germans had advanced over twelve miles in the southern sector of the attack.

The defence put up by the 21st Division did not save the Flesquieres salient, however the troops within it were able to be withdrawn, pulling out on 24th March. This withdrawal heralded another retreat by the British; Bapaume fell to the Germans on this same day (24th March), and Albert fell on 26th March. Because of these continuing retirements by Gough's Fifth Army, Byng's Third Army to the left was also forced to give ground.

It was to the north, on the front of the Third Army, that the next Ravensthorpe casualty was suffered.

* * *

Operation *Michael* extended from the 58th (2nd/1st London) Division in the south to the 3rd Division in the north. The 3rd Division held the front line south of the town of Arras.

Harry Armitage was born in Liversedge in about 1889. After going to St. Saviour's Boys' School and the Boothroyd Lane Council School in Dewsbury*, he first of all worked for Hemingway Brothers, grocers in Liversedge, later taking charge of the management of the Lion Stores in Thornhill Lees for two years (this store is where Percy Boothroyd had also worked - see Chapter 10). In July 1916 he

**** This second school was attended probably because the family lived just outside Ravensthorpe at 5 Thornville Street, Dewsbury.***

▲ 126. Harry Armitage

▲ 127. Fred Auty

was called up into the army and was initially drafted into the General Service Cavalry. The term 'General Service Cavalry' was not a unit but a description of terms of service, it described those men who had enlisted for service in one of the Cavalry Regiments.

Later in the war (mid- to late-1917) many men were stripped out of the cavalry and transferred to the infantry. It is likely that Harry was part of this process as before being sent overseas he joined the 1st Battalion, Northumberland Fusiliers. The Dewsbury Reporter indicates that he spent Christmas 1917 at home, implying that this was home leave from France, although it is equally possible that this may have been his last leave before being sent overseas for the first time.

The War Diary of the 1st Battalion, Northumberland Fusiliers (part of 9 Brigade, 3rd Division) describes how, on 21st March, a heavy barrage came down on them whilst they were occupying trenches in the area between Boisleux-au-Mont (where the division had its headquarters) and Heninel. The front line system was captured by the Germans at 7.15am, but the battalion counter-attacked and regained the trench by 9am. A second German attack just before noon again captured the front line. The brigade War Diary states that the Germans advanced *"...from Fontaine Wood. In this attack* [at 3.25pm*] *the enemy succeeded in capturing the front line all along the Brigade front, and as this line was practically obliterated, I* [presumably the Brigadier-General in charge of 9 Brigade] *decided not to attempt its recapture."*

The brigade fell back on to its second system which it occupied overnight. The Germans did not attack again until midday on 22nd March. After beating off

**** This contradicts the battalion War Diary's time of "Just before noon".***

attacks again during the day, the 1st Northumberland Fusiliers withdrew at 1am on 23rd March, concentrating with the rest of 9 Brigade on the village of Mercatel.

In early April, Harry's parents, John and Hannah Armitage, received 'an official notice' that Lance Corporal Harry Armitage had been killed. He was 28 years of age. The Dewsbury Reporter described how the notice said *"...he died from a gunshot wound in the head and a fractured skull on March 23rd in the 43rd Casualty Clearing Station."* The report continued, *"A friend has also written to Mr Armitage to the effect that 'Harry was sniped'."*

There is no clue as to whether Harry received his wound on 21st or 22nd March. The battalion's War Diary indicates casualties for the period of 122 other ranks, of whom, according to S.D.G.W., seventeen were killed on 21st March and eight on 22nd March. Harry was one of four men from the battalion who died of their wounds on 23rd March. Harry is buried at Bac-du-Sud British Cemetery near the village of Balleuval, about ten miles due west of where the battalion was fighting; this cemetery was started by the 7th, 20th and 43rd Casualty Clearing Stations in March 1918 and now contains 743 graves.

Sir Douglas Haig was, after several days of the German offensive, becoming concerned not only at the amount of ground being given up but also at the non-appearance of the French army which would, he had been assured, come to his aid.

In view of the deepening crisis, an inter-allied conference was held on 26th March in the town hall at Doullens. At this conference, Haig swallowed his pride and suggested that an overall Allied commander be appointed to coordinate the British and French armies. Despite having good claims to such an appointment, Haig agreed that the French General, Ferdinand Foch be appointed.

Despite the unified command structure, there were no immediate benefits to the new arrangement, the Germans continued their attacks.

* * *

Following their successful attacks at Cambrai in November 1917, the 62nd (West Riding) Division was withdrawn to a rest area, west of Arras; although periods in the line were undertaken, the division was not involved in any serious fighting. As previously mentioned, the reorganisation that occurred in the army at this time involved a reduction in the number of infantry battalions in a division from twelve down to nine. In the 62nd Division, the three battalions that disappeared were the 2/6th West Yorkshire Regiment, 2/5th York and Lancaster Regiment and the 2/6th Duke of Wellington's Regiment.

In addition to this, three of the 62nd Division's battalions (the 2/8th West Yorkshires, 2/5th Duke of Wellington's and 2/5th K.O.Y.L.I.) were merged with their first line 'sister battalions' from the 49th Division (the 1/8th West Yorkshires, 1/5th Duke of Wellington's and the 1/5th K.O.Y.L.I.). The merged battalions (called the 8th West Yorkshires, 5th Duke of Wellington's and 5th K.O.Y.L.I.) all remained with the 62nd Division.

None of this reorganisation directly affected the 2/7th West Yorkshires, with whom Fred Auty was serving.

Fred Auty was born in about 1891 to Mr and Mrs Richard Auty. On leaving school he worked as a packer for James Walker and Sons of Butt End Mills, Mirfield. He was a regular attender at Ravensthorpe Congregational Church and Sunday School, and a member of the cricket team. Fred joined the West Yorkshire Regiment in June 1917, being sent to France in December.

At midnight on 24th/25th March the battalion, along with the rest of the 62nd Division was ordered to move from Arras, where it had been resting, south to the village of Bucquoy where it arrived at about noon on 25th March. 185 Brigade (containing Fred's battalion) was ordered to take up a defensive position at Achiet-le-Petit (a village to the east of Bucquoy). Due to German successes further south a small retirement was ordered that night, and by dawn on 26th a new line was held east of Bucquoy with 186 Brigade on the right and 185 Brigade on the left.

Shortly before 8am on 26th March the Germans started to attack the division's positions, particularly vulnerable was 186 Brigade on the right whose flank was open; the nearest troops on their right were about three miles away, being the 12th (Eastern) Division.

The 62nd Division was hard pressed but unexpected help was to hand. The commander of the Machine Gun School in France had been ordered to the front, together with his troops who were instructors at the school. Becoming lost he stumbled on Major-General Braithwaite's Divisional Headquarters; Braithwaite asked him to take up positions to relieve the pressure, these positions were probably on the right of the division's front, where the risk of encirclement was at its highest. The machine gunners were faced with hordes of Germans, whose attacks they helped break up.

Although most of the attacks came on the right, heavy German artillery fire was turned on the 8th and 2/5th West Yorkshires who were in the front line. That night (26th/27th March) these two battalions were relieved by the 2/7th West Yorkshires.

At 7am on Wednesday 27th, men of the 2/7th West Yorkshires saw Germans advancing from Achiet-le-Petit and so fire was brought down on them. For the next two hours, the Germans bombarded the village of Bucquoy and the battalions who were holding trenches in and around the village. Again the Germans attacked and again they were beaten off with heavy losses.

The 2/7th West Yorkshires held its position all day, sustaining in the process 25 men killed in action. One of these was Rifleman Fred Auty, aged 26.

Fred's wife received a letter at the house she shared with her parents-in-law at 21 Field Street Ravensthorpe on Tuesday 9th April from the Reverend F.R. Buxton, the chaplain to the battalion. The letter, dated Thursday 4th April, broke the news that Fred had been killed. Besides leaving a widow and his bereaved parents, Fred also left behind a baby girl aged 2 months. It is likely that Fred (who had been sent to France in December 1917) had never seen his daughter.

Neither Fred nor the other 24 soldiers of the 2/7th West Yorkshires who were killed on 27th March have known graves, and they are all therefore commemorated on the Arras Memorial to the Missing.

The 62nd Division, although attacked on 28th March gave little ground, and the German assault in this northern sector of the Operation *Michael* front started to run out of steam. The division lost 98 officers and 2,084 other ranks killed, wounded and missing between 25th and 31st March. The officer casualties included two battalions' commanding officers killed and three wounded; one of the two to be killed, Lieutenant-Colonel O.C. Watson of the 5th K.O.Y.L.I. was

Map 28. Bucquoy

awarded a posthumous Victoria Cross for his actions on 28th March.

It is ironic that ten months earlier in the Second Battle of Bullecourt, the 2/5th K.O.Y.L.I. had lost another commanding officer killed also called Watson - this one being Lieutenant-Colonel W. Watson. After his commanding officer was killed, Major (as he was then) O.C. Watson took over temporary command of the battalion from his name-sake until he was himself wounded in that battle; he recovered to return to the battalion, to be killed during the battle on 28th March.

Lieutenant-Colonel O.C. Watson, V.C., D.S.O. has no known grave and is commemorated on the Arras Memorial to the Missing.

* * *

The situation to the south was still desperate. As a result of the continued withdrawal of the Fifth Army General Sir Hubert Gough was relieved of his command on 28th March, largely at the instigation of Lloyd George who demanded a scapegoat. General Rawlinson, then undertaking a liaison role as the British Military Representative on the Supreme War Council at Versailles, replaced Gough. The Fifth Army was renamed the Fourth Army on 2nd April.

It is necessary to look briefly at how Ludendorff, at this stage, perceived the progress of the battle. The original concept was for a breakthrough followed by a turn northwards to roll up the British line. Following the success in the south and the relative failure in the north, Ludendorff had, on 23rd March, given orders that instead of turning northwards, the breakthrough should continue heading westwards. He therefore reinforced this portion of his armies and did not persist in trying to break through the British line in the north (south of Arras).

Two days later, on 25th March, Ludendorff changed his mind and decided to launch Operation *Mars* against Arras. This attack was made on 28th March, but was repelled by the British who inflicted heavy losses on the Germans.

Faced with this set back, he again changed his mind and ordered a further thrust westwards, directing that Amiens was to be taken. He believed, probably correctly, that the loss of this town behind the Somme battlefield with its vital rail junction would be a disaster for the British. Although this advance caused concern for the British (and led to Gough's sacking), unfortunately for Ludendorff his troops were becoming exhausted, their lines of supply were over-stretched, his best men had become casualties, and discipline was breaking down when his troops came across piles of abandoned stores. Many of his soldiers became hopelessly drunk on looted alcohol, and the advance slowed down. At Villers-Brettoneux on 4th April the German assault was halted. This ended Operation *Michael*.

The Germans had been stopped ten miles east of Amiens. The attack had cost the British 178,000 men (including 70,000 prisoners taken by the Germans), and the French casualties amounted to 77,000. German losses at 250,000 (including over 70,000 men dead) were made worse because many of these were the storm troopers who would be almost impossible to replace. The German armies had advanced over thirty miles, but none of the ground they had taken was strategically vital; Ludendorff still had, however, further plans to attack and knock the British army out of the war.

Chapter Nineteen

Backs to the Wall
The German Lys Offensive

After Ludendorff closed down Operation *Michael* there were two further fatalities to Ravensthorpe's soldiers before the next phase of Germany's attacks began.

Mystery surrounds Arthur Hampshire. Arthur, who was 34 years old, went to France in February 1918, joining the 1/4th K.O.Y.L.I. in the 49th (West Riding) Division. The only reference to him in the local newspapers is an appeal for information in January 1919 when his wife, Lavinia Hampshire of 40 William Street, Ravensthorpe asked for anyone who had news of her husband. The only other information this article contained was that Arthur was in 'W' Company and that before joining up he worked at Lee & Nephew's mill in Ravensthorpe. The article said he had been missing since 20th April (1918), although this is most likely a mis-print for 2nd April because this date does not tie in with other sources. The C.W.G.C., S.D.G.W. and the Medal Rolls at the Public Record Office at Kew all give his date of death as 2nd April 1918 (the Medal Rolls saying 'presumed dead').

Whilst this contradiction may be explained as a typographical error creeping into the newspaper's report, the confusion really starts when the battalion's War Diary is examined. The 1/4th K.O.Y.L.I. had been holding a position in the front line in the Menin Road sector at Ypres. The War Diary in the days leading up to 2nd April is very sparse:

28th March - *Holding the line, one killed, three wounded.*
29th March - *Holding the line, one wounded.*
30th March - *Holding the line, no casualties.*
31st March - *Holding the line, no casualties.*
1st April - *Battalion holding the line in the Menin Road sector. Battalion relieved by the 1/6th West Yorks and proceeded to Otago Camp.*
2nd April - Battalion at Otago Camp, resting and training.

The battalion's fatalities mentioned in the War Diary are more or less confirmed by S.D.G.W., which gives casualties as follows:

28th March - 1 killed, plus two died of wounds.
29th, 30th and 31st March - none killed.
1st April - two killed.
2nd April - 1 killed (Arthur Hampshire), plus one died of wounds.

Why Arthur is reported as killed in action on a day when the battalion was in camp cannot be explained, whatever happened to Arthur Hampshire, he has no known grave and is therefore commemorated on the Tyne Cot Memorial to the Missing.

The second of Ravensthorpe's casualties in this period was Charles Ellis. Charles was born in Dewsbury in about 1895. Until he joined up in August 1915 he worked as a farm labourer for Charles Fearnley of Ravensthorpe. Like Harry Harris (see Chapter 11) and the Duxbury brothers (see Appendix 2), he joined the Miners' Battalion, despite having no mining connections. He probably joined up on 9th August, being given the regimental number 1755*. Charles (like Harry Harris) was destined not to stay with the Miners' Battalion, instead being transferred to the Royal Welsh Fusiliers, joining the 4th Battalion which was the pioneer battalion to the 47th (2nd London) Division. It is not known when he joined the battalion in France.

In early April 1918, the battalion was at Senlis, a village 3½ miles north-west of Albert. Based in the village chateau, it was providing working parties in the front line at the village of Bouzincourt. On 4th April the battalion was unexpectedly given a rest from its normal duties in order to recuperate prior to going up to the front line where the men were to be used as infantry. The order to rest was no doubt met with mixed feelings.

At 1pm on 5th April, the battalion was ordered to the front line, to take up positions at a crossroads between the villages of Bouzincourt and Martinsart. Placed under the orders of 142 Brigade, the battalion was told it would be delivering a counter-attack against the Germans. In moving into position north-west of Martinsart, the battalion suffered three other ranks killed, plus sixteen wounded (S.D.G.W. states four killed in action on 5th April).

The battalion's War Diary describes how, by 4am on 6th April, two of the battalion's three companies+ ('A' and 'B' companies) were *"...assembled for the attack along the bank to the west of Aveluy Wood....'B' on the right, 'A' on the left....companies advanced in extended order to the edge of the wood where snake formations were adopted. Zero hour was fixed* [for] *5.55am. The attack failed owing to the intensity of the hostile machine gun fire and the inefficiency of our own artillery barrage. Having sustained very heavy casualties 'B' Company fell back to their original line....*[a] *machine gun was silenced in the wood by bombing and killing the crew. The position was held and consolidated. As the other machine guns were out of bombing distance, no further advance could be made....At 7pm before the relief took place a violent enemy barrage was put down behind our front line and on the village of Martinsart lasting 20 minutes....Thus ended the most disastrous day in the history of the battalion."*

The battalion and the rest of 142 Brigade were relieved that night. The battalion's War Diary lists casualties as:

7 officers and 15 other ranks killed,
1 officer and 1 other rank died of wounds,
2 officers and 71 other ranks wounded,
10 other ranks gassed,
49 other ranks missing.

**** Harry Harris, who joined up in July 1915 was given the regimental number of 1605; John and Arthur Duxbury, who joined up on 10th August were allocated numbers 1788 and 1789.***

+ As part of the reorganisation earlier in the year, pioneer battalions had been reduced from four to three companies.

Of the 65 other ranks killed, died of wounds or missing, S.D.G.W. gives a figure of 40 men killed in action or died of wounds on this day; of these 40 men, eight had formerly been with the K.O.Y.L.I., their regimental numbers indicate that, like Charles Ellis, they were drafts from the 12th (Miners') Battalion.

One of those killed was Charles Ellis, who died aged 22.

Charles was initially posted as missing. His mother, Elizabeth Ellis who lived at 97 Garden Street, Ravensthorpe, made an appeal for information about her son in the Dewsbury Reporter in July.

Nearly half of the 40 men from the 4th Royal Welsh Fusiliers who lost their lives on 6th April have no known grave, whilst a similar number of the 'other ranks' plus six of the eight officers are buried at Martinsart British Cemetery.

Whilst Charles, having no known grave, is commemorated on the Pozieres Memorial to the Missing, it is highly likely that he is buried in Martinsart British Cemetery, which contains the graves of nearly 500 soldiers, about one quarter of whom are 'unknown'.

* * *

Although Ludendorff had stopped the Operation *Michael* offensive, he believed he could still win the war before the Americans were able to exert their influence.

It will be recalled how several plans had emerged from the original *Kaiserschlacht* concept. Two of these, *Michael* and *Mars* had been tried. The third, *George*, was now put into operation, although it was scaled-down in size, and thus became Operation *Georgette*. This attack was to become known to the British as

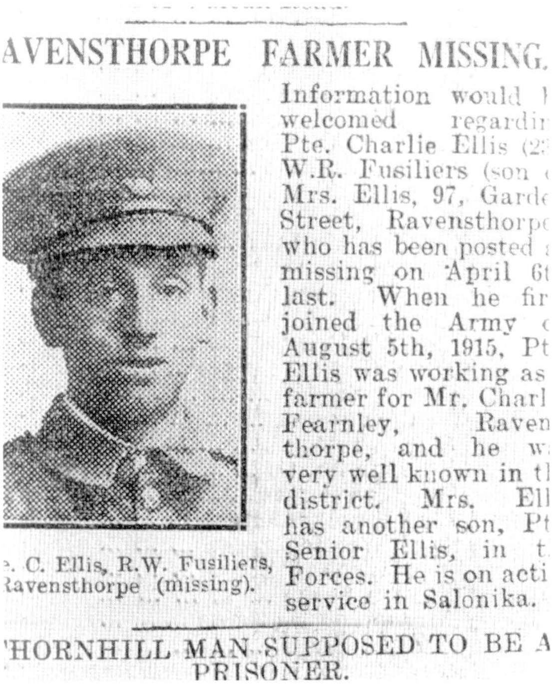

AVENSTHORPE FARMER MISSING.

Information would
welcomed regardi
Pte. Charlie Ellis (2
W.R. Fusiliers (son
Mrs. Ellis, 97, Gard
Street, Ravensthorp
who has been posted
missing on April 6t
last. When he fir
joined the Army
August 5th, 1915, Pt
Ellis was working as
farmer for Mr. Charl
Fearnley, Raven
thorpe, and he w
very well known in t
district. Mrs. Ell
has another son, Pt
Senior Ellis, in t
Forces. He is on acti
service in Salonika.

. C. Ellis, R.W. Fusiliers,
Ravensthorpe (missing).

'HORNHILL MAN SUPPOSED TO BE A PRISONER.

▲ 128. Charles Ellis

▲ 129. The headstone of an unknown Royal Welsh Fusilier, in Martinsart British Cemetery.

the Lys Offensive as it was centred around the River Lys which ran through the Flanders plain on the Belgian/French border.

Whilst *Michael* had been a success in terms of ground gained, none of this was strategically important to the Allies; it was a different matter to the north, a similar loss of ground would leave the British army in dire straits.

At 8.45am on Tuesday 9th April 1918, after a 4½ hour artillery bombardment, fourteen German divisions attacked on a front of twelve miles, aiming at capturing Hazebrouck with its vital rail junction. Although attacking with significantly less than the 64 divisions they had used for the opening of the *Michael* offensive, and with some of these divisions being 'trench holding' rather than attack divisions, a significant breakthrough was achieved. This was partly due to the fact that the full weight of the attack fell on the 2nd Portuguese Division* which was holding part of the British front near Neuve Chapelle. The two Portuguese Divisions were considered by both British and German army intelligence to be of dubious quality, and although attacked by overwhelming numbers of German troops, their collapse was rapid. The Germans advanced 3½ miles at this point in the line. To the south, the 55th (West Lancashire) Division put up a brave defence, and despite being forced to give a little ground, inflicted heavy casualties on the Germans.

To the north of the Portuguese was the valley of the River Lys; in this sector was the 40th Division. Under the cover of fog, the Germans forced a crossing over the river.

The following day a further series of attacks were made by the Germans to the north, forcing the abandonment of the Messines Ridge and the town of Armentieres on 11th April. It was on 11th April that Haig issued a 'Special Order of the Day', which included *"...There is no other course open to us but to fight it out. Every position must be held to the last man: there must be no retirement. With our backs to the wall and believing in the justice of our cause each one of us must fight on to the end."*

It is unlikely that three of Ravensthorpe's soldiers would have heard this message as two were killed and one captured on this day. Possibly as a result of the chaotic conditions at this time, little information about these three soldiers is available, either from their respective battalions' War Diaries or from accounts in the newspapers.

Jack Whiteley was born in either 1899 or 1900 to Mr and Mrs Fenton Whiteley. Nothing is known of his education or employment. He was sent to France in March 1918, joining 'B' Company of the 1/6th Battalion, Northumberland Fusiliers (part of 50th (Northumbrian) Division). The War Diary of the division's 149 Brigade (made up of the 1/4th, 1/5th and 1/6th Northumberland Fusiliers) states that the brigade (*"400 all ranks"*) was relieved on 1st April, moving to the town of Lillers. There, the battalions were made up to strength with men drafted from home. It is likely that Jack was with this large group of reinforcements. From Lillers the division moved north to Merville. [See Map 34 in Appendix 2].

At Merville, on 9th April (the opening day of the *Georgette* Offensive), the 1/6th Northumberland Fusiliers was ordered to be prepared to move at short notice, probably to support the 40th Division who were holding the line astride the River Lys. At 7.30am, the battalion, together with the 1/5th Northumberland Fusiliers were moved up to Le Trou Bayard, a small village east of the town of Estaires.

**** Portugal had entered the war on 8th March 1916 when Germany declared war on her.***

From there, a series of small moves were ordered, but no contact was made with the Germans; the situation must have been very confusing for the battalion and brigade commanders, with reports of German advances and the sound of heavy fighting nearby. The division was in the vicinity of, and behind the 40th Division which had (as the unit to the north of the Portuguese) been attacked early that morning but had managed to keep the Germans more or less at bay.

On 10th April, nervous of being attacked from the south, where the Germans had broken through, the 1/6th Northumberland Fusiliers was ordered to form a defensive flank facing the line of the German breakthrough. At 7.15am, the battalion was ordered to attack and retake Estaires which had fallen into German hands, and they were successful in regaining most of the town. The battalion was shelled for the rest of the day, incurring heavy casualties and was forced to give up part of Estaires that evening. S.D.G.W. gives casualties for 149 Brigade on 10th April as exactly 100 men killed or died of wounds.

On Thursday 11th April, the 1/6th Northumberland Fusiliers was placed into brigade reserve. Despite this, there was to be no rest for the men. At 7am a report arrived to say that the Germans had occupied Le Trou Bayard, and the battalion was therefore ordered to move forward. By 1.50pm the battalion's advance had been halted, and due to German pressure, was being forced back. The battalion was in serious trouble. With an open flank to the right, the brigade (according to its diary) *"...seemed to be in touch with the 29th Division on the left."* A verbal report that Neuf Berquin (a village north-west of Estaires) was in the hands of the enemy put in doubt the existence of troops on the left. At 11pm that evening, after consulting with brigades from the 29th Division, 149 Brigade fell back to Vierhoek.

Further withdrawals proved necessary on following days, but in this confused fighting*, the 1/6th Northumberland Fusiliers lost (according to S.D.G.W.) 98 men. One of these was Jack Whiteley.

No obituary appeared for Jack in the local newspapers; there was, however an appeal in January 1919 by his parents who lived at 273 Scout Hill for information concerning their son.

Jack has no known grave and is commemorated on the Ploegsteert Memorial to the Missing. This Memorial, actually in southern Belgium, lists the names of 11,500 soldiers killed in the area throughout the 1914-1918 period and who have no known grave.

The account of Jack Whiteley mentions the 29th Division. This division was theoretically a regular division, but by this stage in the war it would have received numerous drafts of conscripts thus making it virtually indistinguishable in character from any other division of the British army; one of the division's battalions was the 2nd Battalion, Royal Fusiliers.

The 2nd Royal Fusiliers, part of 86 Brigade, was, on 10th April in the Merville area. The following day the battalion was put under the command of 151 Brigade (50th (Northumbrian) Division) whose battalions were in reserve positions. At

**** The fighting was so confused and the fighting so heavy that the battalion's War Diary was not written up; instead, it contains a statement to the effect that the War Diary could not be provided due to the fact that the only surviving officer, Major J.G. Leathart is at Le Touquet (the home of Number 1 British Red Cross Society Hospital, otherwise known as the Duchess of Westminster's Hospital). The statement went on to say that the War Diary would be forwarded at the earliest possible moment, but clearly this did not happen. Such instances of there being no officer to write up the War Diary are quite rare.***

◂ 130. Jack Whiteley

▾ 131. The Ploegsteert Memorial to the Missing.

noon the battalion was moved to the village of Doulieu (2½ miles north of Estaires), where they again came under the orders of 86 Brigade. The War Diary states that *"At 3pm the enemy became very lively and troops showing a tendency to retire....Sharp fighting all that afternoon and night when we were ordered to evacuate Doulieu, this about 2am on 12th April."*

The battalion's War Diary does not mention the casualties, but S.D.G.W. gives fatalities for the 2nd Royal Fusiliers on 11th April as seven killed in action. Amongst this number was John Blakeley. There are hardly any facts available about John. According to S.D.G.W. he was born in Mirfield and after joining the army initially served in the York and Lancaster Regiment. He did not go overseas with this regiment, however, as the Medal Rolls at the Public Record Office indicate that he went to the Western Front with the 1st Battalion, Royal Fusiliers (part of the 24th Division) in June 1917, serving with them until November 1917. It is likely that he was injured in November 1917, possibly during the German counter-attack at Cambrai, in which the 24th Division was involved. As a result of these injuries, he spent the next three months recovering before being posted to the 2nd Battalion. He then served with the 2nd Royal Fusiliers from the end of February 1918 until his death.

The only references to John in the newspapers appear in February and March 1917. The newspapers at this time carried reports from local tribunals which heard appeals against conscription; one of the articles, only a few lines long, referred to John, aged 18, appealing against being called up. His employer, Mr C. Fearnley (possibly the same individual who had employed Charles Ellis - see the beginning of this chapter), a carting agent operating in Ravensthorpe, made a statement to the tribunal in which he said that it was difficult obtaining men *"...due to his work which included scavenging."* The first report, in the Dewsbury News went on to say that John *"...was the oldest of seven children and the widowed mother was dependent* [on him]."

The appeal was dismissed although 'one month's grace' was allowed conditional upon no further appeal being lodged. The condition was refused and the case went to appeal. This was heard three weeks later and seems to have been dismissed again, although he was 'given grace' until 1st April.

The appeals made by John and his mother are typical of this period of the war. The Military Service Act had been in operation for over a year, and the local tribunals (like the one John attended) were set up to hear the appeals of those men who believed they had a case for not being called up (the usual grounds being either having a reserved occupation or as a conscientious objector).

John Thomas Blakeley has no known grave and is commemorated on the Ploegsteert Memorial to the Missing. He was probably aged 19 when he died (the newspapers indicated he was 18 when the appeals were being made, some 14 months before his death). It is likely that he served overseas before his 19th birthday due to the fact that during the German's spring offensive, the Government was forced to increase the upper age limit of conscripts to 50 and also go back on its undertaking not to send young soldiers overseas until after their 19th birthdays.

There was one other event on 11th April that affected a Ravensthorpe family.

Frank Bower was born in Huddersfield in about 1899 to John and Mary Ellen Bower. Until he joined up on 13th April 1917 he worked as a clerk in the goods department of the London and North West Railway Company in Dewsbury, at the same time studying at Dewsbury Technical School. He lived with his parents at 4 Netherfield Road, Ravensthorpe, attending the Parish Church, and being a member of St. Cuthbert's Bible Class.

After joining the army, he had a prolonged period of training which was probably due to a combination of Lloyd George's policy of keeping Haig short of reinforcements, and the fact that he had not reached his 19th birthday. Frank was sent to France in early April 1918, joining the 22nd Battalion, Northumberland Fusiliers, part of the 34th Division who were in the Houplines sector, near Armentieres. Although in the sector facing the full weight of the *Georgette* Offensive, Frank was destined to see no fighting. He was admitted to hospital (possibly a casualty clearing station) on 9th April, suffering from a poisoned stomach. He was taken prisoner, probably when the hospital or casualty clearing station was over-run.

Although they had received a letter from him dated 6th April, saying he was in the trenches, the next his parents heard was a report stating that he was missing *"...as between April 11th and April 14th"*. A further letter came to them on 4th May from a comrade of Frank's giving them the news that Frank had been in hospital. Desperate for information, they wrote to both this correspondent and to his commanding officer, but without receiving any reply. It was not until early June that they received a field postcard from him to say that he had been made a prisoner and he was at Limburd on the Lahn in Germany. Although no doubt worried about their son, Frank's parents were no doubt relieved that he was alive, and would have been confident that he would eventually return home. Unfortunately this was not to be the case.

In mid-October they received a letter from him (he was now at Friedrichsfeld) to say that he was 'in the pink'. He went on to say that amongst the soldiers in his hut was George Hargreaves of 25 Back North Road, Ravensthorpe and Harry Gibson of 17 Anroyd Street, Westborough, Dewsbury. It is likely that this was his last letter home as on Tuesday 29th October, Private Frank Bernard Bower died, aged just 19.

Frank was buried at Heilsberg* Prisoner of War Cemetery. This was a very large cemetery containing several thousand burials, mainly of Russians and other eastern Europeans who had died, presumably as prisoners of war. The number of British prisoners (39) was a very small proportion of the total burials, which were made in a series of mass graves. The local authorities left the cemetery unattended.

The Imperial War Graves Commission (as it then was) realised in 1931, presumably when they first visited the site, that the 39 British burials could not be located amongst the mass graves. As part of the Commission's policy of ensuring all soldiers are commemorated, there is a small memorial at Malbork Commonwealth War Cemetery on which the names of the 39 soldiers are carved, including that of Frank Bower. Malbork is 25 miles south-east of Gdansk; although the cemetery is predominantly a Second World War cemetery it does also contain the remains of thirteen soldiers from the First World War which were concentrated into it in 1960 from a cemetery in Gdansk which could not be maintained.

***** *Heilsberg (originally in Germany) is now Lidzbark in Poland. It is 80 miles east of the city of Gdansk.***

It is not known on which day Frank was captured, but around this time, another soldier from Ravensthorpe was killed. The story of John Duxbury and his brother Arthur (who were members of the 12th K.O.Y.L.I., the Miners' Battalion) and their involvement in an important action at La Couronne (a village west of Doulieu where Jack Whiteley had been killed) is told in Appendix 2.

John Duxbury was killed on 13th April, and it was on this day also that William Harry Griffith lost his life.

Harry, as he was known, was born in Crewe to David William and Elizabeth Griffith in 1897 or 1898. He enlisted in Dewsbury, joining the Royal Field Artillery, being posted to the 38th Brigade. He arrived in France on 26th August 1915, aged just seventeen years old.

Although changes in artillery brigades had occurred throughout the war, by 1918 each artillery brigade contained 3 six gun batteries (ie. eighteen guns) of 18-pounder guns plus 1 six gun battery of 4.5" howitzers. The change that brought about this structure reduced the number of artillery brigades per division from four down to two, although the actual reduction in number of guns per division was only 25%. As outlined in Chapter 10, the surplus guns were allocated to Corps and Armies to be used as reserves.

Harry Griffith, as has been mentioned, was part of the 38th Brigade, R.F.A. The brigade was originally part of the 6th Division but had become an 'Army' brigade in February 1917. 'D' Battery, which was Harry's battery within the 38th Brigade, was armed with 4.5" howitzers. In the hectic days of the German Lys offensive, the 38th Brigade was moved from division to division in order to help stem the German tide.

▲ 132. Frank Bower

▲ 133. Harry Griffith

On 10th April the Brigade was put under the control of the 25th Division being in the Ploegsteert area of southern Belgium. On this day, the officer commanding 'D' Battery, Major L.E. Booth, together with some men of the battery, retrieved a 4.5" howitzer out of Ploegsteert Wood, where it had been abandoned by another battery.

Due to German pressure, the following day the infantry of the 25th Division were forced to retire, all batteries of the Brigade assisted the retirement by firing on the Germans, in the words of the brigade's War Diary *"over open sights*....did great execution. Finally withdrew battery by battery, getting all guns, ammunition and stores safely away."* Having been forced to retire from their positions south-east of Neuve Eglise, they took up new positions probably between Neuve Eglise and Dranouter.

The 12th April was a quiet day, the War Diary reporting *" 'D' Battery engaged in silencing a German 4.2* [inch] *battery."*

On Saturday 13th April, the Germans again attacked in force, making for Neuve Eglise. New positions were taken up a mile south-east of Dranouter, from where the brigade fired on the Germans. There were, however, losses to the brigade; two officers, including Major Booth were killed (he is buried at Wulvergem-Lindenhoek Road Military Cemetery) along with nine other ranks; a further two officers and eighteen other ranks were wounded. One of the fatalities was Harry Griffith.

The only references to Harry in the local newspapers are very brief; one was a 'thank you' message from his parents, who lived at 583 Huddersfield Road, Ravensthorpe, for the sympathy shown to them. The other was an extract from a letter written by a lieutenant which said: "...[Harry] *has always done well in the battery. We had been heavily shelled and all the men did excellent work in staying by the guns."*

Gunner William Harry Griffith, a veteran of nearly three years of warfare died aged 20. He has no known grave and is therefore commemorated on the Tyne Cot Memorial to the Missing.

* * *

Over the following days the crisis caused by the German Lys offensive eased. Although Haig had issued his uncharacteristic 'Order of the Day' on 11th April at the height of the crisis, it was more likely the arrival of reinforcements in Flanders that helped to resolve the situation than the effect of Haig's words on the ordinary soldiers.

A sign of Ludendorff's desperation came when the next attack was launched back on the Somme, at Villers Bretonneux on 24th April. The Operation *Michael* attack here had long since been abandoned, and there was no possibility of a strategic victory being forced in this locality. Although the village was lost (the

**** Firing directly at the Germans rather than indirectly (which was the usual method). With indirect fire, the fall of the shells had to be seen by observers who were watching the barrage either from aeroplanes or from trenches well forward of the battery's position.***

German attack was notable in that they used thirteen tanks*), a counter-attack that night re-took the village.

Back in Flanders, the French army lost Mount Kemmel to the Germans on 25th April; this large hill dominating the otherwise flat landscape of southern Belgium was of vital importance, but this was the last success of their Lys offensive. A final attack was made on 29th April, but it made little ground; that evening Ludendorff called off the *Georgette* Offensive.

The artillery bombardment in support of this final attack by the Germans on 29th April was to lead to the death of another of Ravensthorpe's soldiers.

Leonard Calvert was born in the Howden Clough area of Birstall, near Batley, on 3rd August 1891 to George and Annie Calvert. Leonard attended Birstall Central School until the family (which included another son, John) moved to Leeds. In about 1904 the family moved again, this time to Ravensthorpe. It is possible that there may have been another move at around this time, as the Dewsbury News indicates that Leonard attended the Jubilee School whilst living at Savile Town, Dewsbury.

◂ 134. Leonard Calvert

**** The first tank versus tank fight took place that day when three German tanks met three British tanks. Two of the British tanks were knocked out, however the third British tank then destroyed two of the German tanks. The third German tank was surrendered by its crew after coming under heavy machine gun fire.***

In 1911 there was yet another move for the Calvert family, this time to Batley Carr, the family living at 18 Warwick Road; it is possible that this was a result of George Calvert chasing employment in the local mills. George Calvert was at this time employed as a head tuner at Joseph Newsome and Sons' mill in Batley Carr; Leonard followed him into this type of work, being a tuner at G.H. Hirst & Co.'s mill, also in Batley Carr.

Leonard was called up into the army in 1916, joining the K.O.Y.L.I.; he was sent to France, initially joining the 2/5th Battalion, but after just four days he contracted trench foot and rheumatism which led to him returning home, where he spent the next twelve months. On Easter Monday 1918, Leonard returned to France, joining the 9th K.O.Y.L.I. in the 21st Division.

Following the loss of Mount Kemmel on 25th April, the 21st Division, in conjunction with both British and French troops launched an attack on 26th April. Unfortunately, possibly due to the attack being planned at the last moment, the battalions on either side of the 9th K.O.Y.L.I. failed to join in the attack when they went over the top; as a result the battalion lost heavily, S.D.G.W. indicating 65 men from the 9th K.O.Y.L.I. were killed on this day.

After being withdrawn and moved back to Red Horseshoe Camp, south-west of Ypres, the 100 men left out of the attackers were joined by the 155 men who had been left as the nucleus of the battalion back at the transport lines. Understandably, the 9th K.O.Y.L.I.'s commanding officer was somewhat bitter about the turn of events and sent a letter of complaint to Brigade Headquarters criticising not only the lack of movement on either side of his battalion, but also the feeble barrage that had been put down.

On 28th April Red Horseshoe Camp was bombarded by German artillery, and the battalion was ordered to move to defensive positions in case the Germans attacked; no attack developed.

The following day, Monday 29th April, another bombardment commenced at 4.30am. At 5.30am the battalion was moved into the same positions as before, and at 6.30am the road on which they were deployed was shelled. It was during the shelling on 29th April that Leonard Calvert, aged 26, was killed.

An article appeared in the Dewsbury Reporter on the 25th May describing "*...Miss Laycock of Eastfield Road, Northorpe**" who was Leonard's fiancee, receiving a letter from Private G. Metcalfe. Private Metcalfe told how "*...Leonard had been left out of the line to stay with the transport where he had the misfortune to be killed.*" He went on to say that he had helped to bury Leonard, and had "*...taken possession of Leonard's pocket wallet from which I got your address and also a letter which you had sent to him. I will get his personal belongings and send them to his home as soon as I can.*"

Leonard Calvert (who the article said was connected with Ravensthorpe Church as well as Ravensthorpe Wesleyan Cricket Club) has no known grave and is commemorated on the Tyne Cot Memorial to the Missing.

After the war, Leonard's parents moved again, this time to live in Heckmondwike.

* * *

**** Presumably a sister of Joseph Laycock who was to die in Mesopotamia in September (see Chapter 11).***

Although the Battles of the Lys officially ended on 29th April, and the roads to Ypres and the Channel Ports were barred, Ludendorff still had not given up hope of winning the war. Repulsed three times (Operations *Michael*, *Mars* and *Georgette*), he now turned his attention away from the British and looked to the south, where the French armies were holding the line. If he could divert the Allies' attention to this sector, committing their reserves, he believed he would subsequently be able to renew the offensive against the British in the north.

The first of the next wave of offensives was code named Operation *Blucher*, and was also known as the Third Battle of the Aisne, it was mounted against the Chemin des Dames Ridge and commenced on 27th May. Seventeen German divisions attacked across a nine mile front, preceded by the usual artillery bombardment; just four French and three British divisions stood in their way, although a total of nine further divisions were in reserve. (Ironically, the British divisions in this area had been sent there to recuperate after being in the thick of the earlier fighting; these British divisions were the 8th, 9th (Western), 21st, 25th and 50th (Northumbrian) Divisions.)

A high level of surprise was achieved, with the Germans capturing several bridges across the River Aisne; advances of between ten and twelve miles were made on the first day of the attack, although the British divisions did well in preventing the Germans from widening the frontage of their assault.

Having achieved the limited objectives of the attack, Ludendorff once again changed strategy to take advantage of this local tactical success, and continued the battle, aiming for Paris, which was only 80 miles away. Further advances were made but the attack was stopped at Chateau-Thierry, just 56 miles from Paris, with the help of two American divisions; although this was not the first time the American soldiers were in action in the First World War, it was the first major battle U.S. divisions were involved in during this conflict.

The Germans were now in a salient, in an attempt to widen this, another attack (code-named *Gneisenau*) was launched on 9th June; this, it was hoped, would link up with the Amiens salient (created by the Operation *Michael* offensive) to the north. Despite being warned of the attack, the French were unable to prevent a German advance of six miles. A counter-attack on 11th June, besides driving the Germans back to their starting line, did much to restore the morale and prestige of the French army.

* * *

It is necessary to turn away temporarily from the fighting in the south, as back in the British sector, Ravensthorpe was about to lose another soldier.

George Herbert English was born in Ravensthorpe to Edwin and Annie English in about 1889. Before joining the army in September 1916 he worked as a willeyer for Robert Swire and Sons. (A willey is a cylindrical machine with internal spikes which opens and cleans wool.) George was married to Sarah Jayne English, they had three children and lived at 31 Havelock Street, Ravensthorpe. After his call up (he enlisted in Heckmondwike) George was drafted into the Army Service Corps, being sent to France in August 1917. In December his wife had their fourth child. He was destined never to see it.

◄ 135. The shoulder tabs on George's unform indicate this was taken whilst a member of the Army Service Corps, before his transfer to the Northumberland Fusiliers.

▼ 136. Havelock Street, Ravensthorpe. *Photograph courtesy of Kirklees Community Service*

During May 1918 he was transferred from the A.S.C. to the Northumberland Fusiliers, joining the 1st Battalion, part of the 3rd Division. The division was, in mid-June, in the vicinity of the town of Bethune.

On 13th June, 9 Brigade (of which the 1st Northumberland Fusiliers was a part) issued an order calling for an advance on the night of the 14th/15th June on the east bank of La Bassee Canal. The operation was to be carried out by the 4th Royal Fusiliers, with three platoons of the 1st Northumberland Fusiliers attached. The attack was carried out at 11.45pm on 14th June and according to the brigade War Diary all objectives were gained.

The following day, the German artillery retaliated with a barrage of the British lines. The numbers of men killed on the 14th and 15th June, according to S.D.G.W., were twelve men from the 4th Royal Fusiliers (plus four died of wounds) and fourteen from the 1st Northumberland Fusiliers. One of these was George English, who was killed in action on 15th June; it is not known if George was killed during the attack or in the subsequent bombardment. Like six of his comrades, George is buried at Sandpits British Cemetery just south-west of Bethune. Lying alongside him are three other men from the 1st Northumberland Fusiliers who died at this time.

Sandpits British Cemetery was used between April and September 1918 and contains nearly 400 burials. Just a few yards from the cemetery runs the busy A26 motorway, the main route from Calais into northern France.

* * *

The next significant event involving the British Empire's armies on the Western Front involved the Australian Corps. This corps had been formed in November 1917 from the two Anzac Corps and contained the five Australian Divisions in France. Lieutenant-General Birdwood had been in command of the corps until his promotion to command a re-formed Fifth Army*. His replacement, Lieutenant-General John Monash was unusual in gaining such an elevated command, not being a professional soldier, he was a civil engineer of German-Jewish origin from Melbourne.

The Australian Corps undertook a small operation on 4th July which was carried out by the 4th Australian Division, together with four companies of American troops. The aim of the attack was to iron out a small German salient at Hamel, between Villers-Bretonneux and the River Somme. This operation became the model for the B.E.F.'s attacks for the remainder of the war. Monash planned the assault to use the fullest co-operation between all arms of the B.E.F. Aeroplanes from the newly formed R.A.F. plus tanks and artillery were to assist the infantry in their attack, which was an unqualified success. The use of aircraft to parachute supplies to forward troops and the arrival of the new Mark V tanks helped to keep the casualties suffered by the Australian and American troops to a minimum. The assault lasted just 90 minutes and cost less than 1,000 casualties.

**** See Chapter 18 - following Gough's dismissal in March 1918, the Fifth Army was taken over by Rawlinson and was renamed the Fourth Army. In May, Lieutenant-General Birdwood, commander of the Australian Corps, was promoted to command a new Fifth Army.***

Despite the warning at Hamel, Ludendorff still had hopes of victory. On 15th July he launched the sixth, and what was to be the last, all-out offensive by the German army in the Great War. The attack was once again made against the French army near the city of Reims, this assault and subsequent Allied counter-attack became known as the Second Battle of the Marne. By now, the Allies had learned how to cope with these attacks, and to the east of the city the German attack was halted by 11am on the first day. To the west of Reims there was some German success, and an advance of four miles was made, however by 17th July this attack, too, was halted by the French army, with support from British, American and even Italian units.

The following day, 18th July, a French counter-attack was launched against the Marne salient, supported by four British and four American divisions (it should be noted that American divisions were approximately twice the size of British and French divisions). The British divisions (part of XXII Corps) were the 15th (Scottish), 34th, 51st (Highland) and 62nd (West Riding) Divisions.

The 62nd (West Riding) Division had arrived in the area on 17th July, the divisional headquarters being at Tours sur Marne. Alongside the 62nd Division was the 51st (Highland) Division, the other two British divisions that had been sent to this area were some miles away to the west, on the other side of the German salient.

The French counter-attack on 18th July was aimed at cutting off the German troops in the bulge between Soissons and Reims, which were 25 miles apart. On 19th July orders were given to the 51st and the 62nd Divisions to continue the attack. The 8th Battalion, West Yorkshire Regiment (part of 185 Brigade) was one of the battalions which were to take part in the attack. The 8th West Yorkshires' War Diary describes its march forward towards the concentration area. Setting off at about 6am from Tours sur Marne, the battalion found the dusty roads crowded with transport and it was not until the evening that the battalion arrived at St. Imoges. Over the next few hours the 8th West Yorkshires moved up to its assembly positions at Bois de Pourcy.

The countryside was different from anything previously encountered, there were no trench systems but instead thick woodland and forests which had to be negotiated. Whilst passing along forest tracks German artillery shells came down, hampering their progress. The scene was chaotic; struggling along in the depths of a dark forest, with French guides leading the way to an un-reconnoitred rendezvous, the battalion became mixed up with units from other armies, not only French but Italian. Eventually they arrived at their allotted positions.

It was likely that Rifleman John Arthur Barnes, aged 19 and from Ravensthorpe, a member of the 8th Battalion, West Yorkshire Regiment, was by this time in a state of near exhaustion.

Arthur, as he seems to have been known, was born in Ravensthorpe on 2nd May 1899, the youngest of nine children. After leaving school he went to work for Rawdon, Briggs and Co., in their finishing department; he attended Ravensthorpe Congregational Church and Sunday School. His 18th birthday in 1917 meant that he had to follow two of his older brothers into the army, and he left his widowed father, William, at 5 Dearnley Street, Ravensthorpe to enlist.

His papers, which have survived, show that John was 5' 3½" tall and weighed 7 stones 6 lbs. His chest was measured at 30" (32" when fully expanded). He was sent home for a few days, but was ordered to report back on 21st May when he joined

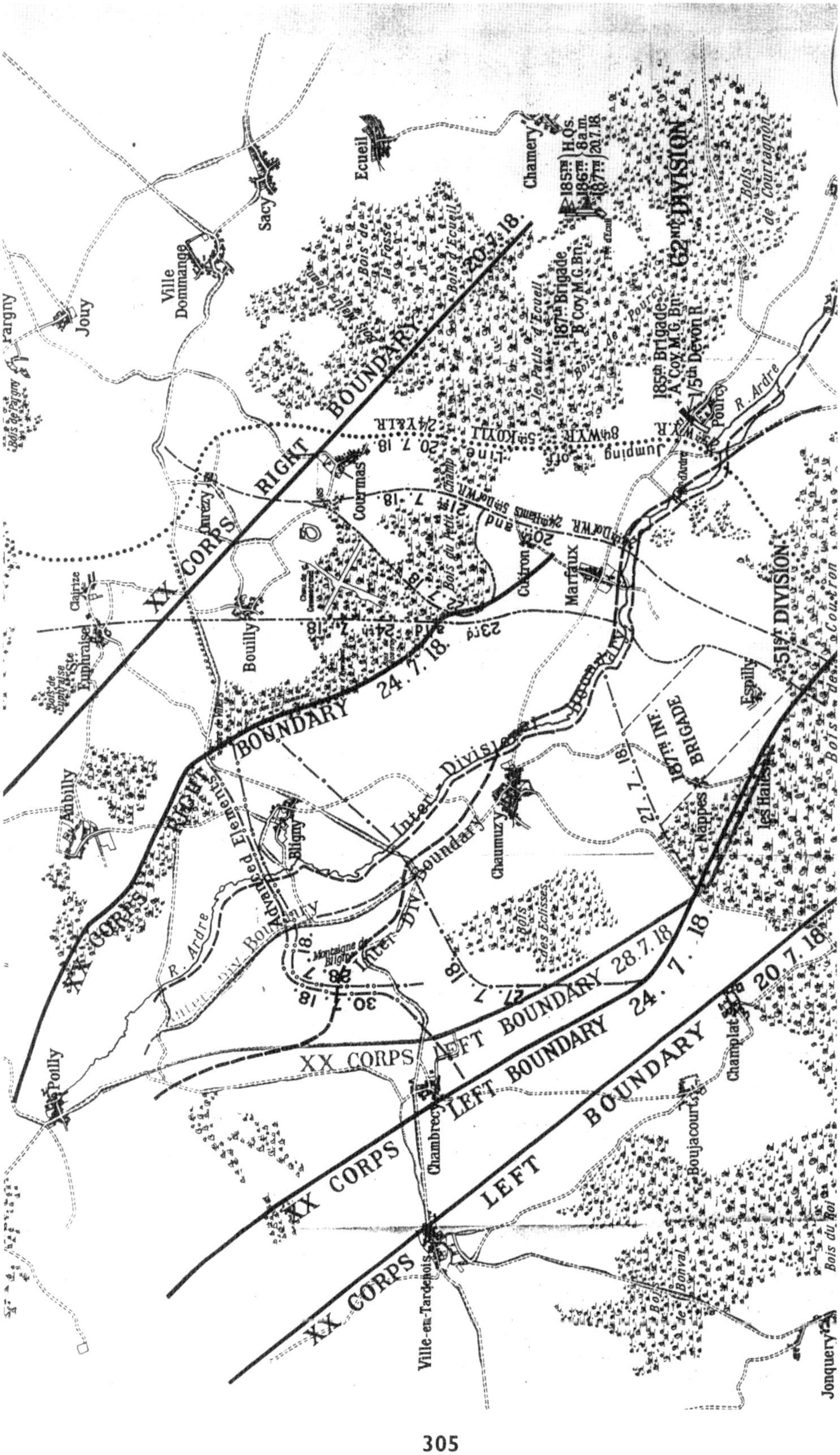

▲ Map 29. The 62nd Division's attack at Marfaux

the 7th Battalion, Training Reserve. In July he was examined by a dentist and although he refused treatment, he was passed as 'Dentally Fit'.

On 18th August 1917 he was transferred to the 10th Battalion, Training Reserve where he remained until 30th March 1918 when he was posted to the 15th/17th Battalion, West Yorkshire Regiment. This battalion, part of the 31st Division, had been formed following a merger of the 15th West Yorkshires (The Leeds Pals) and the 17th West Yorkshires.

After crossing to France on 31st March, he spent a few days at the Infantry Base Depot, Etaples where he would have received some harsh, last minute training, and joined his battalion on 5th April. Arthur did not stay long with this battalion, and was posted to the 8th Battalion of the regiment, part of the 62nd (West Riding) Division on 24th June, which he joined the next day.

He wrote home on 18th July, probably describing the long rail journey down from the Somme.

The attack on Saturday 20th July started promptly at 8am. Unfortunately the barrage by French artillery was too far in front of the division's jumping off positions. As a result, the German machine gun nests were left untouched. The attack, in brilliant sunshine through golden fields of corn with vineyards in the distance must have been a surreal experience for the troops. Two companies led the 8th West Yorkshires' advance towards the village of Bligny four miles away.

Shortly after leaving the protection of the woods, the battalion came under heavy machine gun fire from the villages of Cuitron and Marfaux. These machine gun nests were invisible to the troops, being amongst trees or hidden in the high corn. The attack ground to a halt in front of these two villages. The War Diary reports the battalion's casualties as:

Killed - *7 officers and 43 other ranks,*
Wounded - *3 officers and 199 other ranks,*
Missing - *23 other ranks,*
Gassed - *26 other ranks.*

Arthur's service records indicate that he was originally posted as wounded. By 11th August, he was deemed to be wounded and missing, and on 3rd October, it was decided that Arthur had been killed in action or died of wounds on or shortly after 20th July.

According to S.D.G.W., six officers and 73 men of the battalion lost their lives on 20th July. Arthur Barnes is amongst the one officer and 17 men who have no known graves and who are commemorated on the Soissons Memorial to the Missing.

The Soissons Memorial commemorates men killed in the campaigns of 1914 as well as those killed in 1918. The vast majority of those commemorated (nearly 4,000) are men who were killed in the Third Battle of the Aisne and the Second Battle of the Marne from May to July 1918 and who have no known grave.

Curiously there is a note on Arthur's file which states *"Recovery of body reported by 2/4th West Riding Regiment* [ie. the 2/4th Duke of Wellington's]". This note is undated, and if Arthur's body was recovered and identified, it must have subsequently been lost again.

Out of the 79 officers and men from the battalion who were killed on 20th July, over fifty are known to be buried in Marfaux British Cemetery. It may be assumed that Arthur lies beneath one of the 300 or so headstones within this cemetery that

◂ 137. Arthur Barnes

▾ 138. The Soissons Memorial to the Missing.

mark the resting place of an 'Unknown British soldier'. The cemetery contains over 1,000 graves.

The attack continued for a week, incurring heavy casualties. The Germans, fearing being cut off, withdrew from the salient. The offensive was halted on 6th August, by which time the British divisions had returned to the north.

The enforced retirement made Ludendorff abandon his plans for Operation *Hagen*, which was to be the next attempt at attacking the British in an effort to break through to the Channel Ports.

Despite having advanced many miles, and having gained hundreds of square miles of French territory, all of the attacks had been halted by the Allies. None of the six all-out assaults made by the Germans had achieved their strategic objectives and Ludendorff had shown himself to be indecisive, often changing strategy in the midst of the battle because of the successes being achieved locally.

The German army had lost many of its best soldiers and had lost its numerical superiority as well. The initiative had now passed to the Allies.

Chapter Twenty

The Hundred Days (1) The Battle of Amiens and The Battle of Albert

William Kendall was born in Ravensthorpe in April 1896; he was the second son of William and Elizabeth Kendall. Willie, as he was known, attended St. Saviour's Boys' School and Ravensthorpe Congregational Church and Sunday School. Prior to the war he worked as a hurrier at the Three Nuns Pit in Mirfield; in June 1915 he joined the King's Own Scottish Borderers. It seems that he served in several battalions of this regiment, initially joining the 6th Battalion (9th (Scottish) Division) in France in September 1915. At some stage he transferred to the 2nd Battalion (5th Division); it is possible that he was with this battalion when he contracted trench foot, and as a result may have been invalided home. He next joined the 1st Battalion (29th Division) and was probably with this battalion in its attack on 1st July 1916 as around this time he received serious shrapnel wounds in both legs (see Chapter 7). As a result of these injuries he was hospitalised from July to December 1916. After recovering he rejoined the 2nd Battalion.

The 2nd Battalion K.O.S.B. was (as part of the 5th Division) sent to reinforce the Italian army in December 1917, returning to France in early April 1918 at the height of the German's *Georgette* offensive. By this time Willie would have been regarded as a veteran, despite being just 22 years of age.

In July 1918 he enjoyed a period of home leave, returning to the battalion in the middle of the month, and finding himself a job as an officer's servant; these jobs were much sought after as they were perceived as being 'cushy'.

The battalion, at the end of July, was in the Merville area of northern France, and on 25th July took over in the front line. It was, as a matter of course, necessary to know which units of the German army were on the opposite side of No Man's Land; the only way of discovering this information (other than from a deserter) was to carry out a raid on the German trenches in order to take a prisoner. Such a raid was organised for Tuesday 30th July, and was undertaken by one officer and seventeen other ranks. At 1am, under covering fire from artillery, trench mortars and machine guns the party went over and headed towards the German trench 300 yards away. It seems that due to German posts (which had been pushed out into No Man's Land) not being bombarded, and the large amount of barbed wire, the party were unable to force their way into the German trench. Casualties amongst the raiding party were two killed and seven wounded.

During the rest of the day the battalion's War Diary indicates that the 2nd K.O.S.B. suffered two further fatalities plus one officer wounded. These further casualties were probably due to German artillery retaliating following the abortive raid. S.D.G.W. indicates the battalion lost three men on 30th July (plus two who died of their wounds on the following day); one of these fatal casualties was Private Willie Kendall.

Willie's father had died within the previous three years, therefore it was his mother who received a letter at the family's home at 11 Dearnley Street, Ravensthorpe on Tuesday 13th August from Second Lieutenant William MacDonald, the officer for whom Willie had acted as servant. The letter described how Willie was killed *"...at 7.30pm on the 30th July...I* [MacDonald] *came upon him in the trench just after he was hit: he was unconscious and he died in a few minutes without regaining consciousness, so that I am assured he suffered no pain. We took his body back with us* and he was buried with full military honours on the 31st July in a little cemetery where his grave will be well tendered. I am sending you his cap badge..."*

Private Willie Kendall is buried at Tannay British Cemetery, Thiennes. The cemetery contains 363 British and Commonwealth Graves.

* * *

▲ 139. Willie Kendall

▲ 140. The headstone of Willie Kendall, in Tannay British Cemetery.

** The battalion was relieved that night and moved back from the front line.*

At the beginning of August 1918 the B.E.F. comprised five armies, these were, from north to south, the Second (under Plumer); the Fifth (under Birdwood); the First (under Horne); the Third (under Byng); and the Fourth (under Rawlinson). The 69 divisions* under Haig's control were organised into eighteen corps (excluding the Cavalry Corps); of these divisions, the Australian, Canadian and the single New Zealand Division were considered the best that Haig had available. The five Australian and four Canadian divisions were formed into two corps: the Australian Corps (under Lieutenant-General Monash) and the Canadian Corps (under Lieutenant-General Currie). These were the only Army Corps in the B.E.F. which had a permanent establishment, the other corps had divisions rotating in and out of them on a regular basis.

The permanency of these divisions within the Australian and Canadian Corps undoubtedly contributed to these formations' high morale and elite status. Unlike their British counterparts, they had played little part in the German spring offensives - the Canadians had not been committed at all, and the Australians had played only a small (but crucial) role during the German Lys offensive. As has been mentioned in Chapter 18, the Canadian and Australian divisions had been exempt from the drastic restructuring during January and February 1918 and had retained their four battalion brigade structure, and were therefore correspondingly stronger than their British equivalents.

After the success of the Australian attack at Hamel on 4th July 1918 (see Chapter 19), Rawlinson started working on plans for a much larger attack on the Germans. At this time his Fourth Army comprised just two corps, the Australian Corps and III Corps; for the purposes of this operation, Rawlinson also wanted the Canadian Corps. In order to avoid alerting the Germans to the arrival of the Canadians in this sector (which was just south of the old Somme battlefield of 1916), a great deal of deception was needed.

The Canadian Corps (with the exception of two battalions) was transferred to the south in great secrecy and prepared to take over the southern sector of the Australian Corps' front. The two battalions which remained in Flanders were ordered to use their wireless equipment so as to make the Germans believe the Corps was still in the north.

The Fourth Army's front was arranged with III Corps (comprising one American and four British divisions) on the left, stretching from Albert in the north to the River Somme. The Australians, in the centre, were to jump off on a line from the River Somme to Villers-Bretonneux, and the Canadians were to be to the south (they were to take over at the last moment from a skeleton force of Australians). The French, on the Canadian's right, were also to take part in the attack. The city of Amiens lay just over ten miles to the west of the proposed battlefield.

In a similar way to the attack at Cambrai, the part played by the artillery and the tanks was to be vital to the success of the operation. The Tank Corps assembled ten battalions of heavy tanks (improved versions from the 1917 models) - these totalled 342 machines. There were also two battalions (72 machines) of the brand new Whippet tank; this was a smaller and faster tank (it could achieve 8

**** Of these 69 divisions, five were American (three of these would soon be transferred to the American army's control when General Pershing, the Commander-in-Chief of the A.E.F., demanded their return); two were Portuguese; and ten were Dominion. The remaining 52 were British, including three cavalry divisions.***

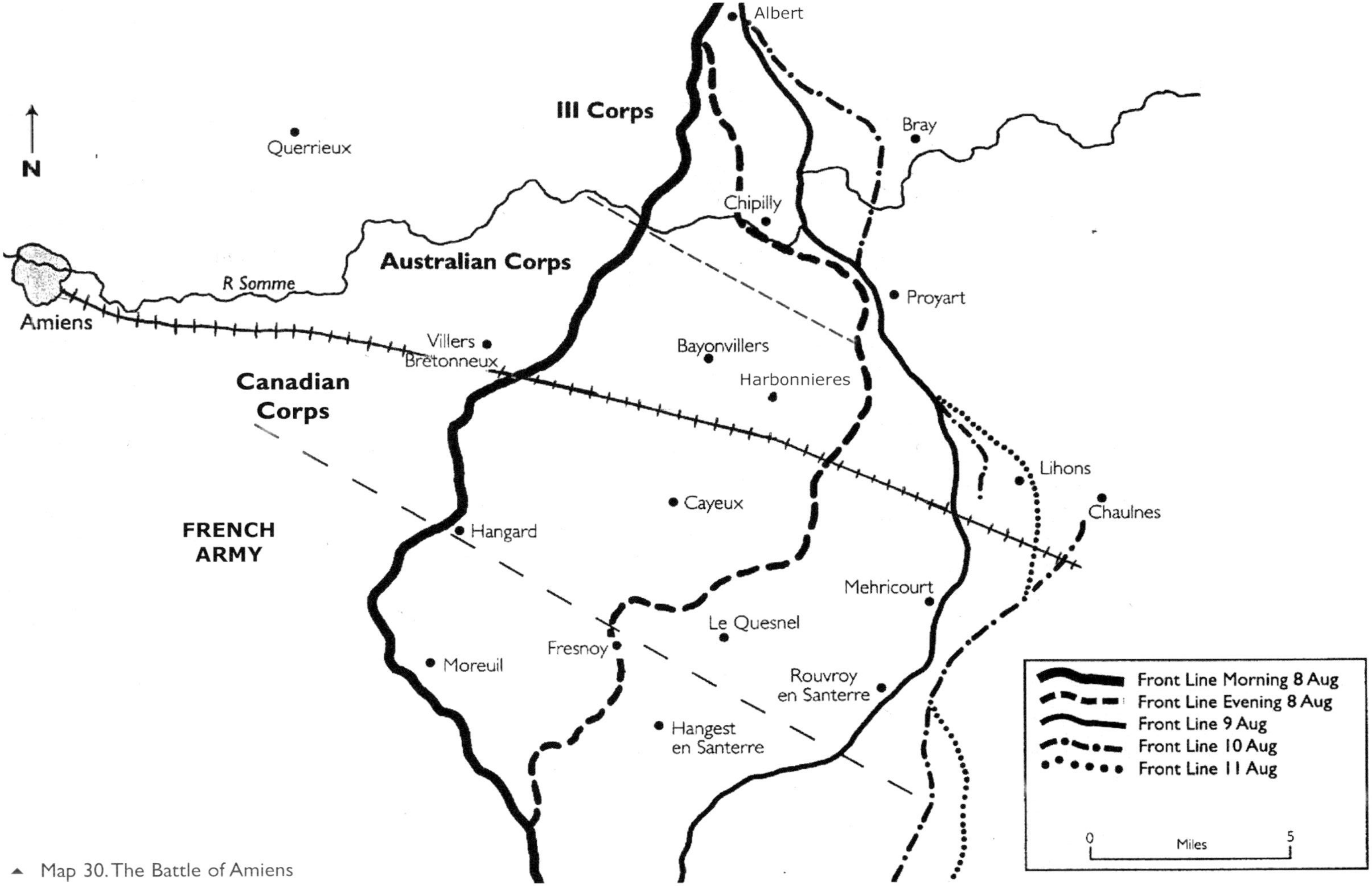

Map 30. The Battle of Amiens

mph!) which was to be used for exploitation. There were also to be 120 supply tanks and even a battalion of armoured cars. The artillery had been considerably strengthened with nearly 2,000 pieces of varying calibres.

In addition the Cavalry Corps and Royal Air Force were to be used in the forthcoming operation.

The attack was planned for Thursday 8th August, but just two days before 'Z' day*, on 6th August the Germans launched a major raid on the 18th Division, on a front of two miles. The raid captured 200 prisoners and badly dislocated the division's preparation for the forthcoming offensive.

Despite this set-back, at 4.20am on 8th August, two thousand guns from the Fourth Army's artillery roared into life and started battering the German trenches and artillery positions. Across the fourteen mile front, British, Australian and Canadian infantry advanced, helped in no small way by fog which shrouded their movements in a similar way to those of the German infantry during the opening of the *Michael* offensive just over four months previously.

There was at least one soldier from Ravensthorpe taking part in this attack, which was to become known as the Battle of Amiens.

Neville Tattersfield, after taking part in the operations on the Somme when the tanks made their debut, was granted leave in England in April 1917. Returning to his unit on Good Friday (6th April), he was immediately returned to England as his application for a commission had been accepted. Within days of returning home, he was to lose his father who died on 19th April.

He was ordered to join the Number 2 M.G.C. Officer Cadet Battalion, at Grantham on 4th May, this was the Cadet School Preliminary; from 2nd July he attended Pirbright Cadet School until October. On 3rd November 1917 he was appointed to a temporary commission for the duration of the war. In December 1917 he was sent on a further course at Wareham. It was not until 13th March 1918 that he returned to France, arriving in Boulogne. He was posted to the 2nd Battalion, Tank Corps + and joined his unit on 21st March.

Although the details of his actual involvement are not known, it seems that Neville may have been involved in the counter-attack by the 2nd Battalion, at Beugny, a village four miles east of Bapaume on the Bapaume to Cambrai road on 22nd March, the second day of the German Operation *Michael* offensive (see Chapter 18). This counter-attack came at a crucial stage in the attempt to stem the German tide; it was made without infantry support and with minimal assistance from the artillery. Although many casualties were incurred in the 2nd Battalion, Neville came through this unscathed. The counter-attack was successful as it stopped the German advance here for twenty-four hours.

The battalion refitted and by August was once again ready for action; some weeks before the Battle of Amiens the battalion undertook training with Australian troops and for the battle was selected to be in support of the 2nd and 5th Australian Divisions on the southern half of the Australian sector. (The 5th Australian Division was to pass through the 2nd Australian Division once the latter had taken its objectives.)

***** *The First World War equivalent of the more familiar D-Day.*

\+ *There had been a further reorganisation within the Tank Corps when the battalions' designations had changed from letters to numbers.*

On the evening of 4th August the three companies (each comprising twelve tanks) of the 2nd Battalion set off from Querrieu on the Amiens to Albert road in order to get to the assembly position at Fouilloy. The roads were packed with heavy artillery, ammunition lorries, battalions of infantry and numerous other units needed to support a major offensive; as a result the tanks were able to make only slow progress. At a point approximately mid-way between Querrieu and Fouilloy is the village of Daours. This proved to be a severe bottleneck and the tanks had great difficulty in negotiating the two bridges and two right-angled corners. Despite these problems, the tanks were able to be hidden before daybreak on 5th August, and remained out of sight from German aerial observation until the evening of 7th August. At midnight on 7th/8th August they completed the penultimate leg of their journeys and switched off their engines near Villers-Bretonneux.

One hour before 'Zero' the tanks of 'B' and 'C' Companies moved the last ½ mile to a point in front of the waiting infantry.

'B' Company was to lead the 5th Australian Brigade and 'C' Company was to lead the 7th Australian Brigade; both of these infantry brigades being part of the 2nd Australian Division. The objectives of the Australians were the villages of Warfusse and the ground to the south of the village, and the village of Bayonvillers.

'A' Company, meanwhile moved into position, they were to lead (together with twelve tanks of the 13th Battalion, Tank Corps) the 5th Australian Division onto the second phase objective of Harbonnieres.

It was planned that the tanks of the four companies (three companies of the 2nd Battalion and one company of the 13th Battalion) would rally at Harbonnieres. In the event only five of the 48 tanks reached the village.

Despite the losses to the tanks, the attack here was a stunning success. To the south, in the Canadian Corps' sector there was further success except on the extreme right where co-ordination with the French attack proved difficult.

To the north, in III Corps' sector, the victory was less clear cut. The relative failure by the British troops, when compared to the victorious assault to the south by the Australians and Canadians, has been the subject of much debate. There are, however, a number of factors to explain this apparent 'failure' (which, if compared to other attacks earlier in the war, was highly successful).

III Corps was not intended to make as deep a penetration of the German lines as the two Dominion corps to the south; the German raid on 6th August had an adverse impact on the plans, necessitating the withdrawal of some units and their replacement with others from a different division. In addition the land over which III Corps' divisions were expected to advance was significantly easier to defend. The fact that the Australian and Canadian divisions had retained their four battalions to a brigade structure must not be forgotten. Finally, it has been said that the German troops north of the Somme (in III Corps' area) were of a higher quality than those to the south of the river.

* * *

The successful attack of 8th August was not as a result solely of the Tank Corps' part in the action, nor of any other single factor. Each part of the army (and

R.A.F.) contributed to the most successful day of the war so far for the British: it was the successful integration of all arms that ensured the victory.

The Canadians had advanced up to eight miles, the Australians in the centre up to six miles, whilst the British III Corps still managed a creditable two mile advance. (The American troops in III Corps were not used on 8th August.)

The French, to the south of the Canadian Corps, advanced up to five miles, mainly as a result of the Canadian success on their left, but their main function was to guard the southern flank of the battle, a task they accomplished.

Nearly 400 guns were captured form the German artillery in this advance together with 18,500 prisoners. In addition the Germans lost 9,000 men killed or wounded. The Allied losses (killed and wounded) were also in the region of 9,000 men. Ludendorff described the 8th August as *"The Black Day of the German Army."*

Notwithstanding the arrival of German reinforcements and the exhaustion of the Allied troops the attack was resumed on 9th August. Despite having advanced beyond the range of the artillery and without telephone links to headquarters in the rear there was still an average advance of three miles, this was with only about half the number of tanks that had been available on the first day.

Second Lieutenant Neville Tattersfield took part in this, the second day of the Battle of Amiens. The 2nd Battalion, Tank Corps, which was down to about seventeen tanks, mustered south of Bayonvillers and at 1pm moved off in support of the attack by the 2nd Australian Division. Despite the German infantry surrendering in large numbers, there was a great deal of hostile shell-fire which hit three tanks as they approached the railway station at Rosieres. Further artillery fire was directed onto the tanks from German batteries on high ground at Lihons, this fire knocked out a further five tanks.

The tanks were unable to advance in the face of this hostile shelling; the infantry, too, were held up. Eventually Australian artillery was brought up and managed to silence one of the German batteries allowing the objectives to be reached. The remaining tanks withdrew. It was during the course of this day's fighting that Neville was injured.

A brief article in the Dewsbury Reporter stated that Neville had been wounded when a shell burst near him when he was attempting to unditch his tank whilst under heavy machine gun and shell-fire (it is possible he was saved from serious injury or death by a hip flask which bore the brunt of the impact). His sergeant and two gunners were, according to the report, wounded at the same time. His medical records indicate that he incurred gun-shot wounds in a buttock and upper left arm.

Neville was taken first of all to the 15th Australian Field Ambulance, from where he was sent the following day (10th August) to the 20th General Hospital, where he was operated on for the removal of shrapnel. Eleven days later, on 21st August, Neville was evacuated to England to recuperate.

* * *

On Saturday 10th August, a further advance of two miles was made but the attack had now run out of steam, German resistance was stiffening, and ahead lay the trenches of the old 1916 battlefield of the Somme. In view of this the Fourth Army's advance was called off; the fighting dying down by 11th August.

▲ 141. Neville Tattersfield (on the right), with two other, unidentified, officers. Neville is wearing a mourning band on his sleeve, indicating the photograph was probably taken shortly after the death of his father. On his left sleeve is a single 'wound stripe'. It has not been possible to establish when Neville was wounded, although there is evidence this may have been in the latter stages of the Battle of the Somme.

◄ 142. Willie Allott

In order to keep pressing the Germans, Haig instructed General Byng, whose Third Army had thirteen infantry and three cavalry divisions under its command, to prepare to attack. This next attack was launched on 21st August, it stretched from the southern end of the line assaulted in the 1917 Battle of Arras down to the northern end of the area attacked in the 1916 Battle of the Somme. This was the start of the Battle of Albert.

The initial attack lasted for just one day and was a success. Because the assault was called off after just twenty-four hours, the German commander in the area believed his army had halted the British and therefore ordered a counter-attack to be launched on 22nd August; this was easily defeated by the British, seriously weakening the German divisions.

Haig, frustrated at Byng halting the attack, ordered the assault to be continued; this was organised for 23rd August. The Germans had played into British hands and were in a poor condition for the resumed attack. Byng, stung by Haig's criticism made the second attack a much larger affair. In the northern part of the front assaulted by the Third Army, VI Corps advanced between 1 and 2½ miles on a front of about seven miles; part of the attack here was launched from the village of Gomiecourt towards the villages of Ervillers, Behagnies and Sapignies. Although Ervillers was taken, Behagnies and Sapignies were not.

In the centre, IV Corps attacked towards Achiet-le-Grand and Irles. Meanwhile in the south, V Corps pushed on to take positions to the east of Albert, on the western edge of the old Somme battlefield of 1916.

This attack by the British divisions (plus the New Zealand Division) was highly successful, and was without the element of surprise that was available on 8th August; there was also much less reliance on tanks.

* * *

It is necessary to break off at this point from the Battle of Albert. At the northern end of the British line, around Ypres, the painful decision had been taken, in April, to give up much of the ground wrested from the Germans during the Third Battle of Ypres in 1917. It was in this sector that Rifleman Willie Allott* was to be killed.

Willie was born in Dewsbury in 1893 or 1894 to James and Emma Allott who lived at 4 Church Street, Ravensthorpe. He is one of the few soldiers on the War Memorial for whom no obituary can be traced in the local newspapers, therefore nothing of his life is known.

After originally being drafted into the K.O.Y.L.I., it was with the King's Royal Rifle Corps that he was probably sent to the Western Front, joining the 18th Battalion of the regiment, part of the 41st Division.

The 18th K.R.R.C.'s War Diary describes how the battalion moved up to the front line, south of Ypres on 22nd August; there was little activity on this day and the next, except for a small amount of German shelling. On Saturday 24th August, however, a heavy German barrage commenced at 3.45am; an hour later the Germans attacked. It seems that the British front line was not held in strength,

**** The War Memorial miss-spells his name as 'Allatt'.***

instead there was a series of posts, each probably manned by a platoon or section; these posts were numbered. The War Diary states: *"...the enemy attacked from number 3 post to number 8 post inclusive, number 4 post was thought to have been taken but was later found to be intact. Number 5 post was lost, also number 6. Number 7 post was obscure, no one knowing anything about it......Casualties two officers and six other ranks killed; twelve other ranks wounded; seven other ranks missing."*

The War Diary continues: *"At 11.15pm four fighting patrols of one platoon each were directed against numbers 4,5,6 and 7 posts. 4 and 7 were reached and found to be occupied by our troops. The platoon against number 6 found the post occupied by the enemy and after some bombing and rifle fire entered the post. The platoon against number 5 failed to make any progress through Clydesdale Camp and dug in on the line of the light railway. Casualties one other rank killed, two other ranks wounded."*

Although the War Diary indicates two officers and seven men were killed on 24th August, the fatalities were slightly higher* as a result of some of the injured men dying of their wounds. One of the men to die from wounds was Willie Allott. Of the fourteen men and two officers to be killed in the period from 22nd to 25th August, twelve (including both of the officers) are buried in Lijssenthoek Military Cemetery; of these, six (including Willie) are buried together in one row.

* * *

Although the Germans were now withdrawing in the south, this was not a full-scale retreat. They managed to cover their withdrawals with machine gunners and other reliable troops. Sir Douglas Haig was hopeful of finishing the war in 1918 but many others, including the politicians believed that it would take well into 1919 to defeat Germany, by which time the Americans would be fully effective.

Haig maintained it was necessary to keep pressing the Germans back in order to prevent them organising a strong defensive line; if the pressure could be maintained, he believed his hoped-for victory might be achieved.

Ludendorff, following the heavy defeats in the Battle of Amiens and the commencement of the Battle of Albert realised he would have to withdraw to a winter position, this was to be a line based somewhat in advance (ie. to the west of) the Hindenburg Line. A northern extension of the Hindenburg Line, known to the British as the Drocourt-Queant Line, was also to be used as part of this defensive position.

Ludendorff authorised the withdrawal to this line on 26th August, but he was unable to carry out this operation without interference as the Third and Fourth Armies were continuing to push the Germans backwards; it was in these operations that the 62nd (West Riding) Division was to be involved.

**** S.D.G.W. states:***
22nd August - 1 officer killed in action;
23rd August - 2 other ranks k.i.a.;
24th August - 1 officer k.i.a. plus 6 other ranks k.i.a. and 5 other ranks died of wounds;
25th August - 1 other rank died of wounds.

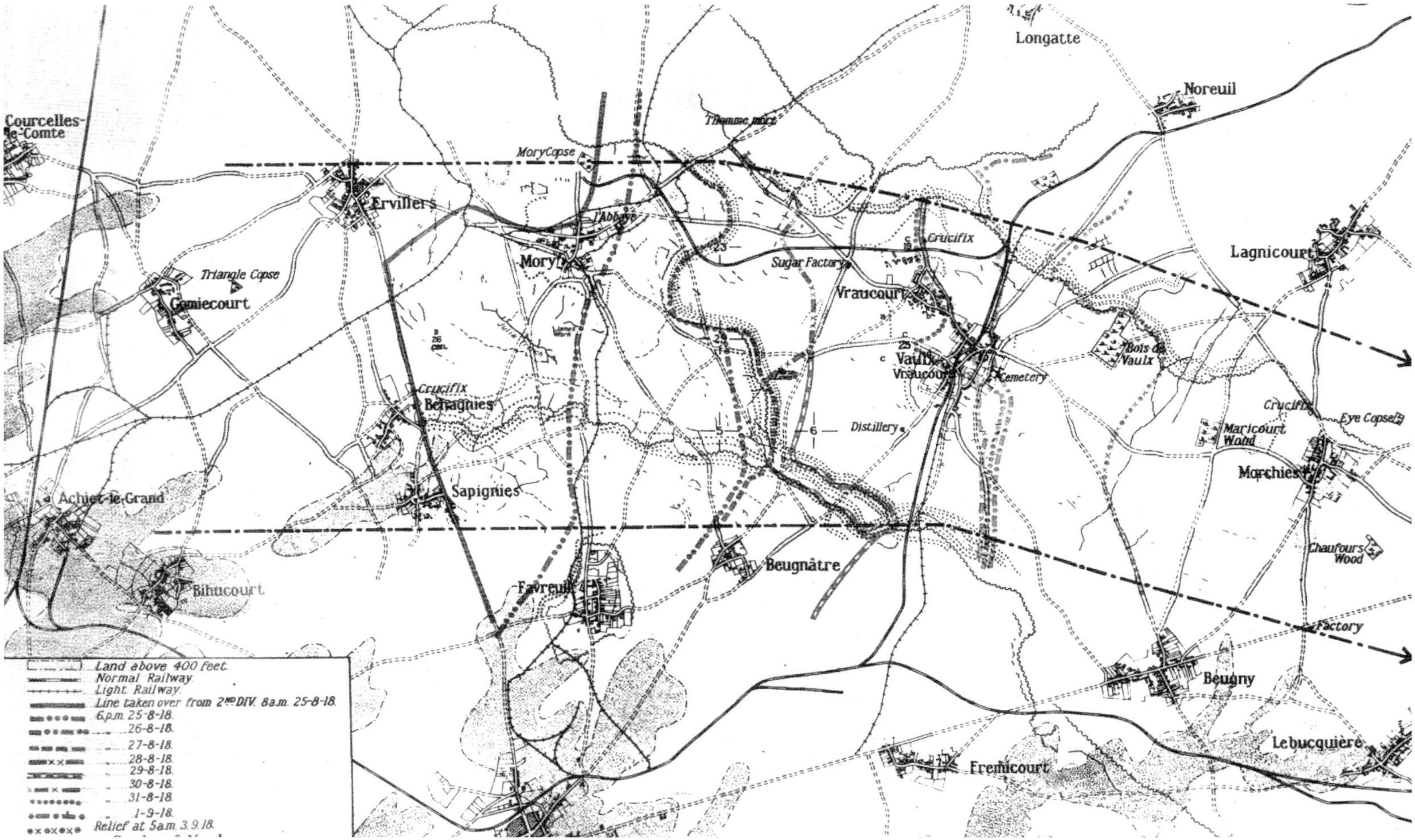

▲ Map 31. Behagnies/Sapignies

It will be recalled how, after defeating the German counter-attack, Byng was stung into action by Haig's criticism; his Third Army assaulted again on 23rd August, the attack being continued over the following days.

On 24th August the 62nd (West Riding) Division were ordered to relieve the 2nd Division; they moved forward to the Achiet-le-Grand area and took over the front line from two of the 2nd Division's brigades. The remaining brigade of the 2nd Division (5 Brigade) was ordered, at 7.45pm on 24th August, to take Sapignies and Behagnies. This attack was launched in the early hours of Sunday 25th August and was successful. The way was therefore prepared for the main attack; this was to be launched at 9am the same day with the 5th Duke of Wellington's on the right and the 2/4th York and Lancaster Regiment on the left.

The 5th Duke of Wellington's, advancing through Behagnies and Sapignies, at first encountered no opposition, but once through these villages and beyond the Bapaume to Arras road the attacking companies ('B' and 'C') came under machine gun fire, incurring heavy casualties. The attack was now continued by 'A' and 'D' Companies, but just east of a light railway that ran from Favreuil to Mory, the attack ground to a halt. This was due to the battalion's flanks being exposed; the 37th Division to the south and the 2/4th York and Lancasters to the north had been unable to advance in line.

At 5pm the Germans started to shell the British positions and at 6.15pm launched a counter-attack. This was repulsed with rifle and Lewis gun fire and with the assistance of the artillery. Casualties according to the battalion's War Diary amounted to two officers and 33 other ranks killed or died of wounds plus seven officers and 212 other ranks wounded (36 of the latter gassed) plus a further five other ranks missing; S.D.G.W. gives figures of seventeen men from the battalion losing their lives.

Two of these fatal casualties were men from Ravensthorpe.

John Edward Schofield was born in about 1894 to Joseph and Priscilla Schofield. John (or Teddy as he was known to his family) was the youngest of three sons, all of whom joined up. Fred, aged 43 was a veteran of the Boer War and was stationed in Ireland. Joe, the middle son, aged 35, had seen active service but had been discharged due to ill health. Before the war John worked as a tenterer for Rawdon, Briggs & Co., he had joined up early in 1914 and probably went to France with the 2/5th Battalion, Duke of Wellington's Regiment in January 1917.

An article in the Dewsbury News reported how, on Thursday 19th September 1918, Mr and Mrs Schofield received a letter at their home at 13 Field Street, Ravensthorpe stating John had been killed. The letter said that John *"...was always of a cheerful disposition and his loss is much felt by the rest of the company."*

John, who was 24 when he lost his life is buried in Gomiecourt South Cemetery. The cemetery was started by the 62nd Division's Burials Officer and contains 206 British and 27 German graves.

The second soldier from Ravensthorpe to be killed in this action was Harry Ross Eastwood. Harry's younger brother, Fred, had been killed on 3rd May 1917 when the battalion received its baptism of fire at Bullecourt. Since then Harry had been promoted to sergeant and had won the Military Medal during the battalion's attack at Cambrai.

Harry, like Fred, attended Ravensthorpe St. Saviour's Boys' School. After leaving school he worked for the Yorkshire Electric Power Company. He attended

▲ 143. John Schofield

▲ 144. The small bar on Harry's lower sleve is a wound stripe, however it is not known when he was injured so as to be awarded this.

St. Saviour's Parish Church and played in the church football team; he was also a member of the Church Institute and a member of Ravensthorpe Cycling Club.

Like John Schofield, Harry was 24 years of old. Harry is not buried with John in Gomiecourt, it is likely his original grave was subject to a post-war concentration, resulting in him now being buried in Douchy-les-Ayette British Cemetery. This cemetery contains over 700 graves.

* * *

The description of the 5th Duke of Wellington's attack coming to a halt mentions the 2/4th York and Lancasters on the Duke's left. This battalion's attack was stopped in its tracks after less than 500 yards when it ran into strong German defensive positions in the village of Mory. The 5th K.O.Y.L.I., who were in support of the 2/4th York and Lancasters, had been ordered to push patrols south of Mory; besides doing this they also managed to capture the village. It seems that German resistance in Mory had melted away by the time of the 5th K.O.Y.L.I.'s attack, as the battalion lost only seven men killed during the course of the day compared to the York and Lancaster's 21 fatalities.

Part of the 5th K.O.Y.L.I.'s attacking force was Company Sergeant Major Fred Watson. It will be recalled that Fred was a pre-war regular, who, when war broke out was a sergeant instructor at Goole. Fred had been awarded a Distinguished Conduct Medal within weeks of his arrival in France, and since then he had experienced further highs and lows of army life.

Shortly after he was awarded the D.C.M. in March 1917 the battalion's Regimental Sergeant Major was commissioned, and a replacement R.S.M. was therefore required. Fred was chosen and on 21st April was appointed Acting R.S.M.; within two weeks the appointment was confirmed and on 2nd May 1917 Fred was promoted to Temporary R.S.M. for the duration of the war. The promotion was made the day before the Second Battle of Bullecourt, in which the battalion was engaged.

Fred was destined not to keep his exalted rank for long. As the senior N.C.O. in the battalion, he would have wielded a massive amount of power; many junior officers would have, no doubt, looked to him for guidance. Perhaps he was unable to cope with the demands made upon him, or possibly he was just unlucky to be caught, but on 4th August 1917, Fred was discovered drunk whilst on duty. He was placed under arrest and tried by a Field General Court Martial a week later on 11th August. Fred was found guilty of the charge and the sentence passed on him: *"To be reduced to the rank of Sergeant (Recommended to mercy on grounds of long and gallant service)."* The sentence was confirmed by the Brigadier-General commanding 187 Brigade.

From the end of September to the middle of November, Fred left the battalion and acted as an instructor for the division. Upon rejoining the 2/5th K.O.Y.L.I. he was once again appointed to the acting rank of Company Sergeant Major. He was home on leave between 22nd December 1917 and 5th January 1918 after which he rejoined the battalion and was confirmed in his rank of C.S.M. Within five months of returning to his battalion, he was again granted home leave, but this was no routine leave. As he had now served a total of twenty one years in the army, he would, under normal conditions have been discharged*. Fred was a vastly experienced N.C.O., and even had he wanted to, it is unlikely he would have been able to avoid further military service. He therefore signed on again 'for the duration of the war'. After a month's leave at home, when he saw his wife and three sons for what was to be the last time, he returned to his battalion on 11th June, and recommenced his duties as C.S.M. for 'D' Company.

His service record gives further details of his last period with the army. On two successive days, 20th and 21st July he was wounded. At this time the battalion (and indeed the entire 62nd Division) were in the Marne sector, operating with the French army (see Chapter 19). It seems that his wounds were not sufficiently serious to warrant evacuation to England.

Although the action in which it was earned is not recorded, it was possibly during this operation on the Marne that Fred was awarded the Military Cross. This award was mainly made to officers and it is relatively rare for it to be made to Warrant Officers. The citation for the M.C. reads - *"5441 CSM Frederick William Watson, D.C.M., Yorkshire Light Infantry: For conspicuous gallantry and good leadership. When the officers of two platoons became casualties he took command and led the men forward with great dash and skill. He was cut off with part of his*

***** ***He was awarded a bounty of £25, probably due to him for having served the full 21 years.***

platoon but fought his way back to his company. His courage and resolution were remarkable and his cheerfulness inspired all who were with him."

It is, of course, equally possible that the award was earned during the action on the 25th August, but the fact that the award mentions being cut off and fighting back to the company does not seem to conform with the successful action on this day.

* * *

Orders for the continuation of the 62nd Division's attack were received during the afternoon of 25th August. This was to commence at 6am on 26th August following a barrage by British artillery.

Half an hour before the barrage was due to commence, it was realised that patrols from the 5th K.O.Y.L.I. were already in the area in which the barrage was due to fall, and runners were despatched with orders for these patrols to pull back, and once the barrage had lifted to then re-establish themselves. Fortunately the withdrawal was carried out just in time and upon regaining their positions, they were able to fire on the German troops who could be seen withdrawing.

Further orders were received that afternoon for a continuation of the attack the next day (Tuesday 27th August) at 7.30am, the battalion's objectives being a sunken road running north-south about 1/2 mile west of the village of Vraucourt; on the sunken road, at a cross roads, lay a sugar factory. Fred Watson's 'D' Company was to lead the attack, with 'B' Company in support. The assembly positions were to be on the railway east of Mory, and to avoid the British artillery barrage that was to be put down, the attacking companies were ordered to stay to the north of the sunken road leading east from Mory.

Everything was going well until the attacking troops came to the road junction north-east of the sugar factory when they were hit by fire from German machine gunners who had managed to survive the artillery barrage. The War Diary of the 5th K.O.Y.L.I. states: *"During the attack 2/Lt. Logan with his Company Sergeant Major* and one runner showed great coolness in capturing seven officers and one hundred other ranks.....in dugouts."*

On realising the attack was stalling the officer commanding the support company ('B' Company) formed a defensive line; parties of the attacking company ('D' Company), which was by now cut off, dribbled in that afternoon and evening.

The 5th K.O.Y.L.I. suffered 24 other ranks killed plus four officers and 114 other ranks wounded; a further 15 other ranks were reported missing; (S.D.G.W. indicates 22 killed plus three died of wounds).

One of the fatal casualties was Company Sergeant Major Frederick William Watson, M.C., D.C.M. and Bar +.

**** If this is taken to be an account of 'D' Company, the Company Sergeant Major must be Fred Watson.***

+ The C.W.G.C. record him being awarded the D.C.M. twice, and this is confirmed by his entry in S.D.G.W.; however there are no other records of this award. The Dewsbury News also implies that he had been awarded a bar to his D.C.M. shortly before he was killed, a report on the 7th September stating that "....a short time ago he received the D.C.M. ribbon for bravery in gaining a trench but up to his death had not been presented with the medal itself." This is different from the citation to his award for the M.C. and whilst similar to that for his first D.C.M., it seems unlikely that he could not have been given the medal when the act of bravery took place eighteen months prior to his death.

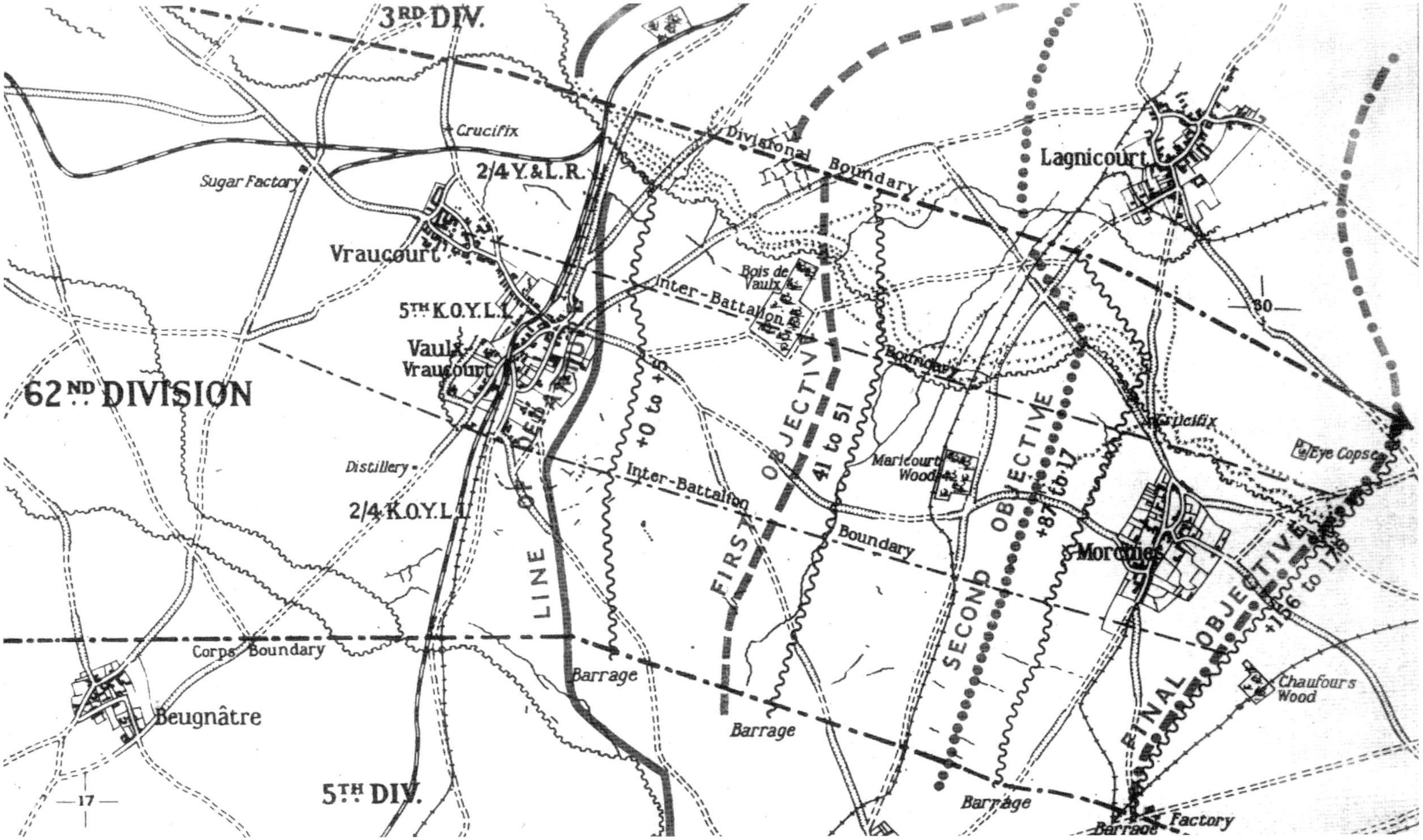

Map 32. Vraucourt

Fred's wife, Ada, received a letter at their house at 3 William Street, Ravensthorpe from a Quartermaster Sergeant, which told how Fred *"...met his death from an enemy machine gun bullet, which hit him in the back of the neck. He died in a few minutes."* Fred was aged 39 when he was killed.

Fred Watson, like John Schofield who died two days earlier, is buried in Gomiecourt South Cemetery.

* * *

The next soldier from Ravensthorpe to be killed was Horace Scott.

Horace was born in Armley, Leeds in February 1898, the youngest of two sons of Robert and Sarah Scott. He was brought up in Ravensthorpe, where he probably went to school, attending the United Methodist Church. He went to work at the same woollen mill as his father, F. Doble & Sons, where he worked as a twister (the person who twists together the ends of yarns of the new warp to those already woven).

Horace was called up, aged 18 in May 1917 and joined the Durham Light Infantry. After completing his training in late summer 1917 he would normally have sent to the Western Front, he did not, however, go overseas at this stage.

In February 1918 Horace reached his 19th birthday; one of the less welcome presents he received was a posting to France. Upon being ordered overseas it is likely that he was transferred to the East Lancashire Regiment, being sent to the 2/4th Battalion. This battalion was, on 19th February, merged in the restructuring

▲ 145. Fred Watson

▲ 146. Fred Watson's headstone at Gomiecourt South Cemetery.

that was then being undertaken with the 1/4th Battalion of the Regiment. Because there was a surplus of troops in the combined battalion Horace was probably immediately sent to make up the numbers in another battalion of the East Lancashire Regiment - the 1/5th Battalion, part of the 42nd (East Lancashire) Division.

The 42nd Division had taken part in the Battle of Albert which, it will be recalled, had started on 21st August. By the time the battle had officially ended, on 29th August, the division was south of Bapaume, and was being employed in the continuing operation of pushing the Germans backwards.

In late August the 1/5th East Lancashire Regiment moved from Warlencourt, on the Albert to Bapaume road, to the village of Thilloy (due east of Warlencourt); the battalion being in support of other battalions of the 42nd Division which were making the advance. Thilloy was entered without opposition on 29th August, and the advance continued due east towards the village of Riencourt. To get to this village, the main Bapaume to Peronne road had to be crossed, and it was here that strong opposition was met, probably at the village of Beaulencourt, being astride the Bapaume to Peronne road.

The 1/5th East Lancashires were ordered to push the advance forward, and they started out at 2pm on 29th August from Thilloy. As they moved east along the road towards Beaulencourt they came under long range machine gun and shell-fire (they were still 1½ miles short of Beaulencourt), the battalion therefore diverted northwards. Coming under further fire, the battalion dug in on the ridges and waited for the 1/8th Manchester Regiment to come up and pass through their positions to make an assault on Riencourt. Unfortunately, due to heavy machine gun fire, the Manchesters were held up.

At 6pm the Brigadier-General came to investigate the reason for the delay. He ordered that the Manchesters should attack Riencourt from the west, whilst the East Lancashires should co-operate from the north. As it was dark, it was decided to wait until the next morning before making the attempt. Further attacks were made the following morning (30th August), but it was found that any movement brought down a hail of fire from German machine gunners, many casualties being incurred. Despite this, an attack was made on some German held trenches which was successful, thus enabling the Bapaume to Peronne road to be crossed, and clearing the way into Riencourt; however further enemy fire prevented them reaching the ridge for which they were aiming. The battalion was forced to pull back and dig in just west of the road. A bombardment of the ridge was ordered, but the Germans, even after this still hung on. During the rest of the day the battalion was shelled and trench-mortared by the Germans. A further attempt, in conjunction with the Manchesters on the right was made, but again without success.

That night, patrols were sent out and they discovered that the Germans had slipped quietly away.

The exact involvement of Horace Scott during this action is not known, but it is likely that he was injured and evacuated, via a casualty clearing station, to hospital. He was probably not too seriously injured as he remained in France (he was probably most disappointed not to have received a 'Blighty' wound).

A Field Post Card from Horace was received by his parents at their home at 11 Hebble Street, Ravensthorpe on Wednesday 4th September to say that he had been wounded. A letter was received the following morning, again from Horace, saying

"Don't bother, Father & Mother about me, because I shall get better sometime." He failed however to mention the nature of his injury, which was a wound to his left arm.

His parents relief was short-lived, despite receiving on Monday 7th October a cheerful letter from him informing them that he was *"in the pink"* only a few days later, on Friday 11th they heard that he had been admitted to the 73rd General Hospital with pneumonia. The following morning they were informed that he was dangerously ill, and by that same Saturday evening they had received a further communication saying that Horace had died on Thursday 10th October.

Horace is buried at Tourgeville Military Cemetery in Normandy, close to the town of Le Havre (clearly he was in the Le Havre area, recovering from his wound when he was taken ill). The cemetery was used by three hospitals (including the 73rd); besides these hospitals, there were also three convalescent depots in the area.

* * *

This phase of the war (commonly called the 'Hundred Days') is somewhat different to the common perception of the conflict; British and Dominion divisions were moving forward in conditions of semi-open (as opposed to trench) warfare. Bapaume was taken by the New Zealand Division on 29th August whilst the divisions in Monash's Australian Corps pressed forward to the River Somme.

DEATH FROM DOUBLE PNEUMONIA.

A few weeks ago we noted that Pte. Horac
ott (19), East Lancs., son of Mr. and Mr
obert Scott, Hebble Street, Ravensthorpe, ha
been wounded in th
left arm on Augu
30th. He notified hi
parents to that effec
but assured them tha
they had no need t
bother about him, be
cause he would get be
ter. Evidently he di
so, but he subsequentl
contracted lun
trouble, and he was ad
mitted to the 73r
General Hospital i
France, and died from
double pneumonia las
week-end. He was
fine lad, connecte
with the Unite
Methodist Chapel, Rav
ensthorpe, and ver
cheerful and well-like
y everybody. Prior to joining up, in May
17, he was a twister at Messrs. F. Doble an
o.'s mill, Ravensthorpe, where his father i
so employed as a tuner. He went to Franc
February, 1918. His brother, Driver Georg
cott, R.F.A., is in Belgium.

Pte. Horace Scott,
E. Lancs., Ravensthorpe
(died).

▲ 147. Horace Scott

RAVENSTHORPE FAMILY'S SECOND LOSS.

An "official" from the War Office anno
Saturday that Pte. Joseph Harris, (23)
orks. Regt., had been killed in action in F
September 4th. Pte. Harris was a nat
Worcestershire, h
parents, Mr. and
Joseph Ha
migrated to R
thorpe 18 years
and they have
settled there sinc
are now living in
mercial Street.
to the outbreak o
Pte. Harris worl
the Ings Pit, T
hill. He, however
out of the pit, and
to Messrs. F. Dob
Co.'s warehouse,
he left on do
khaki in January
His military care
not one of the luc
and he longed for
and a safe return
July, 1916, he came to England with shr
his back. In November, 1917, he was afl
h trench feet, and he had only been ba
ance about ten weeks when he fell. His
d brother, Pte. Harry Harris, died in

Pte. Joseph Harris,
st Yorks., Ravensthorpe
(killed).

▲ 148. Joe Harris

The harassment of the withdrawing Germans was not undertaken by just a few divisions up and down the Third and Fourth Armies' fronts; further to the north, General Sir Henry Horne's First Army advanced towards the Drocourt-Queant line, using the Canadian Corps which had now been moved into this area. The advance was difficult against determined German resistance but by 2nd September the First Army had managed to win ground to enable an attack to be launched on the Drocourt-Queant line. The Canadians attacked on 2nd September and broke through this strong position.

As a result of this victory, the Australians taking the town of Peronne on the River Somme, and the pressure exerted by the Third Army between the two Dominion Corps' attacks, the Germans were forced to abandon their winter position and fall back to the Hindenburg Line.

Another effect of the Canadian Corps' victory was the Germans abandoning the territory they had gained in their *Georgette* offensive in April; they therefore withdrew from the Lys salient between Ypres and Lens, thus allowing Plumer's Second Army and Birdwood's Fifth Army to advance.

It was in this area, on the French-Belgian border, that the next Ravensthorpe soldier was to be killed.

Joe Harris was born in Dewsbury in about 1895, the second son of Joseph and Lizzie Harris. Before the war Joe worked at Ings Pit in Thornhill, later working as a warehouseman at F. Doble & Sons. He lived with his parents in Raven Street and attended Ravensthorpe United Methodist Church. Joe joined the army in January 1916, being sent to France with the 10th Battalion, Yorkshire Regiment in May of that year. He was injured on the opening day of the Battle of the Somme (see Chapter 7) and returned to England, being sent first of all to a hospital in Birmingham for two days, and then to a convalescent home in Blackpool.

It was from Blackpool he wrote to the parents of another injured soldier *"...I was going to have to go under an operation but they have decided to leave the metal in (so I shall weigh a bit more)."*

Within a few days of writing this, his older brother, Harry, died of sunstroke in Mesopotamia (see Chapter 11). Joe returned to France, joining the 8th Battalion Yorkshire Regiment (23rd Division) and later the 1/5th Battalion of the regiment (50th (Northumbrian) Division). It was probably whilst he was with the latter unit that he contracted trench foot in November 1917 and returned home again to recover. In June 1918 he once again returned to France, this time with the 10th Battalion, East Yorkshire Regiment (31st Division).

At the beginning of September the battalion was at Meteren, east of Bailleul, on the French side of the French-Belgian border. On 3rd September orders were received to proceed to the village of Nieppe, just west of the town of Armentieres, a march of some nine miles. One platoon of the 10th East Yorkshires, whilst passing through the village of Nieppe on the way to the front, must have been observed by the Germans who sent over some shells, killing one officer and ten other ranks. As a result of this, the battalion's relief of the troops in the front line was delayed until 4am the next day.

On Wednesday 4th September the battalion received orders to push patrols forward (presumably to keep in touch with the withdrawing Germans). The battalion's War Diary describes how, at 8.35am, the patrols started moving forward, but without any artillery support: *"....enemy opposition was very strong and seemed to be very much on the alert. The ground over which the attack was made was very flat and in many places devoid of cover with the result that most of our casualties were caused by machine gun fire."*

The battalion lost five officers and 69 other ranks killed and wounded. S.D.G.W. indicates two officers plus ten other ranks were killed.

Private Joseph Harris, aged 23, was one of the soldiers killed during the course of the advance made on 4th September. His parents, then living at 20 Commercial Street, Ravensthorpe heard the news of his death towards the end of September.

Like six of his comrades Joseph has no known grave* and is commemorated on the Ploegsteert Memorial to the Missing which is situated just three miles to the north of where he was killed, over the border in southern Belgium.

Of the two officers and three men who have known graves, one is buried in Trois Arbes Cemetery, one at New Irish Farm Cemetery and three in Le Grand Beaumart British Cemetery.

Chapter Twenty-One

The Hundred Days (2) The Breaking of the Hindenburg Line to The Armistice

At the southern end of the B.E.F.'s front, the Third and Fourth Armies were now approaching the Hindenburg Line. This was, of course, the same line that the Germans had constructed during the summer and autumn of 1916 in order to allow their army to fall back to seemingly impregnable positions after the Battle of the Somme. Unless the Hindenburg Line was to be broken quickly the momentum the B.E.F. had so far built up would be halted and the Germans would have a chance to regroup over the winter of 1918/1919 and hold out for a negotiated peace treaty on more favourable terms. It was therefore vital for this major obstacle to be comprehensively breached.

The first chip in the wall of the Hindenburg Line was made by the 62nd (West Riding) Division. Operating as part of the Third Army, the division attacked the Germans in their Hindenburg Line defences at Havrincourt on 12th September and took the village, just as they had done ten months previously. This operation (made in conjunction with the 37th and New Zealand Divisions) was met with the most fierce resistance, preventing further exploitation of their initial success.

Although the outer defences of the Hindenburg Line had been breached, it did not lead to any major strategic benefits. It was going to be necessary for a much larger attack to be made to break the Hindenburg Line.

Whilst the Third Army was now up against the Hindenburg Line defences, Rawlinson's Fourth Army had first to cross the old British defensive positions that the Germans were now holding. These were partly broken on 18th September when the Australian Corps together with III Corps and IX Corps inflicted a further major defeat on the Germans in what became known as the Battle of Epehy. The IX Corps, it is of interest to note, was commanded by Lieutenant-General Sir Walter Braithwaite who had been promoted from command of the 62nd (West Riding) Division.

This advance, most successful in the Australian sector, had brought the Australian Corps up to the Hindenburg Line, but in order to have a good position from which to launch an attack, Rawlinson wanted the rest of the Fourth Army's line to be advanced. Attacks by III Corps, to the north of the Australian Corps' frontage, over the next few days were unsuccessful, but after resting his troops, Braithwaite's IX Corps (to the south of the Australians) managed, on 24th September, to advance its line.

* * *

In an attempt to widen the attack, Foch, the General-in-Chief of the Allied armies on the Western Front, gave orders in mid-September for attacks to be launched in the south (by combined French and American armies) and in the north by an Army Group commanded by Albert, King of Belgium. King Albert's Army Group (known as the Flanders Army Group) comprised the Belgian army (which the King had commanded since 1914) and the British Second Army under General Plumer, it also contained some French divisions in reserve. This meant that for the duration of this offensive, the British Second Army was not technically part of the B.E.F.

In the centre, between these two attacks, the B.E.F. was to assault the German lines using its remaining four armies (from north to south, the Fifth, First, Third and Fourth) - a total of 55 divisions (including three Cavalry divisions and two American divisions) on a front of 67 miles. The attack in this central sector was the most difficult task, as the B.E.F. faced the strongest fortifications and a larger number of German troops.

On 25th September, the Franco-American offensive opened on a 44 mile front. Although initially successful the gains in ground were relatively small and the attack, especially in the American sector, bogged down largely as a result of logistical problems caused by inexperienced American staff officers.

The next attack was launched by the B.E.F. on 27th September. This was in the First and Third Armies' areas, and was launched towards the Canal du Nord, Bourlon Wood and Cambrai. Once again the Canadian Corps was to have a prominent part to play. As had come to be expected, the Canadians achieved magnificent results, crossing the potentially lethal obstacle of the (dry) Canal du Nord and by the evening of the 28th had advanced up to six miles on a front of twelve miles. Use of the vital rail head of Cambrai was denied to the Germans as a result of the advance.

The Flanders Army Group joined the offensive on 28th September. Of the 37 mile front held by this army group, 16 miles were held by Plumer's Second Army, running from just north of Ypres to the River Lys at Armentieres in northern France.

Despite the Germans expecting an attack, when it was launched the assault advanced with relative ease against crumbling opposition, it even went beyond its objectives. On the first day of the attack, an advance of up to six miles was made, which was about the same as was managed during the entire Third Battle of Ypres in 1917; that battle having lasted for over three months.

As was usual in Flanders, the weather broke, rains turned the battlefield into a morass, making relief and resupply of the troops in the front line very difficult; this was especially true of those positions which had to be supplied across the moon-scape of the old 1917 battlefield. The battle had therefore to be broken off. To the north of Plumer's Second Army, the Belgian army did well in keeping pace with Plumer's troops.

It was now the turn of Rawlinson's Fourth Army to join the offensive again. Whilst good results had been achieved elsewhere on the Western Front, especially in Flanders, it was in the central sector where the most spectacular and telling results could be achieved.

* * *

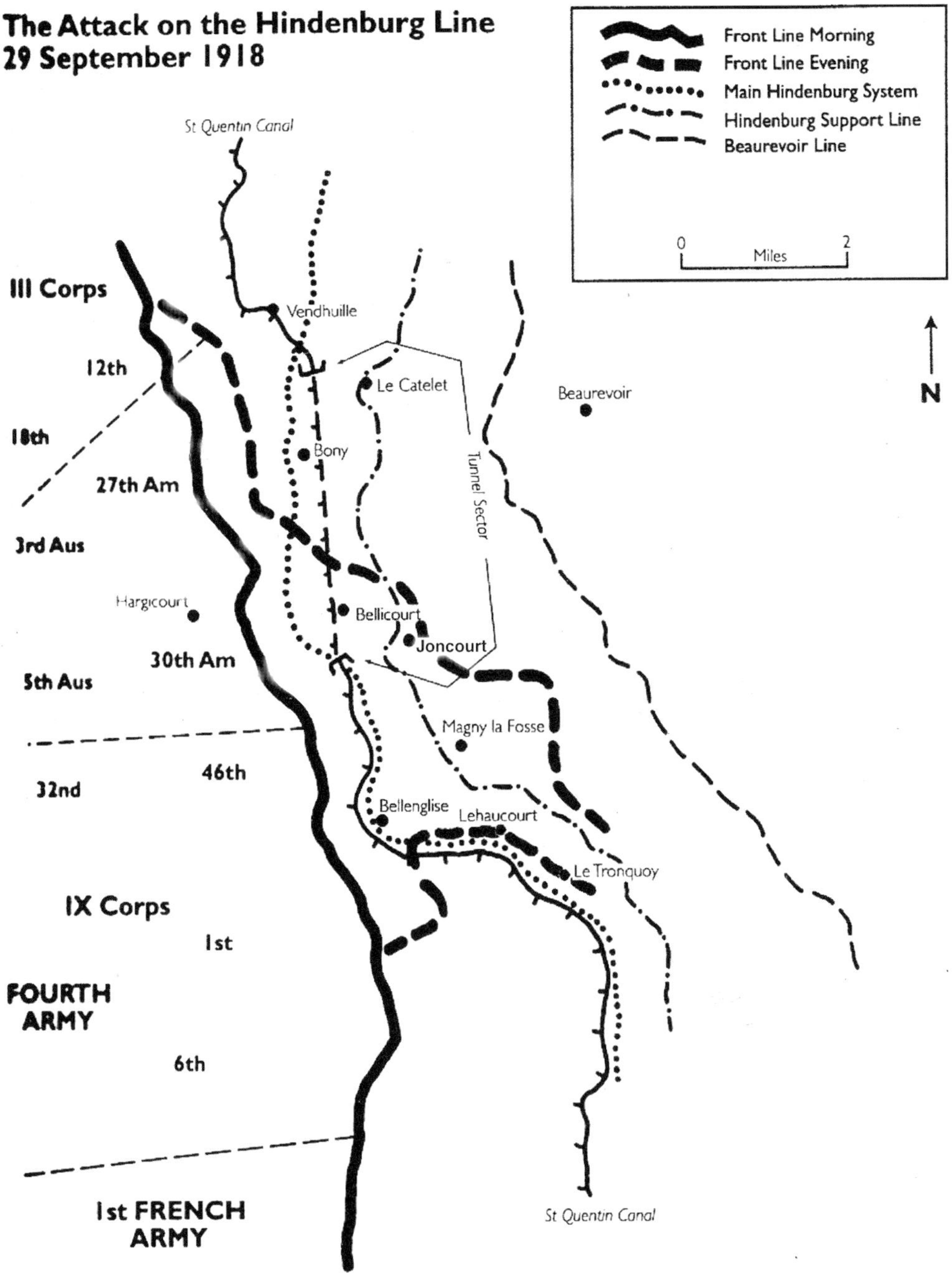

▲ Map 33. The Hindenburg Line

As has been mentioned, by 24th September the majority of the Fourth Army was up to the Hindenburg Line defences which were based in this area on the St. Quentin Canal; unlike the Canal du Nord, this canal was complete. It was 35 feet wide with mud and water standing to a depth of about six feet; it was likely to be a formidable obstacle. The canal did, however, have an Achilles heel - a three mile stretch of the canal ran under a tunnel. Realising the weakness here, the Germans had moved the main trench system at this point in front of the canal rather than behind it. The tunnel itself was turned into a massive artillery-proof barracks with troops being accommodated on barges.

Rawlinson, together with Monash, the Australian Corps' commander, drew up plans for breaking through the Hindenburg Line, and chose to put the main weight of the attack across this three mile 'bridge'. The Australian Corps was to be reinforced by the two American Divisions (the 27th and 30th) which had remained part of the B.E.F.

Ludendorff was under no illusion about how important the Hindenburg Line was to the German army. Behind the main defences ran the Hindenburg Support Line, behind this was the Hindenburg Reserve Line (otherwise known as the Beaurevoir Line), beyond this was the open countryside which was devoid of trenches and prepared defence lines.

Although the B.E.F. was faced with an awesome obstacle, it had one major advantage. On 8th August, during the Battle of Amiens, detailed plans of the defences in the tunnel area of the St. Quentin Canal in the Hindenburg Line had been captured.

Not content to rely solely on Monash's plan, his fellow Corps Commander, Braithwaite, commander of IX Corps, proposed to Rawlinson that he could get a division across the canal itself using a combination of life belts (from cross-channel steamers), portable boats, ropes and ladders. The division proposed for this seemingly impossible task was the 46th (North Midland) Division. Rawlinson supported the amendment and plans were advanced. Tanks, employed only sparingly since 8th August, were again to be used in large numbers, but because of the canal these would all have to be concentrated in the tunnel sector.

On 27th September British artillery started its bombardment of the Hindenburg Line defences, and on 29th September at 5.50am, shrouded by a thick fog, the tanks and infantry advanced.

Despite a failure at the northern end of the tunnel area, a limited breakthrough was achieved at the southern end of the tunnel. Against all odds the greatest results however, were achieved by the 46th (North Midland) Division who succeeded in crossing the canal. Possibly due to surprise at being attacked here at all, or possibly because of the support from the tanks who had managed to advance across the tunnel sector and swing south, an advance of up to 3½ miles was made by the territorials of the 46th Division.

Although somewhat disappointed at the results of the attack and unfairly blaming the inexperienced American troops, Rawlinson, by breaching the Hindenburg Line, had destroyed virtually the last hope the Germans had of delaying the inevitable defeat.

Ludendorff and von Hindenburg after discussing the recent series of disasters went to see the Kaiser on 29th September. They recommended that an armistice be negotiated. Within a few days the German Government had made contact with the American President, Woodrow Wilson; negotiations were to be conducted secretly over the forthcoming weeks.

* * *

This is perhaps a suitable point at which to summarise the position along the Western Front. In the south the American offensive had ground to a halt with severe logistical problems. In Flanders, the driving rain and then the arrival of German reinforcements had halted the offensive by the Flanders Army Group. Only in the centre, where the B.E.F. was in the line, was there a chance of continuing success in the immediate future.

The success of the Fourth Army's breach in the Hindenburg Line, it should be borne in mind, whilst spectacular, was only on a narrow front. In addition, the B.E.F.'s First and Third Armies had halted in front of the city of Cambrai. It was therefore imperative that the breach in the Hindenburg Line be exploited, and the 32nd Division (who had been in support of the 46th Division on 29th September) was the unit which was to start this operation. The next soldier from Ravensthorpe to be killed was serving in one of the 32nd Division's battalions.

Private Harry Hemingway was 33 years of age and a member of the 15th Battalion, Lancashire Fusiliers. The battalion had been raised (along with three others) in Salford in November 1914 by the town's Member of Parliament and carried the sub-title '1st Salford Pals'. Since being raised, the four Salford battalions had suffered heavy casualties, and had lost much of their local identity. Harry Hemingway was one of the soldiers who had been drafted into the battalion to make good its losses, joining it on 12th September 1918.

Harry's battalion crossed the St. Quentin Canal on Monday 30th September and moved up towards the village of Joncourt which lay between the Hindenburg Support Line and the Beaurevoir Line. The village was attacked at 8am, the 15th Lancashire Fusiliers, with the assistance of tanks and a heavy artillery barrage making the assault. 'A' and 'B' Companies received many casualties from machine gun fire; despite being reinforced by 'C' Company, they were unable to take the village, but did manage to enter the its western outskirts.

The 15th Lancashire Fusiliers lost according to S.D.G.W. one officer and 56 men killed in action on 30th September; a further 150 men were wounded, ten of these men succumbing to their wounds over the course of the next week.

Harry Hemingway was one of the battalion's fatal casualties. Born in Leeds in about 1885 he attended the Holy Innocents' Church School in Thornhill Lees, as well as singing in the church choir. Before being called up Harry worked as a hydraulic press operator at Wormald and Walker's mill in Dewsbury; he was also a member of Ravensthorpe Conservative Club. In May 1918 he was drafted into the army, joining the East Yorkshire Regiment and being trained at Hornsea on the Yorkshire coast. After just four months training he went to France, joining his battalion, as previously mentioned, on 12th September.

Harry wrote his last letter to his wife at their home at 19 Field Street, Ravensthorpe, on 25th September, in which he told her they were going to the front. According to an article which appeared in the Dewsbury Reporter on 14th December, Mrs Emma Louisa Hemingway wrote eighteen letters to her husband, all of which were returned to her. When the first of these was returned, she made enquiries about her husband to be told that he was wounded and ill; this was subsequently amended to wounded and missing. It was not until 2nd February 1919 that she received official confirmation that Harry had been killed.

Harry Hemingway is buried in Joncourt East British Cemetery. This small cemetery contains 71 graves, eleven of which are from the 15th Lancashire Fusiliers; the majority of the battalion's remaining casualties are buried close to Joncourt at Uplands Cemetery.

Although not connected with the attack on the Hindenburg Line, another Ravensthorpe soldier was to receive fatal injuries on 30th September.

Albert Dent was born in about 1899 to Mr and Mrs James Dent. Before the war Albert worked as a mule minder at F. Doble & Sons until being called up; this did not mean that he worked with animals, a mule (otherwise known as a spinning mule) was a machine used for spinning cotton into yarns and then winding the yarns onto spindles.

After training he was sent to France, joining the 10th Battalion, Lincolnshire Regiment (the Grimsby Chums). According to the Dewsbury News he joined the battalion 'at Easter' (presumably his 19th Birthday), but within a month had contracted trench fever. This disease was passed by body lice; lice were a severe irritant to the troops, and despite strenuous efforts, their spread could not be

▲ 149. Harry Hemingway

▲ 150. A confusingly captioned photograph. Albert Dent was not a member of the West Riding Regiment (Duke of Wellington's Regiment); the 'WRR' is clearly in error. Albert however seems to be wearing on his jacket collar a badge of the West Yorkshire Regiment; again, as far as is known, he was not a member of this Regiment.

prevented in the insanitary conditions that were prevalent in the trenches.

At around the time Albert contracted trench fever, the Grimsby Chums were disbanded, and Albert was transferred to the 2nd Lincolnshires, part of 62 Brigade, 21st Division. The division was operating as part of the Third Army's push on Cambrai, 62 Brigade being in the line just west of the village of Gouzeaucourt (south of Havrincourt and south-west of Cambrai). On 27th September the 2nd Lincolnshires were in support of an attack on African Trench, the next day patrols found Gouzeaucourt to have been abandoned by the Germans.

On 29th September an attack was launched from Gouzeaucourt towards the village of Gonnelieu, a smaller village 1½ miles to the east of Gouzeaucourt. The attack went in at 3.30am, with the 1st Lincolnshires on the right and Albert's 2nd Lincolns on the left. Unfortunately Albert's battalion was not in position when the attack was launched, and therefore did not have the full support of the artillery barrage; nevertheless the men caught up with the attack despite heavy enemy machine gun fire. The attack did not dislodge the Germans from Gonnelieu, and casualties to Albert's battalion, according to S.D.G.W., amounted to fourteen men killed in action.

In the early hours of 30th September patrols reported that the Germans had evacuated Gonnelieu, and the 2nd Lincolnshires moved up to occupy the village.

It is likely that it was during these operations that Albert received a severe gunshot wound to the chest. Evacuated to a casualty clearing station, Albert died on 5th October aged 19; his parents received notification of their son's death at their home at 23 Aire Street in the middle of October*.

Albert Dent is buried at Thilloy Road Cemetery south of Bapaume; the cemetery was started in September 1918 by a field ambulance unit and used until early October by the 3rd, 4th and 43rd Casualty Clearing Stations. It now contains 240 graves.

* * *

Returning south to the front of the Fourth Army, the attacks on the St. Quentin Canal and nearby villages had broken not only the main Hindenburg Line but also the Hindenburg Support Line. The last remaining obstacle before open countryside, the Hindenburg Reserve Line (the Beaurevoir Line) was now within reach.

On 1st October parts of the Beaurevoir Line were taken but it was not until 3rd October that a full scale attack was launched. The Germans, under orders to hold the line 'at all costs' hung on grimly to their positions and even counter-attacked in some places; within three days, however, the fighting for this line was over, and the Fourth Army was at last in countryside which bore little sign of warfare.

Because of this breach in their last prepared line of defence, the Germans were forced, at last, to abandon the city of Cambrai and began to pull back from here towards the River Selle; Canadian patrols entered Cambrai on 9th October.

**** A newspaper report indicated that Albert Dent and Horace Scott (who was to die of pneumonia five days later - see Chapter 20) knew each other, which seems reasonable as they were the same age and before the war had worked together at F. Doble & Sons.***

Part of this follow up to the German withdrawal was made by the 11th (Northern) Division which was operating to the north of Cambrai. Although the Germans were now effectively in retreat, they continued to use rearguards to keep the following British troops at bay. It was equally important that the British kept in touch with the Germans in order to deny them any breathing space in which to prepare a line of defence.

One example of this continually-applied pressure was the attack on 10th October by the 6th Battalion, Lincolnshire Regiment (part of 33 Brigade, 11th (Northern) Division) on the village of Hem-Lenglet, 5½ miles due north of Cambrai. Private Fred Preston, aged 19 and from Ravensthorpe, was a member of this battalion.

On the morning of 10th October orders to attack Hem-Lenglet were received by the 6th Lincolnshires' commanding officer; patrols were sent out in order to undertake a reconnaissance, but these came under fire and sustained casualties. Despite these casualties, information was obtained, and drawing on this, plans were laid for an attack that night, in conjunction with the 7th Battalion, South Staffordshire Regiment, also part of 33 Brigade.

Patrols were again sent out that evening, one of which was fired upon by a machine gun. The position was rushed, the gun put out of action and the crew killed. A further two machine guns were captured soon after, and the patrols, on entering the village, met little resistance.

The battalion's casualties in this operation, according to the War Diary, were one officer and four other ranks killed plus four other ranks wounded and missing. S.D.G.W. indicates the battalion's fatalities were eight men killed in action plus one who died of wounds; one of these fatal casualties was Fred Preston.

Fred was the only son of John and Emily Preston of 783 Huddersfield Road, Ravensthorpe; he was born in Ravensthorpe on 3rd January 1899. After attending St. Saviour's Boys' School, Fred later went on to Mirfield Grammar School. Leaving school he started working for his father's joinery firm of Preston and Burnett as an apprentice, also attending Dewsbury Technical School. Besides being a server at the church, Fred had been a member of St. Saviour's Church Choir since the age of seven.

Fred was called up in March 1917 and undertook training for the next eleven months; before being sent to France in February 1918 he was granted home leave, during which he attended church, and took his usual place in the choir, albeit dressed in his khaki uniform.

The Dewsbury Reporter, quoting a letter from Second Lieutenant C. Watson and Sergeant T.S. Royle, stated that *"...during the taking of a village Private Preston was killed by machine gun fire....he was a good soldier, always willing and ever ready and cheerful."*

Fred, along with four of his comrades who were also killed on 10th October is buried some distance away at Naves Communal Cemetery Extension, having being exhumed from the original place of burial and moved to this cemetery in a post-war concentration.

Fred's parents donated the cross and a pair of candle sticks in his memory which to this day stand on the high altar at St. Saviour's Church; this fact is recorded by a small brass plaque on the wall to the side of the altar.

*   *   *

▲ 151. Fred Preston

▲ 152. Fred Preston's headstone at Naves Communal Cemetery Extension.

The pursuit to the River Selle continued on the fronts of the Third and Fourth Armies over the next few days. On 17th October, the same day as elements of Birdwood's Fifth Army liberated the city of Lille, divisions of the Fourth Army commenced an attack against the Germans who were holding the British up at the River Selle. Despite the attack being launched after a two day artillery bombardment, the crossing proved surprisingly difficult. After three days fighting the Battle of the Selle, as it was to be called, was over and the Fourth Army had crossed this obstacle; the Third Army, to the north, also crossed the river on 20th October. The Third and Fourth Armies' crossing of the Selle was another major victory for the B.E.F., with thousands of prisoners being taken; the cost in terms of casualties was relatively light.

On the northern flank of the B.E.F., the Fifth Army in France and the Second Army in Belgium were continuing to make substantial progress and on 20th October they reached the River Schelde (otherwise known as the Scheldt to the French), which was the name given to the River Rhine as it flowed from Germany into Belgium.

During October, correspondence had been exchanged between the German Government and President Wilson, who was demanding harsh terms from Germany*. The German Government was prepared to accept these terms but

** Field-Marshal Haig, when he heard of the harsh conditions being made commented that statesmen should "not attempt to so humiliate Germany as to produce a desire for revenge in years to come."*

Ludendorff was not, he reacted angrily and offered to resign, as did Field-Marshal von Hindenburg. On 26th October, the Kaiser accepted Ludendorff's resignation but not that of von Hindenburg.

After having crossed the River Selle, the First, Third and Fourth Armies continued the advance, the First towards the town of Valenciennes, near the French border with Belgium and the Third and Fourth towards the Forest of Mormal and the Sambre and Oise Canal; the canal in particular was likely to be a major obstacle.

Although the Fourth Army was not involved in any major battles in this last week in October, it was during this period that another Ravensthorpe soldier was to lose his life.

Arthur Lister was born in Dewsbury in about 1888 to Alfred and Bertha Lister; they lived at 2 Scout Hill Terrace and Arthur attended Westtown School. In 1914 he married and at the time of his call up in February 1918 was working at Mark Oldroyd and Son's mill in Dewsbury. He went to France on 4th May, joining the Royal Garrison Artillery's 2nd Siege Battery, part of the 85th Brigade, Royal Garrison Artillery. The 2nd Siege Battery was armed with six 6" howitzers and (as part of the 85th Brigade, R.G.A.) was attached to the Fourth Army*.

There is no firm information about what happened to Arthur, but according to a letter from a nurse which was published in the Dewsbury News: *"Gunner Arthur Lister was admitted to this hospital on 28th October with a severe wound in the thigh and died the same day."* According to the article, Arthur was in the anti-aircraft gun section.

Whilst R.G.A. personnel did man anti-aircraft section guns, it is more likely that Arthur was part of an anti-aircraft picquet (possibly armed with a machine gun) within his battery, rather than assigned to a specialised anti-aircraft battery.

Arthur, who was aged 30, is buried at Premont British Cemetery; this cemetery was used in the last weeks of the war by the 20th, 50th, 55th and 61st Casualty Clearing Stations. It contains over 500 graves.

* * *

During October the B.E.F. had, since breaking the Hindenburg Line, advanced twenty miles on a broad front but had also suffered 120,000 casualties. The issue now was whether the German army could be defeated before the onset of winter, and if it could not, could the B.E.F., with its extended lines of supply, keep itself fed and armed. The potential supply problems were of course compounded by the fact that much of the countryside was devastated, with few roads or railways in full working order. Even before the onset of winter, these supply problems were of concern to the military commanders as they were desperate to sustain the momentum of their advance: As the B.E.F.'s lines of supply lengthened, the German lines were shortening.

**** In Chapter 10, reference was made to the R.G.A. batteries being formed into Heavy Artillery Groups. In mid-1917 there had been a reorganisation within the R.G.A. and the batteries were instead formed into Brigades. Some of these Groups or Brigades were under the control of Corps, others, such as the 85th were Army troops.***

▲ 153. Arthur Lister

▲ 156. Maurice Crossley

If the German army was still capable of warding off the Allied offensives and reorganising itself over the winter, there was still the chance of a negotiated peace which would therefore mean a less than outright victory had been won. Anything less than an absolute victory and humiliation of Germany was something which, after all the bloodshed of the previous four years, the politicians wished to avoid.

The pressure on the Germans had to be maintained in order to achieve an end to the war in 1918. The city of Valenciennes, a centre of communication for the Germans, was identified as the hub of the German defence; it was in the sector of the front being attacked by General Horne's First Army. Before the city could be taken, the villages to the south-west had to be cleared.

Even at this stage of the war, German resistance could still be severe, and so it was to prove here. The key to the southern approaches to Valenciennes was a prominent hill called Mont Houy, this hill had, in the last days of October, been captured by British troops, but had fallen to German counter-attacks. On the 1st November another attack was mounted, this time by the Canadian Corps, with the 49th (West Riding) Division on the Canadian's right.

The 49th (West Riding) Division had served for most of the war in the Ypres sector and had failed to achieve a good reputation; the division was now, however, to have an important part to play in this attack.

Maurice Crossley was born in Morley on 1st October 1899 to Mr and Mrs J. Crossley; although there is no obituary for him in the local newspapers, his service record still exists. Maurice was the second child (first son) of ten children. It is not known when his parents moved to 355 Huddersfield Road, Ravensthorpe but his enlistment papers give this as his address. Before being conscripted into the army he worked as a dyer's assistant although it is not known for which firm he worked. Maurice received his call up papers on 10th October 1917, a few days after his 18th birthday, and reported to the barracks at Pontefract on 18th October. He had been medically examined a month earlier, and his measurements give an indication of the lowering of the requirements for army service. Maurice's papers indicate that he was just 5' 1½" tall, weighed exactly seven stones and his chest measured only 33" even when fully expanded.

On 23rd October Maurice was posted to the 6th Training Reserve Battalion, which subsequently became the 53rd (Young Soldiers) Battalion, West Yorkshire Regiment* the training being undertaken at Brockton Camp, between Stafford and Rugeley. It was here that Maurice was confined to barracks for four days as punishment for being absent from a parade on 28th February 1918. On 25th March, he was transferred to the 51st (Graduated) Battalion of the West Yorkshire Regiment at Clipstone Camp in Nottinghamshire, where on 2nd April, he seems to have got himself into trouble again, being confined to barracks for three days, for being absent from guard duties.

Despite not yet being 19 years of age, Maurice was drafted out to France. Leaving Folkestone for Boulogne on 25th April, he arrived at the Etaples training ground the following day from where he was posted to the 1/7th Battalion, West Yorkshire Regiment, part of 146 Brigade, 49th (West Riding) Division.

By the end of October, 146 Brigade's three battalions totalled less than a thousand men, which was less than a full-strength battalion; despite this they were ordered into the attack on Friday 1st November.

Maurice's 1/7th Battalion (which was in support of the 1/5th West Yorkshires) had by 7am crossed the River Rhonelle; by 9am the 1/5th Battalion reported to Brigade Headquarters that they had taken the final objective (being the Marly - Preslau road), but in doing so a gap had appeared in their line and one company of the 1/7th West Yorkshires was sent up to fill this gap.

Despite the claim that the final objective had been taken, it later transpired that this was not the case, and they were in fact 200 yards short of their objective. This may partly explain why, for much of the day, according to the brigade's War Diary the front line was *"seriously troubled by machine gun fire from the steel works."* This steel works was a factory due south of Marly, it was not an objective of the attack.

A German counter-attack at 4.30pm was easily repulsed.

Notwithstanding the West Yorkshires being slightly short of their objective, the attack, especially by the Canadians, was a success; supported by a massive artillery bombardment Mont Houy had been taken.

Casualties, according to S.D.G.W., amongst the 1/7th West Yorkshires were nine killed in action (including one officer) plus three who died of wounds. One of the three who died of wounds was Rifleman Maurice Crossley, aged 19. He is buried at Thiant Communal Cemetery, a French civilian cemetery which contains 72 Commonwealth War Graves. Seven of the men killed in action are buried at Auberchicourt British Cemetery.

The Training Reserve battalions (see Chapter 13) were restructured at about this time and were affiliated to certain regiments, in all cases being designated as the 53rd (Young Soldiers) Battalion of the regiment to which they were affiliated. After receiving their training the recruits were posted to 51st or 52nd Battalions of these regiments, these battalions designated 'Graduated' Battalions. The Graduated battalions were used to provide drafts to battalions of the regiment on active service as well as being used for home defence purposes.

Realising that Valenciennes was untenable, the Germans evacuated the city the following day.

* * *

To the south of Valenciennes, in the path of the advance of the Third Army stood the Forest of Mormal; further to the south in front of the Fourth Army was the Sambre and Oise Canal. These obstacles had the potential to be difficult to overcome if the Germans were to put up a stubborn resistance.

On the morning of Monday 4th November, the final battle of the First World War commenced, when across the fronts of the Third and Fourth Armies, British divisions attacked German positions. At this stage in the war there were no continual trench lines, and the Germans relied on scattered machine gun positions and fortified villages to hold up the Allies' advance. By now German resistance was crumbling and this Battle of the Sambre, as it was to become known, was a relatively inexpensive victory although there was in some areas (particularly just west of the Forest of Mormal) some stiff German resistance early on.

Following this attack, the Germans put up only marginal resistance and from the Belgian coast to the city of Sedan in the south the advance took on the character of a pursuit.

Thursday 7th November was the last day fatal injuries were incurred by a Ravensthorpe soldier.

Henry Davill (the younger brother of John Davill - see Chapter 2) was born in Dewsbury in 1897 to Harry and Mary Davill. He was working for Mr G.W. Walker at Paradise Farm when, on 18th May 1915 (about a month after his brother John had been sent to France), he tried to join up, according to the Dewsbury Reporter: *"...before he was 18 but was sent back home until* [he was] *19* [years of age]*."*

It is unclear when he was sent out to France, where he joined the 9th K.O.Y.L.I., part of the 21st Division. On 6th May 1918 he was awarded the Military Medal, but there is no record of any citation for this award nor any clue in which action he was involved when he earned the decoration.

An order dated 23rd June 1918 was issued, but later cancelled, instructing the battalion to disband. In this order, Henry was on a list of personnel who were to have been posted to the 5th K.O.Y.L.I. It is interesting to note that this order not only listed Henry as a Lewis gunner, but also that he had a bar to his Military Medal; there is, however no other reference to this second award of the M.M., and it is possible the reference to the bar is an error.

Henry remained with the 9th K.O.Y.L.I., and although the 21st Division did not take part in the Battle of the Sambre, the division was moved forward to take part in the pursuit of the retreating German army.

On 7th November the 9th K.O.Y.L.I. was ordered to take the adjoining villages of Limont-Fontaine and Eclaibes (being 5½ miles south-west of Maubeuge and 6 miles east of the Forest of Mormal). The War Diary describes how the attack began at 16.50 hours*.

**** The British Army had gone onto the 24 hour clock system on 1st October 1918.***

◀ 155. Henry Davill

▼ 156. Paradise Way, near Paradise Farm where Henry Davill worked.

"From now on the battalion, ably led, made excellent progress and literally carried everything before it by sheer determination and will to win. A strong stand was made by the enemy but all to no purpose. In the fierce fighting that took place in front and in the streets of the villages the men of the 9th K.O.Y.L.I. refused to be denied victory. Once again the enemy were entirely out-manoeuvred and out-fought. By 21.30 hours so great had been the force of the assault the villages of Limont-Fontaine and Eclaibes were thoroughly cleared of the enemy....".

The victory was not without its price; thirteen men of the battalion were killed in action and a further two were to die of their wounds later that same day. Others were no doubt injured, including Corporal Henry Davill.

Henry received a wound to his chest and was evacuated, arriving at the 21st Casualty Clearing Station at Caudry (between Le Cateau and Cambrai) on 11th November; at first it was thought he would recover. He told the nurses to pass on a message for his mother not to be worried about him. Henry was X-rayed; this revealed there was a small piece of shrapnel behind his heart.

Henry Davill died of his wounds aged 21 on Thursday 14th November and is buried at Caudry British Cemetery. The cemetery contains over 700 graves from the last weeks of the war.

Chapter Twenty-Two

Other Theatres, The Armistice and 1919

Before describing the events leading to the end of the Great War on the Western Front, it is worthwhile to describe the action in other theatres.

Prior to 1914, the Italians were part of a Triple Alliance with Germany and Austria. On the outbreak of the war they stayed neutral but on 26th April 1915 they signed, in great secrecy, the Treaty of London. By signing this, the Italians undertook with Great Britain, France and Russia to declare war on their former allies within a month; this agreement was made on the basis of Italy receiving valuable territorial gains. The Triple Entente thought Italy's entry would be a massive benefit to their war effort. In this they were to be sadly mistaken. On 23rd May 1915 Italy declared war on Austria and three months later, in August, did the same with Turkey. It was not until a full year later that Italy completed its undertaking, declaring war on Germany on 27th August 1916.

Austria had a commanding position along the mountainous Alpine frontier with Italy, as a result the Italian Commander-in-Chief, General Luigi Cadorna, decided to concentrate the army's efforts in the east along the Isonzo River. Because of the lack of preparation by the Italians, their first attack soon broke down, but after reinforcing his army, especially with artillery, Cadorna made further attacks, all however failing to make a breakthrough. As on the Western Front, trench warfare soon developed. There were four Battles of the Isonzo in 1915 alone, followed by five in 1916. An Austrian attack in the middle of 1916 (the Battle of the Asiago) was defeated by the Italians. In 1917 the Tenth and Eleventh Battles of the Isonzo were fought, the Eleventh being successful in that an advance of five miles was made.

In the belief that the Austro-Hungarian forces were about to collapse, Ludendorff agreed to send several German divisions to the Italian front in order to mount a large counter-attack. This, the Battle of Caporetto, was launched on 24th October 1917 in a lightly defended sector to the north of the Isonzo front. After an overwhelming artillery and gas bombardment (a prototype for the German spring offensive of 1918), the unprepared and demoralised Italian troops fell back in the face of the combined German and Austrian attack. General Cadorna ordered a retreat to the River Piave, seventy miles to the rear. This natural barrier proved to be impossible for the Germans and Austrians to cross, and the Italian army, bolstered by the arrival of six French and five British divisions*, held the Austrian and German armies at this river.

** The British divisions were the 5th, 7th, 23rd, 41st and 48th (South Midland), and were commanded by General Plumer, who arrived from Belgium on 17th November, taking over from Lieutenant-General The Earl of Cavan. Plumer returned to the Western Front once the position in Italy was stabilised in March 1918.*

A further Austrian attack was made on 15th June 1918 (The Battle of the Piave); although there was limited Austrian success on part of the front, this was soon halted.

In late 1918, after the successful Allied attacks on the Western Front, General Diaz, who had replaced General Cadorna, launched an offensive. The three British divisions still in Italy, now back under the command of Lieutenant-General The Earl of Cavan, took part in the assault, which started on 23rd October. This was the final campaign in Italy and became known as the Battle of Vittorio Veneto. Against crumbling Austrian opposition, this offensive was highly successful and fighting finished in Italy on 4th November 1918.

* * *

Besides the battles fought in Italy, there was another area of Europe which saw some British involvement during the course of the Great War. The spark that started the First World War, was, it will be recalled, ignited in Bosnia. After the assassination of the Austrian heir Archduke Franz Ferdinand and his wife in Sarajevo, the Austrians were determined to make the Serbians pay for the murders. An invasion of Serbia was mounted by the Austrians on 12th August 1914; four days later, on 16th August, the Serbian army came into contact with the Austrians on the banks of the Jadar River. The Battle of the Jadar River lasted five days, Austrian casualties were heavy, and resulted in the Austrian armies having to withdraw.

Despite this setback the Austrians were determined to crush the Serbs, and further attacks were made. Against the stronger Austrian army the Serbs were forced, over the following months, to give ground.

A Serbian counter-attack was launched in December 1914 (The Battle of the Kolubra River) which forced the Austrians off Serbian soil; although the Serbians had fought valiantly against the Austrians both sides committed atrocities. Austria dare not re-launch its offensive until assistance was likely to be forthcoming. Bulgaria, the most powerful of the Balkan states, entered the war on Germany's side in September 1915. This persuaded Austria that the time was right to attack again and a German-Austrian offensive was launched in October 1915. Along with the Bulgarians, who joined the attack later in the month, the German and Austrian armies drove what remained of the Serbian army into Albania, from where they were shipped (via the island of Corfu) to neutral Greece. The Serbians arrived at the port of Salonika in the spring of 1916.

The only major Balkan state not yet involved in the war was Greece. In the early months of the war, Britain had hoped to use the Greek's traditional hatred of the Turks to the Allies' advantage, especially in view of the planned Gallipoli expedition. This aspiration did not come about, because in March 1915 the Greek Prime Minister (Eleutherios Venizelos) resigned due to his pro-Allied policies being at odds with the pro-German stance of King Constance I, the Greek monarch.

After the Prime Minister was restored to office he gave permission for an Anglo-French force to land at the port of Salonika in an attempt to help the Serbians against the Bulgarians. Shortly before the Anglo-French force landed, Venizelos was once again ousted by King Constance, but nevertheless the landings, made in October 1915, were not opposed by the Greek army.

The Allied force pushed up from Salonika into Serbia although the single British division - the 10th (Irish) Division - went no further than the frontier because the British Government was unenthusiastic about the venture. The French force was forced to fall back after being blocked by a much larger Bulgarian force. The Bulgarians did not cross the frontier into Greece, and the French and British forces stayed in the Salonika area, much against the wishes of King Constance, who unsuccessfully sought German assistance.

In April 1916, the Anglo-French divisions (suitably reinforced and now made up to a total of eleven divisions including five British*) plus the remains of the Serbian army which had just arrived, pushed up from Salonika towards the Bulgarian frontier. The Bulgarians, anticipating the Allied move attacked first, forcing the French back. Fortunately the British under General Milne held the Bulgarian attack. Further pushes, mainly by the French and Serbians, continued for the rest of the year but progress in the mountainous countryside was painfully slow.

In December 1916 landings were made at Athens in order to protect the Salonika forces from interference, followed in May by another large scale offensive which failed. In June 1917 the Allies forced King Constance to abdicate and Venizelos returned as Prime Minister, leading to the Greeks entering the war on the Allied side.

It was not until September 1918 that a further push was made; this attack was successful, mainly due to the withdrawal of large numbers of German troops to the Western Front. The Bulgarians soon collapsed, leading them to be the first of the Central Powers to seek an armistice, which was signed on 29th September. The Serbs marched out of Salonika and re-took their capital city, Belgrade on 1st November 1918. Allied casualties in Salonika were 18,000 from battle but 481,000 from malaria.

* * *

The first shots fired on behalf of the British Empire in the Great War are commonly thought to be by a patrol of the 4th Dragoon Guards on the Mons to Brussels Road at dawn on 22nd August 1914. This is not the case, the first shot fired in anger by a soldier of the British Empire was fired a week earlier a few miles north of Lome in Togoland, west Africa, by a black African of the Gold Coast Regiment, part of the West African Frontier Force. At the outbreak of the war this force consisted of 242 British regular officers, 181 British N.C.O.s and 7,733 African soldiers.

The two German colonies in the area, Togoland and the Cameroons were invaded by British and French forces, although the Germans tried, unsuccessfully to invoke a treaty dating from 1885 in which European powers had agreed, in the event of war, not to carry out that war in Africa.

**** Besides the 10th (Irish) Division which had been in action at Gallipoli, these British divisions were the 22nd and 26th Divisions plus two regular divisions, the 27th and 28th, which had been decimated during the Second Battle of Ypres.***

The conquest of Togoland was very rapid but the Cameroons, larger than Germany itself, presented great difficulties. Although defended by fewer than 1,500 German and about 6,500 African troops, the vastness of the country, and poor road and rail communications together with disease which was rife, made this colony's capture a totally different prospect.

An initial invasion by British, French and Belgian troops from their adjoining colonies was made in August 1914 and although the capital, Duala, was captured in November, unfavourable weather conditions stopped the total conquest of the country for many months. Resistance did not end until February 1916.

Germany's other extensive colony was many miles to the south. German South West Africa (now Namibia) covered an area six times larger than England, much of the interior of the country being desert. The German attitude to the indigenous population was high-handed (this stemmed from the first Imperial Commissioner of the area, Dr Ernst Goering, father of Herman who was to become a First World War fighter ace and later to take charge of the Luftwaffe under Adolf Hitler). There were no black soldiers to support the German troops in the area. The German force consisted of 140 officers and 3,000 other ranks. Within the German colony was Walfish Bay, the only harbour suitable as a naval base. This fact alone made war in the area inevitable.

Adjoining the German colony was the Union of South Africa. This had been the scene of the bitter Boer War at the turn of the century. Since that war, however, Britain had assisted the country in overcoming the effects of the war, and had allowed free elections in 1907; the old Boer leaders coming to power and becoming staunch allies of Britain. The South African Prime Minister, Louis Botha, was asked if his troops could capture German South West Africa, but before a campaign could be mounted, there was an uprising within South Africa by Boers who had German sympathies. This uprising was put down by the end of 1914 and the campaign against the Germans resumed; this lasted until July 1915.

By far the most significant of the African campaigns was the one fought in German East Africa. This campaign opened badly for the British. It was decided to mount an amphibious operation to take the German port of Tanga (north of Dar es Salaam). This was to be undertaken mainly by Indian troops, but a regular British battalion, the 2nd Battalion, The Loyal North Lancashire Regiment, was also involved. The attack was repulsed by a much smaller German force.

Despite this victory, the Germans realised that they could not hope to win against the numerically stronger British, and the commander of the German forces in the colony, Colonel (later General) Paul von Lettow-Vorbeck adopted a raiding strategy, aimed at tying down as many British* troops as possible. In this he succeeded. His small force of 260 Europeans and 2,500 Askaris (African soldiers), although later expanding to 3,000 Europeans and 11,000 Askaris, kept the British forces numbering (at their peak) 150,000 men (plus 200,000 porters) tied up for the rest of the war. Of these British troops, only a small number (about 4%) were actually from Britain, principally 2nd Loyal North Lancashires (who left South

It will be noted that the term 'British' in many of these references means forces under British command; they could be South African troops, British South African Police, Northern Rhodesian Police, soldiers of the Indian Army, or native Africans of the King's African Rifles, Nigerian Regiment, Gold Coast Regiment, West India Regiment, Rhodesia Regiment, East Africa Regiment or East African Mounted Rifles.

Africa in December 1916) and 25th Battalion, Royal Fusiliers. This latter battalion was raised by the Legion of Frontiersmen, and served for a large part of the East African campaign, only leaving the continent at the end of 1917.

It was not until 1916 that an expedition under General Jan Smuts, a Boer who had fought against the British in the South African war and a member of Louis Botha's cabinet, set out to subdue von Lettow-Vorbeck. Although Smuts managed to make sweeping advances, he was never able to pin the elusive German down.

General Smuts left Africa in early 1917, joining Lloyd George's War Cabinet as an advisor. His replacement in German East Africa was no more successful at catching von Lettow-Vorbeck, although in November 1917 a large portion of the German forces surrendered to a small British formation.

It was not until the war in Europe was over that von Lettow-Vorbeck eventually surrendered to the British. He had led a superbly executed guerilla campaign against forces up to ten times the size of his own and although he never had a chance of defeating the British, or preventing the loss of the colony, he had tied down valuable British resources for much of the war.

* * *

Before the war there had been great scepticism about the value of aeroplanes for military purposes. It was not until 1912 that the Royal Flying Corps, with military and naval wings, was created. The Royal Naval Air Service was created in July 1914 when it was hived off from the R.F.C. and placed under the control of the Admiralty. At the outbreak of war the R.F.C. had just 179 aircraft under its control, of which only a small proportion were operational. Virtually the entire strength of the R.F.C. went to France in August 1914; numbers 2,3,4 and 5 Squadrons* crossed the Channel between 13th and 15th August under the control of Brigadier-General Sir David Henderson. Its primary role was reconnaissance for the army, a role previously assigned to the cavalry.

The aeroplanes of the R.F.C. soon showed their value, on 20th August they spotted the German army pushing towards Louvain in Belgium. The R.F.C. again proved their worth in September 1914, when they spotted the movement of the German First Army in front of Paris which allowed Joffre to launch his counter-attack; this led to the Battle of the Marne. In the early days of the war the aircraft were unarmed, but pilots and observers soon started taking pot shots at each other with revolvers and rifles. These first aerial combats were invariably unsuccessful. The later introduction of machine guns ensured the air war would develop into a far less chivalrous affair.

Under Brigadier-General Hugh 'Boom' Trenchard who took control of the R.F.C. in France in August 1915, this early reconnaissance role was developed during the war and expanded to photography and bombing, observation for the artillery, long range (strategic) bombing and, towards the end of the war, ground support of attacking infantry. In support of these activities, and to prevent similar operations by the Germans, a large number of fighter ('scout') aircraft were built. Each side

**** Number 1 Squadron was in the process of re-equipping, having previously had balloons rather than aircraft.***

developed aircraft and tactics throughout the war to achieve supremacy. The Germans achieved this through the Fokker Monoplane from mid-1915 to early 1916, one of the leading German airmen of this period was Max Immelmann. The air war swung the way of the Allies with the arrival of better machines and the expansion of the R.F.C., which had grown to 27 squadrons by July 1916.

The Germans responded and again achieved an advantage with the arrival of the Albatross D.III. This supremacy culminated in April 1917 (which became known as 'Bloody April' to the R.F.C.) when 150 aircraft and 316 airmen were lost during the month. The R.F.C.'s pilots had a life expectancy of only a few hours flying time; particularly vulnerable were the newly-arrived pilots from training schools in Britain. The German ascendancy was overcome with the arrival of yet better machines, these included the SE5 and the Sopwith Camel.

The pilots of these aeroplanes could build up large scores. The first of the famous British Aces was Albert Ball who claimed 44 victims. He was killed at the age of 20 in May 1917. James McCudden (57 victories) started his career as a mechanic with the R.F.C. in 1913. He died in July 1918 when he crashed on take-off whilst on his way to take over the command of a squadron. Raymond Collishaw (60 victories) was the highest scoring pilot in the R.N.A.S. and survived the war. William 'Billy' Bishop also survived and was the second highest overall 'ace' with 72 victories and was the highest scoring Canadian. The top British 'ace' was Edward 'Mick' Mannock who, despite a slow start, amassed 73 'kills'. He may, in fact, have achieved a higher total were it not for his habit of severely damaging his opponents before allowing a novice pilot to come in and make the final kill, so as to give them experience and confidence. A superb tactician and leader, he was killed in July 1918, but his achievements were ignored after the war because of his forthright socialist views. Between them these five pilots won four V.C.s, twelve D.S.O.s, one D.S.C., six M.C.s, two D.F.C.s, and one M.M.

The most famous First World War fighter ace was a German, Manfred von Richtofen, the Red Baron, who scored 80 victories, until his death in July 1918. The command of his unit was taken over by Herman Goering, who was to become the head of the Luftwaffe in the Second World War.

The R.F.C. and R.N.A.S. became the Royal Air Force on 1st April 1918, but Trenchard did not remain in charge largely due to his inability to work with the politicians in Whitehall. It was not long after the R.A.F.'s creation that he was placed in command of the Independent Air Force, which was tasked with the long range strategic bombing of Germany.

* * *

Returning to the Western Front, over the last weeks of the war, Germany's position had been becoming increasingly precarious, with their allies agreeing armistice terms. As has been mentioned earlier in this chapter, the first to sue for peace were the Bulgarians, an armistice being agreed on 29th September. Next were the Turks, who agreed armistice terms at Mudros, on the island of Lemnos on 30th October, after their defeats in Palestine (see Chapter 17).

In Austria the Hapsburg Empire was falling apart, with Hungary and ironically Bosnia (in whose capital, Sarajevo, the heir to the Austrian throne,

Archduke Franz Ferdinand was assassinated) declaring their independence on 31st October. The Austrians, whose actions were a major cause of the war, signed an armistice on 3rd November.

Germany was now left alone and isolated; there was widespread hunger, verging on starvation, throughout the country. When ordered to put to sea in one final mission, on 29th October, the sailors of the High Seas Fleet mutinied. Civil unrest began to spread through the country, leading to riots.

With her army falling back and with no hope of stemming the Allied advances, Germany realised that she had to agree peace terms.

On the night of 7th/8th November a German delegation crossed the Allied lines in order to discuss armistice terms. The terms offered by Marshal Foch, on behalf of the Allies were extremely harsh and only stopped a little short of being a demand for Germany's unconditional surrender. These terms were referred back to the German Chancellor, Prince Max of Baden (second cousin to the Kaiser) who had been sworn in on 3rd October after the Kaiser had dismissed the previous Chancellor. By now Germany was on the verge of revolution, the civil population, weakened by the Allied blockade were dying in their thousands from the influenza pandemic.

In order to try and pacify the agitators, and without consulting him, Prince Max announced the abdication of the Kaiser on Saturday 9th November, this led to the collapse of the Government and the proclamation of a republic.

On Sunday 10th November, the Kaiser fled to neutral Holland* and the signing of the Armistice was authorised. The signing took place at 5am the following morning in a railway carriage in a siding in the Forest of Compiegne. The British representative, Vice-Admiral Sir Rosslyn Wemyss, the First Sea Lord, suggested that the Armistice should come into effect at 11am that day; so at 11am on Monday 11th November 1918 up and down the Western Front the guns fell silent. Orders were issued for there to be no fraternisation with the Germans.

In Belgium the Canadians had entered the town of Mons earlier that morning, Mons was of course the site of the first battle involving the B.E.F. over four years previously. The Canadians delayed their official entry into the town for several hours in order to enable an escort to be provided by a detachment of the 5th (Royal Irish) Lancers, a regiment which had, as part of the 3rd Cavalry Brigade, been present at the Battle of Mons in August 1914.

* * *

It is impossible to calculate exactly the cost of the Great War in human lives. The French dead amounted to approximately 1.4 million, Germany lost approximately 1.8 million, and the British and Empire dead totalled about 900,000. American deaths were over 100,000. Of course, many more men were injured, the total casualties (killed as well as injured) amounted to nearly 9 million for the Allies plus 6½ million for Germany. How many of those who were injured never made a full recovery and died prematurely cannot even be guessed at.

** Where he was to die in 1941.*

▲ 157. Neville Tattersfield, before his promotion to Second Lieutenant.

▲ 158. The headstone of Neville Tattersfield in the graveyard at Wareham Parish Church, Dorset. *Photograph courtesy of Mr R Tattersfield*

▼ 159. North Road, Ravensthorpe. *Photograph courtesy of Kirklees Community History Service.*

In 1918 a much greater threat to the worldwide population occurred when the Spanish 'flu epidemic broke out. This was to sweep round the world from 1918 to 1919 killing many times more people than had been killed in the conflict; estimates range from 21 to 40 million people worldwide succumbing to the illness. Many of these deaths were of soldiers who had survived the war and, weakened by their injuries, were more vulnerable to the effects of the disease.

Such a fate befell Second Lieutenant Neville Tattersfield. Neville's enlistment has already been described, as has the deaths of his parents. Following his injuries at the Battle of Amiens in August 1918 and his subsequent convalescence, Neville stopped with his brother, John, and his sister-in-law, with their 8 year old son, Maurice, at 64 North Road, Ravensthorpe in order to complete his recovery. It was probably about this time that John borrowed Neville's 'Wolf' motorbike and crashed it coming down the steep Shillbank Lane in Mirfield; Neville, it seems was none too pleased.

Although engaged to a local girl called Elsie Fawcett, Neville, upon recovering from his injuries, decided to visit another girlfriend in Scotland. Neville, at this time had a heavy cold, and his sister-in-law tried to dissuade him from making the journey. Against this advice Neville went up to Scotland. Upon returning home his cold was much worse but he was now due to return to the Tank Corps depot in Dorset. He insisted on making the journey, and reported to Swanage on 3rd November. Within a week he had contracted influenza and was admitted to a military hospital in Wareham on Monday 11th November. His brothers John and Clifford went down to Wareham to visit him on Saturday 16th November, after which they returned home.

A telegram was received in Ravensthorpe on Monday 18th November to say Neville's condition had deteriorated and so they set about the long journey back to Wareham.

Neville died, aged 26, on Wednesday 20th November, with his brothers present. He was buried two days later in the churchyard at Wareham Parish Church.

Unlike Neville, there is little information about the next two men named on the Ravensthorpe War Memorial. Harry MacDonald was born in Mirfield on 4th March 1888 to John and Mary MacDonald. Before being called up in October 1916, he worked for Mr A. Algate, a tailor in Ravensthorpe (it will be recalled from Chapter 4 that George Hammond also worked for this gentleman). Rather than being called into the army, Harry joined the Royal Navy. A letter from him (published in the Dewsbury News in January 1917) in which he acknowledged a parcel from the Ravensthorpe and Northorpe Soldiers and Sailors Christmas Parcel Fund described how he had seen "*...a batch* [of men] *going to France. They were playing tin whistles and singing to their hearts' content....I don't wish to come home until victory is gained.*"

Harry was posted to the Mediterranean where he served on motor launches, working from H.M.S. Europa, an old cruiser which had been built in 1897. Europa, until 1915, was part of the 9th Cruiser Squadron working off West Africa, but had become a depot ship later that year and was now based in Mudros harbour on the island of Lemnos in the Aegean Sea near the Gallipoli peninsular. It was in Mudros harbour that the Turks signed their armistice at the end of October.

Harry contracted pneumonia and was transferred to a hospital ship, the Ferashon, where he died on 6th December 1918, aged 30. His parents, who lived at

RAV[illegible]STHORPE MINE-SWEEPER [illegible]IES OF PNEUMONIA.

The m[illegible] friends of Seaman Harry Mac-[illegible]onald, w[illegible]se wife and two children live at 6, Duke Street, Ravens-thorpe, will regret to hear that he died from broncho-pneumonia on December 6th, on a hospital ship in the Eastern Mediterranean. Seaman Macdonald joined the Navy in August 1916 and was attached as a deck-hand to one of H.M. motor-launches and was eng[illegible] for a time in the [illegible] occupation [illegible] mine sweeping. [illegible]e came through man[illegible] difficulties without wound to die as sta[illegible]d on a hospital ship. Before he joined up [illegible] was a [illegible]ailor [illegible]mployed by Mr. Howgate, at Ravens-[illegible]horp[illegible] and he was a member of the Ravens-[illegible]horp[illegible]beral Club.

Seama[illegible]arry Macdonald, Ra[illegible]sthorpe (died).

▲ 160. Harry MacDonald

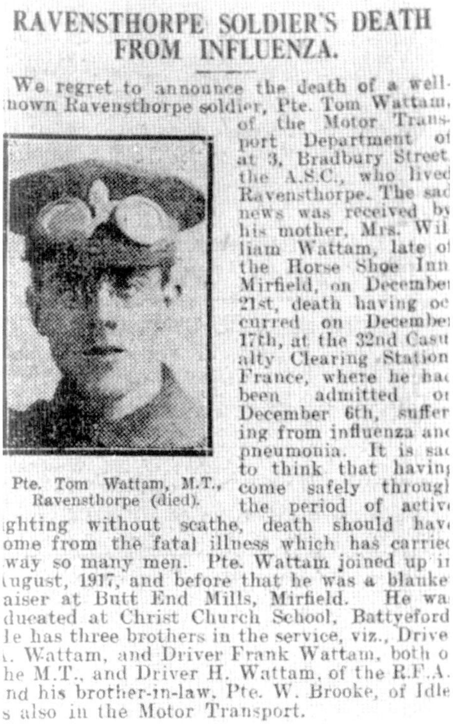

RAVENSTHORPE SOLDIER'S DEATH FROM INFLUENZA.

We regret to announce the death of a well-[illegible]nown Ravensthorpe soldier, Pte. Tom Wattam, of the Motor Transport Department of at 3, Bradbury Street, the A.S.C., who lived Ravensthorpe. The sad news was received by his mother, Mrs. William Wattam, late of the Horse Shoe Inn, Mirfield, on December 21st, death having occurred on December 17th, at the 32nd Casualty Clearing Station, France, where he had been admitted on December 6th, suffering from influenza and pneumonia. It is sad to think that having come safely through the period of active [illegible]ghting without scathe, death should have [illegible]ome from the fatal illness which has carried [illegible]way so many men. Pte. Wattam joined up in [illegible]ugust, 1917, and before that he was a blanket [illegible]aiser at Butt End Mills, Mirfield. He was [illegible]ducated at Christ Church School, Battyeford. [illegible]e has three brothers in the service, viz., Driver [illegible]. Wattam, and Driver Frank Wattam, both of [illegible]he M.T., and Driver H. Wattam, of the R.F.A. [illegible]nd his brother-in-law, Pte. W. Brooke, of Idle [illegible]s also in the Motor Transport.

Pte. Tom Wattam, M.T., Ravensthorpe (died).

▲ 161. Tom Wattam

▼ 162. East Mudros Military Cemetery, on the island of Lemnos. *Photograph courtesy of the Commonwealth War Graves Commission.*

11 Duke Street Ravensthorpe, and his wife Lilian (with two young children) who lived at 6 Duke Street, were informed of his death in mid-December.

Harry MacDonald is buried at East Mudros Military Cemetery on Lemnos which contains nearly 900 graves, many of these are of soldiers who died of wounds on the island following the Gallipoli campaign of 1915.

The last Ravensthorpe soldier to die in 1918 was Tom Wattam, who was born in 1895, one of four sons of William and Ellen Wattam. It is likely he was born in Mirfield as he attended Christ the King Church School in Battyeford, where his parents (or at least his mother, following the death of his father) ran the Horse Shoe Inn. Until his call up in 1917, Tom worked as a blanket raiser at James Walker and Sons at Butt End Mills, Mirfield, where he was probably a work mate of Fred Auty (see Chapter 18).

Tom was posted to the Army Service Corps, being employed in the Motor Transport Section of 'L' Siege Park, attached to XI Corps' heavy artillery units; he would have been responsible for transporting ammunition from railheads to the ammunition dumps nearer the guns. The unit's War Diary does, however, mention them carrying other materials such as on 26th October 1918: *"During last 5 days an average of 50 lorries have been detailed daily....to convey road and bridging materials."*

On 6th December 1918 Tom was admitted to the 32nd Casualty Clearing Station suffering from influenza and pneumonia. Ten days later on 16th December he died. The Dewsbury Reporter stated in an article dated 4th January 1919 that Tom *"...who lived at 3 Bradbury Street, Ravensthorpe* [died] *on December 17th* [sic]*....It is sad to think that having come safely through the period of active fighting....death should have come from the fatal illness which has carried away so many men."*

Tom, who was aged 24, was buried at Valenciennes Communal Cemetery in which there are nearly 900 graves, mainly from November and December 1918, when four casualty clearing stations were located in the town.

* * *

In order to come to an agreement on the terms of the peace settlement, the Allied powers (principally Britain, France, U.S.A. and Italy) held a conference in Paris. The conference itself lasted just three days from 18th to 20th January 1919, but the details of the agreement were delegated to ministers and officials of the governments. These further negotiations were to drag on for six months due to disagreements between the parties over territorial concessions, especially in the Balkans, and arguments over the role of the League of Nations, which was to be set up as an early prototype of today's United Nations.

France demanded the harshest of settlements to be imposed whilst the U.S. Government tried to be more reasonable towards Germany and the other defeated nations.

It was whilst the politicians were squabbling over the destiny of Europe that the last three men named on the Ravensthorpe War Memorial lost their lives.

Stanley Fisher was born in 1893 to Fergus and Elizabeth Jane Fisher. After attending Ravensthorpe St. Saviour's Boys' school, he moved on to the Wheelwright Grammar School in Dewsbury, for whom he played football. Leaving school he went to work first as an errand boy and later as a clerk for the Yorkshire Electric Power Company. Outside school and work Stanley was a bugler in the Church Lads' Brigade, and a member of St. Saviour's Church Choir.

Leaving his widowed mother, he enlisted in the Royal Field Artillery in Huddersfield on 1st June 1915. After training at Ripon and on Salisbury Plain he was sent to France, arriving on 29th December 1915 as part of the 32nd Division's artillery.

It is known that Stanley joined the 168th (Huddersfield) Brigade, R.F.A. as it was with this unit's headquarters that he is listed in the War Diary. According to this diary, the headquarters of the brigade comprised four officers and 43 other ranks. For reasons that will be explained shortly, it is possible that his role within this unit was that of signaller; he may have volunteered or have been selected for this type of work as a result of his pre-war employment.

In April 1917 a letter from Stanley to 'a lady friend' appeared in the Dewsbury Reporter. In this letter he describes the devastation caused by the Germans during their withdrawal to the Hindenburg Line: *"Most of the villages we have passed through have been gutted by the Germans and everything of value has been taken away. All the main roads have been mined, we have been held up at times until large craters were filled up and the guns could pass along. In one French town the civilians gave us a cordial welcome and gave us either tea or coffee to drink and they declined to take any payment. The Bosche cleared out on the Saturday and we were the first British soldiers to enter the town at 10am so I do not think we did badly. The place has been in the hands of Fritz since the commencement of the war. We were billeted in houses but the dirty blighter had broken every piece of furniture in the place we occupied. He had also written on the walls "Gott Strafe England". They are a nation aren't they? The town we are in is one from which Fritz had made a hurried exit, otherwise I have no doubt he would have gutted it as he has done the villages, where he has blown the churches up. In our journey through the villages we slept in holes or any sort of temporary shelter we could find. We are now in action on the outskirts of a ruined village so we set to work, cleaned up a cellar and put a top on it, and there we are living for the time being."*

Stanley's name is listed on the strength of the headquarters of the 168th Brigade, R.F.A. until September 1917 when his name disappears. It can only be assumed that it was at this point he was transferred to the Royal Engineers, with whom he served as a signaller attached to the R.F.A. It is possible he stayed with his unit, the 168th Brigade, simply being absorbed into the Royal Engineers but continuing with the same duties as before.

Stanley's last home leave was in March 1918, after which he returned to his unit and served until the Armistice according to the Dewsbury Reporter 'without a scratch'. In November or early December 1918 he fell ill and was sent to a military hospital at Rouen. After spending some time there he was brought back to England, being admitted to the Bermondsey Military Hospital in mid-December. It seems that Stanley's condition deteriorated and a telegram was sent, resulting in his mother, who lived at 10 Field Street, Ravensthorpe, and his sister-in-law (the wife of his elder brother, Herbert) going down to London. They arrived on Thursday 8th January, but Stanley died four days later on Sunday 12th January from a heart attack. The newspapers, probably quoting a hospital report put his death down to over-exertion and exposure which together with influenza resulted in the 'heart trouble'.

After a service at Ravensthorpe Parish Church (the attendance was described as 'large') Stanley was buried at St. Mary's Parish Church, Mirfield. A military escort was provided, and the Last Post was sounded over the grave.

Compared to the detailed information known about Stanley Fisher, there is very little known about Robert Ouldridge. Robert was the son of Willie and Lillian Ouldridge of 10 Craven Street, Ravensthorpe; he seems to have served in 886 Battery, Royal Field Artillery, although no trace of this unit can be found. He did not serve abroad, and it can only be assumed he was another victim of the influenza epidemic. He died aged 20 on 7th February 1919 and, like Stanley Fisher is buried at Mirfield Parish Church; according to the Ravensthorpe Parish Church magazine he was buried on 11th February. The magazine makes reference to both Stanley Fisher and Robert Ouldridge, indicating they were both *"...well known and loved at our church and were devoted in their attendance as servers at the altar."*

A gap of four months occurred during which there were no additions to the long list of Ravensthorpe's war dead. During this time, many men would have been returning to their homes after receiving their discharge from the army; however men were still required not only for the occupation of part of Germany, but also for the continuing garrison duties in the far-flung corners of the Empire. It was in India in June 1919 that tragedy was to strike, causing the death of the last man to be named on the Ravensthorpe War Memorial.

Harold Vivian Hickling, the son of William and Alice Hickling, was born on 20th April 1891. After attending St. Saviour's Boys' School and later Wheelwright Grammar School in Dewsbury he was apprenticed to a firm of lithographers in Leeds probably as a result of his natural talent for drawing; he subsequently

▲ 163. Stanley Fisher

▲ 164. Robert Ouldridge

worked in Skegness. It was in Skegness that Vivian (as he was known) found himself when war broke out, and volunteered for the army in September 1914. A local 'pals' battalion was being raised at the time under the title 'The Grimsby Chums', which when incorporated into the army became the 10th Battalion, Lincolnshire Regiment, part of the 34th Division. Vivian, together with Fred Holmes (see Chapter 7) are the first of Ravensthorpe's soldiers to gain a mention in the local newspapers, both being listed in the Dewsbury News in December 1914 as *"Wheelwright* [Grammar School] *'Old Boys' serving with the forces."*

The 34th Division went to France, Vivian's battalion landing on 9th January 1916. From a letter written a little time later, it seems that Vivian's active part in the war was not to last very long. According to the letter written to his mother (his father had died), it seems that within a month of arriving in the trenches he was gassed; he wrote: *"....I didn't get long in the trenches did I, just over a month although we had it very bad a time or two. The third time we went in was the Kaiser's birthday (27th January)....the salient at Bois Grenier, where we were, was nearly levelled off...."* Vivian's letter goes on to describe some spy stories that he had heard (such stories were rife at this stage in the war). After being gassed he was sent to Wimereux, near Boulouge to recuperate, from where he sent further letters to his brother and sisters. In these letters he describes gardening and working in the convalescent camp's theatre where he had *"Collared the scenery painting job"*. It seems he spent some considerable time at this camp.

During his stay in the camp, a letter from him to his sister, Beatrice, was reproduced in the Dewsbury Reporter. Part of the letter reads:

"I am getting on as well as can be expected, but am still rather weak. That isn't to be wondered at as I was in bed for nearly three weeks. It is a pleasant change to be here and to walk about without any equipment on, much different from being up the line, where, as you will see (Private Hickling encloses a very clever sketch of himself in full pack) [unfortunately the drawing has not survived] *we carry 'our houses on our backs'. There is a good recreation room here, with billiard tables etc. and for the thirsty a bar where one can get French beer, of which the more one drinks, the more sober one gets - so I am told. We had a thunderstorm last night and it is very warm today. I hope it continues so.......A character I have come across here is Johnson of Shoreditch, who on pay nights is generally to be found in some neighbouring estaminet, making an offer in his native tongue of '50 Francs for any man in the haase as'll stand up and 'ave free raands wiv'im'....In spite of* [Johnson's] *little idiosyncrasies* [he has] *his tender side which is laid bare in his affection for 'Spot'. Spot is a canine acquisition with a wealth of affection, an appalling appetite and no family tree. He has come to stay, at least his collar has disappeared. How's golf going? I wouldn't mind a walk round Coxley* [valley - an area of woodland about four miles from Ravensthorpe] *though I'm afraid it would be rather a slow one."*

A further mention of Vivian appears in the Dewsbury News in May when he writes again from the convalescent camp to the Headmaster of St. Saviour's Boys' School, thanking them for a parcel: *"The contents were very acceptable indeed and they were appreciated greatly by the chaps in our tent. At present I have not much news as a convalescent camp is scarcely a place for excitement."*

After his recovery, Vivian would have been medically examined, and was declared unfit for the rigours of the Western Front. Parts of the British Empire, however, still required a military presence and he was therefore transferred to the

◂ 165. Vivian Hickling

▾ 166. The Kirkee Memorial to the Missing at the rear of the Kirkee War Cemetery. *Photograph courtesy of the Commonwealth War Graves Commission.*

South Staffordshire Regiment, and after a period of leave at home was posted to 'A' Company, 1st Garrison Battalion, and sent out to India in March 1917. The journey, via Sierra Leone, and Cape Town and Durban in South Africa took many weeks, but gave him ample opportunity to draw and paint the various things he came across, including the shipping in the harbours and the docks at the ports en-route.

He arrived in India, probably in May 1917, being stationed near Bombay. Whilst he was away from the Western Front, he was not exactly out of danger; in his weakened condition he would have been more prone than others to the illnesses that can be caught in that part of the world. Over the next two years he contracted dysentery, typhoid fever and at Christmas 1918, influenza; thankfully he managed to survived all these.

A letter to his mother dated 6th February 1919 describes a *"Big Hindoo wedding....the bridegroom was 10 years old and is the heir to £7,000,000. The bride was only six years old but she chucks another £4,000,000 into the pool. There were all kinds of entertainment, Hindoo plays, Dancing Girls and jugglers etc..."* He went on to describe how he was there as a member of the battalion band, but they were not overworked, all they were required to do was *"...play 'Tipperary' about twenty times by request, it is the only English tune they know...."*.

Another letter, dated 18th March was received by his mother in Ravensthorpe, this described the arrival of Earl Jellicoe (*"an insignificant little beggar"*), the former First Sea Lord (*"...of course we had to stand in the sun for a few hours waiting"*).

At the end of May 1919 he wrote to his mother at 719 Huddersfield Road, Ravensthorpe, indicating he was in good spirits; the letter added that he was at Calabar, near Bombay on India's west coast.

On Tuesday 3rd June 1919, Vivian was on the jetty at Pilot Bunder, near Calabar, when a huge wave swept him into the water. Despite a boat being launched to try and save him, because he was a non-swimmer, he had drowned before it reached him. Vivian was 28 years of age.

Vivian Hickling was buried at Bombay (Sewrie) Cemetery, but following India gaining independence it was anounced in 1950 that the cemetery was one of those now deemed to be in an unmaintainable position and he is therefore commemorated on the Kirkee Memorial to the Missing at Poona. The Memorial lists more than 1,800 men who died in the service of the army between 1914 and 1919 whose graves are either unknown, are lost, or are inaccessible.

*   *   *

Meanwhile, in Paris, the negotiations were continuing between the Allied powers as to the terms of the peace treaty to be imposed on Germany. The German High Seas Fleet had, under the terms of the Armistice, been surrendered to the British on 21st November 1918, and since then had been interned at the Royal Navy's base at Scapa Flow in the Orkney Isles pending the signing of the peace treaty. Realising the surrender of the fleet was imminent, the German sailors successfully scuttled their ships on 21st June; this was to be the last wartime act of the German forces. Exactly a week later on 28th June 1919 the Treaty of Versailles was signed in the Hall of Mirrors in the Palace of Versailles.

The treaty was only signed by the Germans under protest, its terms were harsh; France recovered the territories of Alsace and Lorraine it had lost to Germany in the Franco-Prussian War of 1870-1871, and Germany was also forced to cede other areas to Belgium, Denmark and Lithuania. In addition the Rhineland was to be occupied by the Allies for a period of 15 years. Germany's army was to be limited to a maximum of 100,000 men and restrictions were to be placed on the size of her navy. Germany lost all her colonies, which were placed under the control of the League of Nations and massive reparations were ordered to be paid to the Allied nations.

The signing of the peace treaty with Germany signalled the end of the war, although this had effectively been months earlier when the Armistice was signed. To celebrate the treaty, a victory parade was held in London; planning for this had been taking place for months. The celebrations were to take the form of a march-past involving nearly 15,000 troops, with King George V reviewing them from Buckingham Palace. The highlight of the parade, which was held on Saturday 19th July 1919, was when the seemingly never-ending column of troops marched past the temporary structure that had been designed by Sir Edward Lutyens and built in Whitehall. This structure was there to represent the fallen, and took the form of a column of stone, on top of which was a representation of an empty tomb. So popular did this become that the Cenotaph was made permanent, and unveiled on Armistice Day, 1920.

Further peace treaties were imposed on the other enemy nations. In September 1919, the Treaty of St. Germain with Austria effectively broke up the Hapsburg (Austro-Hungarian) Empire; Italy, Rumania, Czechoslovakia and Yugoslavia being the beneficiaries of the subsequent territorial reorganisation. The Treaties of Neuilly (with Bulgaria) in November 1919, Trianon (with Hungary) in June 1920, and Sevres (with Turkey) in August 1920, were also signed, although the Turks were able to renegotiate their treaty to a more favourable one in 1923.

Inevitably, it is the Treaty of Versailles that is remembered; the impositions were to lead to much bitterness amongst the German people for many years, and the world-wide economic slump of the late 1920's and early 1930's together with hyper-inflation in Germany ensured the German population suffered severely during this period. Whilst this may have brought about a sense of satisfaction, especially amongst the French who had suffered themselves at the hands of the Germans, this was ultimately to prove counter-productive.

In Germany the myth grew that the army had not lost the war, but had instead been 'stabbed in the back' by politicians. Field-Marshal Paul von Hindenburg became Chancellor, and presided over the country during the dark years of the depression, but in 1933 following elections, handed over power to a new man, a corporal who had served in The Great War - Adolf Hitler.

Epilogue

In the early months of the Great War, an unframed Roll of Honour was hung at the west end of St. Saviour's Parish Church, this was replaced in November 1916. The new 'war shrine' was dedicated at a memorial service held on Sunday 5th November 1916, it is probable that the new war shrine was placed in the same position as the previous roll of honour, in the south-west corner of the church. According to the Parish Magazine the war shrine contained three rolls: *"Two listing Ravensthorpe Boys who were on active service (and included on one of these a special list of our own Church Lads); the third list will bear the names of the dear, brave fellows from this place who have made the great sacrifice, and who, alas, we shall not see again in this life."*

"Underneath the Rolls of Honour," continues the article, *"will be placed vases of flowers as simple tributes."* A rota was to be organised so that fresh flowers could be placed there each week. Photographs of the soldiers were also provided, which was the start of the invaluable collection now held by St. Saviour's Parish Church.

The dedication service for the new war shrine went on to remember by name 28 local soldiers, although according to the list of names now present on the War Memorial, an additional seven soldiers had been killed by this stage in the war (early November 1916).

A second memorial service was held on 10th June 1917. A further fourteen names had been added to the list of the fallen, although three of these should have been included in the earlier service. Curiously, two of the fourteen (Fred Duxbury and Henry Carter - see Appendices 2 and 4) have not been included on the present day memorial. Again, a number of men were missed off the list of those remembered at this second service and who are now named on the memorial; some of these omissions however, are due to men being posted as 'missing' rather than 'killed'.

Other details about the service include the fact that the organist, Mr Cooper, played the Dead March in 'Saul' and the collection for the Y.M.C.A. realised £2-13s-0d.

On Sunday 28th April 1918, a meeting of the church congregation elected a committee whose role was to consider the construction of a permanent War Memorial.

The Parish Magazine for June 1918 gave notice of another meeting of the congregation at which the findings of the committee would be revealed. A summary of these findings was printed in the magazine. The committee had concluded that a memorial should be built for *"...all Ravensthorpe Men and Lads who shall have fallen in the war, whether definitely connected with the church or not."* Two alternative schemes were put forward.

Scheme 1 was for both a large stone cross outside the church (on the base of which the names of the fallen would be inscribed) and for the completion of the east window. The cost of this scheme *"...should not be more than £1,000."*

Scheme 2 was for the construction of a new tower to the church (the church had, and still has only a small spire). The estimated cost would have been £5,500.

Over the next few months these rather ambitious schemes must have been dropped, as the magazine for January 1919 reported how *"After many schemes had been discussed, the committee arrived at the conclusion that the best War Memorial would be to make the war shrine in church a permanent one, and at a meeting of the congregation in December, they accepted the recommendation."*

An architect, Mr Bilson of Hull was consulted. It was estimated that £150 would be needed and donations would be received on behalf of the committee by Mr J.E. Oldroyd of 116 North Road, or by Mr H. Rothwell of 785 Huddersfield Road.

In February 1919 an invitation was made by the committee for *"The names of all the soldiers and sailors who have fallen in the war, whose parents or friends reside in the parish and who desire to have their names inscribed on the Memorial."* The estimated cost had been revised to £175, of which £45 had already been subscribed.

By May 1919 the estimated cost had again risen, this time to £187, and it was hoped that the Memorial would be in place by the Dedication Festival (the anniversary of the Parish Church's consecration) in September. So far the committee had been promised £117.

The committee met on 27th May 1919. It must have been with some alarm that they heard the estimated cost had again risen, this time to £212, and only £130 had been raised. Despite this, the decision was taken to proceed. The first steps were to obtain consent from the Bishop, (a 'faculty' was required) and to obtain this a 'Vestry Meeting' had to approve the plans. A notice was placed in the porch of the church, giving warning of the meeting, which was to be held on 8th June 1919*.

The formal process of obtaining the Bishop's permission for the construction of the Memorial was completed by August, and at a meeting of the committee on 14th August, the order for the construction was given according to Mr Bilson's design. Unfortunately, there was still a shortfall of £80 and a second appeal had to be launched.

In October's magazine it was announced that a firm in Halifax had started work on the Memorial and that £25 had been promised from the funds of the Men's Bible Class.

For the next eleven months, there was no mention of the new Memorial or whether the required sum had been raised. No doubt news leaked out, but it was not until the September 1920 edition of the magazine that there is any further news of the Memorial. This edition goes into some detail about the dedication of the War Memorial *"...which will take place on Sunday 5th September at 3.00pm."* The article continues, *"It has been erected against the south wall at the west end of the church in place of the temporary shrine, which has been given special sanctity to that corner of the church. The result is pleasing beyond expectation, though nothing could be too good for the purpose..."*

The article goes on to say: *"The Memorial is made from English Wainscot Oak. The panels, on which the names have been inscribed in English gold, have been painted several coats and finished in dark green with flatting varnish. The central figure representing Our Lord in Majesty, the gift of Mrs Beverley+ and Mr B.B. Beverley."* The article concludes by saying that the photographs which surround the temporary shrine would be re-hung opposite the memorial, and shelves would

**** Just before this, on 3rd June, the death occurred, in India of Vivian Hickling (see Chapter 22) - the last man to die who is listed on the Memorial.***

+ The widow of Cecil Beverley (see Appendix 1) who died whilst serving with the army in Salonika. Surprisingly his name is not amongst those listed on the War Memorial, although a brass plaque to the side of the memorial records the fact that the statue forming the centre of the Memorial was given in his memory.

◂ 167. The Ravensthorpe Parish War Memorial, immediately after its installation.

be provided for those who wanted to bring flowers. Dr Walker was thanked for the gift of the carpet.

An article describing the service appeared in the Dewsbury Reporter on 11th September 1920. The church, it said, was *"filled almost to capacity."* Various dignitaries were there and numerous clubs and organisations were represented. The clergy present were Archdeacon How of Halifax; the Reverend R.H. Sutch (vicar); Father Sampson (who had been in charge of the parish whilst Rev. Sutch was with the army as a chaplain); and the Reverend M.A. Maddocks who had left St. Saviour's in 1917 for the Parish of Elland. The hymns included 'Think O Lord in Mercy', 'For All the Saints', 'When the Strife is Fierce' and 'God of Our Fathers, Known of Old'.

Further detail appears in the October magazine, but this contradicts the previous criteria for eligibility on the Memorial by stating that *"Only names of men who lived in Ravensthorpe at the time of enlisting were regarded as being eligible for inscription on the Memorial. However every effort has been made to compile a complete list of names entitled to be inscribed on the shrine but it is just possible that some names have been omitted. The war shrine's committee will deal with any application in the endeavour to rectify any omission."* It is of course unclear how they intended to do this, and it is possible that John Duxbury (see Appendix 2) was such an omission, like his brother Fred, and Henry Carter who have been mentioned earlier.

The final mention of the construction of the War Memorial came in the magazine for March 1921 when the accounts for the memorial committee were published. The carver had charged £218, the architect £22 and other expenses amounted to

£7. These expenses had been funded by donations of £230 and service collections of £21. Other sources brought the total to £266; the surplus of £19 was paid over to the churchwardens towards the cost of alterations to the church that were needed to allow the War Memorial's installation.

*   *   *

The War Memorial has stood in the same place in Ravensthorpe Parish Church since 1920, the only alteration being the addition of 22 names following the end of the Second World War (see Appendix 7) and the removal of the three large frames containing photographs from a nearby wall when the church was redecorated in the 1980's.

It seems that the carpet standing just in front of the memorial is the same one that Dr Walker donated all those years ago.

Whilst the War Memorial has been the focus for the Remembrance Sunday service at church every November, it is likely that, apart from on Remembrance Sunday, an ever diminishing number of people were routinely aware of its presence. Possibly the last people to pay their respects at the memorial on a regular basis were Amelia and Eveline Beckett, the two spinster sisters of Ernest Beckett, who was killed in September 1915. The sisters each lived to a ripe old age, only dying in the 1980's.

By the time of Ernest Beckett's death, a poem had already been written, part of which is repeated in front of War Memorials up and down the country every November; the poem itself is not particularly well known, apart from its middle stanza. It is perhaps fitting for three of its seven stanzas to be reproduced here in memory of the men of Ravensthorpe whose names appear on the Parish War Memorial.

With Proud thanksgiving, a mother for her children,
England mourns for her dead across the sea.
Flesh of her flesh they were, spirit of her spirit,
Fallen in the cause of the free.

They shall grow not old, as we that are left grow old:
Age shall not weary them, nor the years condemn.
At the going down of the sun and in the morning
We will remember them.

As the stars that shall be bright when we are dust,
Moving in marches upon the heavenly plain;
As the stars that are starry in the time of our darkness,
To the end, to the end, they remain.

Lawrence Binyon:
'For the Fallen' (September, 1914)

Appendix I

After the victory parade related in Chapter 22, there was over the following months, a feeling throughout the country that the sacrifice made by the nation in the Great War had to be commemorated; this was in part satisfied by the building of the Cenotaph. As the mammoth task of constructing permanent war cemeteries was started by the Imperial War Graves Commission, this also to a great extent satisfied the public's need for recognition of the war dead; however it was felt that there had to be a focus in this country for the bereaved relatives who had no grave at which they could mourn. A suggestion was made in the Daily Express in September 1920 that the body of an unknown soldier be brought back from France and be buried beneath the Cenotaph.

The vicar of Holy Trinity Church in Margate, the Reverend David Railton, a former army chaplain, suggested that a more suitable place for this soldier to be buried would be within Westminster Abbey. The idea was taken up by the founder of the Imperial War Graves Commission, Fabian Ware and the Dean of Westminster Abbey. After consultations with Buckingham Palace, the proposal was agreed by the Cabinet that the body of an unknown soldier should be exhumed, and reburied in the Abbey.

Arrangements for the selection of the body were put in hand, and the battlefield clearance teams who were combing the former battlefields were ordered to bring the bodies of six unknown British soldiers from the areas they were searching to the town of St. Pol. On the night of 7th/8th November 1920, in a chapel near the St. Pol British Cemetery were collected the bodies of six soldiers, one from each of the battlefields of the Somme, Ypres, Arras, Cambrai, the Marne and the Aisne. An officer, who did not know from which battlefield each of the bodies came, then made a random choice.

The body of this unknown soldier was transported back to London and on 11th November 1920 his coffin was carried on a gun carriage from Victoria Railway Station to the permanent Cenotaph. The streets were lined with huge crowds, and with soldiers with reversed arms and bowed heads. After the King officially unveiled the new Cenotaph at 11am there was a two minutes' silence, and the cortege then moved on to Westminster Abbey. At the Abbey, a burial service took place with full field-marshal's honours. With the highest ranking generals and admirals in attendance, and with King George V as chief mourner, the body of the Unknown Warrior was laid to rest at 11.20am.

* * *

I have, in the course of the book, related the stories of 113 out of the 114 men whose names are listed on the Ravensthorpe War Memorial located within St. Saviour's Parish Church. Many of these men have no known grave and are therefore commemorated on Memorials to the Missing. Unfortunately one name has defied all attempts at investigation, and is therefore Ravensthorpe's own 'Unknown Warrior'.

Upon the panels of the Memorial is listed the name of Charles A. Matthews, his regiment being stated as the K.O.Y.L.I. No man by this name was killed whilst serving with this regiment during the course of the First World War. There is no photograph of him amongst those of the other soldiers' photographs held in the church, and no obituary appeared in either the Dewsbury Reporter or Dewsbury News during the war years. Neither the electoral rolls or the census information so far made available indicates anyone of this name living in Ravensthorpe. There are numerous men of this name (both with and without the middle initial) who were killed in the Great War, but so far I have been unable to link any of them to the Ravensthorpe area.

It is of course possible that whilst Charles Matthews served in the K.O.Y.L.I., he may have been killed whilst serving with another regiment. He may not even have served in the K.O.Y.L.I. at all, but in, for example the Yorkshire Regiment; there are of course other examples of the War Memorial being wrong with details of the regiments (see Chapter 9). The Memorial may have mis-spelt his name (Mathews, for example) or have his Christian name incorrect; he may equally have been from outside Ravensthorpe, this would certainly explain the apparent absence of any mention in the local newspapers. From the lack of detailed information on how the names for the Memorial were compiled, it is even possible he may not have been killed at all; his name may have been included by some family friend or distant relative. Whoever Charles A. Matthews was, it is not inappropriate for his story to be told in the same context as the story of the Unknown Warrior who lies in Westminster Abbey.

*   *   *

Although Charles Matthews is named on the Ravensthorpe War Memorial, there are other men from Ravensthorpe (or with Ravensthorpe connections) who are not listed on memorials within the Parish of Ravensthorpe. Whilst this book has always been intended to be about the 114 men named on the St. Saviour's Parish Church War Memorial, for the sake of completeness, I have undertaken research which has produced a list of these other men. Some of their connections are stronger than others; these men are listed on the following pages. It is certain that there are still more who are connected with Ravensthorpe.

1) Harry Armitage. Born Ravensthorpe, resided Batley, enlisted Leeds. Private in 7th East Yorkshires. Killed in action 18th September 1918. Regimental number 35220. Buried at Gouzeaucourt New British Cemetery, France.

2) Herbert C. Barker. Born Ravensthorpe, resided Batley, enlisted Pontefract. Private in 2nd Royal Scots Fusiliers. Died of wounds 28th September 1918 aged 30. Regimental number 43420. Son of the late J.W. and A. Barker of Dewsbury Moor, husband of Edith Barker of 80 Upper Road, Batley Carr. Buried at Haringhe (Bandaghem) Military Cemetery, Belgium.

3) Harry Beldon. Born Ravensthorpe, resided Dewsbury, enlisted Heckmondwike. Private in 6th Loyal North Lancashires. Died of wounds in

Mesopotamia 9th March 1917. Regimental number 23374. Commemorated on the Basra Memorial to the Missing in Iraq.

4) Cecil Alder Beverley. Born Copley, in Yorkshire, resided Dewsbury, enlisted Liverpool. Corporal in 80th Field Ambulance, Royal Army Medical Corps. Died in Salonika 17th October 1918 aged 32. Regimental number 337395. Husband of Mary Beverley of 'Craig-Owen', Ravensthorpe. Enlisted December 1914. Teacher at Birkenhead Higher Elementary School. Buried in Mikra British Cemetery, Greece. The central figure of Christ on the Memorial was given in his memory. A small brass plaque next to the Memorial commemorates this fact.

5) Percy Bowker. Born Batley, enlisted Dewsbury. Private in 1/5th Northumberland Fusiliers. Killed in action 27th May 1918 aged 19. Regimental number 59935. Son of Mrs Alice Swallow of 448 Huddersfield Road Ravensthorpe. Commemorated on the Soissons Memorial to the Missing, France.

6) Edward Burton. Born West Ardsley, enlisted Dewsbury, resided Ravensthorpe. Sergeant in 148th Company, M.G.C. Killed in action 19th July 1917. Regimental number 23580. Commemorated on a Special Memorial in Ramscapelle Road Military Cemetery, Belgium to those men who were buried at Nieuport Military Cemetery and whose graves could not be identified.

7) Fred Cooper. Driver in Army Service Corps. Died 2nd December 1918 aged 37. Regimental number 7/278387. Husband of Jennie Cooper of 57 Back Albion Street, Ravensthorpe. Buried in Dewsbury Cemetery.

8) Harry Crawshaw. Born Ravensthorpe, enlisted Cleckheaton. Private in 15th West Yorkshires (Leeds Pals). Died of wounds 18th June 1917 aged 23. Regimental number 38430. Son of John and Martha Crawshaw of 23 South Parade, Cleckheaton. Buried at Duisans British Cemetery, France.

9) Charles Arthur Dyson. Born Ravensthorpe, resided Battyeford, Mirfield, enlisted Mirfield. Private in 1st Yorkshires. Died in India 22nd October 1918. Regimental number 10001. Buried in Rawalpindi War Cemetery, Pakistan.

10) John William Gill. Born Cleckheaton, enlisted Dewsbury. Private in 22nd Durham Light Infantry. Killed in action 26th March 1918 aged 19. Regimental Number 78658. Son of Daniel and Cecilia Gill of 33 Low Mills Lane Ravensthorpe. Brother of Arthur Gill who is named on the Parish War Memorial. Commemorated on the Pozieres Memorial to the Missing, France.

11) George Clifford Greenwood. Born Ravensthorpe, enlisted Batley. Gunner in 373 Battery, 96th Brigade R.F.A. Died in Mesopotamia 12th August 1917 aged 31. Regimental number 646508. Husband of Annie F. Greenwood of 17 Talbot Street, Batley. Buried in Basra War Cemetery, Iraq.

12) Edgar Broadbent Haigh. Born Huddersfield, resided Dewsbury, enlisted Heckmondwike. Private in 2/4th Duke of Wellington's. Killed in action 3rd May 1917 aged 22. Regimental number 202338. Son of Tom Haigh of 'Thornleigh' 102

North Road, Ravensthorpe. Commemorated on the Arras Memorial to the Missing, France.

13) Cyril Harding. Born Silverdale, Bristol, resided Ravensthorpe, enlisted Lancaster. Private in 4th Yorkshires. Killed in action 23rd April 1917. Regimental number 235055. Son of Hugh and Ada Harding of Birmingham. Husband of Maggie Harding of Blackpool. Commemorated on the Arras Memorial to the Missing, France.

14) John Richard Hitchen. Born Stackstead, Lancashire, resided Waterfoot, enlisted Bacup. Private in 35th Company, M.G.C. Killed in action 17th July 1917 aged 33. Regimental number 83781. Son of Lily Hitchen of 'Rook View' Booth Road, Stacksteads, Manchester and the late William Hitchen; husband of Eleanor Senior (formerly Hitchen) of 32 Craven Street, North Road, Ravensthorpe. Commemorated on the Arras Memorial to the Missing, France.

15) Harold Hopkinson. Born Ravensthorpe, enlisted Huddersfield. Private in the 2/4th K.O.Y.L.I. Died of wounds 30th September 1918 aged 18. Regimental number 63608. Son of James and Emma Hopkinson of 21 Johnson Street, Hopton. Buried at Grevillers British Cemetery, France.

16) James Hosey. Born Ravensthorpe, enlisted Leeds. Private in the 2nd K.O.Y.L.I. Died of wounds 8th July 1917. Regimental number 38668. Buried at Coxyde Military Cemetery, Belgium.

17) Leonard Jackson. Resided Ravensthorpe, enlisted Dewsbury. Private in the 7th South Wales Borderers. Killed in action in Salonika 18th September 1918. Regimental number 64058. Husband of Martha Jackson of 27 Bradbury Street, Ravensthorpe. Buried at Doiran Military Cemetery, Greece.

18) Percy Jeeves. Born and resided in Dewsbury, enlisted Birmingham. Private in the 15th Royal Warwicks (2nd Birmingham Pals). Killed in action 22nd July 1916 aged 22. Regimental number 611. Son of Edwin and Nancy Jeeves of 1A Craven Street, Ravensthorpe. Commemorated on the Thiepval Memorial to the Missing, France. Possibly the most famous of Ravensthorpe's casualties. Played cricket for Warwickshire and England and was the inspiration behind the naming of P.G. Wodehouse's character in his famous Jeeves and Wooster books.

19) John Alfred Lee. Born Ravensthorpe, resided Mirfield, enlisted Huddersfield. Lance Corporal in the 13th Yorkshires. Killed in action 23rd November 1917. Regimental number 25631. Commemorated on the Cambrai Memorial to the Missing, France.

20) J.S. Lockwood. Born Ravensthorpe, enlisted Leeds. Pioneer in the 59th Division's Signal Company, Royal Engineers, attached to M.G.C. Died of wounds 17th April 1918 aged 31. Regimental number 360401. Son of Frederick and Elizabeth Lockwood of 19 Chesney View, Hunslet. Buried at Haringhe (Bandaghem) Military Cemetery, Belgium.

21) James Herbert Midgley. Born and enlisted in Halifax. Gunner in 'D' Battery 104th Brigade, R.F.A. Died of wounds 17th October 1916 aged 34. Regimental number 49455. Husband of Ada Midgley of 17 Craven Street, Ravensthorpe. Buried in Heilly Station Cemetery, France.

22) Edgar Moore. Born Ravensthorpe, resided and enlisted in Leeds. Lance Corporal in the 15th West Yorkshires (Leeds Pals). Killed in action 1st July 1916 age 22. Regimental number 15/663. Son of Alfred and Helena Moore of Morecambe. Commemorated on the Thiepval Memorial to the Missing, France.

23) William Morris. Born Holbeck, Leeds, resided Ravensthorpe, enlisted Dewsbury. Private in 1st K.O.S.B. Killed in action 30th April 1916. Regimental number 20434. Buried in Auchonvillers Military Cemetery, France.

24) Ralph Fernando Morton. Born Ravensthorpe, resided and enlisted in Blackpool. Private in the 20th Royal Fusiliers. Killed in action 20th July 1916. Regimental number 8849. Buried in Caterpillar Valley Cemetery, France.

25) Fred Newsome. Born Batley Carr, resided and enlisted in Huddersfield. Rifleman in 'C' Coy, 13th Rifle Brigade. Killed in action 12th October 1916 aged 23. Regimental number B/203225 (Was previously number C/7672 in the K.R.R.C., which is the next consecutive number after his brother, below). Son of George and Annie Newsome of 7 Lower Fold Honley, Huddersfield. Native of Ravensthorpe. Buried in Maroc British Cemetery, France.

26) Willie Newsome. Born Ravensthorpe, enlisted Huddersfield. Rifleman in the 18th K.R.R.C. Died of wounds 16th September 1916 aged 21. Regimental number C/7671. Son of George and Annie Newsome of 7 Lower Fold, Honley. Buried in Heilly Station Cemetery, France.

27) Charles Norminton. Born Ravensthorpe, enlisted Hull. Private in the 21st Manchesters. Killed in action 3rd November 1918 aged 21. Regimental number 76508. Son of James and Fanny Norminton of 11 Cracrofts Terrace, Normabell Street, Holderness Road, Hull. Buried in Landrecies British Cemetery, France.

28) William Peace. Born Ravensthorpe, resided Mirfield, enlisted Halifax. Rifleman in the 18th K.R.R.C. (same battalion as Willie Newsome). Killed in action 15th September 1916. Regimental Number C/7160. Buried in Bulls Road Cemetery, France.

29) Arthur Pickles. Born Ravensthorpe, enlisted Cleckheaton. Sergeant in the 3rd West Yorkshires. Died in U.K. 14th May 1915. Regimental number 7468. Buried in Birmingham (Yardley) Cemetery.

30) Walter Pollard. Born Heckmondwike, enlisted Halifax. Private in the 2nd Duke of Wellington's. Killed in action 19th March 1915 aged 30. Regimental number 7710. Brother of T. Pollard of 502 Huddersfield Road, Ravensthorpe. Commemorated on the Ploegsteert Memorial to the Missing, Belgium.

31) Joseph Duncan Reekie. Born Perth, enlisted Dewsbury. Private in the 2nd K.O.Y.L.I. Died in U.K. 28th October 1917 aged 31 of the effects of gas poisoning. Regimental number 28808. Son of Joseph and Elizabeth Reekie of Perth; husband of Alice Reekie of 51 Albion Street Ravensthorpe. Buried in Mirfield Cemetery.

32) Joseph Roche. Born and enlisted in Dewsbury. Private in 2nd K.O.Y.L.I. Killed in action 11th August 1918 aged 29. Regimental number 27488. Husband of Lillian Lockwood (formerly Roche) of 47 Albion Street, Ravensthorpe. Commemorated on the Vis-en-Artois Memorial to the Missing, France.

33) Simon Senior. Born Dewsbury, resided Ravensthorpe, enlisted Breary Banks, Yorkshire. Private in 7th Dragoon Guards. Killed in action 24th March 1918. Regimental number 12740. Buried in Creil Communal Cemetery, Oise, France.

34) William Henry Sharp. Born and resided in Dewsbury enlisted Heckmondwike. Private in 1/4th York and Lancaster Regiment. Died of wounds in U.K. 4th November 1918 aged 28. Regimental number 203351. Son of Andrew and Annie Sharp; husband of W. Heald (formerly Sharp) of 26 Myrtle Avenue, North Road, Ravensthorpe. Buried in Dewsbury Cemetery.

35) Fred Sheard. Born Mirfield, resided Ravensthorpe, enlisted Huddersfield. Private in 10th Lincolnshires (Grimsby Chums). Killed in action 28th April 1917 aged 19. Regimental number 40946. Son of James Sheard and Mary Sheard of 27 Fir Parade, Ravensthorpe. Commemorated on the Arras Memorial to the Missing, France.

36) Ernest Langley Spaight. Born Ravensthorpe, enlisted Dewsbury. Private in 2nd K.O.Y.L.I. Killed in action 2nd February 1915 aged 28. Regimental number 3/1349. Son of Mrs H. Eastwood of 26 Brearley Street, Mount Pleasant, Batley. Commemorated on the Menin Gate Memorial to the Missing at Ypres, Belgium.

37) Walter Speight. Born Ravensthorpe, enlisted Dewsbury. Private in 6th Lincolnshires. Died of wounds 20th July 1917 aged 19. Regimental number 31528. Son of Benjamin and Ellen Speight of 14 Thornville Street, Huddersfield Road, Dewsbury. Buried in Essex Farm Cemetery, Belgium.

38) Harold Taylor. Born Ravensthorpe, enlisted Dewsbury. Private in 6th Queen's Own Royal West Kents. Killed in action 30th August 1918. Regimental number G/31761. Commemorated on the Vis-en-Artois Memorial to the Missing, France.

39) Richard Alfred Tennyson. Born Ravensthorpe, resided and enlisted in Leeds. Private in 2nd West Yorkshires. Killed in action 28th June 1916. Regimental number 9512. Commemorated on the Thiepval Memorial to the Missing, France.

40) Fred Tinkler. [C.W.G.C. give the spelling as 'Tinker'] Born Ravensthorpe, resided Honley, enlisted Huddersfield. Private in 9th Duke of Wellington's. Killed in action 25th April 1917. Regimental number 23602. Commemorated on the Arras Memorial to the Missing, France.

41) Willie Walker. Born Ravensthorpe, enlisted Dewsbury. Private in 7th K.O.Y.L.I. Killed in action 20th November 1917. Regimental number 25159. Commemorated on the Cambrai Memorial to the Missing, France.

42) Fred Watson. Born Ravensthorpe, enlisted Dewsbury. Private in 12th K.O.Y.L.I. (Miners' Battalion). Died of wounds 2nd August 1918 aged 24. Regimental number 12/1555. Son of Mark and Elizabeth Watson of 13 Wilton Street, Batley. Buried in Longuenesse (St. Omer) Souvenir Cemetery, France.

43) Joseph Arthur Watson. Born Batley, enlisted Dewsbury. Private in 1/5th York and Lancaster Regiment. Killed in action 15th April 1918 aged 31. Regimental number 204710. Son of James and Lavinia Watson of Batley; husband of Emily Watson of 800 Huddersfield Road, Ravensthorpe. Buried in Le Grand Beaumart British Cemetery, France; his headstone records that he is *"Buried near this spot"*.

44) George Whittaker. Born Ravensthorpe, enlisted Dewsbury. Private in 2nd K.O.Y.L.I. Killed in action 28th October 1914 aged 19. Regimental number 10952. Son of John Whittaker of 51 King Street, Batley Carr. Commemorated on the Le Touret Memorial to the Missing, France.

45) Harry Wilson. Born Ravensthorpe, enlisted Dewsbury. Gunner in 'A' Battery, 95th Brigade, R.F.A. Killed in action 21st March 1918. Regimental number 232937. Commemorated on the Pozieres Memorial to the Missing, France.

* * *

Besides the Parish Church War Memorial, a number of other War Memorials were constructed in the years after the ending of the First World War. These are described in Appendix 4.

Appendix 2

The Preface to the book describes how the 81 photographs I rediscovered in Ravensthorpe Parish Church had been one of the factors that brought out my interest in the First World War. What I also discovered when comparing the photographs to the names on the memorial was that there was one photograph of a soldier called John William Duxbury whose name was not listed. As mentioned in the Epilogue, it is possible that his name was somehow omitted from the list of 114 men named on the War Memorial.

This curiosity was compounded when the Commonwealth War Graves Commission claimed to have no record of the soldier in question.

Whilst his name has been omitted for some reason from the Parish War Memorial itself, I feel it is necessary to include John's story within this book not only because his photograph is one of those held in the church, but also because his story serves as an example of how whole families were decimated by the Great War.

* * *

In Chapter 2 it was mentioned how many local organisations were motivated to assist the war effort by recruiting men who were associated with the organisation or area, and formed these recruits into battalions. The majority of these battalions were recruited geographically, and such battalions as the Leeds Pals, Bradford Pals and Grimsby Chums were formed. Other battalions were formed not on geographic lines, but by such groups as public schools or those with a common interest such as football*. However it was the West Yorkshire Coal Owners' Association which raised the 'Miners' Battalion' that attracted John William Duxbury.

John (aged 26) was probably influenced to join the Miners' Battalion by his elder brother, Arthur (aged 38) who lived at Bradbury Street, Ravensthorpe. On Tuesday 10th August 1915, they went to the recruiting office in Dewsbury and were given consecutive regimental numbers, Arthur was 1788 and John 1789. Another two brothers also joined the army; Fred, aged 22, lived with John and their mother at 76 Sackville Street, Ravensthorpe and joined the 8th Battalion, K.O.Y.L.I. whilst James Duxbury, aged 28 and married, joined up but was sent to India. The Miners' Battalion was clearly open to all trades - whilst Arthur worked for the Mirfield Colliery Company, John was employed by Pickles and Smithson, chemical manufacturers in Ravensthorpe.

After undergoing training at Otley, the Miners' Battalion (which had by now become the 12th Battalion, Kings Own Yorkshire Light Infantry) became part of the 31st Division and in view of the obvious labouring skills of the majority of its

**** The 16th Battalion, Middlesex Regiment and 18th to 21st Battalions, Royal Fusiliers were the 'Public Schools' Battalions and the 17th and 23rd Battalions, Middlesex Regiment were subtitled the 1st and 2nd Football Battalions.***

members, they became the divisional pioneer battalion. Towards the end of November 1915 orders were received to prepare for service overseas.

Much to everyone's surprise the division was not sent to France, but was instead ordered to Egypt where they were to guard the Suez Canal (see Chapter 17). After a short period in Egypt, the 31st Division was sent to France where, on 1st July 1916 they took part in the opening day of the Battle of the Somme (see Chapter 7). The Miners' Battalion was not heavily engaged in the 1st July attack, although many other battalions from the division were decimated in the unsuccessful attack on the village of Serre. Although the Miners' Battalion lost 37 men killed on 1st July, both Arthur and John Duxbury came through unscathed; the battalion's casualties will have been caused as a result of the German shelling of the British trenches, which the Miners had to man after the waves of infantry were either killed or pinned down in No Man's Land.

One uncanny coincidence which the brothers would undoubtably have been aware of was the fact that one of the main British trenches behind the front line was called Sackville Street, John's address in Ravensthorpe!

Despite being wounded in April 1917 (receiving treatment in France), John survived until 1918. In March of that year the Germans launched a series of offensives one of which was aimed at capturing the vital railway junction at Hazebrouck. As described in Chapter 19, two men from Ravensthorpe had been killed in this sector on 11th April, and a third captured; this was one of the severest crises of the war, with Field-Marshal Sir Douglas Haig issuing his 'Backs to the Wall' exhortation to the troops. It is against this background that John and Arthur Duxbury were involved in the battalion's severest fighting of the war.

The Miners' Battalion's War Diary describes how, in early April 1918, the battalion was out of the line, undergoing training. Orders were received on 10th April, giving instructions to move. On the following day the battalion de-bussed near Vieux-Berquin, and from there marched to Merris. At 8pm orders came through to take up positions astride the Estaires to Caestre road, covering the crossroads in the village of La Couronne. The Miners' Battalion was in position by 9.30pm.

On 12th April the battalion was in much the same position; most of the morning was probably spent constructing trenches. The battalion was unable to gain touch with the troops on either their right or their left. At 3pm enemy machine gun and artillery fire became heavy, and troops on the battalion's left (who, according to the War Diary were from the 29th Division) started falling back. In accordance with its orders the battalion *"..refused its left flank, and pivoting on La Couronne covered the village with its right flank facing east and south-east."* They dug in and spent the night there. The War Diary gave casualties for the day as being two officers and 40 other ranks.

The German attack on the following day (Saturday 13th April) developed at 8.30am. The battalion's left flank easily beat off the attacks by the Germans, all four of which failed. At the crossroads in La Couronne, however, the enemy succeeded in working up a trench that the battalion had constructed, but had been forced to abandon the previous day. From this position, with the aid of trench mortars, the Germans managed to dislodge the defenders who, although forced to fall back formed another line under heavy fire.

The new line faced south-east with its right on a stream; the line extended to the main road where the rest of the battalion was holding off German attacks. Despite

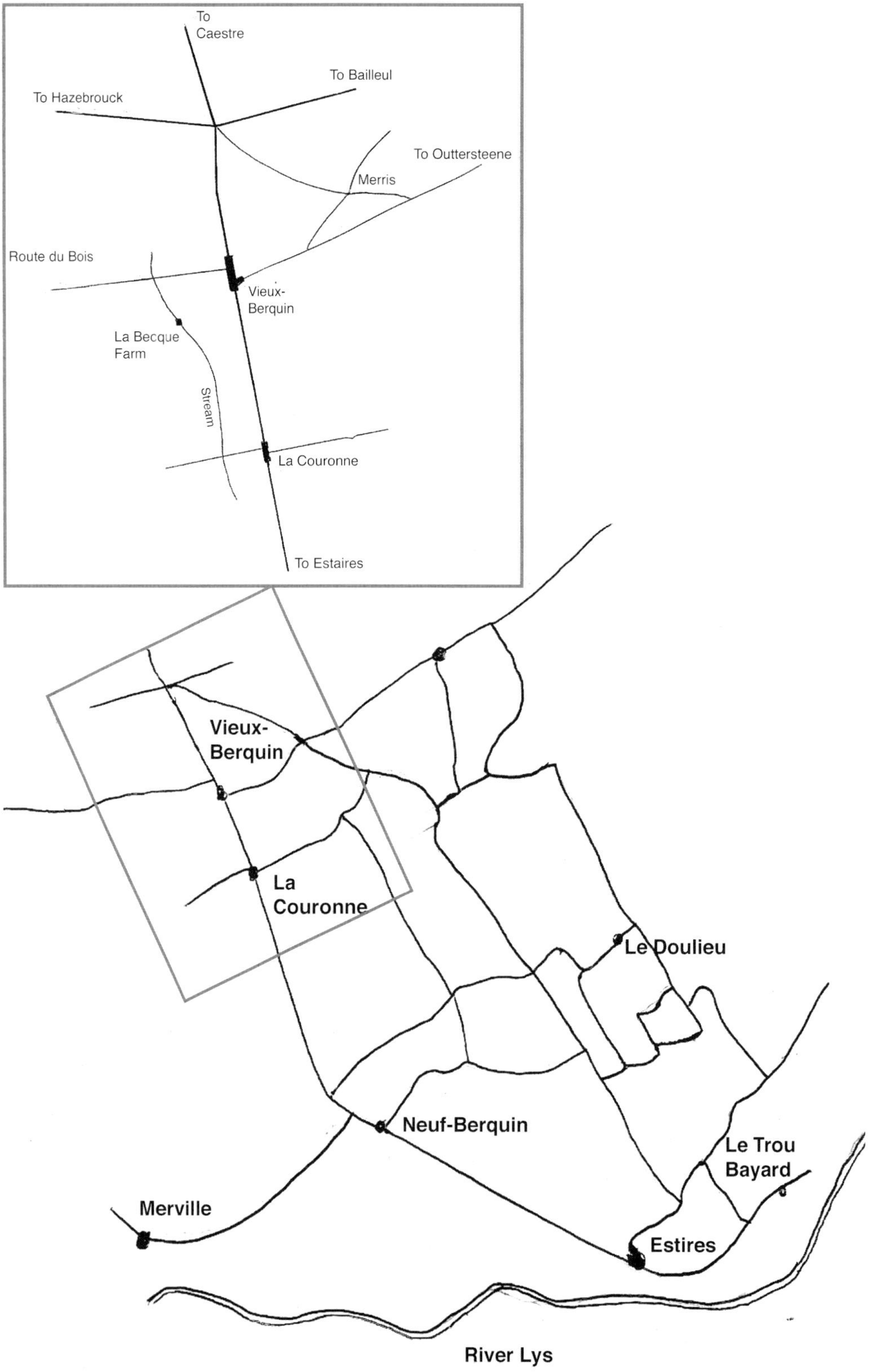

Map 34. La Couronne

◂ 168. John Duxbury, the pick-axe and rifle symbol denoting a member of a pioneer battalion is visible on the collar of his jacket.

now being in touch with the Irish Guards on the right there was a gap here which the Germans exploited and it was from this direction that the battalion was enfiladed at 1.30pm. Shortly after this the Germans, working through the village broke the line. The battalion's right was forced to fall back, and the troops on the left were partially surrounded, many being taken prisoner.

The remnants of the battalion rallied at La Becque Farm, but machine gun fire made the position untenable, and a further withdrawal was made, falling back on posts held by Australian troops on the Route du Bois.

On the morning of 14th April the Miners' Battalion was withdrawn from the line. The War Diary describes how, after going into action with nineteen officers and 510 other ranks, the battalion suffered casualties of twelve officers and about 275 other ranks*. The battalion had, however, accomplished its task, it had delayed the German advance sufficiently to enable troops from the 1st Australian Division to be brought up.

As might be expected, there is no clue in the War Diary of what happened to John and Arthur Duxbury. After sticking closely together throughout the war, on 13th April the brothers' paths diverged. Arthur was captured, probably wounded, by the Germans; he was, together with other prisoners sent to the rear and eventually arrived in Germany, where, just over a fortnight after being captured, he died.

Nothing is known of John's fate. Possibly the family would have realised

***** *S.D.G.W. gives fatalities on 13th April as 59, plus a further two on 14th April.*

something was wrong when they failed to receive a regular letter, or possibly an officer or pal may have written to his mother to say that he had not returned after the battle. Although Arthur was reported as missing towards the end of May, it was not until 29th June that the Dewsbury Reporter printed a few lines to say that *"Private John William Duxbury, son of Mrs Duxbury of 40 Fearnley Street, Dewsbury* is officially reported missing since April."*

The names of 47 of the 59 men killed on 13th April are inscribed on the Ploegsteert Memorial to the Missing, just across the border in southern Belgium. Of the remaining fourteen casualties from the 13th and 14th April, thirteen have known graves +, which leaves one man unaccounted for.

Because of the chaotic circumstances during and after the Great War, it seems that a number of casualties were overlooked by the authorities. It was initially the responsibility of the War Office and not the Imperial War Graves Commission to compile lists of casualties. Somehow the name of John William Duxbury failed to be included in the lists the Imperial War Graves Commission took over from the War Office, and consequently his name was not inscribed on the Ploegsteert Memorial to the Missing. For nearly eighty years, John Duxbury was not officially commemorated by the War Graves Commission.

This oversight was pointed out to the Commission during the course of my research, and after requesting evidence in November 1995, they confirmed (ironically on 14th April 1997, 79 years and one day after his death) that John William Duxbury's name had been added to the Ploegsteert Memorial to the Missing.

John's older brother, Arthur, is buried along with several hundred men who died as prisoners of war in the Commonwealth War Graves Commission plot in Ohlsdorf Cemetery near Hamburg.

Fred Duxbury was one of the casualties of 1st July 1916, he died whilst serving in the 8th Battalion, K.O.Y.L.I. and is commemorated on the Thiepval Memorial to the Missing.

Only James Duxbury came home.

**** Clearly a move from 76 Sackville Street, Ravensthorpe.***

+ One is buried at Ebblinghem Military Cemetery, one at Aire Communal Cemetery and one at Longuenesse (St. Omer) Souvenir Cemetery. A further ten are buried at Outtersteene Communal Cemetery Extension, being two miles north-east of where the battalion fought on 13th April. (It may be fair to assume that some of the unknown headstones in this cemetery stand over the graves of the 47 men named on the Ploegsteert Memorial.)

Appendix 3

Name	Age	Date of Death	Regiment / Corps	Where Buried	Home Address	Employer
1)Willie Allott	24	24th August 1918	18th KRRC	Lijssenthoek Military Cemetery	4 Church Street	?
2)Harry Armitage	28	23rd March 1918	1st Northumberland Fusiliers	Bac-du-Sud British Cemetery	5 Thornville Street, Dewsbury	Lion Stores, Thornhill Lees
3)William Astbury	22	16th June 1915	1/5th Duke of Wellington's	Rue David Military Cemetery	4 Craven Street	'Labourer'
4)Fred Auty	26	27th March 1918	2/7th West Yorkshire	Arras Memorial	21 Field Street	James Walker & Sons
5)J. Arthur Barnes	19	20th July 1918	8th West Yorkshire	Soissons Memorial	5 Dearnley Street	Rawdon, Briggs & Co.
6)Ernest Beckett	25	14th September 1915	1/5th Duke of Wellington's	Bard Cottage Cemetery	12 Calder Road	Armitage & Rhodes
7)William Beckett	24/25	17th December 1915	1/5th Duke of Wellington's	Wimmereux Communal Cemetery	450 Huddersfield Road	?
8)Percy Bennett	24	20th November 1917	2/4th KOYLI	Hermies Hill British Cemetery	32 Netherfield Road	Marshall, Kaye & Marshall
9)John Blakeley	19	11th April 1918	2nd Royal Fusiliers	Ploegsteert Memorial	?	Mr C. Fearnley
10) Charles Blamires	?	18th November 1916	8th Gloucestershire	Thiepval Memorial	35 Albion Street	Kilner Brothers
11) Percy Boothroyd	27	7th December 1916	9th West Yorkshire	St. Sever Cemetery Extension	107 Sackville Street	Co-op Stores, Doncaster
12) Frank Bower	19	29th October 1918	22nd Northumberland Fusiliers	Malbork Memorial	4 Netherfield Road	L&NW Railway
13) Samuel Brierley	27	10th July 1917	2nd Royal Munster Fusiliers	Coxyde Military Cemetery	37 Commercial Street	Armitage & Rhodes
14) Charles Buckley	19	7th March 1918	Royal Field Artillery	St. Mary's Parish Church, Mirfield	57 Clarkson Street	Mirfield Colliery Co.
15) Leonard Calvert	26	29th April 1918	9th KOYLI	Tyne Cot Memorial	18 Warwick Road, Batley Carr	G.H. Hirst & Co.

16) Harry Campbell	32	20th March 1917	221st Siege Battery, RGA	Faubourg d'Amiens British Cemetery	13 Lee Street	Marshall, Kaye & Marshall
17) Fred Cardwell	21	28th July 1916	1/4th KOYLI	Authuille Military Cemetery	31 Commercial Street	Jas Smith & Sons
18) William Cawthorne	21	25th April 1917	27th Northumberland Fusiliers	Arras Memorial	66 Queen Street	G.H. Hirst & Co.
19) James Chapman	33	17th November 1915	21st Trench Mortar Battery, RFA	Hollybrook Memorial	?	Yorkshire Electric Power Co.
20) Philip Chapman	35	26th September 1915	9th Norfolk	Loos Memorial	?	Mirfield Gas Co.
21) Thomas Chapman	38	14th January 1917	XIV Brigade, RHA	Bray Military Cemetery	?	Mirfield Gas Co.
22) Charles Crabtree	40	7th December 1916	Depot, KOYLI	Dewsbury	124 North Road	Chadwick & Son, solicitors
23) Leonard Crane	36	7th October 1916	7th KOYLI	Thiepval Memorial	15 George Street	E.T. Ingham
24) Ralph Crawshaw	32	25th April 1917	9th Duke of Wellington's	Arras Memorial	Spring Place Cottages, Dark Lane, Northorpe	Newsome Brothers
25) Maurice Crossley	19	1st November 1918	1/7th West Yorkshire	Thiant Communal Cemetery	855 Huddersfield Road	?
26) Henry Davill	21	14th November 1918	9th KOYLI	Caudry British Cemetery	79 Sackville Street	Mr George Walker
27) John Davill	22	31st July 1915	West Riding Heavy Battery, RGA	Merville Communal Cemetery	79 Sackville Street	?
28) Albert Dent	19	5th October 1918	2nd Lincolnshire	Thilloy Road Cemetery	23 Aire Street	F.Doble & Sons
29) Ewart Doodson	18	9th April 1917	'D' Battalion, Tank Corps	Arras Memorial	453 Huddersfield Road	Yorkshire Electric Power Co.
30) Fred Eastwood	21?	3rd May 1917	2/5th Duke of Wellington's	Arras Memorial	28 Duke Street	Wormald & Walker
31) Harry Eastwood	24	25th August 1918	2/5th Duke of Wellington's	Douchy-les-Ayette British Cemetery	28 Duke Street	Yorkshire Electric Power Co.
32) Harry Ellam	22	12th February 1917	7th KOYLI	Thiepval Memorial	19 Raven Street	Henry Hamer & Sons
33) Charles Ellis	22	6th April 1918	4th Royal Welsh Fusiliers	Pozieres Memorial	97 Garden Street	Mr C. Fearnley
34) Henry Ellis	23	17th August 1915	7th Royal Munster Fusiliers	Helles Memorial	71 Albion Street	?

35) John Ellis	24	29th March 1917	1/5th York & Lancaster	Pont-du-Hem Military Cemetery	79 Garden Street	Hartley Brothers
36) George English	29	15th June 1918	1st Northumberland Fusiliers	Sandpits British Cemetery	31 Havelock Street	Robert Swire & Sons
37) Frank Fearnsides	20	23rd October 1916	2nd Duke of Wellington's	Thiepval Memorial	5 Cyprus Place, Northorpe	Armitage & Rhodes
38) George Fieldhouse	23	2nd September 1917	2nd Grenadier Guards	Tyne Cot Memorial	19 Armitage Street	Critchley Sharpe & Tetlow
39) Stanley Fisher	25	12th January 1919	Royal Engineers	St. Mary's Parish Church, Mirfield	10 Field Street	Yorkshire Electric Power Co.
40) Herbert Gamble	20	25th February 1917	2/5th KOYLI	Thiepval Memorial	27 Sackville Street	G.H. Hirst & Co.
41) Alfred Gardiner	21	26th September 1915	9th KOYLI	Loos Memorial	9 Armitage Street	Bagley's Glass Works
42) Walter Garfitt	20	5th September 1916	1/5th Duke of Wellington's	Forceville Communal Cemetery Extension	4 Dearnley Street	Howroyd & Oldroyd
43) Lewis Garside	37	8th July 1916	1/4th KOYLI	Serre Road Cemetery Number 2	John Street	Henry Burrows
44) Stanley Gawthorpe	19	3rd September 1916	1/5th Duke of Wellington's	Thiepval Memorial	35 Tanhouse Street	Armitage & Rhodes
45) Arthur Gill	20	21st December 1915	1st West Yorkshire	Lijssenthoek Military Cemetery	33 Low Mills Lane	Rawdon, Briggs & Co.
46) John Gledhill	35	26th September 1917	8th King's Own Royal Lancaster	Tyne Cot Memorial	39 Clarkson Street	Newsome Brothers
47) Cyril Glover	24	20th November 1917	2/4th KOYLI	Hermies Hill British Cemetery	19 Havelock Street	Bell Brothers
48) James Goodfellow	27	19th December 1915	1/4th KOYLI	Bard Cottage Cemetery	3 Bridge Street	G.H. Hirst & Co.
49) William Greaves	21	16th January 1918	1/5th KOYLI	Etaples Military Cemetery	7 Day Street	Rawdon, Briggs & Co.
50) Herbert Greenwood	19	22nd December 1915	1/5th Duke of Wellington's	Talana Farm Cemetery	113 Sackville Street	Henry Hamer & Sons
51)W. Harry Griffith	20	13th April 1918	38th Brigade, RFA	Tyne Cot Memorial	583 Huddersfield Road	?

52) William Haldenby	36	14th October 1917	1st Scots Guards	Bleuet Farm Cemetery	109 Sackville Street	Cottam's Piano Works
53) Clifford Haley	19	13th October 1917	6th KOYLI	Tyne Cot Memorial	65 Sackville Street	Hartley Brothers
54) George Hammond	20	26th October 1915	1/5th Duke of Wellington's	Talana Farm Cemetery	1 Garden Street	Mr A. Algate
55) Arthur Hampshire	34	2nd April 1918	1/4th KOYLI	Tyne Cot Memorial	40 William Street	Lee & Nephew
56) Harry Harris	24	20th July 1916	6th East Lancashire	Basra War Cemetery	20 Commercial Street	Robert Swire & Sons
57) Joseph Harris	23	4th September 1918	10th East Yorkshire	Ploeegsteert Memorial	20 Commercial Street	F. Doble & Sons
58) Harry Hemingway	33	30th September 1918	15th Lancashire Fusiliers	Joncourt East British Cemetery	19 Field Street	Wormald & Walker
59) John Hemingway	26	5th November 1916	7th Yorkshire	Thiepval Memorial	11 Ravenswharf Road, Dewsbury	?
60) Fred Hey	29	14th October 1917	1/5th Duke of Wellington's	Wimereux Communal Cemetery	16 Bradbury Street	?
61)H. Vivian Hickling	28	3rd June 1919	1st Garrison, South Staffordshire	Kirkee Memorial	719 Huddersfield Road	?
62) Ernest Hinchcliffe	21	3rd September 1916	1/5th Duke of Wellington's	Thiepval Memorial	839 Huddersfield Road	Rawdon, Briggs & Co.
63) John Hinchliffe	24	11th August 1916	1/5th York & Lancaster	St. Mary's Parish Church, Mirfield	23 Lee Street	Grimethorpe School
64) Wilfred Hirst	24	26th October 1917	426 Field Coy, Royal Engineers	St. Mary's Parish Church, Mirfield	26 Dearnley Street	Kershaw Brothers
65) George Hoggarth	20	9th October 1916	HMS Mounsey, Royal Navy	Plymouth Naval Memorial	24 Bell Street	Mirfield Colliery Co.
66) Charles Hollingworth	24	30th October 1917	6th Yorkshire	St. Mary's Parish Church, Mirfield	775 Huddersfield Road	Henry Wheatley & Sons
67) Fred Holmes	27	1st July 1916	9th KOYLI	Thiepval Memorial	5 Beacon Street	Marshall, Kaye & Marshall
68) William Hopkinson	32	20th November 1917	7th KOYLI	Cambrai Memorial	20 Beacon Street	Yorkshire Chemical & Dyework Co.

69) Bertie Howroyd	19	6th September 1917	10th West Yorkshire	Brown's Copse Cemetery	93 Clarkson Street	Pickering Greaves & Co.
70) George Jackson	45	7th June 1917	14th Training Reserve	St. Mary's Parish Church, Battalion	40 Crawshaw Street Mirfield	Thornhill Cabine Co.
71) Albert Jewsbury	19	23rd October 1915	1/5th Duke of Wellington's	Talana Farm Cemetery	30 Broomer Street	Yorkshire Electric Power Co.
72) William Kay	30	14th September 1914	1st Northumberland Fusiliers	La Ferte-sous-Jouarre Memorial	16 Aire Street	L&Y Railway
73) William Kendall	22	30th July 1918	2nd KOSB	Tannay British Cemetery	11 Dearnley Street	Three Nuns Pit
74) Arthur Kershaw	24	3rd May 1917	2/5th Duke of Wellington's	Arras Memorial	Gladys Street, Liversedge	?
75) Charles Lapish	29	23rd October 1917	10th KOYLI	Tyne Cot Memorial	36 Clarkson Street	Yorkshire Chemical & Dyework Co.
76) Joseph Laycock	23	15th September 1918	2nd Garrison, Northumberland Fusiliers	Baghdad (North Gate) War Cemetery	Eastfield Road, Northorpe	G. & J. Stubley
77) Luke Leadbeater	19	22nd November 1917	1/5th Duke of Wellington's	Aeroplane Cemetery	636 Huddersfield Road	Jas Smith & Sons
78) Ernest Ledgard	37	20th September 1917	68th Coy, MGC	Tyne Cot Memorial	285 Ravenswharf Hill, Dewsbury	L&Y Railway
79) George Ledgard	19	22nd November 1917	2/8th West Yorkshire	Cambrai Memorial	569 Huddersfield Road	Jas Smith & Sons
80) Arthur Lister	30	28th October 1918	2nd Siege Battery, RGA	Premont British Cemetery	2 Scout Hill Terrace, Dewsbury	Mark Oldroyd & Sons
81) Harry MacDonald	30	6th December 1918	HMS Europa, Royal Navy	East Mudros Military Cemetery	6 Duke Street	Mr A. Algate
82) Charles Matthews	?	?	?	?	?	?
83) Fred Mellor	39	14th December 1916	12th (Labour)Bttn, Lincolnshire	Janval Cemetery	2 Charles Street	Publican - New Albion Inn
84) Willie Mellor	40	21st January 1916	Steam Trawler 'Earl'	Tower Hill Memorial	6 Glasgow Street, Hull	Great Northern Company

85) Herbert Nicholls	20	14th August 1917	87th Battalion, CEF	Vimy Memorial	62 Muriel Avenue, Toronto	'Farmer'
86) Allen Oldroyd	32	16th February 1917	8th KOYLI	Boulogne Eastern Cemetery	4 West Vale, Dewsbury	Standard Patent Glazing Co.
87) Horace Oldroyd	18	14th February 1916	7th Yorkshire	Menin Gate Memorial	49 Garden Terrace	Marshall, Kaye & Marshall
88) Robert Ouldridge	20	7th February 1919	886 Battery, Royal Field Artillery	St. Mary's Parish Church, Mirfield	10 Craven Street	?
89) Hubert Oxley	21	12th September 1915	2/5th Duke of Wellington's	Edgerton Cemetery, Huddersfield	130 North Road	?
90) John Pattinson	38	26th September 1915	10th KOYLI	Loos Memorial	18 Duke Street	Canal Boatman
91) George Pickles	33	5th August 1917	106th Field Coy, Royal Engineers	Menin Gate Memorial	47 John Street	Morton Son & Co.
92) Albert Pizer	20	1st July 1916	10th KOYLI	Thiepval Memorial	98 North Road	Wormald & Walker
93)W. Ewart Popplewell	19	7th November 1915	1/5th Duke of Wellington's	Talana Farm Cemetery	73 Garden Street	Fred Ellis Ltd
94) Fred Preston	19	10th October 1918	6th Lincolnshire	Naves Communal Cemetery Extension	783 Huddersfield Road	Preston & Burnett
95) William Ridley	21	27th August 1917	8th Duke of Wellington's	Tyne Cot Memorial	8 Spen Valley Road	Jas Smith & Sons
96) John Roberts	19	22nd March 1918	2nd Lincolnshire	Pozieres Memorial	26 Lee Street	?
97) John Schofield	24	25th August 1918	5th Duke of Wellington's	Gomiecourt South Cemetery	13 Field Street	Rawdon, Briggs & Co.
98) Horace Scott	19	10th October 1918	1/5th East Lancashire	Tourgeville Military Cemetery	11 Hebble Street	F. Doble & Sons
99) Arnold Sheard	20	14th March 1918	Royal Defence Corps	St. Mary's Parish Church, Mirfield	2 Field Street	Armitage & Rhodes
100) Clifford Simpson	23	16th August 1917	1st KOSB	Tyne Cot Memorial	141 Sackville Street	Rawdon, Briggs & Co
101) Fred Smith	25	26th September 1915	9th KOYLI	Loos Memorial	21 Hebble Street	Marshall, Kaye & Marshall

102)	George Sutcliffe	33	23rd July 1917	1/4th KOYLI	Adinkerke Churchyard Extension	751 Huddersfield Road	Mr Sam Schofield
103)	Fred Sykes	22	3rd May 1917	2/5th Duke of Wellington's	Achiet-le-Grand Communal Cemetery Extension	36 Woodbine Street, Dewsbury	Crawshaw and Warburton's Colliery
104)	Neville Tattersfield	26	20th November 1918	'B' Battalion, Tank Corps	Wareham Parish Church	64 North Road	Jas Smith & Sons
105)	Isaac Thompson	31	13th November 1917	1/5th KOSB	Jerusalem Memorial	35 Bradbury Street	Dewsbury Corporation
106)	Arnold Tompkins	20	31st July 1917	6th/7th Royal Scots Fusiliers	Tyne Cot Cemetery	126 North Road	Self-employed barber
107)	Ernest Walker	20	12th August 1916	6th/7th Royal Scots Fusiliers	Thiepval Memorial	17 Foundry Street	Robert Swire & Sons
108)	John Walker	19	28th June 1916	4th Battalion, Special Brigade, Royal Engineers	Avesnes-le-Comte Communal Cemetery Extension	53 Sackville Street	L&NW Railway
109)	Frederick Watson	39	27th August 1918	5th KOYLI	Gomiecourt South Cemetery	3 William Street	Pre-war regular
110)	Tom Wattam	24	16th December 1918	'L' Siege Park, RASC	Valenciennes Communal Cemetery	3 Bradbury Street	James Walker & Sons
111)	Harry Webster	29/30	3rd May 1917	2/5th Duke of Wellington's	Arras Memorial	20 Charles Street	J. & J. Wilkinson
112)	Jack Whiteley	18	11th April 1918	1/6th Northumberland Fusiliers	Ploegsteert Memorial	273 Scout Hill, Dewsbury	?
113)	Friend Whitwam	42	21st October 1917	13th Durham Light Infantry	Tyne Cot Memorial	11 William Street	Yeast Dealer
114)	Beaumont Wood	28	10th October 1916	26th Royal Fusiliers	Etaples Military Cemetery	34 Myrtle Avenue	Marshall, Kaye & Marshall

◂ 169. The names on the Ravensthorpe Parish War Memorial.

▾ 170. Note the jumbling of the order in the H's.

Appendix 4

The men listed on the Ravensthorpe Parish Church War Memorial (see Appendix 3) were not the only men from the village to lose their lives during the Great War. Although the Parish Church's War Memorial covers the vast majority of the village's war dead, as mentioned in Appendix 1, there were other men who were omitted. Some of these have been named on other War Memorials within Ravensthorpe, others have not been included on any known War Memorial, but were remembered by name in services of remembrance held during the war.

A special memorial service held at St. Saviour's Church on Sunday 10th June 1917 commemorated a total of 41 men who had been killed in the war up to that point; the Dewsbury Reporter dated 16th June gave details of the service and listed the names of the men from Ravensthorpe who were being commemorated (an earlier service had been held on Sunday 5th November 1916).

The list of names provided by the Dewsbury Reporter does have some anomalies when compared to the War Memorial, some fourteen men were omitted from the list:- William Kay, Philip and Jim Chapman (but not Tom Chapman), John Pattinson, Willie Mellor (but not Fred Mellor), Ernest Hinchcliffe, Charles Blamires, Allen Oldroyd, Harry Campbell, Willie Cawthorne, Ralph Crawshaw, Arthur Kershaw, Fred Eastwood and Harry Webster although it must be said that the last four named may still have still been classified as 'missing' and not 'killed'. (It is most surprising that Harry Campbell was not included as he seems to have been very well respected within St. Saviour's; perhaps he was included in the service and his name was accidentally overlooked by the Dewsbury Reporter.)

Curiously, however, the names of two men that did not eventually make it onto the Parish War Memorial were included in the service, being Fred Duxbury (who is mentioned in Appendix 2) and Henry Carter.

Henry Lodge Carter was yet another member of the 1st Battalion K.O.S.B.; the others from this battalion are Clifford Simpson (Chapter 14); Isaac Thompson (Chapter 17); Willie Kendall (Chapter 20); and William Morris (Appendix 1). Henry Carter was born in Kirkheaton, but resided and enlisted in Dewsbury; he died on 28th January 1917 and is commemorated on the Thiepval Memorial to the Missing. He was the son of Alice Sykes of 2 Mitchell's Row, Dale Street, Ossett.

* * *

In the Prologue, I mentioned the various non-conformist churches that were situated in Ravensthorpe at this time. Whilst none of these exist today*, each had its own Roll of Honour.

The Congregational Church building was demolished in about 1974, its successor, the United Reformed Church was built on the site of the old church. The Wesleyan Chapel is still standing, and is now one of the two mosques within Ravensthorpe, which is very much a multi-cultural community.

The Congregational Church - The War Memorial for this church took the form of a font. Now standing in the United Reformed Church, this names fourteen men connected with this church who were killed in the war: W. Astbury; F. Auty; J. Arthur Barnes; R. Crawshaw; E. Doodson; C. Ellis; S. Gawthorpe; J. Gledhill; C. Haley; W. Kendall; C. Oates; H. Scott; H. Sutcliffe and C.G. Walker. All but three of these names appear on the Parish War Memorial.

Cyril Oates, aged 19 was killed in action on 17th September 1918 whilst serving as a private in the 9th Battalion, Duke of Wellington's Regiment. He was the son of Mr and Mrs Thornton of 17 Lee Green Mirfield. Cyril is commemorated on the Vis-en-Artois Memorial to the Missing, France.

Herbert Sutcliffe was a corporal in 9th K.O.Y.L.I. and was killed in action on 7th November 1918, aged 32. He lived with his wife, Gertrude at 'Hazlehurst' 122 North Road, Ravensthorpe. Herbert is buried in Maubeuge Centre Cemetery, France.

C.G. Walker: unfortunately it has not been possible to trace this individual.

In addition to the font, there is a small plaque commemorating seven of these men who, as youngsters, were members of the church's Boys' Club.

The Wesleyan Methodist Church - This memorial is in two parts. The first lists ten men, nine of whom are named on the Parish Church War Memorial. Those listed are: Leonard Calvert; John Hemingway; Bertie Howroyd; Fred Hey; Joseph Laycock; John Roberts; John Schofield; John Schorah; Clifford Simpson and Jack Whiteley. The second part of the memorial names 90 men from the church who served in the armed forces but who survived. John Schorah (the soldier from this Memorial not named on the Parish Church Memorial) was born and resided in Batley, but enlisted in Leeds, in the West Yorkshire Regiment. He died, aged 36, on 30th October 1918 whilst serving in India in the 1st (Garrison) Battalion, Yorkshire Regiment. He is commemorated on the Karachi 1914-18 War Memorial in Pakistan.

The United Methodist Church ("*New Connection*") - On this memorial are listed Percy Bennett; Willie Beckett; Fred Cardwell; Albert Dent; Herbert Greenwood; Joe Harris and his brother Harry Harris; George Hammond; George Ledgard; Luke Leadbeater; and Horace Scott. It also names 55 more men who served and who seem to have survived the conflict.

The Primitive Methodist Church - lists Percy Boothroyd; John Ellis; Herbert Gamble and Friend Whitwam, all four of whom are named on the Parish War Memorial. It also names 38 men who were connected with the church who joined up.

* * *

Besides the War Memorials located in churches and listed above, at least three further War Memorials were built. One of these, in St. Saviour's Church school, has disappeared following the demolition of the building in 1987. The other two were commissioned by the Liberal and Working Men's Clubs.

The Dewsbury Reporter for 5th July 1919 gives a brief description of the unveiling of the War Memorial in the Central Working Men's Liberal Club, on which was listed the names of eleven men. Nine of those named (Harry Campbell, Charles Crabtree, Leonard Crane, John Gledhill, Ernest Ledgard, Harry MacDonald, Fred Mellor, Fred Smith, and Isaac Thompson) also appear on the Parish Church's War Memorial; George Boothroyd and William Sheard do not.

William Duncan Sheard was born in Ravensthorpe and enlisted in Dewsbury. He initially served in the Royal Army Service Corps until being transferred to the Tank Corps. He was killed on 29th September 1918 whilst serving with the 17th Battalion and is buried in Templeux-le-Guerard British Cemetery. He was awarded the Military Medal.

George William Boothroyd was born in Hanging Heaton, Dewsbury but lived in Ravensthorpe. He enlisted in Dewsbury and went to Mesopotamia where he died whilst serving with the 1st Battalion of the Connaught Rangers on 14th October 1916. He has a special headstone in Baghdad (North Gate) Cemetery, indicating he was originally buried at Nisibin, but his grave was lost or was deemed to be unmaintainable.

The Liberal Club, as it was known, fell into disuse and was demolished in the late 1990's; the location of the War Memorial is not known, it is likely to have been destroyed along with the building in which it stood.

After the Second World War, a memorial was erected in the Working Men's Club to the members of the club who had given their lives in the two world wars. Of the twelve men from the First World War named on this memorial, five are 'new' names. Unlike the two 'new' men on the Liberal Club War Memorial, none of these men have an obvious link to Ravensthorpe other than the fact they were members of its Working Men's Club, presumably they had jobs in the village. The men listed on this memorial are: A. Armitage, W. Booth, S. Brierley, J. Chapman, P. Chapman, T.W. Chapman, A. Hampshire, H. Hemingway, G.A. Pickles, J. Simpson, C. Speight, and H. Townend. The 'new' men on this list are:

A. Armitage. Arthur was a member of the 6th Battalion, Connaught Rangers. He was killed on 21st December 1917, aged 28 and is buried at Ronssoy Communal Cemetery, France.

W. Booth. This is either: **Wilfred Booth** of the 1/4th K.O.Y.L.I., killed on 7th July 1916 aged 21 and commemorated on the Thiepval Memorial to the Missing or **Walter Booth** of the 1/5th Duke of Wellington's, killed on 3rd September 1916 aged 39 and buried at Serre Road Cemetery Number Two.

J. Simpson. Probably James Henry Simpson, who was another member of the 1/5th Duke of Wellington's, who was killed on 3rd September 1916, aged 28. Commemorated on the Thiepval Memorial to the Missing.

C. Speight. Charles was a member of the 10th Battalion, York and Lancaster Regiment, and was killed on 15th November 1916, aged 33. Charles is commemorated on the Thiepval Memorial to the Missing.

H. Townend. This could be one of three men but is most likely to be Harry Townend, of the 2/4th K.O.Y.L.I., killed in action on 27th November 1917 and commemorated on the Cambrai Memorial to the Missing.

* * *

In addition to these War Memorials in Ravensthorpe, on Saturday 6th September 1924, Lieutenant-General Sir Walter Braithwaite unveiled the Dewsbury Borough War Memorial in Crow Nest Park. This memorial lists 1,054 men from the various villages and communities that make up the Dewsbury Borough. All 114 men named on the Ravensthorpe Parish Memorial also appear on this memorial.

* * *

In attempting to compile a definitive number of men from Ravensthorpe who were killed in the First World War, many problems are encountered, the main one of which is how one defines "from Ravensthorpe". Clearly Charles Matthews is the most obvious example here, but Herbert Nicholls also has no obvious link with the village. Others named on the Parish Memorial have varying claims to be "from Ravensthorpe" as many lived out of Ravensthorpe's boundary even though they attended the Parish Church. Using the 114 men named on the Parish Memorial as a starting point, and with the four extra men named on the Wesleyan and Congregational Church Memorials, there are 118 men named on Church War Memorials in the village.

The Liberal and Working Men's Clubs between them added a further seven names, giving 125. By adding the two men (Henry Carter and Fred Duxbury) from the Memorial Service who are not commemorated, plus the other two Duxbury brothers whose stories are told in Appendix 2, Ravensthorpe's war dead rises to 129. By adding the 45 named in Appendix 1 this gives a total of 174 men from Ravensthorpe killed during the Great War. Out of a total pre-war population of about 6,400, this was a significant loss to such a small and close-knit community.

May their Names Live for Evermore.

▲ 171. The unveiling of the Crow Nest Memorial to the dead of the Borough of Dewsbury. *Photograph courtesy of Kirklees Community Service.*

Appendix 5

Order of Battle of 49th and 62nd Divisions

Using the two West Riding Divisions, this appendix is an attempt to show how the infantry was organised in the Great War. (These two divisions have been selected because 35 of the men named on the Ravensthorpe Parish War Memorial were serving in battalions from these two divisions when they were killed.)

As can be seen, a massive reorganisation of the structure of British divisions in the B.E.F. was undertaken in the early months of 1918, which resulted in the strength of each infantry brigade being reduced from four to three battalions (see also Chapter 18 for details of this reorganisation).

Unfortunately space does not make it possible to list the Order of Battle for each division mentioned in the book.

49th (West Riding) Division
From arrival in France (April 1915) to re-organisation (January 1918)

146 Brigade

1/5th West Yorks	1/6th West Yorks
1/7th West Yorks	1/8th West Yorks

147 Brigade

1/4th Duke of Wellington's	1/5th Duke of Wellington's
1/6th Duke of Wellington's	1/7th Duke of Wellington's

148 Brigade

1/4th K.O.Y.L.I.	1/5th K.O.Y.L.I.
1/4th York & Lancaster	1/5th York & Lancaster

Pioneers - 3rd Monmouth*

The 3rd Battalion, Monmouthshire Regiment was replaced by the 19th Lancashire Fusiliers in August 1916.

49th (West Riding) Division
From re-organisation (January 1918) to Armistice

146 Brigade

1/5th West Yorks	1/6th West Yorks
1/7th West Yorks	

147 Brigade

1/4th Duke of Wellington's	1/6th Duke of Wellington's
1/7th Duke of Wellington's	

148 Brigade

1/4th K.O.Y.L.I.	1/4th York & Lancaster
1/5thYork & Lancaster	

Pioneers - 19th Lancashire Fusiliers.

62nd (West Riding) Division
From arrival in France (January 1917) to reorganisation (January 1918)

185 Brigade

2/5th West Yorks	2/6th West Yorks
2/7th West Yorks	2/8th West Yorks

186 Brigade

2/4th Duke of Wellington's	2/5th Duke of Wellington's
2/6th Duke of Wellington's	2/7th Duke of Wellington's

187 Brigade

2/4th K.O.Y.L.I.	2/5th K.O.Y.L.I.
2/4th York & Lancaster	2/5th York & Lancaster

Pioneers - None

62nd (West Riding) Division
From reorganisation (January 1918) to Armistice

185 Brigade
2/5th West Yorks*
2/7th West Yorks +
8th West Yorks

186 Brigade
2/4th Duke of Wellington's
5th Duke of Wellington's
2/7th Duke of Wellington's +

187 Brigade
2/4th K.O.Y.L.I.
5th K.O.Y.L.I.
2/4th York & Lancaster

Pioneers - 1/9th D.L.I.

** The 2/5th West Yorks was disbanded in August 1918 and replaced by the 2/20th (County of London) Battalion (Blackheath and Woolwich), London Regiment.*
+ The 2/7th West Yorks and 2/7th Duke of Wellington's were replaced by the 1/5th Battalion, Devonshire Regiment and the 2/4th Battalion, Hampshire Regiment respectively, in June 1918.

Appendix 6

The Western Front Association

The Western Front Association (a Registered Charity) was formed to further interest in the period 1914-1918. Its principal objective is to perpetuate the memory, courage, and comradeship of those, on all sides, who served their country in France and Flanders. It does not seek to glorify war, is entirely non-political and welcomes members of all ages.

There are numerous branches of the Association throughout Britain, there are others in Europe and North America. These branches hold meetings, usually on a monthly basis, at which, typically, a speaker will address members on a particular aspect of the war.

A copy of the Association's magazine 'Stand To!' is sent to members three times a year; the W.F.A. Bulletin, another publication, is also sent to members, again three times a year. Both of these magazines contain articles about the Great War, together with book reviews, lists of future regional and national events, and reports on the Association's activities.

The Western Front Association was founded by John Giles in 1980. Its Patron is John Terraine, Honorary President is Correlli Barnett, and Honorary Vice Presidents are General Sir Anthony Farrar-Hockley; The Earl Haig; The Earl Kitchener; Colonel Terry Cave; John Toland; Professor Peter Simkins; The Burgomaster of Ypres and the Mayor of Albert.

For full details of the Association, send a stamped addressed envelope to The W.F.A., P.O. Box 1914, Reading, Berkshire, RG4 7YP.

Appendix 7

World War II

Following the Second World War, a list of twenty two parishioners who had lost their lives in this conflict was compiled. At a special service on Sunday 22nd April 1951, the addition to the War Memorial was dedicated.

(1) Stanley Armitage. Marine. 4th Royal Marines Light Anti-Aircraft Regiment. 16th December 1944. Aged 31. Son of Florry Armitage of Ravensthorpe. Buried at Schoonselhof Cemetery, Antwerp, Belgium.

(2) Colin Batley. Corporal. 5th Battalion, Northamptonshire Regiment. 17th January 1945. Aged 28. Son of Rufus and B. Batley of Ravensthorpe. Buried at Santerno Valley War Cemetery, Italy.

(3) William Bedford. Private. 2nd Battalion, York and Lancaster Regiment. 1st June 1944. Aged 25. Son of Aquila and Mary Bedford of Ravensthorpe. Buried at Taukkyan War Cemetery, Rangoon, Burma.

(4) Clifford Auckland Bentley. Sub-Conductor. Royal Artillery, attached to Indian Army Ordnance Corps. 18th/19th May 1943. Aged 24. Son of Mr and Mrs C. Bentley of Mirfield. Commemorated on the Rangoon Memorial, Burma.

(5) George Crabb. Sergeant. Royal Air Force Volunteer Reserve. 612 Squadron. 18th March 1944. Commemorated on the Runnymede Memorial, Surrey.

(6) George William Farrand. Private. 3 Sub Depot Royal Army Ordnance Corps. 10th November 1939. Aged 21. Buried at Escoublac-la-Baule War Cemetery, France.

(7) Herbert Richard Gibbs. Gunner. 4 Medium Regiment, Royal Artillery. 2nd June 1940. Aged 32. Buried at Etaples Military Cemetery, France.

(8) Walter Gledhill. Corporal Air Gunner. Royal Air Force Volunteer Reserve. 2839 Squadron, Royal Air Force Regiment. 6th November 1942. Aged 39. Son of Harry and Mary Elizabeth Gledhill of Dewsbury; husband of Florrie Gledhill of Ravensthorpe. Buried at Dewsbury Cemetery.

(9) Ernest Greaves. Corporal. The Black Watch (Royal Highland Regiment). 8th April 1943. Aged 28. Son of Francis and Lona Jane Greaves; husband of Audrey Greaves of Savile Town, Dewsbury. Buried at Dewsbury Cemetery.

(10) Stanley Hepworth. Sick Berth Attendant. Royal Navy. 10th September 1944. Buried at Mirfield (St. Mary's) Churchyard.

(11) Reuben Jackson. Private. 2nd Battalion, West Yorkshire Regiment. 19th June 1942. Aged 21. Buried at Delhi War Cemetery, India.

(12) Harry Harker Marshall. Able Bodied Seaman. Royal Naval Patrol Service. H.M. Trawler 'Colsay'. 2nd November 1944. Commemorated on the Lowestoft Naval Memorial.

(13) William Henry Morton. Marine. Royal Marines. 4th August 1944. Aged 21. Son of Clarence and Martha Morton, of Scout Hill, Dewsbury. Buried at Mirfield (St Mary's) Churchyard.

(14) Arnold Newsome. Able Bodied Seaman. Royal Navy. H.M. President III, lost in S.S. Radhurst. 21st February 1943. Aged 35. Commemorated on the Portsmouth Naval Memorial.

(15) Walter Sampson Poskitt. Lance Corporal. York and Lancaster Regiment. 31st January 1941. Aged 40. Husband of Annie Maria Poskitt of Ravensthorpe. Buried at Dewsbury Cemetery.

(16) Cecil Burnley Robertshaw. Flight Sergeant (Wireless Operator / Air Gunner). Royal Air Force Volunteer Reserve. 514 Squadron. 13th August 1944. Buried at Reichswald Forest War Cemetery, Germany.

(17) Harry Roscoe. Sergeant. Royal Air Force. 18th November 1942. Aged 22. Son of Fred and Elizabeth Roscoe of Ravensthorpe. Buried at Dewsbury Cemetery.

(18) Albert Smith. Able Bodied Seaman. Royal Navy. S.S. Freidig. 7th February 1944. Aged 31. Son of Charles and Isabelle Smith; husband of Phyllis Smith of Ravensthorpe. Commemorated on the Chatham Naval Memorial.

(19) Kenneth Sykes. Fusilier. 6th Battalion, Royal Scots Fusiliers. 26th June 1944. Aged 19. Buried at St. Manuieu War Cemetery, France.

(20) Clifford Tudor. Leading Aircraftman. Royal Air Force Volunteer Reserve. 18th June 1943. Aged 19. Son of Mr and Mrs Reuben Tudor of Ravensthorpe. Buried at Davidson Cemetery, Saskatchewan, Canada.

(21) John Marlborough Wailes. Lance Corporal. 4th Battalion, Coldstream Guards. 28th February 1945. Aged 25. Son of John R. and Dinah Wailes of Ravensthorpe. Buried at Reichswald Forest War Cemetery, Germany.

(22) Frank Webster. Marine. Royal Marines, H.M.S. 'Keren'. 17th June 1944. Aged 29. Son of John and Mary Elizabeth Webster; husband of Annie Webster of Ravensthorpe. Commemorated on the Chatham Naval Memorial.

Bibliography

Besides much use being made of back copies of both The Dewsbury Reporter and Dewsbury News, I have consulted the following publications over the course of my research. I am grateful to all authors and publishers of these books.

Bales, Captain P.G. - The History of the 1/4th Duke of Wellington's Regiment *(Edward Mortimer Ltd., 1920)*

Bannister, Andrew - One Valley's War *(Outremer Publishing, 1994)*

Bolton, Sidney - A History of Ravensthorpe 1759-1960. *(Privately printed)*

Bond, R.C. - The History of the KOYLI in the Great War 1914-18. *(Percy, Lund Humphries & Co., 1929)*

Bruce, Anthony - An Illustrated Companion to the First World War *(Michael Joseph, 1989)*

Bruce, C.D. - The History of the Duke of Wellington's Regiment 1st & 2nd Battalions 1881-1923 *(Medici Society, 1927)*

Bullock, David - Allenby's War *(Blandford Press, 1988)*

Cave, Nigel - Battleground Europe - Sanctuary Wood & Hooge *(Leo Cooper, 1993)*
- Passchendaele - The fight for the village *(Leo Cooper, 1993)*

Cave, Terry - The BEF and the Expansion of the British Army 1914-1918 *(article via Naval & Military Press, 1999)*

Clark, Alan - The Donkeys *(Hutchinson & Co., 1961)*

Crutwell, C.R.M.F. - A History of the Great War 1914-1918 *(Oxford University Press, 1935)*

Edmonds, Brigadier-General Sir James [and others] - Military Operations in France and Belgium. (The numerous volumes are otherwise known as the "Official History of the Great War"). *(Macmillan, and other publishers, 1922-1948)*

Farwell, Byron - The Great War in Africa 1914-1918 *(Viking, 1987)*

Gilbert, Martin - the First World War *(Weidenfield & Nicholson, 1994)*

Giles, John - The Somme Then & Now *(Bailey Bros. & Swifen, 1977)*
- The Western Front Then & Now *(Battle of Britain Prints International, 1992)*

Gill, Alec - Lost Trawlers of Hull *(Hutton Press, 1989)*

Gliddon, Gerald - VC's of the First World War-Somme *(Gliddon, 1991)*

Griffith, Paddy - Battle Tactics of the Western Front, The British Army's art of attack 1916-1918 *(Yale University Press, 1994)*

H.M.S.O. - Soldiers Died in the Great War and Officers Died in the Great War.(1921) *(CD-Rom version - Naval & Military Press).* Republished by J.B. Hayward & Sons in the late 1980's

Hargrave, John - The Suvla Bay Landing *(Macdonald & Co., 1964)*

Harris, J.P. - Amiens to the Armistice *(Brassey's, 1998)*

Hickey, Michael - Gallipoli *(John Murray, 1995)*

Horsfall, Jack & Cave, Nigel - Battleground Europe - Cambrai, the Right Hook *(Leo Cooper, 1999)*

James; Brigadier E.A., O.B.E., T.D. - British Regiments 1914-1918 *(Samson Books, 1978)*

Jane's Fighting Ships of World War 1 *(Studio Editions, 1990)*

Joy, David - A Regional History of the Railways of Great Britain, Vol.8-South & West Yorkshire *(David St. John Thomas, 1984)*

McCarthy, Chris - The Somme - The Day by Day Account *(Arms & Armour Press, 1993)*
- Passchendaele - The Day by Day Account *(Arms & Armour Press, 1995)*

Macdonald, Lyn - 1914 *(Michael Joseph, 1987)*
- 1915, The Death of Innocence *(Headline, 1993)*
- Somme *(Michael Joseph, 1983)*
- They Called it Passchendaele *(Michael Joseph, 1978)*

Magnus, Laurie - The West Riding Territorials in the Great War *(Kegan Paul, Trench, Trubner & Co. Ltd., 1920)*

Magnus, Philip - Kitchener, Portrait of an Imperialist *(John Murray, 1958)*

Middlebrook, Martin - The First Day on the Somme *(Allen Lane, 1971)*
- The Kaiser's Battle *(Allen Lane, 1978)*
- The Somme Battlefields *(Viking, 1991)*
- Your Country Needs You *(Leo Cooper, 2000)*

Moore, William - A Wood Called Bourlon, The cover-up after Cambrai 1917 *(Leo Cooper, 1988)*

Neillands, Robin - The Great War Generals on the Western Front 1914-1918 *(Robinson, 1999)*

Nicholls, Jonathan - Cheerful Sacrifice, The Battle of Arras 1917 *(Leo Cooper, 1993)*

Oldham, Peter - Battleground Europe - The Hindenburg Line *(Leo Cooper, 1997)*

Owen, Edward - 1914, Glory Departing *(Buchan & Enright, 1986)*

Pidgeon, Trevor - The Tanks at Flers *(Fairmile, 1995)*

Richardson, Gavin - After Gallipoli *(Gavin Richardson, 1992)*

Scott, Michael - The Ypres Salient - A guide to the cemeteries and memorials of the Salient *(Gliddon, 1992)*

Simkins, Peter - Chronicles of The Great War. The Western Front 1914-1918 *(Bramley Books, 1998)*

Smith, Peter L. - Yorkshire Waterways *(Dalesman Books, 1978)*

Smithers A.J. - Cambrai. The First Great Tank Battle, 1917 *(Leo, Cooper 1992)*

Spagnoly, Tony & Smith, Ted - Salient Points. Cameos of the Western Front *(Leo Cooper, 1994)*

Stedman, Michael - Salford Pals *(Leo Cooper, 1993)*
- Battleground Europe - Thiepval *(Leo Cooper, 1995)*
- Fricourt-Mametz *(Leo Cooper, 1997)*

Tempest, Captain E.V. - The History of the 1/6th West Yorkshire Regiment *(Percy Lund, Humphries & Co. Ltd., 1921)*

Terraine, John - Essays on Leadership and War *(Privately published)*

Westlake, Ray - Kitchener's Army *(Nutshell, 1989)*

Western Front Association - Stand To! *(The journal of this organisation) (Numerous articles)*

Wolff, Leon - In Flanders Fields *(Longmans, 1960)*

Wyrall, Edward - The West Yorkshire Regiment in the War 1914-1918 *(John Lane, The Bodley Head Ltd., undated)*
- The History of the 62nd (West Riding) Division *(John Lane, The Bodley Head Ltd., undated)*

Index

C

D